P9-DMB-291
DISCARD

Ancient Ideals

VOLUME I

ANCIENT IDEALS

A Study of Intellectual and Spiritual Growth from Early Times to the Establishment of Christianity

VOLUME I

Henry Osborn Taylor

FREDERICK UNGAR PUBLISHING CO.
NEW YORK

Republished 1964

Second Edition first published 1913

Printed in the United States of America

Library of Congress Catalog Card No. 64-25564

PREFACE TO THE SECOND EDITION.

SAVE for a few verbal changes, this edition is a reprint of the first, which was published in 1896. It is difficult to put new cloth into an old garment. Our opinions may hold fast; yet the mystery of things deepens as the shadows lengthen with us; and we do not speak at one time of life as at another. Any revision of the present work might have impaired the equal temper and conviction which seem to me to give it unity.

Ancient Ideals was intended to set forth human growth. The archæological data of the first six chapters were subordinate. They are still substantially sound; except that the chapter on "Greek Beginnings" makes no reference to Crete. Yet I think the chapter suggests correctly the manner in which the Hellenic race gradually became itself. The recent Cretan discoveries serve to carry this inchoate Hellenic story back many centuries and further illuminate it. For this fascinating matter I would refer the reader to the writings of Sir Arthur J. Evans (the article in the *Encyclopædia Britannica* on Crete offers a summary from his pen), and to such books as *Crete, the Forerunner of Greece*, by Mr. and Mrs. Hawes, or Messrs. Fowler and Wheeler's *Greek Archæology*. For recent authoritative statements of the thoughts of ancient Egypt and Mesopotamia, the reader may be referred to Breasted's *Development of Religion and Thought in Egypt*, and Jastrow's *Religious Belief and Practice in Babylonia and Assyria*.

HENRY OSBORN TAYLOR.

NEW YORK, March, 1913.

FROM THE PREFACE TO THE FIRST EDITION.

IN view of the progress of historical research, causing some modification of opinion,—and our judgment of the past alters not merely through the increase of our knowledge, but likewise because of changes in ourselves in these progressive decades,—I have ventured to hope that a new historical survey of the mental and spiritual growth of mankind may be of interest to the scholar as well as to the thoughtful general reader.

The present work is an attempt to treat human development from the standpoint of the ideals of the different races, as these ideals disclose themselves in the art and literature, in the philosophy and religion, and in the conduct and political fortunes of each race. It has been my endeavor to preserve a unity of plan in setting forth the part taken by each race in the human drama. I have sought to make clear the nature of the contribution made by each to the stages of human growth reached before the Christian era; and to indicate in what respects these contributions became permanent elements of humanity and thus elements of its further possibilities,—possibilities that find in Christianity perfect conditions for their final realization.

CONTENTS.

CHAPTER I.

CHAPTER II.

CHAPTER III.

CHAPTER IV.

CHAPTER V.

CHAPTER VI.

CHAPTER VII.

CHAPTER VIII.

CHAPTER IX.

CHAPTER X.

CHAPTER XI.

CHAPTER XII.

CHAPTER XIII.

ANCIENT IDEALS.

CHAPTER I.

INTRODUCTORY.

IT is the instinct of every living organism to maintain its existence, live its own life, fulfil itself. Essentially and simply, this is to live. Life consists in the lives of individuals: species, racehood, is the means of their propagation. This instinct, many-phased, on which hangs all organic life, exists in man not as with beasts and plants, but more clearly, in accordance with the larger measure and lucidity of human consciousness; and in him this fundamental energy of life is made anew by qualities which vindicate the truth that he, and he alone, uses rational discrimination in living, he alone thinks,—this is well, that is not well, he alone may be thought capable of eternal life freed from conditions of the flesh. Only man can desire better things, form an ideal, know God.

Life.

Man lives fulfilling his desires in discrimination and advance. All his capacities are latent cravings, reaching consciousness as life greatens. He passes from savagery; human potentiality becomes fact. More potently reason discriminates, and human nature overtops the brute. In the conflicts of desires he chooses what will be followed by no ill, and what is better in itself, lasting, not transient, in noble fulfilment of himself, rather than brutally selfish, spiritual rather than material: in the end he chooses the eternal spiritual rather than matters of the flesh's quick satiety, emblematic of mortality, presaging dissolution.

Parallelisms of Development.

Though men differ, there is a foundation of common human trait. And despite differences of land and clime, the habitable earth presents many things alike to all. Everywhere shines the sun, and over all lands arches the high heaven with its starry night and changing moons; and everywhere night passes into day and evening comes again. No land without some change of seasons and the mysterious blowing of the wind. Injury and disease come to men everywhere, and men find themselves powerless before the ills which master them; and everywhere men die. So is there everywhere pressed down on man a sense of something stronger than himself, something to fear. But all men are born of parents, nourished and protected in their infancy, and eat the fruits of earth; they themselves yearn in desire, beget, bring forth and nourish, care for, even cherish, and so hand life on. Hence rise thoughts and sentiments the opposite of fear and hate, and men begin to trust and love.

Thus wherever man dwells, his environment presents like features, and human life is moulded by similar experiences; while everywhere man has the same sentient and percipient faculties and the faint waverings of rational apprehension with its will-o'-the-wisp hints of cause and effect. So from the beginning, men have a like enlightenment and rude appreciation of the facts of life. With shades of difference life teaches them alike, and alike they learn. Hence everywhere appear parallelisms of thought, analogous conceptions and modes of reasoning, and similar opinions ethical and religious. So over all the world men have passed through—or not passed through!—broadly similar cosmogonic conceptions, usually set in myths of primordial engenderings between sky and earth:

everywhere men have projected their crude self-consciousness into the world without, confusedly conceiving all facts as acts of living beings: they have everywhere worshipped the sun and moon and hosts of heaven, and their own ancestors, in fear of ill and hope of good, and buried food and weapons with their dead. And they have worshipped tribal gods, allies against hostile gods and hostile men. So have they gradually evolved like fundamental thoughts of conduct, and with increase of knowledge and experience broadened their ethical conceptions, from the family to the tribe, and from the tribe to men beyond it. They have passed—or failed to pass—through roughly similar rude efforts to think matters they could not see or handle, endeavoring to imagine the human mind and spirit, and some have reached the finer ethical conceptions which lay determining stress on the intent with which an act is done. Through these stages men have helped themselves to thoughts of that which is spiritual, and still help themselves, by like images and modes of reasoning taken from the analogies of material things;[1] and closely parallel have been the lines by which men have reached like opinions.

The Primitive Disquietude.

Primitive man thinks in myths; instead of reasoning, he imagines. Having but begun to classify his experience, he draws no clear distinctions between all the manifold forms of the phenomena which surround him. His sentiments towards them correspond to his nature, and yet vary in accordance with his diverse thoughts of everything with which or in despite of which he maintains his life. According as these sentiments relate to matters mysterious and powerful, he

[1] *E. g.:* "The primitive notion of the [Egyptian] word maāt seems to be the geometrical one 'right,' as in 'right line,' as opposed to χab, 'bent,' perverse. Maāt as a noun is the 'straight rule,' 'canon.'"—Renouf, *Religion of Ancient Egypt* (Hibbert Lectures, 1879), p. 71. Similar derivative senses of the words "right" and "straight" and of many other like common words, run through the Indo-Germanic languages, ancient and modern.

is afraid; but inasmuch as sustenance and means of living come from this vague enchanted region of the world without, sentiments of expectation, nay, of confidence, join with his fears. These mingled sentiments shape his ideas of the extra-human, the super-human, the divine. And from the very first and rude beginnings of his dim child's thought, he knows all is not right between him and the potencies which form this irresistibly infolding world, from out of which he faintly distinguishes the god. Gradually gods, spirits, or demons are separated from his visible and invisible environment, and conceived as moving and controlling it. Towards them he must adjust himself, through them keep his lot favorable. But never wholly favorable is the lot of man; rarely does primitive man feel himself in sure benign relationship to his gods; rarely is he without fear lest the god be, as in the past he may have been, baneful or vengeful. Then with advance from savagery, with the clearing up of thought and sense of self and what self fails to be, the mirror of man's fears turns on himself and shows him his shortcomings. Thus a feeling comes that he has not done all he might to propitiate the powers of life, that he has been remiss in sacrifice or prayer, remiss in honors due the god, or disobedient to such rules of conduct as he is beginning to think laid on him. As towards the powers without, he deeply fears; as towards himself, he is dissatisfied.

In this state was the human race as its branches advanced far enough to be perplexed. Well-nigh universal is the tradition of impiety resulting in destruction from the gods: Chaldæa has it, and the Hebrew race, and all the Aryan races, likewise the Egyptian, though in Egypt the destruction came not through a deluge. But the "deluge" was very wide or very ancient; Chaldæa, Israel, India, Iran, Greece, and peoples of America remembered it in tradition.[1] These thoughts of fault,

[1] See François Lenormant, *Les Origines de l'Histoire*, vol. i, ch. ii and viii.

shortcoming, and destruction involve the contrast of a time before, when men were innocent. And thus this first tradition carried the thought of Eden and the Golden Age, when God walked on the earth and gods were kings of men.

So starts the human race most emblematically of coming failure and endeavor to retrieve unto a new advance. Men have not done well, and God has punished them. But there is hope, for the wrath is stayed; and that people which knew God best most clearly sees His bow of promise in the firmament. Let man endeavor and strain on revering God. With small self-satisfaction and great fear and sorrows manifold, toil and childbirth's pang, foes' onslaught, tyrant's cruelty, mysterious disease, death lowering and sure, the race in little, foolish knowledge lives along. Thought may look back over this ancient past, trace its grim lines, note the broad parallels of like environment within the variances of which, beneath the leadings of God's immanence, the human consciousness with self-asserting individuality attains itself, and men fare on along the triple path of knowledge, fear, and love.

Desire and Endeavor.

Whatever any men have done, what knowledge and accomplishment they have reached, have never been entirely the doer's work. All deeds hang from a past, and are conditioned on a present. No man can sever his attainment, or even his desire, from all that makes it possible. Yet palpably accomplishment depends on things without, while man's desire is more nearly his; for it is he. That which has ever purest human interest, is the endeavor and the aim. The true human story is not a story of what has been done on earth, but rather what man has set before him to desire and has striven to reach; not the story of the veiling deed, but the story of the yearning life, which never can expand to quite the form it would—the story of what man has sought to be and do, and so has really been. What has been brought to pass upon the earth is a story of what

God has done; man's part, which may be also God's one-step-removed efficiency, is his desire and will, his forming to himself a thought of what were best, his power of endeavor thereunto. The efficient part in every man, which makes him what he is distinctively, is his conception of himself and God. And God sets this in man even as He gives him all he has, in answer to what man is and strives for.

Individuality.

Primitive men lack that individuality which partly lies in choice of what is not thrown in the path by circumstances. The savage is drawn on by the visible pleasant, and repelled by the visible ill; when hungry he seeks food, and terrified he worships the terrifier. Slowly, influenced by environment, the rational selecting nature asserts itself, if faintly, and then man learns confusedly. But experience is bringing further knowledge which shall aid discrimination; and as each race emerges into history, it has characteristics which appear not simply the fruit of its environment, but rather of its selection as it were of self from out of self's environment. Each group of men has been selecting, necessarily with reference to circumstances, but still selecting, and in selection lie the beginnings of race individuality asserting its distinctness.

Thereupon, onward from the advent of periods which have left their records, the characteristics of each race, becoming more distinct, combine to form a more distinct race individuality. This, as the race matures, will evince itself in the choice of objects deemed worthy of attainment, and in the form and manner and substantial measure of achievement actually reached. Races, as the Egyptian, or the people of Sumer-Accad, which at an early period possess a considerable civilization, evince little conscious selection as to objects of attainment. They appear to take what their lives offer and suggest. Somewhat later races select with clearer and more consistently discriminating thought, till at last a highest stage of self-assertive individuality appears among the Hebrews and the Greeks. From the times of their advent as races, their choice and endeavors conform, with the one race, to ever larger thoughts of divine righteousness, with the other to ever clearer conceptions of the beautiful and good.

More palpably race individuality declares itself in the form and manner and extent of actual accomplishment; for what the land affords, what it suggests, what it withholds, what it subjects the race to, is enough to render the works and institutions of its dwellers different from those of other peoples. Environment continually conditions the plastic process through which in the course of years the actual achievement of a race—its religion, knowledge, ethics, social institutions, art—becomes distinctively its own, a reflection of itself.

Personality; Modes of Human Growth.

The ideal and the aim becoming ever clearer are not the whole of human progress; and individuality is, as it were, the differentiating aspect of the more positive and complete conception, personality. Human growth consists in two ceaselessly complementing modes,—desire, and action entered upon in consequence of it. The action results in some realization, which represents a growth of personality and in turn becomes an element of further desires leading to further acts. And although untoward circumstances and human weakness may thwart achievement, no endeavor falls to the ground; but according to its strength and correspondence to the best the man conceives, greatens the personality of him who has striven. All endeavor for the best reaches spiritual attainment. Even as this is true of each man, is it true of the races of mankind from generation to generation. The complete story of human progress is the story of ideal conception and of endeavor, and the unfailing realization of ideals in the growth of human beings with ideals uplifted and enlarged. This makes the narrative of the enlargement and greatening of human life; it is a history of the growth of human personality; of the age-long development of the personalities of men and women.

Human life lies in spirit and intent. Apart from motives and desires, intelligence and will, the deeds of men are meaningless: and environment is insignificant save in relation to the soul which feels and loves and loathes, appreciates and understands. Life's furthest finite fact, the human personality, is an enigma which with its growth ever unfolds mystery. Yet it consists, in the individual consciousness, in feelings and desires, and their ordering; it consists in the sum of intellectual faculties and their content of thought; it consists in the sum of emotion and desire mentalized in the intellect, transformed to discriminating and self-ordering spirit. All this is self; and its growth lies in the enlargement and intensifying of consciousness; in the enlargement of conception and the uplifting of desire.

From the beginning man is social, and personality grows through his enlargement of the conception of his relationship towards others, his family, his tribe, mankind at large; it grows in the extension of his loves and sympathies and of his thought of duty. Neither is human consciousness ever void of sense of self's relationship to what is not man, to objects and the powers of nature which affect him, but which at first are hardly distinguished in essence and in mode of action from himself and other men. Gradually, from out of the palpable elements of his environment, he shapes his thoughts of spirits, demons, gods, in modes conforming to the consciousness of himself, to which, as his perception and intelligence sharpen, he perceives that natural objects and the powers of nature do not correspond. But the presence and brute force of things remain, though he has severed from them his disposing gods. Thereupon will he recognize a general force in things, tending to become fate and law apart from the powers of the gods; and his reason grows in finer ethical apprehension of this law of fate. Or else he raises his conception of divinity to all-embracing omnipotence, holding it ever in archetypal correspondence to consciousness of self, holding it therefore as conception of a person. And it may be that he will rise to apprehend God's personality in its perfectness and universal beneficent relationship to mankind. And then may come the more than thought of all men as God's creatures, cared for by Him, beloved by Him, sons of a common Father. The individual's thought and feeling of his relationship to other men is enlarged and unified in his thought of God. Men are members of society, members one of another; this thought is made perfect in the truth that all are members of God. Personality grows in the growth of these conceptions and the endeavor to conform life to them.

Through all of this the man's thought of himself has become clearer, clearer too his thought of the individual personalities of other human beings; and his ideas of pity, love, and justice have developed. Men have disengaged their individualities; they have come to know themselves loving or hating, good or bad, culpable or free from guilt, in themselves apart from family or tribe: and thus has man's personality advanced through better recognition of his own and others' individualities and individual relationships to God and men.

As the human personality enlarges, it intensifies through consciousness of its increased content, its broadened relationships, its greater manifold of desires, its greater sum of worth unto itself. Each man's life becomes more precious; enhanced is his capacity for happiness in being man and living, and using and fulfilling the faculties and modes of human life. With this clearer consciousness of the joy and worth of life comes more intellectual prizing of it and discrimination of its true elements, rejection of its dross, and then again enhanced appreciation of the transcendent value of these truer, better, finer matters, till in each and all of its chosen elements with their circumstantial vantagings life grows in desirability, in loveliness and joy. And this intensifying of the joy of living, with the truer discrimination of what is felt and adjudged best, is another phase of growth of personality, of life. Through these long strainings to reach its best desires, which ever rise and broaden, the human personality has greatened totally; deeper its sense of happiness, broader its loves, farther its intellectual scope. Its growth has been in all its elements; not alone in reason and intelligence; not alone in the moral qualities thereto related; not alone in the emotional qualities of human nature; but in all of these,—in the whole man.

Topics of Inquiry.

In tracing the ideals of different peoples and the growth of human personality, evidently the subjects of inquiry will vary with the genius of each race. The main endeavors of the earliest civilized races being directed by the demands and suggestions of environment, their indistinct conceptions of what is best for men are to be gathered from the general tenor of their lives and the more marked features of their material accomplishment. But as a race reaches more definite conceptions of man's furthest good, its ideals direct themselves towards certain departments of high conception and endeavor. These will lead the inquiry to definite topics. One race conceives an ideal of character: this is to be traced throughout the thoughts of conduct and civilities wherewith it sought to form and clothe itself. Another race, spurning its land's munificence and all life's fleeting gifts, fixes its mind on the Eternal Absolute; its yearnings should be sought for where they are disclosed,—in its religion and philosophy. Another race accepts all, and then discriminates with clearest vision and intelligence, proportioning life's factors, seeking to combine them in beauty's perfectness, and searching out a furthest knowledge of them all. Its ideals are to be sought for in the keen endeavorings of individual life, in art and poetry, and in philosophy. Again, the ideals of another people are religious, comprised within its thoughts of a personal righteous and almighty God, and the desire to hold a right relationship with Him. They must be sought in the record of these thoughts and in the waveringly accordant conduct of the people.

The present work would tell these various ideals of men, seeking them wheresoever with the different races they come to most distinct expression. Of necessity the data of the inquiry in its different fields will be the actual accomplishment which has been wrought, the actual attainment which has been reached. But the writer's purpose is to mark the ideal endeavor which, through its ever incomplete achievement, strives onward somewhither, somehow, to more perfect life,—and thereby gains it.

The work does not touch the problems of the savage state nor the elusive question of the place or many places of origin of mankind. It does not look beyond the records and monuments of those races which have reached a measure of civilization; and within that limit, so far as possible, it seeks to draw its inferences from matters as to which there is some concurrence among scholars. Yet it cannot avoid debatable ground; indeed, the whole past is debatable! But there is little utility in discussing controverted matters except fully, and that were impossible in a work like the present, which, however, the writer trusts is such as to indicate a knowledge on his part of these many controversies which he omits, but has not ignored.

Arrangement.

It seemed manifestly expedient that racehood should determine the larger divisions of the work. Then arises the question of their order. Evidently when a mature race, coming in contact with another, aids its spiritual growth or hastens its corruption, the former has a logical precedence which should be recognized and followed. But it is often impossible to trace a consequential connection between the thoughts of contemporary or succeeding races; and the matter of priority in time may be of no great interest if relations of antecedent and consequent do not exist. When races do not appear to have influenced each other, the fact that one of them flourished at an earlier period may afford but a superficial reason for deciding the order of treatment. In view of parallelisms of thought and the usual course of development, this would turn more properly on the stage of civilization reached by the different races, or rather on the degree of intellectual perspicacity with which they formulated ideals distinct from the suggestions of their environments, and on the measure of the human personality they reached. Savagery logically precedes civilization, vague apprehension goes before a more discriminating understanding of the elements of life, and undeveloped personality, however stricken with case-hardening years, is antecedent to that which holds a larger growth.

Egypt presents itself as the country whose known history extends farthest, whose civilization appears original. And though the Egyptians early made great progress in the arts, they never laid their mental crudities aside, but remained a race ancient and primitive, a great doer in the way of material accomplishment, a universal conserver of all elements of its self-retarded growth. It is for us the earliest example of a civilization material, peaceful, and benign.

Yet only for us at present, since many considerations point to Chaldæa as the first home of culture. The ancient people of Sumer-Accad offer this general resemblance to the Egyptians that their civilization in the main was one of peace. But the history of Chaldæa is still a babel; dim struggling peoples come and go; one drives another out and is expelled in turn, or destroyed, or pressed into traceless existence. All is built up to be obliterated. Chaldæa has no ancient monumental record consecutive and voluminous like Egypt's. Nevertheless she discloses most archaic elements and many indications of her ancient sourceful past, whence issued to fare westward, northward, and it may be even unto the far east, strange mingled streams of foolishness and knowledge. Along currents of Chaldæan influence one may travel into Phœnicia or Asia Minor, from either of these countries pass to Greece, and track the Babylonian numbers on to Rome.

Assyria was Chaldæa's foster-child, which for a thousand years or more should look upon its parent as a font of knowledge and a prey. While Assyria stood, she was the warrior, the plunderer, the uprooter, the impaler and the torturer, and Jehovah's rod.

In the far east another race was in some respects to form an analogue to Egypt. Its culture was not altogether underived, for the rudiments may have come from Chaldæa, but most original in subsequent development. The civilization of the lands bordering the Yellow River was one of peace, and as conservative as Egypt's. The Chinese were not possessed with Chaldæa's superstitious fearfulness, and in their mental progress they surpassed the Egyptians through their capacities of ethical formulation. They evolved a clear ideal of character which, however, never freed itself from a complexity of ceremonial conduct.

A different Nemesis awaited the Vedic Aryans in India, the land which they had conquered in the joyousness of strength, trusting their bright gods. In them and their descendants was a mighty power of thought. They used it to show how thought's consistent power, misguided by the darkening moods of men, might reach the full periphery of all life's nothingness. The Avesta branch of kindred Aryans thought too, yet kept their minds from India's many sloughs. For thought, like life, to them was conflict of the good with bad, the lie with truth. It may be this Avesta folk became the Persian race, and broke itself first against Greece, then in its own corruption, for though Aryan it was Asian.

All this forms the background of Greece, and in part

was her inheritance. But whatever Greece received she transformed, and more did she create. She cleared up the human consciousness and the laws of thought, for herself thinking in truth and beauty on all the manifold of human life, loving its fullest compass.

Politically, Alexander made ready the Mediterranean lands to become the Roman Empire ; and in every way Greece taught her conqueror Rome. The Græco-Roman world politically, socially, intellectually, and in mood, became ready for new life. Jesus showed it. Israel's inspiration led up to Christ's revelation. To an apprehension of Christianity is needed an understanding of its direct antecedent. Hence Israel's topical position immediately precedes Christianity, the new power in the world, but follows Rome and Greece, the ingatherers of the elements which made the time.

CHAPTER II.

EGYPT, CHALDÆA, AND CHINA.

FROM time immemorial the fertility of river valleys, rather than desert and mountain barriers, has stayed the wanderings of men, and the most ancient civilizations appear as the work of peaceful peoples. No echoes of any strife of early self-establishment remain in the traditions either of Sumer-Accad or of Egypt; and while even the Egyptians, and much more the Sumerian people, had need of valor to defend their lands, nevertheless the life and interests of both races centre in peace. It is somewhat different with the story of those "black-haired" tribes who, twenty-five centuries before Christ, established themselves by the Yellow River. Since these ancestors of the Chinese entered China at this comparatively late period, accounts survive of their conflicts with surrounding tribes; yet—here the likeness with Egypt and Sumer-Accad reasserts itself—the civilization which had begun and was to develop with great originality in China was one of peace and toil. Any race which, through some superiority, establishes itself in a fertile valley, finds toil better than warring with less favored tribes, and tends to become a peaceful people.

Elementary Humanity of Early Races.

From Menes to Ptolemy, Egyptian thought was characterized by crass confusion. It analyzed nothing, had neither clearness nor consistency, nor power to discriminate and classify. In consequence ethics remained unsystematized precept; with all the picturesque elaboration of a future life, no thought of spiritual immortality was reached; the religion saw no inconsistency between one god and many; and the race's mighty material accomplishment lacked ennobling aim.

Egyptian Mental Crudities,

Scant record of a primitive Egypt remains. The earliest monuments presuppose an unmeasured past. With her first historic dynasties, Egypt reaches her best. In excellence of building, she never surpassed the Great Pyramid; nor did her artists ever make better statues than some of the oldest; and Ptahotep's precepts[1] were scarcely improved on. Egypt offers the longest of histories, and has no advance to show. She is astounding at the time of her monumental beginning; but this strange ancient child fulfils no promise as the centuries pass.

and Unprogressiveness.

The conceptions of savages are indistinct. Their consciousness of self is undeveloped; they have no thought of existence unlike their own, or of power save as animated by something like human will. Thus they project their inchoate self-consciousness into the external world. It requires some clear thought to think of anything as definitely ceasing. A savage does not think of death as ending man's existence. Plainly, the moveless body cannot help and feed itself; but no thought has come of a spirit needing no bodily nourishment. Out of the dilemma issues the universal though variable conception of a ghost or shade or double, a material yet impalpable survival of the man. Its thin life hangs on conditions of mortality, without the body's substantial power to fulfil them; so it must be provided for by others.

Conceptions of Life after Death.

As a race progresses, it may reach a conception of mind as essentially different from body; and with clearer conception of spirit, thoughts of responsibility for wrongful

[1] V dynasty.

acts lay stress upon the intent with which an act is done. Therewith, thoughts of a future life undergo a change and become ethical. The human lot after death is conceived to depend less on funeral rites, the fate of the body, or the survivors' care, and more on the moral worth of the deceased's earthly life. A final stage is the conception of a spiritual immortality freed from conditions of life in the body.

The Elaborate Egyptian Scheme.

The Egyptians elaborated in unparalleled detail their notions of a future life. Gradually they made that life dependent on the good conduct of the man on earth; yet they never passed beyond thoughts of mortality indefinitely, but precariously, extended under conditions to which life on earth, while similar, was preferable. Apparently, their earliest conception was the *ka*, or double, the body's strengthless equivalent in form. As a basis for its existence the body, or images of the body, must be preserved; and the *ka* had to be lodged and fed. Lodged it was in the Mastaba,[1] the walls of which were covered with all imaginable pleasant scenes from the deceased's earthly life, which should project their reality into the double's shadowy existence. Yet the double was but a poor impotency. So human elements surviving death were given more active powers,[2] and grouped together in the conception of a voracious hawklike soul, the *bi*. Finally was added the conception of the *khou*, according to which the soul was as a pale bluish flame. And, as in Egypt no notion once held was ever abandoned, men came to have a *ka*, a *bi*, and a *khou*. The Egyptians saw no inconsistency; man's post-mortem self might be different things, need not be one thing or another. From adjacent walls

[1] For the details of these tombs of the old empire, see Perrot and Chipiez, *Histoire de l'Art dans l'Antiquité*—" L'Egypte."

[2] By the time of the V and VI dynasties, see Maspero's translations of the inscriptions from the pyramids of Unas, Teti, and Pepi, in *Recueil des Travaux.*

of the same tomb, what survived of the dead man might climb upon a ladder and soar as a hawk.

The history of beliefs in a future life has nothing as picturesque as those of the Egyptians under the eighteenth and nineteenth dynasties, when Egypt was preeminent in art and fancied knowledge as in arms. Death is still a dark vicissitude of life and an imperilment to be passed through. The defunct has a long voyage to accomplish, for which his mummy is elaborately equipped and his tomb so prepared as to facilitate. The ceremonies of interment rendered visible its perilous progress. One episode of the funeral rites was the hysterical banquet at the tomb, in which the dead man shares. Singers sing and dancers dance; the harper plays on his harp bidding the dead man to take his cheer[1] and admonishing the living to make merry until they go to the land which loveth silence. That was a place of darkness and of danger. Perhaps only the great possessed the means of passing through its perils; and a continuance of existence may have been the lot of few;[2] at least, but few could have a comfortable, unlaborious life in the world of the departed, nor there be subject to the corvee of the gods, and forced to till the fields and carry grain, like laborers on earth.[3] Such fortunate ones might reach a life palely reflecting earthly joys of sense.

The *Book of the Dead*[4] is the collection of incantations, composed and collected through a period extending over many centuries, knowing which the defunct shall escape the dangers of his journey. They almost form an epic, whose magic hero is the composite personality of the de-

[1] See Maspero, *Journal Asiatique*, 1880, pp. 393 *et seq.*

[2] See Maspero, "Livre des Morts," *Revue des Religions*, vol. xv, pp. 266–316; republished in *Études de la Mythologie des Egyptiennes*, vol. i, pp. 325–387.

[3] Little figures of men tilling, harvesting, etc., placed in the tomb might serve as the defunct's substitute in such labors.—*Ib.*

[4] See Maspero, "Livre des Morts," *Revue des Religions*, vol. xv, pp. 266–316.

ceased. "The Osiris," for thus is he identified with the principal god of the dead, has first to recover the use of limbs, voice, heart, by means of magic utterances. Then he passes through perils which he wards off, using words of charm to repel scorpions and crocodiles, as well as hunger and thirst. In due time he is re-united with his *ka*. In mystic formulæ also he proclaims, and so effects it, that his nature is that of all the gods, and he gains the powers to transform himself into various animals and birds. Finally with the Osirian circle of ideas there joins confusedly the circle of Ra, that of the fortunes of the Sun, in which "the Osiris" is mystically enabled to participate;—he voyages with Ra. At the end of his voyagings and adventures he undergoes judgment in the "Hall of Truth," where he proclaims his innocence of every crime. But magic elements enter even this judgment scene: the righteousness of "the Osiris" would not save him, could he not pronounce the names of the bolt of the door of the Hall of Truth, of the left and right panels, of the sill, of the door, the lock, the door-posts, and the door-keeper, each name at the bearer's demand. Egypt's *Book of the Dead* abandoned no crude material notion from the past; hence no consistently high thought was reached. There was no thought that a future life is a life of spirit, and not a magically wrought continuance of the life of earth.

The Savage Babylonian Thought.

The Sumerian-Semitic people of Mesopotamia had no conception of life beyond the grave to rival in elaboration the Egyptian scheme; nor is it plain that they attached importance to the ethical character of the deceased's life on earth. They were further than Egypt from a spiritual conception of immortality, and their thought of existence in and beneath the tomb outdid in horror the grave-encircling fantasies of other ancient peoples.[1]

[1] See, *e.g.*, *Ishtar's Descent*, for translation and bibliography of which see Maspero, *Dawn of Civilization*, p. 693.

As Egyptian conceptions of life after death, held for four thousand years or more, indicate mental limitations which the race showed no capacity to pass, so is like witness borne by the conceptions of the gods. Confusion and absence of consistently progressive thought characterize the Egyptian pantheon. It is difficult to separate early from late beliefs, and impossible to pronounce with certainty whether one god or many was first in the Nile Valley.[1] Semi-barbarous notions of gods extend through the entire series of Egyptian monuments; and likewise at any period may be found pantheistic or even monotheistic expressions. These use the word *nutr*, which in modern language can be rendered only "God." Yet whatever fulness of meaning be ascribed or denied this word, the manner of its use shows that there were at the same period—as is always the case everywhere—opposed conceptions of divinity. The nomarch Ptahotep, living under the fifth dynasty, expresses thoughts of God lofty and ethical, apparently monotheistic, at all events removed as pole from pole from the barbarous superstitions which cover the walls of the pyramids of Unas, Teti, and Pepi, where the *ka* of the defunct prevails upon the gods, not by prayer or righteousness, but by magic charm and incantation, overcomes them with fear, and hunts and feeds on them. Similarly, two thousand years later there is like contradiction between the scribe Ani's thoughts of God and those prevalent under the twentieth dynasty, when he lived.[2] Even then the Egyptians did not clearly sever the concept of a god

Egyptian Gods.

[1] See Wiedermann, *Die Religion der Alten Ægypter*, Einleitung (1890); and generally Maspero, "La Mythologie Égyptienne," *Revue de l'Histoire des Religions*, vol. xviii, pp. 253–278, and vol. xix, pp. 1–45 (1889), republished in vol. ii, Maspero's *Études de Mythologie*, etc.

[2] On the other hand, it would be incorrect to regard Ptahotep and Ani as speaking the thoughts of the educated, while the inscriptions reflect popular superstitions. Undoubtedly these moralists expressed the best of Egyptian thought; but all our knowledge of Egyptian belief comes from royal temples or tombs of kings, priests, and nobles, and so must also be taken as representing beliefs of the educated classes.

from that of a man, and regarded the gods as only in degree less subject than mankind to old age, hunger, poison, wounds, and death.[1]

With the Egyptians, religion—prayer, worship, amulet or incantation—was a means of bending to the fulfilment of their desires the vague mass of powers and influences which made their environment and fate. These powers, real or imagined, took shape and name in multitudinous gods. Nor did the Egyptians rest with giving name and active attribute to creations of their fantasy and to the overarching powers of day and night. From out of the aggregate of all outside of man they distinguished nothing as being not divine, and so requiring neither worship nor deprecatory charm. Any object might in some way be some sort of god; and from the earliest to the latest times they worshipped animals.[2] But the same animals were not worshipped, alike over all Egypt; nor were the imagined gods gods equally throughout the land. Ptah was the god of Memphis, as Amon of Thebes, and Ra of Heliopolis; each and every god becoming of wider exaltation as his locality became capital in dignity or power. These gods of local origin were not distinct, and, besides supplementing each other in a common Egyptian pantheon, might readily unite in compound divinities like Amon-ra.

Beneficent Givers of Life.

A basis for the growth of gods and a mythology lay in the action, co-operative or conflicting, of the powers of nature which as to man are beneficent or noxious. In other lands the same phenomena at times bring life and death; but in Egypt flood was benign, drought always noxious, and good and bad were clearly typified in the Nile's conflict with the desert. Here, or in the conflict of the Sun with darkness, might the Egyptians find a quasi-ethical starting-point for

[1] The Turin papyrus (XX Dyn.) which contains the legend of Ra and Isis, speaks of Ra as self-existent and yet as growing old and feeble. See *Ægyp. Zeitschr.*, 1883, p. 27, etc.; also Wiedermann, *Religion*, etc., p. 29; and Erman, *Aegypten*, p. 359, etc.

[2] See Wiedermann, *Religion*, etc., ch. vii.

their religion. Both were illustrative of the more mysterious conflict of life and death, and seem to have formed the basis of the Solar and Osirian groups of myths. Perhaps in the steady and recurrent course of these phenomena, affecting men uniformly throughout the Nile Valley, some Egyptians may have also found suggestion whereby to generalize the divine nature, and find it as a principle of life assuming different forms. At all events, both on the earth and in the land of the departed, the gods were always givers of life. Throughout the famous hymn to Amon–ra[1] is he life-giver. The worshipper views him as the sun that shines and traverses the heavens, then as the life-giving principle of all things, then as kind and merciful, and also as the local god of Thebes.

The Egyptians related everything in life to the powers without them and so, confusedly, to God. By themselves they would attempt nothing; charms, incantations, sacrifices, were means efficacious in all affairs of life on this earth and hereafter. But with the milder and benevolent spirit which was Egypt's best, thoughts of man's relationship to God and of the divine beneficence and justice rose with some men. And so to some, God, or the gods or garbed life-principles, appeared as just, benevolent, and merciful. Such men transformed the ways of amulet and incantation, and the power of the correctly spoken word, into the thought of reverence before God and endeavor to conform human conduct to such modes as such a god would sanction.

Egyptian Ethics.

Egyptian ethics, like the Egyptian pantheon, reflect the kindly, peaceful disposition of the race, and also its inaptitude for rational systematization or consistent thought. The absolute dominion of a king always constituted the government of Egypt. For the times of the Old Empire, the contrast

[1] Wiedermann, *Religion*, etc., p. 64. Translation also in vol. ii, *Rec. of the Past*. Similar thoughts are expressed in the hymn to the Nile, *Rec. of the Past*, N. S., vol. iii.

between the pyramids of the kings and the tombs of Egypt's unroyal worthies present the difference between king and subjects as absolutely as was possible with a people who had no clear conception of difference in kind, and hence could express only a colossal difference in degree. For the later Empire the inscriptions pronounce the pharaoh a god in no uncertain voice. Round him revolved the people's life. Yet between the time of the Old, the Middle, and the New Empire, views of a king's right function may have altered. At first it seemed natural that absolute power should exert itself in favor of its possessor. The early pharaohs employed the resources of the realm in building pyramids. No reason was yet reached why the disposer of his subjects' lives should not employ them on his tomb. Here was no wanton tyranny. The action of Khufu and Khafra was representative of the action of men under the Old Empire towards dependants within their power.

By the time of the twelfth, the great dynasty of the Middle Empire, there had arisen broader conceptions of the duties of a pharaoh. These Usertesens and Amenemhats constructed works of national utility. Says one of them[1] after his death appearing to his successor in a dream: "Listen to what I speak unto thee. Now thou art a king on earth, act even better than did thy predecessors. Let concord be kept between thy subjects and thyself, lest people should give their heart up to fear. Being among them, do not isolate thyself, and let not the lords and noblemen alone fill thy heart; but grant not access to thee to people whose friendship has not long been tried. As for myself, I have given to the humble and made the weak to be. My image lives in the hearts of men, for I have made those who were afflicted free from their afflictions, and their cries are heard no more. Whether locusts were drawn up to plunder, whether I was assaulted by seditions in the interior of my house,

[1] Instructions of Amenemhat I, *Rec. of the Past*, vol. ii.

whether the Nile waters were too low and wells dry, whether my enemies took advantage of thy youth for their deeds,—I never drew back since the day when I was born. I stood in the boundaries of the land to keep watch on its borders. I was a maker of bread, the lover of Nepra.[1] He granted me the rising of the Nile upon the cultivated lands. There was no creature hungry through me, no creature thirsty through me. All my orders increased the love my people bore me. I hunted the lion, I fought the Nubians and the Asiatics. I built myself a house adorned with gold; its roof was painted blue, the walls were of stone bound together with metal. Made for eternity, time shrinks before it." After the Middle Empire had been overthrown, and its conquerors, the Hyksos, in turn expelled, then with the great conquering Thothmes and Ramses of the New Empire comes a novel vaingloriousness. Nevertheless the thought that a pharaoh should be a beneficent god to his subjects was not lost.[2]

The ancient ethical ideals of Egypt may be found in the *Precepts of Ptahotep*,[3] "son" of King Assa of the fifth dynasty. They are shrewd and kindly, and express that conservatism which Egyptians and Chinese have possessed beyond other races. Ptahotep disclaims originality; what were that but innovation? He would set forth the wisdom of former days: "Seek the most perfect way that thy conduct may be above reproach. Justice is great, invariable, and assured: it has not been disturbed since the age of Osiris. God will take away the bread of him who enriches himself by inspiring fear.

"If thou art a leader of peace, listen to the discourse of the petitioner. Be not abrupt with him; that would trouble him: Say not to him: 'Thou hast already recounted this.' Indulgence will encourage him to accom-

[1] The Corn-god.

[2] See *e.g.* Harris Papyrus, "Annals of Ramses III," *Rec. of the Past*, vol. viii.

[3] Translated by P. Virey, *Rec. of the Past*, N. S., vol. iii.

plish the object of his coming. . . . The way to obtain a clear explanation is to listen with kindness." Ptahotep urges gentleness in overcoming opposition. "Let thy love pass into the heart of those who love thee: cause those about thee to be loving and obedient." And "if thou hast become great after having been little . . . rich after having been poor, head of the city, . . . harden not thy heart because of thy elevation; thou art become the steward of the good things of God. Put not behind thee thy neighbor who is like unto thee; be unto him as a companion."

The concluding pages of these Precepts set forth the advantages of filial obedience, how it profits the son in every way, bringing greatness, dignity, and long life; "It produces love, the good thing which is twice good." When the son receives his father's instruction, there is no error in all his plans:—but "the man without experience, who listens not, effects nothing whatsoever. He sees knowledge in ignorance, profit in loss; he commits all kinds of error, always choosing the contrary of what is praiseworthy. . . . Let no one innovate upon the precepts of his father; let the same precepts form his lessons to his children." [1]

But the most authoritative expression of Egyptian ethics is the famous negative confession in the *Book of the Dead.* "The Osiris" has done no fraud nor oppression, has caused no one to hunger or weep, has not robbed the mummies, nor falsified the weights of the balance, nor taken milk from the mouth of children;—better ethics could scarcely be put in precepts unsystematized, related to no controlling principle. They are set in elements of mystic incantation, showing thus that clear thought of meritoriousness was hardly Egypt's, even as she had no clear thought of human immortality or the divine nature.

[1] Two thousand years after Ptahotep may be found like maxims, only a little sharpened. See for instance "Les Maximes du Scribe Ani," trans. by F. Chabas in *L'Egyptologie.*

Puerility of Egyptian Literature.

The character and intellectual qualities of a race show themselves not only in the contents of its writings and the thoughts which it would carry out in architecture, sculpture, and pictorial decoration, but also in the style in which it expresses itself in literature and art. For style is an exponent of perception and discrimination, and betrays the presence or the absence of the artistic intelligence which uses effective means and avoids what is superfluous or incongruous. The creative arts, moreover, are intellectual in so far as accomplishment depends upon man's higher intellectual faculties, and unintellectual in so far as accomplishment may result through adventitious circumstances, or from manual skill and that lower form of patience, physical insistance as it were, whereby manual skill is reached or, without it, substantial results are had. Only the most intelligent peoples have excelled in the literary art; while in the constructive and the plastic arts much has been wrought by races lacking in the higher perceptive, reasoning, and proportioning faculties. Yet architecture, sculpture, painting, afford scope for supreme intelligence, and without it cannot reach the higher modes of beauty.

Thus comes it that Assyria for example accomplished much in building and sculpture, nothing in literature; and while the art of Egypt has striking excellence, the literature is puerile. It was the fault of her intelligence. The Egyptians in matters above the range of common life lacked thoughts clear and distinct, which bring with them a sense that the matter not only is as conceived, but cannot also be otherwise. Hence their slight sense for inconsistency and the incongruous. Nor did they perceive a matter so clearly as to see its limits, where it ceased, and something else began: in consequence they had no sense of the superfluous, no sense of interruption of the thought, no sense of departure from the main idea, the thing itself.

So Egyptian narrative has slight merit. Its defects are

least striking in unambitious popular tales where inconsequence is not without an effect of its own. The autobiographical narratives are monotonous successions of flat statement.[1] The royal inscriptions are monotones of bombast with no connection between successive vaunts. Most famous is the poetical inscription of Pentaur, telling of the combat of Ramses with the Cheta. Ramses' prayer to Amon is vigorous, but the courtly narrative forgets to move in waiting on the royal boasting.

The Egyptians had another intellectual shortcoming which alone might have prevented any noble literature; they never reached an understanding of the force and import of generalized statement. Magical incantations do not trust to generalization, but must particularize every detail. The *Book of the Dead* is illustration. Its magic formulæ were not content to procure for the defunct the power of motion and the right to pass throughout this and the other world: they could not trust to such a generality; so must they bring to him and vitalize each organ of his body, and separately insure each function against every evil power; likewise these formulæ give the defunct, not only power to live, but power not to die. The Egyptian mind was sodden with their spirit; and the incapacity to feel the force of generalized statement affects all parts of Egyptian literature. In the hymns to Amon or the Nile, there is no lyric movement, no gathering up of previously stated thought or feeling, and carrying it on in generalization, or in lines which imply all that has gone before. In these, as in inferior compositions, broad statements are made, but the writer seems not to feel their content, and may return to the preceding order of detail. Nor is there an approach to a logical presentation of a subject with the deductions drawn therefrom. It is significant of the limitations of the Egyptian mind that, while Egypt has left exhaust-

[1] The best of these, perhaps, is a tale of the xii dynasty—the adventures of Sinuhit, vol. ii, *Rec. of the Past*, N. S.

less records, no Egyptian conceived the thought of history.

Monumental remains tell the full story of the Egyptian not unkindly, indiscriminate greed for life's bulk rather than life's best. And since a large proportion of the religious belief related to life after death and the means of insuring its continuance, and as these means lay so largely in building, pictorial representation, and sculpture, Egypt's monuments express these beliefs and embody them. Likewise, the temples tell the beliefs as to the gods, and the king's relationship to them in matters pertaining to the domain of earth. And finally the art entire of Egypt tells the experience and knowledge of the Egyptians, and displays their mental qualities in the modes in which they sought to effect their ends.

Qualities of Egyptian Architecture,

The Great Pyramid is the most admirably built of Egyptian structures. Its marvellous excellence of construction, in some parts more careful than in others, might excuse the absurd ideas which men have held regarding it. Its base lines for example are almost absolutely correct in levelling as well as angle; and well-nigh mysterious is the skill with which the huge limestone slabs of the "grand gallery" are dressed and cemented together.[1] Yet when the construction has been admired, admiration ceases. The architectural design is simple; the fundamental idea is barbarous;—that of ensuring the man's eternal existence by protecting the body with a heap of stone. Moreover the excellences of the pyramid, which lay in its construction, depended not on the higher qualities of the human mind, so much as on adventitious circumstances and that knowledge which is the accumulation of centuries of experience. The Nile inundation floated the blocks of granite and limestone to the spot, and, stopping for the time all works of agriculture, placed the entire population of the country at the disposal of the

[1] See Flinders Petrie, *Pyramids and Temples of Giseh.*

king. Undoubtedly he had also thousands of masons to dress the stones; there are even suggestions that the methods and tools employed were excellent.[1] Intelligence is needed to measure the Great Pyramid, and mathematical knowledge to calculate its angles. Its builders did not have such knowledge. Egyptian arithmetic was crude, and geometry never passed beyond the simplest propositions.[2]

The Theban temples are not as excellently built; and their columns have fallen, and still fall, because insecurely based. These temples are impressive because they are immense, a matter dependent on the wealth of the pharaoh, and the vainglory of his prodigality. No single thought shapes their entire construction. When the temple was begun there doubtless was a plan and grouping of the parts around a centre. But in successive reigns new halls and added galleries made all into a planless aggregate.[3] Here as elsewhere in creations of the Egyptian mind, there is no sense of inconsistency or superfluity, no consciousness of unity impaired. Nor was there always an intelligent use of structural forms. The diameter of a pillar is not kept proportioned either to its height[4] or to the weight which it sustains.[5] And it is curiously characteristic of the Egyptian race, that these pillars from century to century show no progressive modification of form, no increase of height in proportion to diameter, as the Greek columns showed, progressing from early to later Doric, then to Ionic and Corinthian.[6]

The pictorial representations with which Egyptians covered tombs and temples were sometimes slightly in relief, and sometimes slightly sunken in the stone. In

[1] See Flinders Petrie, *ib.*, ch. xix.

[2] See Erman, *Aegypten*, ch. xiv.

[3] The example here is the great temple at Karnak.

[4] As in Greek temples.

[5] As frequently in Gothic or Norman cathedrals.

[6] See Perrot and Chipiez, *Histoire de l'Art dans l'Antiquité*—"L'Egypte," p. 574.

the tombs of the Old Empire they represent the dead man with his wife, and also acts and services performed by his dependants. When the owner of the tomb was drawn, the matter of main interest was the man himself; and the idea seems to have been to render as much of his form as possible, and each part thereof in its most prominent aspect. That the figure as a whole might be out of harmony and truth was not considered. Accordingly the face is always in profile, save the eye, which is rendered in the full.[1] Then the chest and shoulders are drawn in front view; hence the neck is necessarily turned, as are the loins, where a transition is needed from the front presentation of the chest to the legs, which are again in profile, one advanced before the other. When these figures are drawn facing to the spectator's right, the left arm is advanced,[2] the hand grasping a staff on which it supports itself, while the right arm is extended downward back of the body. Thus both arms are completely shown and no part of the body hidden. The feet are drawn wrong, both right and left foot, so as to present its inner side, showing the great toe. Whether or not these peculiarities began as errors of primitive attempts to draw the human form, at all events they became conventionalities which were never given up. The drawing of each member considered by itself was substantially correct; the error lay in the impossible combination, an error not disturbing to the Egyptian mind.

Drawing,

Passing from the representations of the principal figure in these tombs of the Old Empire to those of his servants, one notices that the latter are engaged in acts useful or pleasant to the deceased; and the important matter is to represent, not their persons, but what they are doing. They are drawn with legs and arms in positions which

[1] This fact cannot be regarded as a matter of archaic inability with Egyptian artists; for it held till Ptolemaic times.

[2] Likewise the left leg.

show the act engaged in, and so are drawn more naturally than their masters.

These characteristics of the drawings from the Old Empire continue through the Middle Empire and the New. Yet an element of progress is noticeable: the profiles of the important personages become gradually more refined, attaining to great beauty and to a royal dignity in some of the drawings of the eighteenth and nineteenth dynasties; while on the other hand, as in the tombs from the twelfth dynasty at Benihassan, the painter gives to his wrestlers and tumblers distinctly vulgar features.[1]

and Sculpture.

Sculpture in the round does not lead to the same conventionalities as drawing. It may develop conventionalities of its own, occasioned by the nature of the material worked in. As the Egyptians sought in their statues qualities of endurance, the tendency, especially in the statues of kings who need spare no expense, was to select harder material than could be freely worked. The tombs of the Old Empire furnish statues of two kinds, corresponding to the two kinds of figures represented on the walls: portrait statues of the deceased, and statuettes of minor personages in some act of useful service. The portrait statue was to furnish a support for the double; and the closest likeness to the deceased was sought. This tended to keep such statues lifelike, and the best must have been the counterpart of the living man. On the other hand, the endeavor effectively to represent the act engaged in kept lifelike the ancillary statuettes. Both classes contain works of striking excellence.[2]

[1] Of all Egyptian paintings none are more typical than the battle pictures of the New Empire. There is little variety in them. Erect in his chariot the giant pharaoh advances through his pigmy enemies, who in absurd perspective and impossible positions tumble over each other in their flight. Yet the picture conveys the main idea: that of the superhuman force and majesty of pharaoh.

[2] For example, the famous seated scribe in the Louvre and the wooden statue at Cairo and a number of statuettes at Cairo.

The likeness to the deceased sought in the portrait statues precluded idealizing of form or feature. Yet since the pharaoh was a different being from his subjects, that difference must be shown. Soon were his statues made colossal, a material way of expressing his superiority. But the artists also endeavored to give these statues dignity. It might be that the skill of man, working in diorite and granite, which were the royal stones, reached not to the lifelike delineation of each feature of the pharaoh's face. But then the pharaoh was high and lifted up, a god in flesh; mortal eye shall look beneath the incident and see the real unending life and power divine; the artist must render that, as he did in the leonine calm of Khaphra's statue from the Sphinx's temple. In the end, however, the endeavor for the ideal pharaoh-type, both in painting and colossal statues, weakened to mere conservation of forms perhaps become hieratic.

It was in statues and drawings of the pharaohs that Egyptian art touched endeavor for the beautiful, reaching towards a conscious selection of the better, the more perfect, rather than the less; yet it was held down by blind conservatism and failure to perceive that bulk is not dignity nor hardest stone immortal life. Indeed, the sardonic element in Egyptian art was its misdirection, that with massive structures and colossal statues it thought to insure man's life beyond the grave.

Mesopotamian Culture.

As far back as the monuments of lower Mesopotamia reach, they tell of Semitic people occupying Babylonia, and another race dwelling towards its southern sea-borders, the "black-head" people of Sumer and Accad. In culture, and apparently in possession of the soil, the Sumerian-Accadians were prior, and the spectacle presented from the first is that of the Semites pressing in, politically predominant, absorbing the greater culture of the prior race. Babylonia affords the earliest example of that principle of progress, human or divine, which distinguishes the wars of ancient men from the preying of brutes upon each other: when a fresher, stronger race subdues one more advanced in knowledge and the arts, it acquires the civilization of the conquered.

The names are known of many early Mesopotamian kings and of their cities; their racehood, epochs, and political relations remain largely surmise. Wide-reaching would appear to have been the dominion of the ancient Sargon of Accad and his son.[1] Fifteen centuries later, the great King Hammurabi,[2] of the first dynasty to reign at Babylon, subjected all Chaldæa to his sway. He was a protector and a benefactor to the conquered southern lands, a constructor of canals, and a restorer of temples. From his inscriptions it appears that in Chaldæa beneficence was expected of a king, as in the Egypt of the Middle Empire. "As Anu and Bel granted to me to subject the people of Sumer and Accad, I dug the canal 'Hammurabi is the people's blessing,' which carries water of the inundation for the people of Sumer and Accad. Its banks on both sides I set for nourishment. Measures of corn I poured out. Unfailing water I created for the people of Sumer and Accad; I brought their multitudes together, I created food and drink for them. With blessing and abundance I presented them; I let them dwell in quiet dwellings."[3] Under Hammurabi and his successors the union of Sumerian culture with the stronger Semitic spirit was completed, and hymns and myths and legends were given literary form.[4]

An ancient Sumerian god was Ea. He was worshipped as the demiurge, but wider was his fame and divine sig-

[1] 3800 B.C.?

[2] B.C. 2264–2210.

[3] Winckler, *Geschichte Babyloniens*, p. 64.

[4] In large part the old Sumerian thought furnished the contents of these writings; but the living language of Babylon, in which the genius of the time was finding natural expression, was a Semitic tongue closely allied to the Assyrian.

nificance as the wise sea-god, who civilized the people of Sumer-Accad.[1] Ea stood for the Sumerian consciousness of the worth of civilization and the knowledge whereby man guards his life and gains his ends. In accord with this consciousness the people of Sumer-Accad had developed the arts and faculties of settled life, together with a mass of knowledge real and fanciful; and they delivered all that they had gained to the like-minded yet more masterful race which was making Babylon the dominant centre of a national life. The latter people added further attainments to their heritage, till they could read the heavens, the times and seasons of the earth, and the presageful flight of birds. Along the paths of foolishness comes knowledge. Babylonian astrology held some knowledge of astronomy and mathematics, out of which the ancient world should draw, as it also drew from Babylonian foolishness.[2] In all the elements of material civilization Babylon was to be pre-eminent for two thousand years; a swarming centre of industrial and social life, and the focus of the commerce of the ancient world. Her merchants were princes. In later times Babylonia was the richest province of the Persian Empire, and later still, at Rome, Babylonian vestures fetched their weight in gold, and Babylonian numbers still disclosed the future. For all of which the fame of Babylon has never faded. The matter of chief human interest is the strength and practical intelligence of toil which created this civilization, and sustained it amid the push and tumult of invading arms for twenty centuries.

Toil's peace and comfort lie in the assurance of result. Perhaps because of the land's security, and the certain recurrence of Nile inundation and propitious seasons, the Egyptians rarely felt the bitterness of the labor which

[1] The story of Ea (Oannes) coming out of the Persian Gulf to civilize men is handed down from Berosus in extremely antique guise. See Cory's *Ancient Fragments*, p. 57.

[2] See *Le Divination et la Science des Presages chez les Chaldéens*, Fr. Lenormant; *Die Kosmologie der Babylonier*, P. Jensen.

may end in nought. But life was not secure in Chaldæa, for enemies were never far; nor was the land healthful as Egypt; the plague demon was more frequently to fear. So the Chaldæan view of life lacked the Egyptian calm. Sombre and full of terror is the Gilgames epic,[1] which forms Chaldæa's heroic background. Its plot turns on a goddess' hate; its twelve tablets are filled with dreadful labors undergone, uncouth struggles with monstrous brutes and demi-men, weird voyagings to be cleansed from foul disease, and fruitless questings of the Tree of Life. It closes darkly with burial chant and hideous suggestion of the underworld: "Tell, my friend, tell, my friend, open the earth." "I cannot tell thee, my friend, I cannot tell thee; if I should open the earth to thee, terror and weeping would overcome thee, thou wouldst faint away." So is life a thing of toil, and painful toil; it must encounter perils and overcome or escape them; yet is it run to earth at last. It was fitting that this epic should contain the story of the Deluge; the thought of destruction from the gods was very native to Chaldæa.

Sombreness of Babylonian Thought.

The people of Sumer-Accad and the later dwellers at Babylon were very fearful of the world without. The spirits were malevolent, the great gods were often angry. From the earliest times, when the Chaldæan conscience was still unawakened, there is reflected fear of evils threatening and falling upon man. Blind and arbitrary is the way of the powers without till a moral nature be ascribed to them. In time there came the thought that the great gods might be benign and merciful; and since evils ceased not to come on men, there dawned a sense of shortcoming, sin, and penitence.

The Incantation and the Sense of Sin.

The early Babylonian incantation was full of fear. Troubles which came were either the onslaughts of foes

[1] For translations, see Smith's *Chaldæan Account of Genesis*, Sayce's Ed.; Jeremias' *Izdubar-Nimrod;* Sauveplane, *Une Épopée Babylonienne;* Maspero, *Dawn of Civilization*, p. 574, etc.

or the diseases and accidents of life. Pain and ill seemed to come from beings outside the man, and should be warded off by incantation aiding practical exertion. But magic sought to move solely the other, the extrahuman, superhuman being: it did not contemplate betterment of the man himself; for it was conscious of no human shortcoming. But a sense of sin is a sense of shortcoming in the man; it presupposes the standard of the ways, the power, the nature, or the character of the man's god, his lord whom he must obey, whom he displeases at his peril. It means that religious thought has reached a certain stage of clearness. A savage with his fetish, his totem, his sorceries and incantations, can have no sense of sin; for he has no sufficiently clear standard to give rise to any sense of shortcoming in himself. Hence, consciousness of sin means dawning ideality; means that man conceives what, according to his ethical standards, is better than himself. And as his nature rises and expands, he must conceive his god as just and mighty.

Thus, as it would seem, man's early knowledge of life's pains and ills, and life's destruction, turned with the Babylonians to the thought that all was not right in the sufferer; that his ills were not altogether to be ascribed to arbitrarily malignant forces, but also related to some shortcoming in himself. With these advancing thoughts regarding human ills, the powers of the world without took on a nobler form; no longer altogether brute, malignant, arbitrary, but rather adjudged to be superior where-ever man felt himself wanting. So, when ills threatened men or came on them, when aid was needed or protection, instead of using magic rite and spell, men addressed themselves to their higher gods in prayer and worship, in confession of themselves, what they were and were not, so in penitence. They implore deliverance or aid, not only from the power and favor, but from the mercy of their god. Yet though the Babylonians came thus to address their gods in prayer, they did not expand their thought of prayer's efficiency to the exclusion of the use of magic. Spells still constituted means of protection against malignant powers ; and the strongest spells might consist in conjuring with the names of the mightier gods. So the gods are frequently conjured with rather than prayed to. Finally the worshippers indeed ascribe all power to the god who fills their vision at the time ; but no conception of a god in Babylon or Nineveh rose to such high power of consistency as to dispel all thought of other gods. Of Semitic peoples, Israel alone reached monotheism ; and accordingly only in Israel were magic rites abominated, and reliance placed—at least by Israel's true leaders —solely on penitence and prayer and God's forgiveness.

There is a quality which men feeling their sins must soon attribute to their god, whose nature they should resemble and do not, whose commands they should obey, and do not, the quality of mercy, whereby the god does not destroy, but forgives. Races with no abiding sense of sin do not emphasize this quality in their gods, who rather are beneficent freely or in return for sacrifice, and it may be just.[1] But a sense of sin looks for mercy, and hence Babylonians and merciless Assyrians ascribed it to their gods. Perhaps a step beyond the quality of mercy and forgiveness on repentance is that of unsolicited pity, which also is a quality of Babylonian and Assyrian gods. Merodach is spoken of as the "merciful lord who loves to raise the dead to life."[2] In *Ishtar's Descent* that goddess weeps over human lots, as, in the story of the Deluge she leads the gods in lament over the destruction of mankind.

"Magic Text," "Hymn" and "Penitential Psalm."

Babylonian hymns were largely magic, their recital accompanying the magic ritual. A hymn often passes from lofty thought to merest incantation ; as in the following (Semitic) hymn to the Sun-god :

[1] Neither Egyptians nor Greeks nor Romans laid emphasis on this quality.

[2] Sayce, *Hib. Lect.*, 1887, p. 98.

"O Sun-god, king of heaven and earth, . . .
Thou that clothest the dead with life, delivered by thy hands,
Judge unbribed, director of mankind.

. . . .

O bird stand still and hear the hound!
O Sun-god stand still and hear me!
Overpower the name of the evil ban that has been created,
Whether the ban of my father, or the ban of my begetter, or
The ban of the seven branches of the house of my father. . . .
For father and mother I pronounce the spell;
And for brother and child, I pronounce the spell. . . ."[1]

A mixture of contrite or fearful thought and magic spell also appears in certain compositions of the nature of penitential Psalms:

The heart of my lord is wroth; may it be appeased!
May the god whom I know not be appeased!
May the goddess whom I know not be appeased!
[repetitions similar]
The sin that (I sinned I) knew not,

. . . .

The cursed thing of my god unknowingly did I eat;
The cursed thing of my goddess unknowingly did I trample on.
O my god, my sins are many, my transgressions are great.
[repetitions similar]

. . . .

The cursed thing that I trampled on, I knew not.

. . . .

The god whom I know and whom I know not has distressed me.

. . . .

I sought for help and none took my hand;
I wept and none stood at my side;
I cried aloud and there was none that heard me.
I am in trouble and hiding; I dare not look up.
To my god, the merciful one, I turn myself, I utter my prayer.

. . . .

[1] Sayce, *ib.*, p. 320.

The transgressions I have committed may the wind carry away!

. . . .

O my god, seven times seven are my transgressions; forgive my sins.

. . . .

May thy ban be removed.

. . . .

Colophon,—Psalm of 65 lines; a tablet for every god.
Its repetition insures my peace."[1]

Assurbanipal's Prayer and Nebuchadnezzar's Inscription.

The above "psalm" is preserved in Accadian with an Assyrian interlinear translation. We may pass on two thousand years or more to a prayer of Assurbanipal and the inscription of Nebuchadnezzar.

"I confess to thee, Nebo, in the assembly of the great gods

. . . .

I prostrate myself at the feet of Nebo . . . in the multitude of my sins.
I will cause thee to live, Assurbanipal, even I, Nebo, to everlasting days;
Thy feet shall not be weary, thy hands shall not tremble,
These thy lips shall not fail for praying to me.

. . . .

Bowing down in his sanctuary,
Assurbanipal made his prayer to Nebo, his Lord:
I have given myself unto thee, Nebo,
Thou wilt not forsake me.
My life in thy presence is governed, my soul is held in the embrace of Beltis.
I have given myself unto thee, Nebo, mighty one,
Thou wilt not forsake me in the midst of my sins.
Thy sins, Assurbanipal, like ripples on the face of the water shall they be.
Thou shalt stand in the presence of the great gods; thou shalt magnify Nebo."[2]

[1] Sayce, *ib.*, p. 349. See also *Proceedings of Society of Biblical Archæology*, 1895, p. 139.
[2] *Records of the Past*, N. S., vol. vi, p. 102.

Not many decades after the Assyrian king's death, though in the meanwhile Nineveh had fallen, was written Nebuchadnezzar's inscription. It begins:

"Nebuchadnezzar, King of Babylon, the king exalted, the favorite of Merodach, the pontiff supreme, the beloved of Nebo, the serene, the possessor of wisdom, who in the way of their godhead regardeth, who feareth their lordship; the servant unwearied, who for the maintenance of Esagilla and Egida [chief temples of Babylon and Borsippa] daily bethought him, and the weal of Babylon and Borsippa regardeth ever; the wise, the prayerful, the chiefest son of Nebopolassar, King of Babylon am I. After that the Lord my God had created me, that Merodach had framed the creature in the mother; when I was born, when I was created, even I, the holy places of the god I regarded, the way of the god I walked in. Of Merodach, the great lord, the god, my creator, his cunning works highly do I extol. Of Nebo, his true son, the beloved of my majesty, the way of his supreme godhead steadfastly do I exalt; with all my true heart I love the fear of their godhead, I worship their lordship. When Merodach, the great lord, lifted up the head of my majesty, and with lordship over the multitude of peoples invested me, and Nebo, the overseer of the multitude of heaven and earth, for the governing of the peoples a righteous sceptre placed in my hands: for me, of them am I heedful, I have regard unto their godhead; for the mention of their glorious name, I worship the god and Ishtar. To Merodach, my lord, I made supplication, prayer to him I undertook, and the word which my heart looked for, to him I spake: 'Of old, O prince, lord of all that is, for the king whom thou lovest, and whose name thou callest, that to thee is pleasing; thou directest his name, a straight path thou appointest him. I am a prince obedient unto thee, a creature of thy hands. Thou it was that madest me, and with sovereignty over the multitude of the peoples thou didst invest me; according to thy goodness, O Lord, wherewith thou crownest all of them. Make loving thy supreme lordship and cause the fear of thy godhead to be in my heart. . . . Like as I love the fear of thy godhead, and seek unto thy lordship, favorably regard the lifting up of my hands, hear my prayers.'"[1]

Assurbanipal's prayer discloses a sense of sin, and he casts himself upon his god's forgiveness, doubtless in a tim of distress. Nebuchadnezzar recognizes his relation of creature and minister to Merodach; he knows that Merodach and Nebo have placed a righteous sceptre in his hands[2]; he desires to be obedient, that they may be gracious, and he "loves the fear of their godhead." When words like these are used, it still remains to determine what significance the speaker attaches to them. The conception of religion as an alliance between god and man against other peoples and their gods, never ceased in Mesopotamia. A late Assyrian king needed rather the forgiveness of all the earth, than of the god who had marched with Assur and Ishtar at the head of Assyria's armies. Yet according to his standards, Assurbanipal professes to have sinned and to need forgiveness. What Nebuchadnezzar meant by "righteous" must be inferred from his acts and from his satisfaction with his long reign. Undoubtedly, he wishes to obey, he looks unto his god, will regulate himself by that god's standard; and whatever he may mean by the word "love," he approaches the Hebrew psalmist and prophet when he asserts that he loves the fear of Merodach his creator. Such prayers seem far removed from magic incantation; yet Assurbanipal's library preserves the one and the other with the same reverent care. Far be it from him to have risen above presages and divination, or above the spells which ward off various ills.

[1] *Records of the Past*, N. S., vol. iii, pp. 104–106, 122.

[2] The thought of a sceptre of righteousness or "sceptre of the temples" may be as old as 1800 B.C. See Brünnow, *Zeitschrift für Assyriologie*, 1890, p. 70; Boscawen, *Bible and the Monuments*, p. 32.

The conception of sin is the matter of main human interest in the religion of Babylonia, which in other respects was sufficiently archaic. So is it in the Assyrian religion which in somewhat stricter grooves followed its elder sister. That neither Babylonians nor Assyrians perceived any incompatibility between magic and prayer is one element placing them on the same intellectual level with the Egyptians. The material accomplishment of these races was stupendous; nor did either lack in manifold development of custom and social institution. The Egyptians occupied themselves with varied toil and diversion. Babylon, with its commerce, its banking-houses, its loans and pledges, its developed contract law, may arouse astonishment. Not because of any lack in the bulky composite of common life were these two races what they were, primitive always; but through lack of consistently progressive thought respecting the human spirit; and through lack in consequence of the definite formulation of ideals suited to the higher discriminations of man's nature. Egyptians and Babylonians remained undeveloped in the intellectual and spiritual elements of personality; nor in these respects did the Assyrians show advance.

Egyptians and Chaldæans Intellectually Undeveloped.

They were a Semitic people who had established themselves in northern Mesopotamia before the fifteenth century, B.C. They took to themselves the literature, the arts, and the religion of the south. As a military power, they fixed themselves in their land and set their cities; with arms they conquered, and with arms they held the empire of western Asia; and when their military might was broken, they and their cities ceased.

Assyrian Rudimentary Humanity

Human personality grows as men perceive that only in correlation with the welfare of others can they fulfil themselves. This is early recognized within family and tribal circles; the far goal is its recognition as to all mankind. It is evident that a race entirely occupied with slaying other people and seizing their possessions has but a rudimentary humanity, a narrow ethics, a narrow religion. The latter has not passed beyond the stage where the god is conceived as the ally, who crushes the common foe. The god may become, however, an exacting ally, who will not aid his own except they punctiliously minister to him ; nay more, it may be will not help them unless they maintain themselves at the standard of his excellence ; and in correspondence with this thought, overthrow or ill-success may rouse in the race a sense of shortcoming and of sin. Assyria might order her pantheon more scrupulously than did the Babylonians ; she might restrict her devotions to a few mighty gods ; and bitterly was she in the end to feel how she had fallen below the standard of their excellence of power. But never did she pass beyond the ethics and religion of the race which smites and spares not.

This may be clearly read in those records of war, rapine, and ruin, and of war's diplomacy, which constitute the annals of the Tiglathpalesers, of Assurnazirpal, of Sargon and Sennacherib, and of Assurbanipal, the last great monarch. Under a near successor, Nineveh went down in night, leaving no trace on earth,[1] or record of her ruin. Two or three broken tablets seem to refer to the time of destruction ; they speak darkly of Medes and Cimmerians, proclaim propitiatory rites to be observed for a hundred days, and preserve the fragment of a prayer,—" O great god of fixed destiny, remove our sin ! "[2]—then silence. Writings of the Greeks throw but a faint gleam on the fate of the empire of blood, while the Jew cries out his fierce prophetic hate over her ruin. For indeed, " upon whom had not her wickedness passed continually ? "[3]

[1] Xenophon, two hundred years after, while Babylon was still a great city, saw and heard nothing of Nineveh.

[2] See texts relating to the fall of the Assyrian Empire, vol. xi, *Records of the Past*, p. 79.

[3] Nahum.

There must have been domestic life in Assyria, though it was not thought worth recording. The extant monuments are from the royal palaces. There is enough of bas-relief and inscription, but it is all record and illustration of the story of Assyria's well-organized might, her rapacity, destructiveness, and unique delight in cruelty. Bas-relief and inscription alike tell of the king and his royal strength; they tell of his officers and state and armies, his chariots and horsemen and bowmen going forth to war; they tell of crossing deserts, fording rivers, climbing mountains, in pursuit of enemies; they tell of the devastation of the land, the cutting down of palm-trees, the besieging and the tearing down of cities; they tell of the Assyrian victories, pyramids of heads and trunks, prisoners impaled or flayed, burned alive or blinded. The king himself is seen thrusting his spear into the eyes of men held by hooks through their lips. So they show all manner of torture of vanquished men, and then the long trains of spoil, beasts of all kinds, and women, and the wealth of lands, driven or carried off to glut Assyria's palaces and temples.

Shown in Assyrian Art.

There is power in Assyrian sculpture, even a calm strength in the winged bulls. But the figures in the bas-reliefs are usually in violent motion badly drawn. Two prominent types appear, the bearded monarch and the beardless eunuch, both drawn with over-heavy muscle. These types vary slightly from reign to reign, but the sculptor does not seek to individualize the features. The Assyrians had the Semitic dislike of the uncovered body, and there is no fine modelling of the human form. The only naked figures are those of men impaled on stakes or flayed. The best Assyrian works are the reliefs of animals, dogs or horses, or the hunted beasts, especially the lions transfixed with arrows.[1]

[1] Every one knows the splendid Wounded Lioness, from Assurbanipal's palace, in the Assyrian Basement of the British Museum. An arrow has pierced her back; with a marvellously rendered snarl of rage, she drags her paralyzed hindquarters forward in a death struggle to reach her foe.

The battle scenes are failures of composition; they are panoramic, with neither perspective nor centring of interest. Except for the accompanying text, it might be difficult to distinguish the main characters in the fight. Clearly, whatever adaptation there may be of means to ends in Assyrian art, the higher qualities of human intellect are absent more strikingly than from the art of Egypt. Those qualities had not been shown in the dreary waste of Babylonian writings, and the Assyrians had no literature of their own. The library of Assurbanipal contains only reproductions of Babylonian magic, astrology, science, and religion; largely, indeed, interlinear translations of Sumerian or Accadian texts. In this scribe activity, there was no new creation.[1]

Chinese Characteristics and the Early History.

If the "black-haired" people who became Chinese ever came from Mesopotamian lands,[2] their travels across Asia dispelled Chaldæan vapors, for they were not possessed with the vampire spirit of superstitious fear which overhung the land of Sumer and Accad; nor had they the Semite's sense of sin. They had, however, a mighty power of industry with extraordinary capacity for being governed as a national aggregate. Their most marked superiority over Babylon and Egypt was the faculty of ethical formulation. They related rules of conduct to fundamental principle, constructed a system of ethics, and set before themselves an ideal of character expressing itself in conduct. Under the inspiration of this ideal, the history of China was written; for it formed a standard of remembrance by which certain aspects of fact and story should be preserved, others forgotten; and it was this same ideal which Confucius and his school, who stand for China's very self, formally systematized.

[1] See Winckler, *Geschichte Babyloniens*, etc., pp. 300–302.

[2] See Terrien de la Couperie, *Western Origin of Early Chinese Civilization*; C. J. Ball, "Accadian Affinities of Chinese," *Trans.*, *Ninth Congress of Orientalists* (1891), ii, p. 677.

Thus is it peculiarly enlightening as to the ideals of China to notice the records which the race kept of itself.

Yao is the first emperor told of in the *Shu King*, the ancient canonical collection of historical memorials.[1] He was reverential, accomplished, thoughtful, and courteous.[2] He adjusted the calendar, regulated agriculture, and "united and harmonized the myriad states; and so the black-haired people were transformed. The result was concord."[3] Yao, growing old, wished to nominate the chief councillor as his successor. The latter declared his virtue unequal to the ruling of the realm, and told of one Shun, whose father, step-mother, and half-brother, with whom he lived, were bad and quarrelsome; yet by his filial piety Shun had lived harmoniously with them, and led them to mend their ways. "I will try him," said Yao. "I will wive him, and thereby see his behavior with my two daughters."[4]

Shun, married to the emperor's daughters, displayed a completely virtuous character. He was thereupon made General Regulator, and after three years, in spite of his modest reluctance, was named emperor by Yao. As ruler he was irreproachable, conducting the appropriate sacrifices, regulating ceremonies, weights and measures, and punishments. "Let me be reverent," said Shun, "let compassion rule in punishment."[5] A great organizer was Shun, forming many departments and setting tried ministers over them.

The great Yu had been Shun's General Regulator. When he had set in order the provinces, he said, in reverent response to the Emperor: "If the sovereign can realize the difficulty of his sovereignty, and the minister

[1] It is translated by Dr. Legge in his *Chinese Classics* and (a revised edition) in vol. iii, *Sacred Books of the East*.

[2] *Shu King*, i, 1.

[3] *Shu King*, i, 1, from Dr. Legge's revised translation in *Sacred Books of the East*, vol. iii.

[4] *Shu King*, i, 3.

[5] *Shu King*, ii, 1.

the difficulty of his ministry, the government will be well ordered, and the black-haired people will sedulously seek to be virtuous."[1] Yu overcame the great inundation; he opened passages for the streams, drained the lands, sowing grain and teaching the people. Shun knows him for his true successor, and so calls him to rule. Yu would decline in favor of the Minister of Crime, who on his part will hear only of Yu. Shun, too, is set in his determination, telling Yu that he excels all in ability and merit. "The determinate appointment of heaven rests on your person."[2]

Its Moral.

"The favor of Heaven is not easily preserved. Men lose its favoring appointment because they cannot carry out the reverence and virtue of their forefathers."[3] To a dynasty, Heaven's high commission is during good behavior; when its rule becomes bad, it ceases to be legitimate. The recurrent fact with mighty moral in the *Shu King* is that ruin overtakes a dynasty grown evil, and, as commissioned by Heaven, the founder of the new dynasty overthrows it. Let his descendants revere his ways. Throughout the *Shu King* the virtue of reverence is inculcated, reverence for Heaven, reverence for the people, reverence for ancestors and their customs. It meant the due performance of every duty and the fitting observance of every ceremony and propriety.

The teachings of Confucius and his followers represent

[1] *Shu King*, ii, 2.

[2] The great Yu was the founder of the Hsia dynasty, which came to an end about 1766 B. C. Regarding the truth of these narrations, Legge says: "The results which I have endeavored to bring out in this chapter are, first, that Yu is an historical personage and was the founder of the Chinese Empire, but that nearly all that the *Shu* contains of his labors is fantastical exaggeration; and second, that Yao and Shun were also real men, chiefs of the earliest Chinese immigrants into the country, but we must divest them of the grand proportions which they have, as seen through the mists of legend and of philosophical romance."—Prolegomena to the *Shu King*, p. 80.

[3] *Shu King*, part v, book xv, 1.

a system made from the best elements of China's past as mirrored in its records and traditionary usages and reflected in the life of Confucius himself.[1] The master was a transmitter, but not of disconnected facts with unrelated significance; he sought to learn a unity all-pervading.[2] His teachings are a system holding as an ideal the perfecting of character in modes of conduct accordant with the nature of man conferred by Heaven.

Confucianism.

"What Heaven has conferred is called the nature. An accordance with this nature is called the Path of Duty. The regulation of this path is called the System of Instruction."[3] Evidently the nature which Heaven has conferred on man would bear some likeness to its source, whose way it is to duly recompense, and would include the benevolent faculties, the works of which Heaven prospers and rewards. Hence might Confucius say: Benevolence is man.[4] Also, should it not be germane to man's nature to reverence and fulfil the relationships and duties ordained by Heaven?[5] Very exacting are these relationships, of ruler and minister, son and father, wife and husband, elder brother and younger, friend and friend.[6] So can the master say with definite meaning: "Fidelity to one's self and the corresponding reciprocity are not far from the

"What Heaven has Conferred."

[1] The best understanding of Confucius may be had from reading his life and sayings in the *Lun Yu*, translated by Dr. Legge in his *Chinese Classics*, vol. i (second edition, 1893). Confucius was born 551 B.C.

[2] *Lun Yu*, xv, 2.

[3] *Kung Yung*, i, 1. This treatise forms book xxviii of the *Li Ki*, but is often printed separately. It is the most authentic compend of Confucius' teachings. See Legge's "Introduction to *Li Ki*," vol. xxvii, *Sacred Books of the East*.

[4] *Kung Yung*, ii, 6 Mencius afterwards stated more explicitly the doctrine here involved, that men are by nature good. See Mencius, book vi, i, 6. "The great man is he who does not lose his child's heart."—*Ibid.*, iv, ii, 12.

[5] See *Shu King*, ii, iii, 3.

[6] See *Kung Yung*, i, 35; ii, 9.

path. What you do not like when done to yourself, do not do to others."[1] You would not, when yourself concerned, like to have others fail in the fulfilment of the duties of these relationships: do not you fail in their fulfilment.

State of Equilibrium and Harmony.

Man's nature and the Path which is accordance therewith are set forth as the State of Equilibrium and Harmony. "When there are no stirrings of pleasure, anger, sorrow, or joy, we call it the State of Equilibrium. When those feelings have been stirred, and all in their due measure and degree, we call it the State of Harmony. This Equilibrium is the great root, and this Harmony is the universal path."[2] All men should observe in feeling, thought, and correspondent action exactly what the proprieties of the situation demand, fulfil its requirements, nor exceed them. "The superior man does what is proper to the position in which he is; he does not wish to go beyond it."[3] This principle of propriety of conduct combines with the idea of reciprocity. Confucius was asked whether injury should be recompensed with kindness. He answered: "With what, then, will you recompense kindness? Recompense injury with justice, and recompense kindness with kindness."[4]

The Ideal of Propriety of Character.

Thus, excellence is fundamentally a matter of man's inner nature forming itself in character; the fruit of this character is unfailing propriety of conduct. The former of these principles was carried out consistently: "The superior man, even when he is not acting, has the feeling of reverence; and when he does not speak, he has the feeling of truthfulness."[5] From the formalistic tendencies of the Chinese, rules of conduct before Confucius' time had become rules of propriety and ceremonial usages. In heart-

[1] *Kung Yung*, i, 32.
[2] *Kung Yung*, i, 5.
[3] *Kung Yung*, i, 36.
[4] *Lun Yu*, xiv, 36.
[5] See *Kung Yung*, ii, 60, 63, 64.

felt earnestness, he sought to conform his life to them,[1] feeling them to be expressive of universal propriety and adapted to establish a perfect character.[2] They were the visible frame of the State of Equilibrium and Harmony, a frame which might not be departed from.[3] By them the ancient kings sought to present the ways of Heaven and regulate humanity.[4] They are the bond holding the multitude together; they check depravity. Every act of life, every act of intercourse among the living or between the living and the dead, should conform to them.[5]

Filial Piety.

The Chinese have always thought that to hold office under the government is the goal and highest excellence of human careers.[6] Yet government, in which not all men can take part, has its prototype in the family; and all men are sons, and all wish to become fathers. That a man should leave father and mother and cleave unto his wife is a progressive principle which hands life on, rather than endeavors to repay it to the past. It is the opposite of everything Chinese. In Confucian China the vital principle of the family was to be the relationship of parents and children,[7] rather than that of man and wife; and the pre-eminent virtue of the land was to be filial piety. This virtue includes all duties, social and political; it binds the family together, and forms the basis of government.[8] The master said: "The laying the

[1] *Cf. Lun Yu*, xv, 17.

[2] *Lun Yu*, viii, 8.

[3] *Cf. Lun Yu*, viii, 2.

[4] *Li Ki*, vii, i, 4.

[5] *Cf. Lun Yu*, x, 2, 5, 9, 16. A conception of the enormous import of ceremonies and strict propriety in Chinese thought may be had from the *Li Ki*, or "Collection of Treatises on the Rules of Propriety and Ceremonial Usages," perhaps the most characteristic work in Chinese literature. It is one of the five "King," or classics, and is translated by Dr. Legge in vols. xxvii and xxviii, *Sacred Books of the East.*

[6] See *e. g.* Mencius, book iii, part ii, chap. iii.

[7] See *e. g. Li Ki*, xli, 1.

[8] The father's power has always been and still is autocratic. See F. Scherzer, *La Puissance Paternelle en Chine.*

foundation of [all] love in the love of parents teaches people reverence."[1] "Filial piety is the root of all virtue."[2]

Confucian Conception of Poetry and Music.

Besides direct ethical instruction and example, with teaching of the rites and ceremonies, the system of Confucius sought to use subtler instruments for the perfecting of that character which should display itself in unfailing propriety of conduct. These were poetry and music. In the *Shu King*,[3] the Emperor Shun appoints a Director of Music "to teach our sons, so that the straightforward shall yet be mild; the gentle, dignified; the strong, not tyrannical; and the impetuous, not arrogant." This is the ancient statement. Says Confucius: "It is by the Odes that the mind is aroused. It is by the rules of propriety that the character is established. It is from music that the finish is received."[4]

When Confucius urged his disciples to study the Odes of the *Shih King*,[5] he urged them to study what was a collection of ancient poems, written at various epochs, prosperous or disastrous, virtuous or licentious, of the people's history. These, in the view of Confucian commentators, express sentiments appropriate to the conditions under which they were composed. They are duly joyful over righteous prosperity, duly resentful at disorder, duly mournful over disaster. That is to say, they are moral or, in more Chinese phrase, correct.[6] Odes stir the feelings of the hearers, and, if correct, rouse the feelings aright, all in due measure and proportion,—the State of Harmony. This is the function of poetry, corresponding to its nature. As is said in the "Great Preface": "Poetry is the product of earnest thought. Thought [cherished] in the mind becomes earnest; exhibited in words, it becomes poetry. The feelings move inwardly,

[1] *Li Ki*, xxi, i, 15.
[2] *Hsiao King*, chap. i.
[3] II, i, 5.
[4] *Lun Yu*, viii, 8.
[5] *Lun Yu*, xvii, 9.
[6] See the "Great Preface" to the *Shih King*.

and are embodied in words. When words are insufficient for them, recourse is had to sighs and exclamations; when these are insufficient, recourse is had to the prolonged utterances of song; when this is insufficient, unconsciously the hands begin to wave and the feet to dance."

"From music the finish is received." It is the finer analogue of poetry: "All modulations of the voice spring from the minds of men. When the feelings are moved within, they are manifested in the sounds of the voice; and when these sounds are combined so as to form compositions, we have what are called airs."[1] Conversely, as with poetry, music influences the dispositions of the hearers, hence has an ethical effect. It should not be inappropriate, licentious, rousing feelings improper to the situation. The ancient kings, in their institution of music as well as ceremonies, meant to teach the people to direct aright their likings and dislikings.[2] Both ceremonies and music are needed for the perfection of character. To the performance of the one, as to the utterance of the other, there must be a correspondence in man's inner nature; otherwise, at least for him, they are nothing.[3] It is, however, the special function of music to promote union and affection, while ceremonies preserve distinctions and respect.[4]

It accords with the inwardness of the Confucian ideal of character that music ideally conceived should be an inner harmony without sound, and that ceremony, likewise ideally conceived, should be unembodied in any prescribed form. "When there is that ceremony without embodiment, all the demeanor is calm and gentle, when there is that music without sound, there is no movement of the will in opposition to it."[5]

The ancient Chinese sacrificed to the hills and rivers and

[1] *Li Ki*, xvii, i, 4.

[2] See *Li Ki*, xvii, i, 10, etc.

[3] See *Lun Yu*, iii, 3.

[4] *Li Ki*, xvii, i, 15. 23, 24, 29.

[5] *Li Ki*, xxvi, 5.

other natural objects; more earnestly they worshipped their ancestors with sacrifice and prayer. Divination was the means employed to know the future.[1] Above all these matters was the thought of the supreme and distant Heaven with its ordainments. Sometimes, instead of Heaven (Thien), the word "Ti" is used, which is translated "God." The Chinese terms seem equivalent in import. Heaven orders the world aright; it is intelligent and observing,[2] compassionate, and again angered and unpitying, even unjust, sending down ruin.[3] Distant is it and vast.[4] Of no clear efficacy are prayers and sacrifices. Man must conform to its ways and hold its appointment by obeying its ordinances:[5] "Shall not those whom great Heaven does not approve of, surely as the waters flow from a spring, sink down together in ruin?"[6]

"Heaven" and Human Ethical Endeavor.

The conception of Heaven tended to lift itself farther above men, out of reach of their prayers; it tended toward the thought of ethical law, sure and universal, but impersonal. Heaven was the source of man's nature, and in conformity to its ordinances must men live. Had Heaven possessed a vivid personality, Chinese thought of human shortcoming might have contained a sense of sin. Practically, in the system of Confucius, man must look to himself and his endeavors after right thought and act. Worship and prayer have become a part of human propriety and ceremonial. Not an atom of the rites and ceremonies due to ancestors or to Heaven would the reverent-minded master have disregarded; but his earnest thought was directed to the proper performance of these

[1] See the *Shu* and *Shih King*, *passim*.

[2] *Shu King*, iv, viii, 2.

[3] See *Shu King* iv, xi, 2; v, i, 1 and 2; *Shih King*, Minor Odes of the Kingdom, Fourth Dec. Ode 7 and Ode 10; Fifth Dec., Ode 1; Major Odes, Dec. ii, Odes 10 and 11; Dec. iii, 10.

[4] *Shih King*, Minor Odes of the Kingdom, Fifth Dec., Ode 4.

[5] *Shu King*, iv, ii, 4.

[6] *Shih King*, Major Odes of the Kingdom, Dec. iii, Ode 2.

matters on the side of man. Righteousness, though it be conformity to the nature implanted by Heaven, must be reached through human exertions; Heaven helps not here. Confucius' teachings related not to God, but to human character and human conduct.[1]

Quietistic Tendencies; Taoism and Buddhism.

Confucianism was the ethical expression of the Chinese formative power and capacity. Before this power was spent, the race had realized its destiny in stable nationality under a not intolerable government. There had always been reactionary modes of inert quietism. These found expression in "Taoism," whose founder Lao–tze, was not in all respects an originator,[2] for in his system appear certain thoughts which Confucius also had taken from the past and adjusted to Confucianism. Lao-tze set forth his system darkly in terms of an ill-conceived absolute and the ineffable union of contraries; for such is the Tao, the causative principle of all existence as well as the way or rule of conduct which men must hold to. The operation of the Tao is motiveless; it is neither self-seeking nor benevolent.[3] In no way does it assert itself; yet it is the source and sustaining principle of life, and men must strive to hold it and imitate its ways. The sage will have no desires and do nothing with any purpose, either self-seeking or benevolent, so can he not fail to be beneficent.[4] Thus will he in absolute contentment preserve the Tao within him. If this fills him fully, there is in him no place for injury or death; his is indefinite and undefined longevity.[5] Likewise the Taoist sage-ruler should set the example of doing nothing with a purpose, and seeking no

[1] See *Lun Yu*, vii, 17; *ib.*, vii, 24; *ib.*, vii, 20; *ib.*, vi, 19; *ib.*, xi, 11.

[2] See *Les Origines du Taoisme*, Jean de Rosny, "Revue de l'Histoire des Religions, vol. xxii (1890) p. 161. Lao-tze's interesting but somewhat incomprehensible book is the *Tao-teh-king*, translated by Dr. Legge, vol. xxxix, *Sacred Books of the East*.

[3] See *Tao-teh-King*. 5, 7. 10, 34, 51.

[4] See *Tao-teh-King*, 5, 10, 12, 15, 16, 22, 24, 27, 28, 32, 34, 35, 64.

[5] *Ib.*, 16, 44, 45, 50, 52, 55, 59.

knowledge outside the Tao. Thus will he bring men back to the state of primitive simplicity. Taoism for its ideal looked back to an age of idyllic ignorance, when the people needed neither ruler nor laws, but all had the Tao. The first stage of degeneracy was the conscious exercise of benevolence and knowledge in the conduct of affairs.[1]

In such profound absurdities, which Taoism before its degeneracy drew from its principles, it showed the same thorough-going consistency as Confucianism. But that upheld the state, while Taoism, in any imagined application to affairs, was a more than reactionary dream.[2] It logically had no place for God; but its history bears witness how that the prayerful spirit of man, when it has reached forward to the thought of a single God, if it be cut off by some philosophy, may yield itself to every superstition. Long since has the philosophy of the Tao become idolatry mixed with magic seekings for elixirs of longevity. The course of its debasement is similar to that of Chinese Buddhism, though the latter system had fallen from its strenuous self-reliance before reaching China, where it was not introduced till the first century after Christ.[3] Thereafter, though occasionally persecuted, its spread was rapid, and its influence helped to turn Taoism into a religion. Side by side the two systems sank to kindred forms of superstition, both appealing to the inert, ignoble sides of Chinese character. China was not India, where grief at life's fleeting change might hold itself erect

[1] See *Tao-Teh-King*, 3, 17, 18, 19, 58, 60, 61, 64, 65.

[2] From ancient China comes the noble thought of the silent, undirected, almost unintended, working of a perfect character on the characters of other men. Herein the influence of the Confucian superior man was like the ways of Heaven, while the influence of the Taoist sage was like the rule and principle of life,—the Tao. The active energies of Confucianism kept the application of this idea within the limits of reason. But this same thought, comporting with the rest of Taoist principles and balanced by no teachings of endeavor, confirmed that system's uselessness and sealed its fate.

[3] See Beal, *Buddhism in China*, p. 47, etc. Some slight account of it may have reached China a century or two before.

on the strength of its high despair. China's strength and virtue lay in its toiling hands and toiling character. Doubt of the worth of endeavor and attainment meant life, not grieved over, but besotted.

The civilizations of Egypt, Mesopotamia, and China are primitive, not on account of their antiquity alone, but by reason of their quality and the undeveloped humanity which they present. Alike they stand for that ancient pre-requisite of civilization, ant-like, patient toil, which builds and gathers and preserves according to the calls of material well-being. They also represent a social ethics suited to the complex conventions of established and stationary societies, an ethics roundly well-intentioned, with a great fund of precepts shrewd and benignant, yet, save in the case of China, related to no fundamental principles. Politically, the ideal is that of absolute monarchs wisely ruling, and constructing works of large beneficence.

Spiritual Limitations of these Primitive Races.

As free-will is an element of the concept man, it is evident that no full humanity can exist among people who, through incapacity for social freedom,—which is self-assertion self-restrained,—are incapable of forming a free community. Here was a striking race deficiency in these early peoples. From the first historic periods the rulers of Egypt, Mesopotamia, and China, however wide or narrow the territory over which they ruled, or however insecure their power, were absolute rulers; and nothing points to a previous time when the people's life was not subject to a single will. Nor has capacity for free self-government ever been shown in any of these lands. Even the Chinese, with all their admirable thoughts of right conduct in the ruler and his ministers, never evolved an idea of political representative freedom in the people.

A more general, less tangible, deficiency in the peoples of Egypt and Babylonia was the undiscriminating nature of their desires, and their failure to formulate distinct ideals. China's superiority lay in the Confucian ideal of character; but this failed to break through its material encumbrances, and in the end became sheer ceremonial husk. This best ideal of China, bound as it was by formalities prescribing each detail of conduct, lacked in the vital quality of freedom. Despite the conception of character as inward, there was no trust placed in its spirit growth; it must be bandaged, like the women's feet. Evidently, such character was doomed to final incompleteness. Possibly, had the Chinese been capable of holding to the thought of Heaven's personality, they would have had an ever-heightening standard of will and personality, rather than of form and law, from which continually to vitalize their ideal of character. Such power they lacked; and Chinese limitations showed themselves in a race inability for spiritual concepts transcending the one clogged thought of a character correctly established in actions immemorially prescribed. They might not move onward in conception and endeavor toward ideals growing in correspondence to larger spiritual judgments of the verities of human nature; so they failed to know the freedom and the infinite craving which is man. Together with the Egyptians and the peoples of Mesopotamia, they represent positive limitations, a personality matured, yet incomplete, incapable of larger thought and fuller manhood.

CHAPTER III.

INDIA.

AS excavation and research open new vistas of the human past, a larger estimate is formed of the gulfs of years, the accumulations of experience, and the greatness of attainment, separating the earliest recorded periods of the culture races of antiquity from their own beginnings. Though there be discovered no earlier monuments of a race than those already known, light may be reflected on its past, and its extant records more correctly judged, from the standards of comparison afforded by increasing knowledge of the cruder thoughts of other peoples. The *Rig-Veda* is no new discovery. It is and may remain the oldest extant record of the Aryan spirit. India, at least, will have nothing more ancient to show. But wider knowledge of the ancient world, as well as better understanding of the Vedic text, makes clear that the Vedic Aryans, through the times of their victorious establishment in India, were a race whose institutions and advanced humanity pre-suppose a lengthy past of growth in the qualities which make men men. The circumstances of their previous life in mountain lands to the northwest of India had not evoked in them such monumental builder's faculties as built the temples and the tombs of Egypt, or such artistic skill as filled those tombs and temples with statuary and decoration; nor had they the manufacturing or commercial experience of Babylon. It was not in such trappings of civilization that the Vedic

The Vedic Aryans.

Aryans were rich ; but in human capacity, which is human attainment strictly speaking. The settings of their lives were simpler, but they were more of men. From the time of their first appearance in India, they possess qualities of mind and spirit out of the reach of Egyptians, Babylonians, or Chinese.

A lack of direct knowledge of the primitive life of the Aryan race is but poorly compensated by knowledge of a number of institutions common to apparently early stages of all Indo-Germanic peoples.[1] Yet it may be inferred that prototypes of these institutions existed with the old Aryan stock before any group had begun its journey towards a separate home and a distinct nationality. Ancient Aryan peoples show a like social and political organization. The tribal divisions are similar ; the final social unit is the family. The king or leader is chosen by the tribe, or the leadership is hereditary, but conditioned on popular ratification. Wherever the Aryan tribes first appear, whether spreading through the Punjab, advancing into Greece, or wandering in the German forests, one race characteristic always asserts itself : there are no absolute rulers as against whom other members of the community have not rights, sanctioned by general recognition and maintained, if needs be, by the sword. Primitive Aryan peoples were free, free with such freedom as might not exist beneath the shadow of a Pharaoh's divinity, the spear of an Assyrian monarch, or the paternal rule of a Chinese emperor.

The hymns of the *Rig Veda* were composed during the centuries while the Vedic Aryans were spreading through the Punjab to the heart of India and the Ganges land. It was a period of frequent wars, waged with the tribes of prior races whom the Aryans were subjugating or expelling, also among the Aryans themselves. The social insti-

[1] The word Aryan is properly applicable only to Iranians and Indians, who alone call themselves Aryans. Yet it is commonly used more loosely as equivalent to Indo-Germanic.

tutions shown in the *Veda*[1] are typical products of the Aryan genius; and the political organization corresponds to the primitive organization of the German, Iranian, Slavic, and Italian races,[2] the correspondence holding as well during war in the constitution of the host, as in peace. Kingships were hereditary or elective. The king had the right to command in war; his was the duty to sacrifice for the people or host.[3] The people on their side owed him obedience and gifts. To him fell a large share of booty, and of conquered lands and slaves; splendid his attire, and great the household he maintained, wherein were bards who sang his praises. His power was limited by the people's will expressed in assemblies.

The Vedic Aryans did not live in cities, nor is there evidence that they could write. The art which had reached excellence among them was the one least dependent on material conditions, but most imperatively demanding the finer qualities of human nature, the art of poetry. The *Rig Veda* consists mainly of hymns to the gods for use at sacrifices.[4] They were not the spontaneous outpourings of nature's children,[5] but well-considered and artistic compositions. With great pains, and duc regard to established metrical laws, the bards "stretch" and "weave" and "build" their poems, like careful artisans. But inspiration has its portion too: the thoughts rise in the poet's soul, or come to him from the gods; he sees them —and then duly fashions them. In a hymn to Agni a young man must contend with an older poet—how shall he? Yet—that man who knows to reverence the god, knows aright how to weave the hymn to him: there is the

[1] *Cf.* Zimmer, *Altindisches Leben;* Hopkins, *Religions of India*, ch. ii.

[2] See Maine's *Village Communities*, lecture iv; Maine's *Early Law and Custom*, ch. viii.

[3] Like the Homeric king. Compare Oldenberg, *Religion des Veda*, p. 370, etc.

[4] See Oldenberg, *ib.*, p. 10, etc.

[5] See Pischel and Geldner, *Vedische Studien*, Einleitung, Heft ii, vol. i, p. xxi, etc.

immortal light—Agni—in the singer's heart it breaks as well; and afar draws his spirit in the quest of song.[1]

The Vedic Aryans esteemed honesty and justice and liberality; strong was their sense of chivalric honor; they loved to meet in festivals, and there contend in chariot racing and in song, and enjoy music and the dance; they loved gold and splendid garb, women and drinking. Among them also flourished lust and treachery and greed. Their thoughts were far from primitive. In the hymns, vices are satirized, as well as openly condemned.[2] The *Rig Veda* is not the voice of the people, but courtly poetry in honor of the bright and high-born gods, rulers of the world, bringers of rain, bringers of wealth to noble and royal sacrificers.

The Gods.

These great bright gods appear as nature's powers endowed with life and will. Some of them reach back to the times of Indo-Iranian, even Indo-Germanic, life;[3] and in so far as Vedic people had traits common to all Aryans, the Vedic pantheon would reflect common Aryan traits. The Aryan man was first of all a freeman, and, whether Homer speaks or Vasishtha, man's conceived relationship to his gods is one of freedom and self-respect, even friendship. Otherwise the Vedic pantheon is early Indian, with its conceptions developed in accordance with the Vedic temperament and the Indian environment.

It was a period of advance and acquisition, growth and victory. No reason why the Vedic man should not with open trust face his gods and look to them for help. Enemies quailed before the Aryan hosts, and bountiful was the new home which was becoming theirs—and they its children. So speak the hymns to Indra, the very Vedic god, child of the Indian seasons, god of the towering storm, who swings the lightning, vanquishes the robber

[1] *Rv.*, vi, 9.

[2] *Rv.*, ix, 112; drunken Brahmans are satirized in vii, 103.

[3] *Cf.* Oldenberg, *ib.*, 26–38.

demons, brings back those cows, the clouds of heaven, breaks the drought with rain, increases the wealth of those who sacrifice to him, goes before them also in war—Indra, to whom the warrior calls in battle not in vain ; "the hero-god who as soon as born shielded the gods; before whose might the two worlds shook—that, ye people, is Indra; who made fast the earth and the heaving mountains, measured the space of air, upheld the heaven—that, ye people, is Indra ; who slew the serpent and freed the seven streams, rescued the cows, the pounder in battle—that, ye people, is Indra ; the dread god, of whom ye doubting ask, 'Where is he?' and sneer 'He is not,' he who sweeps away the enemy's possessions, have faith in him—that, ye people, is Indra; in whose might stand horses, cattle, and armed hosts, to whom both lines of battle call—that, ye people, is Indra; without whose aid men never conquer, whose arrow—little thought of!—slays the wicked—that, ye people, is Indra." [1]

The Vedic people fashioned Indra out of the Indian rainstorm, a marked phenomenon, terrific yet benign. The storm winds became the Maruts, while the storm's destructive yet disease-dispelling force was the "howler," Rudra.[2] These gods were personifications of phenomena marked in their appearance yet somewhat irregular in their action. The finer Indian poetic spirit would note their beauty,—call the Maruts "golden-breasted"; and the Indian ethical consciousness would gradually attribute to all of them ethical qualities, making them punishers of sin. But it was to other more regular and all-compassing phenomena that the deifying Vedic spirit turned for personifications with which to connect its broadening conceptions of order, rule, custom, and right. These were the sky which overarched the earth and what took place thereon or in mid-air, and the unfailing light that from the sky flooded the world, wide fearless light, everywhere

[1] *Rv.*, ii, 12. See also *Rv.*, iv, 19 ; iv, 24 ; iv, 30 ; i, 165.

[2] Rudra is also interpreted as the Red God, lightning (Pischel).

penetrating, and disclosing all. This was the home and elemental origin of Varuna and Mitra, and of the cognate gods of sure recurring light, the Riders (Açvin, Dioscuri), the first streams of gray light which lead in the Dawn (Ἠώς, Aurora), close followed by the sun, Surya (Ἥλιος), the golden-haired,—the "eye" of Mitra-Varuna.

The religions of Semitic races, culminating in Israel's conception of Jehovah, developed the thought of divine personal will as immediately all-efficient in the regulation of human affairs and all things. The deity's will was not conceived as limited by any potency or law outside himself; but only as self-limited by the righteousness of his personality. The ways and will of God remained the sole source and standard of human righteousness, morality, and rightly existing law. Hence with Semitic peoples—and here is Israel again the more than typical example—human guilt or criminality remained shortcoming or transgression determined by reference to the commands and ways of the deity; that is to say, remained sin. Sin and righteousness continue a matter of personal relationship to God; and the conception of that relationship grows with the growing compass and content of human life.

Semite and Aryan.

Aryan races tended to form their deities by investing with life and personality the grand recurrent phenomena of nature. The personifications might be vague or monstrous, as were many of the Indian gods, or distinct and only too human, like the gods of Greece. In the background, however, was still the natural phenomenon, which, in so far as it was not the deity, existed of itself if subject to him. Moreover, if the deity's functions came to transcend the character of the phenomenon of which he was a personification, and became ethical, nevertheless the phenomenon remained visibly correlated with other phenomena; and the observed manner of their occurrence would come to be regarded as arising from the nature of things and dependent thereupon as much as on the will of the deity. With Indians as well as Greeks, the material order of the world became a linked and self-conditioned system. And the relationship between this outcome of the correlated nature of things and the power of the deity or deities touched both extremes, identity[1] and independence,[2] and all intermediate modes of dependence. In the ancient Greek world the power of the co-ordinated nature of things came within the conception of unpersonified fate, later becoming impersonal law, while the Vedic Indians regarded it as *rita*. The Vedic *rita* as well as the Greek fate—turning to law,—could form the starting-point of ethical systems based on the fitness and the nature of things, and not finding their standards in the will or ways of a personal god. And whatever names be applied to transgressions of such natural righteousness, they are not sins, because the criterion of transgression is not divine will. There is, however, an intermediate conception, when the standard is a god's command which, by its manifest correspondence to the fitness and nature of things, has come to coincide with fate or natural law.

Rita and Sin.

Rita, like the cognate words in Indo-Germanic tongues other than Sanscrit, had many meanings. It meant at all events what is set or ordered, in the sense of ordained for always. The primary emphasis lies in the fact of the ordainment, without regard to the cause or author or to the character of the matter which is ordered. That might be a physical event or condition, like the coming of dawn or the flowing of a river;[3] or it might be a matter of human conduct. In the world of physical phenomena invariable recurrence may have suggested the conception; and in the moral world, observance of a custom. A like thought could apply in both provinces, since the Vedic gods, notwithstanding their ethical qualities, were personifications of

[1] Pantheism.

[2] Epicurianism (Democritus), Buddhism.

[3] Oldenberg, *ib.*, p. 196.

physical phenomena. The question of the relationship of *rita* to the gods is a question as to its source; that which is *rita* throughout the world must be so by virtue of self-ordainment, or through the inherent principles of things, or by the ordinances of the gods. The Vedic poets spoke of *rita* simply, or of Varuna's *rita*, as indiscriminately as Homer speaks of *Μοῖρα* or *Μοῖρα θεῶν*. Yet *rita* becomes a universal principle of physical and moral order, and though by no means identical with the Greek "fate," it likewise served as starting-point for the conception of universal law, self-ordered or springing from the nature of things, at least not dependent on the will of any god.

Varuna and Mitra, before all other gods, uphold the physical and moral order of the world; they are "Lords of Rita," Watchers over it, its Charioteers and Guides. The more prominent is Varuna, who sees all, knows all, orders all; from whom nothing can be hid.[1] He is the protector of the good. Whoever transgresses, sins against Varuna,[2] and may be punished by him. Yet he is a god of pity and forgiveness. His hymns express the loftiest ethics of the *Veda*. In the following a sinner prays forgiveness:

"Wise and great is verily his being, who set apart the two worlds, uplifted the firmament, and spread out the stars and the earth.

"And I say to myself, When shall I be near Varuna again? What sacrifice will he accept without anger? When shall I, encouraged, behold his pity?

"I search for my sins; I long to see them. I go to enquire regarding them of such as understand. With one voice the wise answer me: It is Varuna who is angry with thee.

"What was the great sin, Varuna, for which thou wilt slay thy singer, thy friend? Tell me that, thou unfailing one, thou free; through my devotion will I speedily atone.

[1] See *e.g.* Rv. i, 25.

[2] Transgression may be a sin against other gods as well. See *Rv.* ii, 27, 14; vii, 57, 4; vii, 58, 5.

"It was not my own will, Varuna; madness was it, drink, play, passion, thoughtlessness. From the youth's error, shall the older man take counsel. Even sleep frees us not from wrong.

"As a servant will I satisfy the gracious one, the zealous god, so that I may be guiltless. The god of the Aryans has given foresight to the careless, the Wise One calls the intelligent to riches." [1]

Immortality.

The *Veda* contains no distinct authoritative formulation of belief as to life after death; yet there was an expectation of happiness for the good in the heaven where King Yama, the first mortal, ruled.[2] Immortality might be conferred by Soma, the divine drink of Indra: "Where there is exhaustless light, where is set the sun, place me there, O Soma, in the lasting world of immortality. Where Vivasant's son (Yama) is king, where the eternal waters flow, where are the worlds of light, there make me immortal. Where there is joy and bliss and pleasure, where the wish's wish is reached, there make me immortal."[3] The import of these phrases may not have been spiritual; yet in their vague and abstract nature they are Indian.

Vedic Questionings.

Long had the Vedic Aryans prayed to Indra and Varuna, and long had they conquered in battle, till there came rest and partial peace. Then had they time to doubt their gods and ponder on life's mysteries, as in the extraordinary, perhaps still misunderstood, hymn to the god Who.[4] Vedic thought was often pleased to muse in modes of cosmogonic speculation. Thus it broached the unanswerable queries, foundation stones of the edifice of human questionings. The *Veda* speaks of the world's origin in various ways, alike illustrative of the primitive confusion of metaphor and fact, which was not to pass away till its place in

[1] *Rv.*, vii, 68. Trans. from Oldenberg, *ib.*, p. 296. *Cf. Rv.*, vii, 89.

[2] There were also forming conceptions of hell. See Oldenberg, *ib.*, p. 536, etc.

[3] *Rv.*, ix, 113.

[4] *Rv.*, x, 121; *cf.* vii, 87, 4, and ii, 12.

Indian thought had been taken by a symbolism and subjectivity disdainful of distinction between desire and realization, the symbol and the symbolized. The Vedic poets speak of the world as built, as a house is built by a carpenter; they also use metaphors of generation as statements of fact; and again the world is regarded as having been brought into being by the power of sacrifice.[1] The spirit of the brooding time to come dawns in a late Vedic hymn of vague and dreamful speculation as to first beginnings:

"Then was there neither Being nor not-Being; neither the air nor the sky above. Did anything stir? and where? under protection of what? Was there water and the Abyss?

"Neither death nor immortality was there. Only One breathed of itself, unbreathed on; beyond this, there was nothing else.

"Darkness sunk in darkness was in the Beginning, everything surged commingled; the void rested on empty space, yet One came to life by the power of warmth.

"In It arose desire, the mind's first seed. The Wise, with insight searching in the heart, found out the way of Being in not-Being.

"Whence the creation came, whether made or not made, he only knows whose eye watches it from highest heaven—or he may know it not."[2]

Soma and Agni: Sacrifice and Subjectivity.

Vedic customs and the notions underlying them are more distinctly connected with the thoughts and institutions of later times through the sacrificial cultus, wherein the two central conceptions were the fire god, Agni, and Soma, the drink-offering, which itself became a god. More than any other members of the Indian pantheon, Soma and Agni represented, symbolized, and became other gods.[3] Vedic and subsequent priestly

[1] See Wallis, *Cosmology of the Rig Veda.*

[2] *Rv.*, x, 129, Kaegi's *Rig Veda*, p. 121; Geldner and Kægi, *Siebenzig Lieder*, lxvii; *cf. Rv.*, x, 72; x, 190.

[3] See *e. g. Rv.*, v, 3; i, 91; ix, 77; *cf.* Hopkins, *Religions of India*, p. 105, etc.

thought regarding them, beginning in unconscious confusion, gives itself over to the unrestricted treatment of symbol as fact, and then to flights of subjective imaginings which become their own realization.

Agni is twofold, the heavenly and the earthly:[1] the heavenly Agni dwells in the fire and light of the sun, and, as the lightning fire, is born in the clouds. Various myths tell how he was brought down to earth.[2] His chief earthly origin is in the two sticks rubbed together to produce the sacred fire. No kindlier friend of man than the Agni of the hearth and sacrificial fire. He was the wise priest-god, knowing well the natures of all the gods and means of moving them to favor sacrificers, the mediating god, descending from the lightning clouds, re-ascending from mankind with the propitiating sacrifice or moving prayer or god-compelling spell. When Indian thought but vaguely distinguished the personalities of gods, and often identified them because of like divine efficiency, Agni could not fail to be identified with all the gods whose functions he quickened to an activity accordant with their worshippers' desires. A god is the personification of power; how sever from that power the power moving it to action, making it efficient? Quite naturally the moving power, the priestly god, unites with all the powers it moves, becomes identical with each of them, even with all of them.

Agni, the bright, beneficent potency of fire, which drove the demons of disease from Aryan hearths, had been a god long before he became the priestly effectuator of the sacrificer's wish. Soma had been the sacrifice itself, the spirituous drink-offering poured to gods before the separation of the Iranian and Vedic stock.[3] In India it held its venerable place as the most sacred sacrificial substance: especially was it the sacrifice offered to that chief Vedic

[1] See *Rv.*, iii, 1, translated and commented on by Geldner, in Pischel and Geldner's *Vedische Studien*, i, 157–170.

[2] See Oldenberg, *ibid.*, p. 121.

[3] It is the Haoma of the *Avesta*.

god, Indra; it inspired him with benevolence towards sacrificing men and the fulness of strength needed in his tempest-conflict with the demon ravishers. From being the substance and the means of sacrifice, which imparted strength to the god as well as rendered him propitious, Soma became the active strength which Indra got from it, as well as the quick benevolence of will which it aroused in him; so it was invested with his living efficiency and became Indra.[1]

As a god its nature was moulded by the nature and the function of that of which it was the personification; that is, by the spirituous, exhilarating, intoxicating nature of Soma as a drink, and certainly by its sacrificial function, which was to inspire Indra with power and good will. Like Agni, Soma the god became a deity which roused other gods to the activity desired by the sacrificer, and like Agni might be identified with all the gods whose efficiency it moved, whose efficiency it was. But the development and changes of Soma's divinity proceeded by a peculiarly symbolic and subjective process, which even in the *Veda* was sufficiently marked to form a connecting link between those ancient poems and the symbolism and subjectivity of the times which were to follow. With many comparisons and metaphors is the sacrifice of Soma represented as effectuating its purpose; then the metaphors became statements of facts.[2] Again, Soma is the visible expression of the sacrificer's wish to move the god to whom it is offered; and the sacrifice has the desired effect: then it becomes not only the symbol of the wish but the symbol of the wish realized, the symbol of the efficiency which brings that wish to realization: and then the symbolism passes away—if indeed there had ever been a clear consciousness that it was symbolism,—and there is left, Soma the wish, Soma the wish realized, Soma the efficiency which realized the wish, Soma the god.

[1] See *Rv.*, i, 91. [2] *Cf. e. g. Rv.*, ix, 36 with *Rv.*, ix, 28.

Post-Vedic Thought.

The Vedic composers had not passed beyond an animistic conception of nature. The more prominent natural phenomena had been personified in gods whose vague and changing personalities tended to confusion with one another; perhaps there may have been the thought of universal deity under many names and forms. Before there was a clearer apprehension of nature, a contemplative, subjective trend set in, which should ring fantastic changes on crude apprehensions of phenomena, and preclude observation or the drawing of clear inference from better apprehended fact. The *Yajur Veda*, put together in the period following the *Rig*, knows no difference between fact and symbol. This *Veda* of the sacrificial words and ritual, the oldest Indian prose composition,[1] is a dreary mass of foolishness, whereby men learn to conduct sacrifices requiring a lifetime for completion and a troop of priests.[2] Unless the officiating Brahman betrays him, the master of the sacrifice obtains cattle or offspring, or effects the destruction of those he fears or hates, or deprives them of cattle or food! The various ceremonial parts of the sacrifice are more than symbolical of various gods and the desires of the sacrificers; they *are* those gods and effect the sacrificer's will.[3] The sacrifice has, in fact, become the greatest power, efficient and creative for men and gods;[4] vitality, breath, eye, hearing, speech, the priest, the lights of heaven, and the sacrifice itself,—all come into being through the sacrifice.[5] And the Brahmans also, who conduct the sacrifices, have become gods.[6]

[1] Schroeder, *Indiens Literatur und Kultur*, p. 88, etc.

[2] See *ib.*, Vorlesung 8.

[3] See *e. g. Satapatha-Brahmana*, *Sacred Books of the East*, vol xii, pp. 78, 158, 159, 299.

[4] "Verily by means of the Great Oblation the gods slew Vitra; by means of it they gained that supreme authority which they now wield; and so does he (the sacrificer) thereby now slay his wicked, spiteful enemy, and gain the victory; this is why he performs this sacrifice."—*Satapatha-Brahmana*, *Sacred Books of the East*, vol. xii, p. 417; *cf. ib.*, pp. 160, 437, 449.

[5] See Schroeder, *ib.*, p. 137, etc.

[6] See Hopkins, *Religions of India*, p. 179.

These notions were the lower products of the spirit which reached the summit of its course of subjectivity along another path. In the *Rig Veda* there appears a god called Brihaspati or Brahmanaspati, the lord of prayer. This god by himself, or with the priests, sang sacrificial songs, or spoke the prayer or magic words; and as prayer and spell, like the warrior's arm, win battles, Brihaspati becomes priest war-god, along with hero war-god Indra.[1] In this conception there might be seen little peculiarly subjective if light were not thrown back upon it by the fortunes which awaited the word forming the first part of the name—Brahma, meaning "prayer." Prayer, persuasive utterance addressed to a being capable of graciousness, readily in India as elsewhere, passes to "spell," the rightly uttered word which compels action or directly compasses a result. This interchange of meaning was analogous to the changing of the thought of sacrifice as a propitiatory offering to sacrifice as magic means of forcing from a god the fulfilment of the sacrificer's wish. And, finally, as the sacrifice, from being efficacious as persuasion or compulsion, itself became efficient, a potency and a god, so in more than corresponding manner, Brahma, prayer, spell, desire expressed, becomes desire attained, spell which has worked, prayer which has wrung its granting—from itself. Ignoring obstacles, ignoring facts, the all-compassing, desirous Indian will conceives its own fulfilment; that conception takes to itself efficiency to do, become, or be, all, absolutely all. Brahma has become absolute, all-inclusive Deity. And Indian brooding, mystic subjectivity, having evolved Brahma, attains it for each man in the conception of the Absolute Self, the Ātmā.[2]

Prayer Becomes Very-God.

As a subject of thought death is not equally absorbing at all times. Men tend to think of the matter in hand; and so long as a race is occupied in strenuous action, it

[1] See Oldenberg, *ib.*, pp. 66, 67.

[2] *Cf.* Deussen, *System des Vedanta*, p. 127 and p. 50 ff.

will not muse overmuch on death. While the Vedic Aryans were conquering India and establishing themselves in their new home, they would hardly pause to ponder on the shortness of life, which indeed might continue in Yama's heaven. Yet the Vedic period had not passed before they began to muse on the world's origin and mysteries. They were an intellectual people, taking pleasure in contests of sharp question and clever answer, as well as in the contest of song with song. The age of conquest spent itself, and the influences of the physically enervating land told upon a race which had been fostered in a mountain home. As centuries went on, this people, having become contemplative, appears as if repelled by the quick growth and quick decay of living things in India. That was all impermanence and limitation; the Indian spirit was questing immortality. The world without was a phantasmagoria wherein change and death seemed the sole realities. The Hindoo turned his mind upon his own desires set on immutability and deathlessness. He had never thought of closely scanning things without; he had never distinguished metaphor from fact; nor was he now distinguishing symbolism from identity. The material and sacred mode of expressing his desires was the sacrifice, which had become all that it symbolized, all that it would effect. This was the priestly mode of effecting whatever was desired: and the sacrifice had become the chief concern of life. To the prevalent conception of it, which stands for the climax of Indian foolishness, there was a more rational counterpart in the philosophy of the metaphysical treatises termed *Upanishads*. Here, still untrammelled by any sense of fact, the Hindoo genius reasons out its reasonings most profoundly.

Death and Impermanence.

One expression of the Hindoo horror of impermanence was the doctrine of recurrent death which awaited hopeless rebirth in forms human or bestial. On re-death rather than rebirth fell the emphasis of the Indian conception of transmigration. The Hindoo

Re-Death; Yearnings.

spirit viewed all things from the side of their change and cessation; hence they were valueless, only lures, torments, pitfalls of death:—Shall we be happy with maidens, horses, wealth, kingship, when we see thee, O Death![1]—this is the Hindoo mood, the Hindoo negation. Its positive side is the yearning for the imperishable and immutable, a yearning to reach a condition not subject to change and death. The teaching of the *Upanishads* is that this absolute condition shall be attained by apprehending and desiring it and nothing else. What and as men know and think and desire they are. Know Brahma, the universal Absolute; know that man's self, the Ātmā, is It; know and desire only It, and It is reached.

Brahma, the Absolute: the Self is It.

The conception of an Absolute has teased the human mind in many lands. In two ways men have tried to reach the thought: by a positive accumulative process—the Absolute is this, and this, and this, and all things; by a negative, abstracting process—the Absolute is not that, nor that, nor that, nor any particular thing.[2] In India, Gotama Buddha was to drive the latter process through to its conclusion; but in the meanwhile the Brahmanical composers of the *Upanishads* pursued for the most part the cumulative way.[3] Brahma, the universal Absolute, was all Being, all that really was, that really saw, heard or knew; Brahma was the essential being and efficient principle of all things; or, by means of the conception of reality as everywhere identical, Brahma might perhaps be conceived as the totality of existence. Having by a process of cumulative symbolism reached a conception of Brahma, the Hindoo genius after its own peculiar modes identified the veritable

[1] See the story of Naciketas in the *Katha-Upanishad;* vol, xv, *Sacred Books of the East*, p. 1, etc.

[2] Of the latter process the philosophy of Plotinus affords the great ancient example. See post, chap. xvi.

[3] See for a prime example the *Chāndogya-Upanishad, passim;* vol. i., *Sacred Books of the East*. The Indian commentators on the *Upanishads*, however, pursued both modes; *cf.* Thibaut, *Vedanta-Sutras*, Introduction pp. xxiv–xxix, vol. xxxiv, *Sacred Books of the East*.

being of each man with this universal Absolute. It did not leap at once to a conclusion by means of a sweeping pantheistic syllogism: Brahma is all; therefore man, with the rest of the apparent manifold of existence, is Brahma. It chose symbols for man's self, and then through modes of subjective thought it distended that self to identification with the sum of the objects of man's knowledge and desires. Thus the self was extended throughout all existence to mutually all-permeating universal identity with Brahma, till the two conceptions became indistinguishable.

Chāndogya-Upanishad; Symbolism and Subjectively.

All this may be traced in the *Chāndogya-Upanishad.* It opens with an injunction to meditate on the syllable Om, the sacred syllable which must be pronounced before and after reading the *Veda.* Om stands for the essence of the *Veda*, which is the essence of speech, which is the essence of man, who is the essence of plants, which are the essence of water, which is the essence of the earth, which is the essence of all things. That is to say, the syllable Om may be meditated upon as the symbol of all these various types of being. Thereupon the *Upanishad* runs the symbolism up and down through all existences, including the elements of human being. "Om is all this" and "all this is Brahma." [1] Then it proceeds: Let a man meditate on all the world as Brahma. "Now man is a creature of will. According to what his will is in this world, so will he be when he has departed this life. Let him therefore have this will and belief," that the intelligent, spirit-like, true-thinking, all-pervasive, all-effecting yet invisible and unspeaking Brahma is the self within the heart, smaller than a mustard seed, greater than the earth and sky.[2]

[1] *Sacred Books of the East*, vol. i, p. 1 *ff.*, pp. 35, 45.

[2] *Ib.*, vol. 1, p. 48. The word "self" is perhaps the best English rendering of Ātmā. Brahma having been declared to be the "self," a symbol for the self is named in a subsequent part of the *Upanishad.* "The person

Subsequently there is given further explanation of what is Brahma, and the result of knowing it. It is said that the *Vedas* are a name; "he who meditates on name as Brahma is, as it were, lord and master as far as the name reaches. Speech is better than a name; he who meditates on speech as Brahma is, as it were, lord and master as far as speech reaches. Mind is better than speech (repeating the "he who meditates," etc.). Will is better than mind. He who meditates on will as Brahma, he being himself safe, firm, and undistressed, obtains the safe, firm, and undistressed worlds which he has willed; he is, as it were, lord and master as far as will reaches. Consideration is better than will (repeating the "he who meditates," etc.). Reflection is better than consideration. Understanding is better than reflection. Power is better than understanding. Food is better than power. He who meditates on food as Brahma, obtains the worlds rich in food and drink. Water is better than food. Fire is better than water. Ether (or space) is better than fire. Memory is better than ether. Hope is better than memory. He who meditates on hope as Brahma, all his desires are fulfilled by hope, his prayers are not in vain. Spirit (prāna) is better than hope; as the spokes of a wheel hold to the nave, so do names, speech, mind, will, etc., hold to the spirit. Father means spirit, mother is spirit, brother, sister, tutor, Brahman, all are spirit. For after the spirit has gone out of them, they are not to be regarded as father, mother, brother, sister, tutor, or Brahman."

It is then suggested that there is yet a broader truth; "The Infinite is bliss. There is no bliss in anything finite. Where one sees nothing else, understands nothing

that is seen in the eye, that is the self. This is the immortal, the fearless, this is Brahma."—*Ib.*, vol. i, p. 67; *Chan.-Up.*, IV, 15, 1. Another important symbol of the self was prāna, the breath of man; which indeed may have been at one time regarded as a satisfactory conception of life, and of the self. See *Kaushitaki-Up.*, iii, 2 (vol. i, *Sacred Books*, p. 294).

else, that is the Infinite. The Infinite is indeed below, above, behind, before, right and left; it is indeed all this. The Infinite is the I. I am below, I am above, I am behind, before, right and left—I am all this. The Infinite is the self; self is below, above, behind, before, right and left; self is all this. He who sees, perceives, and understands this, loves the self, delights in the self, revels in the self: he is lord and master in all the worlds. But those who think differently from this, live in perishable worlds, and have other beings for their rulers. To him who sees, perceives, and understands this, the spirit springs from the self, hope springs from the self, memory springs from the self; so do ether, fire, water, appearance and disappearance, food, power, understanding, reflection, consideration, will, mind, speech, names, sacred hymns and sacrifices,—all, all this, springs from the self." [1]

It is elsewhere taught that there are two kinds of knowledge, first that of the *Vedas* and the sacrificial ceremonies; through practice of these matters a man advances to better conditions of existence; but not to the best. That comes by the higher knowledge of Brahma,[2] by knowing which a man becomes Brahma. It is Brahma which is the self, which sent forth all existence in the beginning; [3] and it is the same self by which we see and hear and smell, and utter speech, and will and know:[4] that is the see-er which cannot be seen, the hearer which cannot be heard;[5] "the one eternal thinker, thinking non-eternal thoughts."[6] He who fails rightly to conceive the self, will perish continually, unable to desire what he does not know.[7] Let a man know that all is Brahma, let him

[1] *Chāndogya-Upanishad*, *Sacred Books*, vol. i, pp. 109–125.

[2] *Mundaka-Upanishad*, vol. xv, *Sacred Books*, pp. 27, etc.

[3] *Aiteraya-Aranyaka*, ii, 4, 1; *Sacred Books*, vol. i, p. 237, etc.

[4] *Ib.*, 6, 1.

[5] *Prasna-Up.*, iv, 7-10.

[6] *Katha-Up.*, ii, 5-13; *Sacred Books*, vol. xv, p. 19.

[7] See *Brihadaranyaka-Up.*, iv, 4, 19; *Sacred Books*, vol. xv, p. 179; *Chāndogya-Up.*, viii, 7-11.

fix his mind on that, understand it, and desire only it. Let him purify his mind from all desires for the manifold of sense, from all the apparent which is subject to change and death.[1] Thereby shall he attain Brahma: "It stirs and it stirs not; it is far and likewise near. It is inside all this, and it is outside all this. And he who beholds all beings in the self, and the self in all beings, he never turns away from it. When to a man who understands, the self has become all things, what sorrow, what trouble, can there be to him who has once beheld that unity?"[2]

Abandonment of Individuality.

Thus has the Hindoo genius conceived Brahma and the self, at first perhaps as correlates, the universal Absolute and the temporarily apparently individualized part thereof, but as correlates never clearly distinguished and soon to be confounded to identity. The use of the term "self" must not disguise the fact that in the process of becoming free from death, from the transient and the perishable, the Hindoo has abandoned individuality and the natural desires of men, whereby they, as individual organisms which they are, must advance and fulfil their lives. The whole content of individual life, the whole content of all the life men know and have experience of or can conceive, this has been sacrificed for a blank dream of oneness with Brahma. Perception, reflection, knowledge, consciousness rest in duality: subject and object there must be. He who has reached the absolute All-one, no longer sees or thinks or knows, and therefore says the sage Yajnavalkya, in the *Brahmana of a Hundred Paths*, "There is no consciousness after death."[3]

[1] See *e. g. Maitrayana-Brahmana-Up.*, vi, 34; vii, 7-8; *Katha-Up.*, i, 2; *Brihadaranyaka-Up.*, ii, 4.

[2] *Isa-Up.*, 5-7; vol. I, *Sacred Books*, p. 312.

[3] It is questionable whether the Upanishads commonly recognize this ultimate conclusion. The thought of absorption in Brahma was of gradual growth, and throughout the Upanishads there is continual reversion to a hope of an immortality wherein the individual consciousness is not lost. Popular beliefs naturally would accord with this hope rather than with the ultimate teaching of the Upanishads.

The higher teachings of the Ātmā and Brahma, the absolute All-One, did not constitute part of Indian popular religion.[1] Instead, there was a vague and various polytheism wherein the gods most prominent perhaps from the end of the Upanishad period were Brahmā, Vishnu, and Siva, who were at a later time to be united in the threefold concept of Creator, Preserver, and Destroyer.[2] Brahmā (masculine) was the personified popular counterpart of Brahma (neuter), and a final stage in the mutation of the word which had once meant "prayer."[3]

Popular Religion.

There are two Indian epics, into which have poured divers streams of all things Indian. The lesser poem, the *Ramāyāna*, makes some approach to being an organic whole. It is a priestly, sacrificial, magic, ascetic story, with slight genuine heroic motive. The *Mahā-Bhārata*, however, has as its epic base the story of a war fought through with hero-valor to the end. This story of the struggle of two rival noble and related races for supremacy underwent extension and revision; and in the course of centuries there was heaped upon it a mass of myth and legend, religious, priestly, and ascetic lore, interspersed with moral discourse and philosophic treatise, till the epic element was overladen, broken, and distorted. The *Mahā-Bhārata* reached its present form through the opposing action of two forces, the epic motive, which spent itself in the composition of the central story, and the Brahmanical tendencies which turn the acts and words of the epic heroes to exemplifications of teachings of renunciation.[4] Both poems are filled with measureless and tedious exaggeration, whereby is rendered dreary compensation for the lack of human reality. Yet in them may be found Indian ideals of heroism, love and devotion,

The Epics.

[1] See Hopkins, *Religions of India*, p. 244, etc., and p. 349, etc.

[2] See Schroeder, *Indiens Literatur und Kultur*, pp. 321 *ff.*, 359.

[3] *Cf. e. g.* Schroeder, *ib.*, p. 244; and *ante*.

[4] See especially the *Bhagavat-gita*, which has been preserved as an episode in the *Mahā-Bhārata*. It is translated in vol. viii, *Sacred Books of the East*.

justice, self-restraint, and righteousness. It is their final teaching that even for the valiant and good, whose righteous deeds have been crowned with glorious success, life and its fruits crumble to derisive dust in the hand of the hero who, through high resolve and happy attainment, has grasped them at last. Valiant should the warrior be, because it is right for him to do his duty as a Kshatrya. Devoted must be the wife, tender must be the husband. Also, justice, truth, and open-handed giving are for all to follow, and the opposite of them brings misery and overthrow even on earth. But foolish is he whose just and righteous acts have for their motives visible good to the doer. And to the strong-armed and enduring hero who sees at last, fair before his eyes, the result of his life's toil and sweat, peace and rest come only when he turns his longing eyes aside, and renounces.

Brahman Ethics.

It were not difficult, from the code of Manu and other legal writings, to obtain more precise expression of Brahman ethics than has been given. But the ethics of pre-Buddhistic Brahmanism, as in the *Brahmanas* and *Upanishads*, are found taken up and carried to sharper expression in early Buddhist writings, and afterwards are again formally expressed in the law books, but with the Ātmā teachings in the place of Buddhist dogma. As the courtly pagan writers at Rome during the second and third centuries ignored the existence of Christianity, so this later Brahmanical literature ignores the existence of Buddhism, while owing to it the sharper development of ethical principles, which existed but crudely in the earlier Brahman compositions.[1]

By the sixth century before Christ, the prestige of the Brahman caste had risen till its members were veritable gods. Hindoo society had become sharply separated into four castes, of each of which there were minor divisions, and had subjected itself to observance of an infinite web

[1] The doctrine of Karma is specially referred to here.

of ceremonial usages regulative of every act of daily life. These usages were in general related to conceptions of ceremonial purity and impurity connected with conditions indispensable for valid performance of sacrifice, and so with the obtaining of all imaginable good. The higher the caste, the greater the complex of performance and conformity required of its members. Above all, the life of the Brahman was prescribed from birth to death. After his childhood, he shall pass the first quarter of his life as a student in a teacher's house; the second quarter as a married householder; then, when he sees his skin wrinkled and the sons of his sons, he shall go to the forest; and for the last part of all he shall, as an ascetic, wander homeless without desires till he die.[1]

Austerities were frequently practised by hermits, to whom merely dwelling in the benign Indian forest was not sufficient purification. It was these wood-dwellers, ὑλοβίοι, that the Greek Megasthenes mentions as the most honored ascetics.[2] But both to the hermit dwelling in a wood and to the beggar-wanderer, asceticism was the prime means of effecting freedom from desire. It had in Buddha's time become the chief Indian meritoriousness of life.[3]

[1] The details of all these matters may be found in the sacred law books, mostly called *Dharma Sutras; Apastamba*, *Gautama*, *Vashistha*, *Vishnu*, and *Manu*; and more especially domestic matters in the *Grihya Sutras*. See for translations, vols. ii, vii, xiv, xxv, xxix, xxx, xxxiii, of *Sacred Books of the East*. The hermit and ascetic life was not for Brahmans alone, though only for them was it the rule.

[2] Says he also, "Much of their talk is about death."—*Fragments of Megasthenes*, quoted by Strabo, xv, 59. Megasthenes was ambassador of Seleucus Nicator to Chandra Gupta.

[3] In striking analogy to the conception of sacrifice had been the growth of the notion of the nature and effect of ascetic penance. The sacrifice is at first propitiatory or deprecatory with a tendency to become magical; then it becomes a potency in itself. Likewise the penance began as an atonement for sin and means of purification, then was practised as a way to positive merit, and then it becomes a means whereby the person practising it acquires might and power over natural phenomena as well as over gods and men. Penance, self-mortification finally, like the sacrifice,

Union with Brahma could not be reached through any acts, not through good deeds, not even by sacrifices or austerities, except in so far as the latter brought cessation of desire. Acts were acts, and could not lift themselves out of the world of action to the Absolute. As the fixing of desire upon the Absolute reached that, so acts begot conditions of phenomenal existence, other states of action;[1] and according as they were good or bad, entailed in this[2] or succeeding lives a better or worse condition. The criterion of what was good and bad was the complex of domestic, social, and ceremonial precept, which had come into existence mainly through Brahman influences. It was a caste morality tempered by the principle that in succeeding lives the effect of good acts might overleap caste divisions.[3] And it was a code which inculcated self-restraint, mild and forgiving conduct, forbade harshness and revenge, and urged charity and kind deeds,[4] especially charity and boundless generosity towards Brahmans. "Not to commit corporal injury, to speak the truth, not to steal, to be pure, to restrain the senses, this condensed rule of duty Manu declared for the four castes."[5] One virtue is not enough; all must be attained. "Austerity is useless to him who is destitute of sacred learning, and sacred learning to him who is destitute of austerity."[6] "The *Vedas* do not purify him who is deficient in good conduct, though he know them all."[7]

With unerring certainty every act brings its result,—a meritorious act, a good result in a succeeding life, a delin-

becomes a cosmogonic power whereby Brahmā creates the world. See Schroeder, *Indiens Literatur und Kultur*, pp. 388–395.

[1] See *Manu*, xii, 88–91.

[2] See *Vasishtha*, vi, 6–8; *Manu* iv, 170–172.

[3] *Cf. Apastamba*, ii, 1, ii, 2. Dreadful was the retribution appointed for the misdeeds of a man of lower caste against a Brahman. A Brahman might vilify a Sudra as he chose. See *Gautama*, xii and xxi.

[4] See *e. g. Vishnu*, xci; *Gautama*, viii, 23; i, 8, 22, 23; ii, 3, 7.

[5] See *Manu*, x, 63.

[6] *Vasishtha*, xxvi, 17; *Sacred Books*, vol. xiv.

[7] *Ib.*, vi.

quent act, a bad result. This ethical code is a system of linked merit and demerit. Good acts accumulate a certain quantity of good result; bad acts diminish that result, or, if greater than the individual's good acts, produce a minus result downward in the stages of existence.[1] The ill results of evil deeds may also be counteracted by atonement or penance performed during the life in which the evil act is done.[2] In such a system as this, by whatever name delinquent acts are called, and the tendency is to adhere to customary phraseology and call them sins, it is clear that they have ceased to come under the stricter conception of sin, as transgression of a deity's command, whereby his displeasure is incurred. In this Brahmanic code, delinquency is that which entails evil results. The effect entailed upon the doer by the act is the sole sanction of conduct; while the criterion, or rather schedule, wherein all acts of life are tabled good or bad, is the complex of rules prescribed by the Brahmans. There is already ceasing to be a logical place for God, his will or ways, his pleasure and displeasure, recompense and punishment, in a world wherein man's good or ill is thus worked out.

Karma.

And already may be noticed, what becomes clearer in Buddhism, how that under this system of transmigration and this doctrine of Karma,—the power of the act over successive existences upward or downward,—human individuality has become relationship, the relationship of a sum of acts and their result to a doer. It is a matter of the connection of that doer's present existence to the next, to which the sum of his acts brings him. His acts are that connection, and keep the individual himself; but no sum of acts leads to a heaven whence man will not be born again; no acts can free from change and death. Such freedom comes through the abandon-

[1] See *Manu*, iv, 238–243; xi, 228-234; xii, 40; *Apastamba*, i, i, i, 5; ii, i, ii, 3; *Gautama*, xi, 29, 30; *Manu*, ii, 2–5; *Vishnu*, xx, 28 *ff*.

[2] See *e. g. Apastamba*, i, 9, 24, to *ib.*, i, 10, 29; *Manu*, xi.

ment of desire and all action done with desire of result, so that the mood may be centred on the final goal of oneness with the Absolute. Of necessity this path lay through renunciation of all acts done with purpose and "attachment to their fruits,"—lay, that is, through the abandonment of that which was the cord of individuality. And the far goal of the final attainment of the absolute All-One meant for such thinkers as would carry the thought out to its conclusion, a merging of consciousness as well. The heart of India was set on an immortality which should attain the unchanging, the eternal, the absolute and infinite. The more strenuous modes of Indian reasonings abandon human individuality as apparently subject to change and death and an impediment to the attainment of the Absolute.

CHAPTER IV.

THE BUDDHA.

THE sixth century before Christ was a time of mental activity in India. The Hindoo genius was pleasurably occupying itself with insoluble problems, the data of which were transcendent or did not exist; the Hindoo spirit, the Hindoo heart, was sick with thinking upon change and death. This Hindoo heart, yearning away from all things transient, has with desire creative in its intensity impelled the Hindoo mind to conceive Brahma and think the Self of man to be that Absolute. It was a dream. The Hindoo metaphysical genius might find ceaseless occupation in its elaboration; but the Hindoo heart, subjectively creative as it was, found the dream vague and the phantom thereof such as might not be clasped. Desire may not forever satisfy itself on fanciful creations. If it do not dissipate to a dialectic and scholastic interest in the creatures of its ratiocinations, it cannot but find their insubstantiality a mockery. In the end, yearning that remains real will be strung to vision, and abandon fulfilments seen to be imaginary. So came it, though argument and metaphysical discussion, with wordy priestly jugglings as to significance of caste and rite and sacrifice, were taking up the minds of many men in India, that there were others whose spirits might not so be quenched. They had had enough of metaphysics; and where was reality in all the fantastic symbolism and subjective fancy of attainment of the heart's desire? Life's

Buddhism a Resultant Revolution.

manifold content of change and death was unsatisfying, loathsome, sorrow-stricken through and through. But recognize it; cease from imaginings; whatever refuge may yet be found, let it be real.[1]

The needs of the time, and that answer to them which was rendered inevitable by the previous courses of Indian thought, reached "name-and-form" in Gotama Buddha. Under the inspiration of his greatness, a renewed reality enters Indian thought. Gotama's system was a marvellous exemplification of one of its fundamental principles, Karma, the power of the previous act. For in Buddhism the necessities of Indian thought reached their issue, and the needs of the tired Indian heart found the only refuge open to the pointings of its mood. It was a further and transcendent greatness of Gotama's teaching that, though an outcome of Indian thought and an answer to Indian needs, it burst through Indian bands of caste and custom, compassed certain broad human, or at least Asiatic, verities, and so was fitted to become, not indeed a universal religion for mankind, but at all events a religious system, or rather congeries of religious systems, for a large part of Asia.

In India, Buddhism was dogmatically a revolution, but a most consequent one, showing how the progress of race tendencies may quite suddenly produce doctrines diametrically opposed to those previously held. The chief practices of Brahmanism were sacrifice and ascetic penance. Buddhism pronounced against both. Brahmanism held to an absolute All-One, Brahma, and to a Self which is It. In the place of a dethroned Absolute, Buddhism set up ceaseless change, nor recognized the existence of a self, or any imperishable entity in man. The deeper philosophic thought of India, having displaced the ancient

[1] Buddhism was not alone in finding all life suffering. The same thought underlies the Samkya philosophy of Kapila, not unlikely an earlier system than Buddhism. It was also atheistic, like Buddhism. See R. Garbe, *Die Samkya-Philosophie*, *passim* and pp. 133 *ff.* and 191 *ff.*

semblances of gods with an impersonal Absolute, might not go back and pray to the old fancies. It must go on. And from the absolute Brahma onwards there was but one step, though it seems a large one—from Brahma to no Brahma,—a step which also involved abandoning the absolute Self in man. With no Absolute nor any god, man, whatever he was, had nothing to rely on but himself. He was his own lord and refuge in a world of change and death, wherein was nothing worth. With this recognition, the Hindoo mood of pain at transitoriness intensified and widened to include all life. So Buddha says all life is suffering; for man there is only detachment. Herein is he lord indeed; he may renounce—no other being for him—and thereby cease from sorrow. Said the young Brahman to Death: "Keep thou thy horses, keep dance and song for thyself. Shall we be happy with these things, seeing thee?"[1] "How is there laughter," says the Buddhist, "how is there joy, as the world is always burning? Why do ye not seek a light, ye who are surrounded by darkness? This body is wasted, full of sickness and frail; this heap of corruption breaks to pieces, life indeed ends in death."[2] "Let no man love anything; loss of the beloved is evil. Those who love nothing and hate nothing have no fetters. From love comes grief, from love comes fear; he who is free from love knows neither grief nor fear."[3]

So Buddhism has no god, no Absolute, and no imperishable human soul. The Blessed One is but the Teacher through whose teachings humanity attains release from suffering. He saves not; each man must save himself: "Rouse thyself by thyself; examine thyself by thyself; for self is the lord of self."[4] Yet the personality of Gotama was of such ineffable comfort, that he was the

[1] *Katha-Upanishad*, i, 1, 26; see *ante*, p. 73.

[2] *Dhammapada*, xi, 146, 148.

[3] *Ibid.*, xvi, 211, 215.

[4] *Ibid.*, xxv, 379, 380. "Wise people fashion themselves."—*Ibid.*, vi, 80.

pattern and the type of human refuge, and Buddhism as a religion to which men cling is the life as well as teaching of Buddha; "I take my refuge in the Blessed One, in his Teaching, and in the Brotherhood."[1]

Gotama.

Gotama the Buddha was born near the middle of the sixth century before Christ, of the Sakya race which dwelt in the northeastern part of India, where Brahman influence was weaker than in the west and south. Little is known of his youth. He married and had a son. When about twenty-nine years old, he left his house, and became an ascetic. For seven years Gotama practised asceticism after the manner of the time. Yet no light came. Realizing the folly of austerities, he stopped them, and resumed an ordinary diet. At this apparent lapse, certain ascetics, who had been his followers, left him—alone. One night, seated beneath a tree in the forest, he saw the principle of causation; he was loosed from cravings and became the Buddha. Moveless he continued in the bliss of contemplation with knowledge perfected. On the seventh evening he allowed to pass through his mind that course of inevitable change to which all life is subject.

Chain of Causation.

"Then the Blessed One, during the first watch of the night, fixed his mind upon the chain of causation, in direct and in reverse order: 'From ignorance spring the samkhāras (conformations, confections, puttings-together), from the samkhāras springs consciousness, from consciousness springs name-and-form, from name-and-form spring the six provinces [of the six senses, eye, ear, nose, tongue, body or touch, and mind], from the six provinces springs contact, from contact springs sensation, from sensation springs thirst

[1] Said by each Buddhist on becoming a monk. This sketch of Buddhism follows the Southern Canon of Pali Books, the *Patimokkha*, *Mahāvagga*, *Kullavagga*, *Dhammapada*, and Buddhist *Suttas*, with a comparison of the later *Questions of King Milinda*, contained in *Sacred Books of the East*, vols. x, xi, xiii, xvii, xx, xxxv, xxxvi. The writer is much indebted to Prof. Oldenberg's *Buddha.*

(or desire), from thirst springs attachment, from attachment springs becoming, from becoming springs birth, from birth spring old age and death, grief, lamentation, suffering, dejection and despair. Such is the origin of this whole mass of suffering. Again, by the destruction of ignorance, which consists in the complete absence of lust, the samkhāras are destroyed; by the destruction of the samkhāras, consciousness is destroyed; by the destruction of consciousness, name-and-form is destroyed; by the destruction of name-and-form, the six provinces are destroyed; by the destruction of the six provinces, contact is destroyed; by the destruction of contact, sensation is destroyed; by the destruction of sensation, thirst is destroyed; by the destruction of thirst, attachment is destroyed; by the destruction of attachment, becoming is destroyed; by the destruction of becoming, birth is destroyed; by the destruction of birth, old age and death, grief, lamentation, suffering, dejection and despair are destroyed. Such is the cessation of this whole mass of suffering.' Knowing this, the Blessed One on that occasion pronounced this solemn utterance: 'When the real nature of things becomes clear to the ardent, meditating Brahman, then all his doubts fade away, since he realizes what is that nature and what its cause, since he has understood the cessation of causation; he stands, dispelling the hosts of Mara, like the sun that illumines the sky.'"[1]

The chain of causation was to Gotama the basis of his system. Life to him was very painful; release from its suffering was the goal and purpose of the way which he set before men. He had no taste for fruitless metaphysical discussion, nor cared for the philosophical establishment of his doctrines further than was needed to support them as a practical system. His followers in more dialectic mode attempted further to substantiate the principles stated in his teachings, or towards which his teachings pointed. His own system consisted in the establishment

[1] *Mahāvagga*, i, i, 1–3. *Sacred Books of the East*, vol. xiii.

of a rule of conduct and a way of life; for the masses in after times it naturally became transformed to a religion. But it were a misnomer to apply the term "religion" to Gotama's system as he set it forth; for it recognized no god nor any all-controlling power without the man, which he should seek to put himself in right relation with. Though hardly a philosophy, it might be called a philosophic way of life, inasmuch as knowledge was its means.

An explanation of Buddha's chain of causation lies partly in the same Hindoo subjectivity that found expression in the *Upanishads*. What one thinks, fixes his mind upon, and absorbingly desires, that he reaches or becomes;[1] and conversely, by ceasing from personal desires he ceases from conditions of their fulfilment, that is, from states of individual existence. From desire of the sense-objects of life comes attachment; from attachment comes becoming; from becoming come birth and rebirth, old age and death, unto the continuance of the evil round, if the subject at death be not free from desires connected with individuality. In Buddhism this is the same as in Brahmanism; except that the final attainment of Brahma differs dialectically from the final release unto Nirvana.

Karma and Selfhood.

The second part of the explanation is the doctrine of Karma and successive lives, which in Buddhism is stated with greater fulness and ethical precision than in the *Upanishads*, and is differentiated from the corresponding Brahman doctrine by a different conception of being. If in Brahmanism, Karma was the cord of individual identity through successive lives, in Buddhism it was more, for it was the sole constituent of self, of individuality. There was nothing in individuality except Karma; Karma is all there is to individual existence.[2] For Buddhism recognizes no essential being, but

[1] For a somewhat later application of this principle, see *Questions of King Milinda*, iii, 7, 9 (vol. xxxv, *Sacred Books of the East*, p. 129).

[2] See *Questions of King Milinda*, ii, 2, 6; iii, 4, 2; iii, 5, 6 (vol. xxxv, *S. B. E.*, pp. 40, 71, 86, 101, 111, 112). "What is it that is reborn?

only a universal linked order of combined causal relationship and ceaseless change. From this continuously, ceaselessly, with an absolute impermanence, result the "conformations," the "puttings-together," the samkhāras, whence spring "consciousness" and that microcosm of all restlessness which Buddha called "name-and-form," but which is usually called a man. To this name-and-form there is no entity, no substantiality, either material or spiritual; there is no body, there is no soul,[1] but only a group of reciprocal causal relations temporarily bound together by Karma, which is the phase of the universal law of causality and ceaseless impermanence relating to this conscious "name-and-form." "Impermanent are all the samkhāras—their vanishing is bliss"—their continuance in consciousness is suffering.

The thought of Māra completes the group of ideas contained in the Buddhist conception of existence. To the simpler view, Māra is a personality, the Evil One, the Tempter, Prince of Death. Between him and the followers of Buddha there is war. But to philosophic Buddhist thought, Māra is the all-pervading principle of evil and of suffering, co-existent, co-extensive with all life. Wherever there is corporeal form, wherever there is life, there is also evil, there is also Māra.

Preaching of the Doctrine.

After seeing the chain of causation, Gotama lingered some days in solitude. He was disinclined to teach, lest he should have his pains for nothing. A great god descends, and kneeling beseeches him to proclaim his doctrine, and the Buddha

Name-and-form is reborn. Is it this same name-and-form that is reborn? No; but by this name-and-form deeds are done, good or evil, and by these deeds (*i.e.* by this Karma) another name-and-form is reborn."—*Ib.*, ii, 2. 6. "Is there such a thing as the soul? In the highest sense there is no such thing. Is there any being who transmigrates from this body to another? No, there is not."—*Ib.*, iii, 5, 6.

[1] It is unlikely that Gotama ever permitted his own discourses to pass into the ultimate denial of any soul or self whatever; he merely pointed out that all things connected with man, material or spiritual, were impermanent and were not the self. See *e. g. Mahāvagga*, i, 6, 38–47; *S. B. E.*, vol. xiii, p. 100.

yields.[1] He resolves to preach to the five Bhikkhus, who had been formerly his followers, and sets out to Benares where they abode. When the Blessed One came to Benares, to the deer-park, Isapatana, where the five Bhikkhus were, they, seeing him, say one to another; "Here comes Gotama, who has turned to a life of abundance. Let us not salute him, nor rise when he approaches, nor take his bowl and robe. We will put there a seat; if he likes, let him sit down." But when the Blessed One approached, they went forth to meet him. One took his bowl and his robe, another prepared a seat, a third brought water to wash his feet.[2] Now they addressed him by his name, and called him Friend. But he said: "Do not address the Tathāgata[3] by his name, nor call him Friend. The Tathāgata is the holy absolute Sambuddha.[4] Give ear, O Bhikkhus![5] the immortal has been won by me. I will teach you. If you walk in the way I show you, you will ere long have penetrated to the truth, and see it face to face; and you will live in possession of that highest goal of the holy life, for the sake of which noble youths give up the world and go forth into the houseless state."

Then the Blessed One convinced them, and they gave ear to him willingly. Whereupon he addressed them thus:

The Eightfold Path and the Four Noble Truths.

"There are two extremes, O Bhikkhus, which he who has given up the world ought to avoid. What are these two extremes? A life given to pleasures and lusts: this is degrading, sensual, vulgar, ignoble, and profitless; and a life given to mortifications; this is painful, ignoble, and profitless. By avoiding these two extremes, O Bhikkhus, the Tathāgata has gained the knowledge of the middle path, which leads to insight and wisdom, which conducts

[1] *Mahāvagga*, i, v, 1–11.

[2] *Ibid.*, i, vi, 9.

[3] This is the term applied by Buddha to himself; it signifies the Completed, Perfect One.

[4] Universal Buddha.

[5] Bhikkhu signifies a beggar-monk, or brother.

to calm, to knowledge, to Nirvana.[1] Which, O Bhikkhus, is this middle path, the knowledge of which the Tathāgata has gained? It is the holy eightfold path, namely, Right Belief, Right Aspiration, Right Speech, Right Conduct, Right Means of Livelihood, Right Endeavor, Right Memory, Right Meditation.

"O Bhikkhus, the noble truth of suffering is this: Birth is suffering; decay is suffering; sickness is suffering; death is suffering; presence of objects we hate is suffering; separation from objects we love is suffering; not to obtain what we desire is suffering; briefly, the fivefold clinging to existence is suffering.

"O Bhikkhus, the noble truth of the cause of suffering is this: Thirst, that leads to rebirths accompanied by pleasure and lust, finding its delight here and there; thirst for pleasure, thirst for existence, thirst for prosperity.

"O Bhikkhus, the noble truth of the cessation of suffering is this: it ceases with the complete cessation of this thirst,—a cessation which consists in the absence of every passion,—with the abandoning of this thirst, with the doing away with it, with the deliverance from it, with the destruction of desire.

"O Bhikkhus, the noble truth of the Path which leads to the cessation of suffering is this: that holy eightfold Path, that is to say, Right Belief, Right Aspiration, Right Speech, Right Conduct, Right Means of Livelihood, Right Endeavor, Right Memory, Right Meditation."[2]

The sermon at Benares illustrates Buddha's restriction of his teaching to the three subjects, suffering, the source of suffering, and how men may attain deliverance from suffering. Ignorance, as it were, of the way out, that is to say, of these four noble truths, is suffering's root. The immediate cause of suffering, which constitutes

[1] For an illustration of Buddha's conception of the "middle path," *i. e.*, a life neither of luxury nor of ascetic penances, see the story of Sona, *Mahāvagga*, v, 1, 12–18.

[2] *Mahāvagga*, i, vi, 17–22.

the sum of individual life, is thirst for life and pleasure: desire leads to rebirth. With the destruction of desire, the round of rebirth and suffering is stopped. The way to the cessation of suffering by the destruction of desire is the eightfold path of the fourth holy truth.

Buddhist Ethics.

The practical ethics of Buddhism burst through the bands of caste and the follies of asceticism, but were otherwise similar to the ethics of Brahmanism. The particular acts approved by a people or sect are often a matter of circumstance and character. A more fundamental question is as to the sanction of the conduct, the principle thereof. Only by understanding that, can one rightly comprehend the meaning of precepts enunciated in a system. It is evident that whatever phrase be used, there can be in Buddhism no principle of sin; no adjudging of an act wrongful because transgressing the will of the doer's god, who is powerful to punish. In Buddhism all is law; wrongful conduct sounds in ignorance with its attendant uncontrolled desires. Lust and anger, for example, represent craving and clinging to existence.[1] Conversely, the great practical Buddhist virtue of benevolence logically sounds in realization that individuality is delusion, and in a consequent discarding of desire for self, a desire which is opposed to sacrifice for others. In fact, there can be no real love without elements forbidden by Buddhism,—attachment, real caring for another, devotion to another.[2] The law of human life, the universal principle of ethics, is Karma, the evil or good result of the act to the doer. The final object is cessation from all personal desire, which shall cut off Karma and rebirth. Logically in such

[1] The man who harbors no harsh thoughts within him, Who cares not whether things are thus or thus, His state of joy, freedom from grief or care, The very gods obtain not to behold.—*Kullavagga*, vii, i, 6; vol. xx, *S. B. E.*, p. 233.

[2] From no Indian point of view could the love between a man and a woman be an ideal, but only temptation and debasement. Here Buddha sees only foulness. See *e. g. Sutta Nipata*, 835. etc. (*S. B. E.*, vol. x.)

a system, devotion to others can be only devotion to abandonment of self. Nevertheless the Blessed One refrained from entering Nirvana, and through a long devoted life exemplified his inculcation of "a love far-reaching, all-extending, all-embracing." By a like devotion must we think that his disciples were inspired.

The precepts of Buddhist righteousness are usually expressed negatively; the Buddhist shall not destroy any living thing, shall take no man's goods, shall not commit adultery, tell no lies, nor drink intoxicating liquor. The precepts inculcating the positive virtue of charity and benevolence towards all living beings are noteworthy: "Do not speak harshly to anybody; those who are spoken to will answer thee in the same way. Angry speech is painful; blows for blows will teach thee."[1] "For hatred does not cease by hatred at any time. Hatred ceases by love; this is an old rule."[2] "Let a man overcome anger by love, let him overcome evil by good; let him overcome the greedy by liberality, the liar by truth."[3] There is a world of progress in the western or Christian acceptation of the thought of overcoming hatred by love; nor are those elements of human truth absent from the Buddhist view.[4] But soon, as with all things Indian, this human truth was carried into the absurd, and there arose the quasi-magical idea that by thinking lovingly of each quarter of the world and all things therein, it was possible to disarm the hurtful power or inclination of all men and animals.[5]

A more advanced stage of holiness, to which good deeds are pre-essential, is self-centred meditation,[6] fortified with knowledge of the impermanence of all things and crown-

[1] *Dhammapada*, 133.

[2] *Ib.*, 5.

[3] *Ib.*, 223.

[4] See the moral narrative of *Mahāvagga*, x, 2.

[5] *Kullavagga*, v, 6; i; *cf. ib.*, vii., 3, 12, and *Questions of King Milinda*, iv, 4, 16.

[6] "If he should desire," *Akankheyya-Sutta* (vol. xi, *S. B. E.*, p. 210).

ing watchfulness over temptations of sense. "Great is the fruit, great the advantage, of earnest contemplation, when set round with upright conduct. Great is the fruit, great the advantage, of intellect when set round with earnest contemplation. The mind set round with intelligence is freed from great evils, from sensuality, from individuality, from delusion and from ignorance."[1]

A little while after the sermon at Benares, when the disciples had reached the number of sixty, the Blessed One said to them: "I am delivered, O Bhikkhus, from all fetters, human and divine. So are you also delivered. Go ye now, out of compassion for the world, and wander for the gain of the many and the welfare of gods and men. Preach the doctrine which is glorious in the beginning, glorious in the middle, glorious in the end, in the spirit and in the letter; proclaim a consummate, perfect, and pure life of holiness. There are beings whose mental eyes are covered by scarcely any dust, but if the doctrine is not preached to them they cannot attain salvation. They will understand the doctrine. And I will go also to preach."[2]

Universal Elements in Buddhism.

It is a characteristic of race religions and all systems of thought showing no tendency to extend beyond national limits, that what there is in them of universal truth and applicability is inseverable from conditions which only the race fulfils, or from peculiar thoughts and customs unsuited to other peoples. Buddhism was not thus limited. Recognizing no castes, it held itself fit for acceptance beyond the pale of Indian society. Suffering weighed on all men, Çudras as well as Brahmans; all were in need of salvation. Caste was a thing of no real import in the way of life towards Nirvana, which Gotama taught. In broad, enlightened, spir-

[1] *Book of the Great Decease*, i, 12. (vol. xi, *S. B. E.*) Buddha set forth different stages of his teaching to householders (lay-brothers) and to monks (*Bhikkhus*). See *ib.*, i, 11, 23, 24; and the beautiful story of the young man Yasa, *Mahāvagga*, i, 7.

[2] *Mahāvagga*, i, ii, 1.

itual mode, early Buddhist writings refute the ethical efficacy of birth or form or ceremony. Not by birth is man an outcast or a Brahman; but by his deed becomes one or the other; the outcast is the angry, hateful man; he who harms living beings, and has no compassion; he who thieves, defrauds, murders; who is an adulterer; who is ingrate to his parents; he who does wrong and conceals it, or pretends to be a saint, and is not,—he is an outcast.[1] It is not by his diet that a man is defiled; nor purified by his formal observances, his tonsure, rough skin, his hymns or sacrifices.[2] He who has cut off all ties; who being innocent, endures reproach; who is free from anger, subdued, clings not to sensual pleasure; who knows in this world the destruction of his pain; he who, without desire for this world, wanders alone and houseless—he is a Brahman.[3]

There was no place in Buddha's system for sacrifices or for prayer; and the teaching that ascetic penances were degrading distinguished his followers not only from Brahmans, but from the many sects and bands of ascetics that filled India. Yet he knew the difficulty of living in the world freed from its attachments; and he may have realized the power which lay in organization. The complete disciple of Buddha must be a monk, a brother, a Bhikkhu. The Buddha himself founded the Order or brotherhood; and the early books ascribed to him its elaborate organization and its many rules.[4] His forty-five years of teaching

[1] *Vasalasutta*, 7; *S. B. E.*, vol. x, p. 20.

[2] *Kullavagga-Amagandha-Sutta*, vol. x, *S. B. E.*, p. 40.

[3] *Mahāvagga-Vasettha-Sutta* (vol. x, *S. B. E.*, p. 112). As is plain from the import of these sayings, the word Brahman is not used in a caste sense.

[4] It was proof of the greatness of Gotama's spirit that, after some misgiving, he permitted women to form Buddhist communities, similar, though inferior, to those of the monks. See *Kullavagga* x, (vol. xx, *S. B. E.*, p. 320, etc.). Compare *Book of the Great Decease*, v, 23 (*S. B. E.* xi, p. 91). Absolute chastity was required of Bhikkhus and Bhikkhunis. For the activity of women in the early Buddhist movement see *The Women Leaders of the Buddhist Reformation*, by C. A. Foley; *Trans. of Congress of Orientalists for 1892*, vol. i, p. 344.

and leadership make this view credible. The brotherhood proved effective for the spread and maintenance of Buddha's teachings. By no means were its rules free from Indian peculiarities. Hindoos were habituated to minute regulations of daily life; it was second nature for Buddhist communities to subject themselves to the like. But Gotama knew that no particular form or regulation was essential, and he is said to have given explicit permission to the Order to change its minor rules after his death.[1] When the Blessed One should be no more, the brethren, in matters touching the Order and all else as well, must heed his final exhortation: "Be ye lamps unto yourselves. Be ye a refuge unto yourselves. Betake yourselves to no external refuge. Hold fast to the truth as a lamp. Look not for a refuge to any one beside yourselves. Let a brother as he dwells in the body so regard the body that he, being strenuous, thoughtful, and mindful, may whilst in the world overcome the grief which arises from the bodily craving; so also, as he thinks, or reasons or feels, let him overcome the grief which arises from the craving due to ideas, or to reasoning, or to feeling."[2]

Death of the Buddha.

Soon after holding the discourse from which these words are taken, Buddha announced his approaching decease:

"My age is now full ripe, my life draws to its close:
I leave you, I depart, relying on myself alone!
Be earnest then, O brethren, holy, full of thought!
Be steadfast in resolve, keep watch o'er your own hearts!
Who wearies not, but holds fast to this truth and law,
Shall cross the sea of life, shall make an end of grief."[3]

Speaking thus, the Blessed One turned to comfort the

[1] See *Book of the Great Decease*, vi, 3; vol. xi, *S. B. E.*, p. 112. There were no prayers in the early Buddhist communities; but frequent public confession as to delinquencies.

[2] *Book of the Great Decease*, ii, 28.

[3] *Ib.*, iii, 66.

disciple who was dear to him: "Enough, Ananda! do not let yourself be troubled. Have I not often told you that it is in the very nature of all things most near and dear unto us that we must divide ourselves from them, sever ourselves from them? Whereas everything born, brought into being, and organized, contains within itself the inherent necessity of dissolution, how can it be possible that such a being should not be dissolved? For a long time, Ananda, have you been very near to me by acts of love, kind and good, that never varies, and is beyond all measure. You have done well! Be earnest in effort, and you too shall soon be free from the great evils, —from sensuality, from individuality, from delusion, and from ignorance."[1]

Then the Blessed One addressed the brethren and said: "Brethren, there may be doubt or misgiving in the mind of some brother as to the Buddha, or the truth, or the path. Enquire, brethren, freely. Do not have to reproach yourselves afterwards with the thought, 'Our teacher was face to face with us, and we could not bring ourselves to enquire of the Blessed One when we were face to face with him.'"

And when he had thus spoken, the brethren were silent. For the second and the third time the Blessed One addressed the brethren with the same words; and they were silent. Then the Blessed One said: "It may be, brethren, that you put no questions out of reverence for the teacher. Let one friend communicate with another."

And when he had thus spoken the brethren were silent. And Ananda exclaimed, "How wonderful a thing is it, Lord, and how marvellous! Verily, I believe that in this whole assembly of the brethren there is not one brother who has any doubt or misgiving as to the Buddha, or the truth, or the path."[2]

[1] *Ib.*, v, 38.

[2] The *Ketokhila Sutta*, on "Barrenness and Bondage" (vol. xi, *S. B. E.*), teaches that a brother cannot become free from spiritual barrenness while he has any doubt in respect of these matters.

Then said the Tathāgata to the brethren : " Behold now, I exhort you, saying, ' Decay is inherent in all component things ! ' Work out your salvation with diligence ! " These were the last words of the Tathāgata.[1]

" Then the Blessed One entered into the first stage of deep meditation, and arising out of the first stage he passed into the second. And rising out of the second he passed into the third. And rising out of the third stage he passed into the fourth. And rising out of the fourth stage of deep meditation, he entered into the state of mind to which the infinity of space is alone present. And passing out of the mere consciousness of the infinity of space, he entered into the state of mind to which the infinity of thought is alone present. And passing out of the mere consciousness of the infinity of thought he entered into a state of mind to which nothing at all was specially present. And passing out of the consciousness of no special object, he fell into a state between consciousness and unconsciousness. And passing out of the state between consciousness and unconsciousness, he fell into a state in which the consciousness both of sensations and of ideas had wholly passed away."

And then the Blessed One passed back by the same stages in reverse order till he reached the first stage of deep meditation, whence he again passed into the second, third, and fourth stage of deep meditation ; passing out of which last, he immediately expired.[2]

Nirvana.

This account of the mode in which Buddha expired is interesting as paralleling the negative or abstracting process[3] by which a conception of the Absolute is reached ; only there is no suggestion of the attainment of the Absolute by the Blessed One. The account is also interesting for the man-

[1] *Book of the Great Decease*, vi, 5–10.

[2] *Ibid.*, vi, 11–13. Compare with this " The Great King of Glory," *Natra-Sudassana-Sutta ;* vol. xi, *S. B. E.*, p. 247, etc., and especially p. 271, etc., and p. 284.

[3] See *ante*, p. 73.

ner in which it turns back just as one expects an account of Nirvana. Buddha's teachings did but make clear that Nirvana is a condition over which the law of causality, with its content of sorrow, death, and rebirth, has no sway.[1] In later Buddhist writings it is explicitly stated that Arahatship, the state of perfect enlightenment and detachment from the cravings of personality, is the attainment of Nirvana;[2] and with this the earlier books accord. But no light is thrown on the condition, existent or non-existent, conscious or unconscious, of the Arahat after death. This question was asked by Buddha's disciples; and the answer was that the Blessed One had not declared it.[3] That condition being a state beyond the pale of the law of causation, nothing might be predicated of it which might be predicated of life, except in this negative mode, that all shortcoming, suffering, need, desire, is satisfied or quenched. But consciousness was one of the links in the chain of causation; and whatever made up that passing delusion, human individuality, was also part of the same chain. Clearly, death released the Arahat from individuality, likewise from consciousness. Buddha's teaching pointed towards extinction, and perhaps so clearly, that the Blessed One never felt called on to declare more explicitly that which was the outcome of his system: if men understood not that, they understood nothing. The whole long round of suffering and rebirth led up to Arahatship, a condition

[1] This point, clear in the early writings, comes to explicit discussion and statement later, *e. g.*, in *Questions of King Milinda*, vi, 7, 13 *et seq.* Nirvana is uncaused, unproduceable, not put together of any qualities.

[2] *Questions of King Milinda*, i, 41; ii, 1; ii., 2, 9; Nirvana is "a state of mind to be realized and enjoyed by a man here, on this earth, in this life, and in this life only."—Rhys-Davids.

[3] In the *Sutta-Nipata*, 342–357 (vol. x, *S.B.E.*), a venerable Bhikkhu asks Buddha whether the Bhikku's teacher, who had gone to Nirvana, was blessed or not; and whether he had been completely extinguished, or still retained some elements of existence. Buddha answers merely: "He cut off the desire for name-and-form in this world. Kanha's (Mara's) stream adhered to for a long time, he crossed completely birth and death."

of intellectual calm and consciousness of release, preceding actual release in the final extinction of that congeries of confections, that conscious "name-and-form" which is called a man.[1] Such result is not preposterous from the standpoint of the long-cumulating Indian yearning for release from mutability and that embodiment of it, the human individuality. Only to the western mind is the system purposeless in its issue, failing to show any ultimate reason for any existence or becoming, or for any objectless law of causality to mould the whole pointless round. The best which can be is but the same as never to have been.[2]

The Result.

The life of the man Gotama, the teachings of the Buddha, represent the sole true consequent ideal of Indian thought. Out of pity, in a world of suffering, he taught through many years. Likewise shall his disciples wander for the sake of men. In itself this pity, which exceeded that of all the Indian gods, was not effectual. The highest of beings, the holy and absolute Sambuddha, the self-enlightened man, the Perfect One, at whose feet the gods fell down, could only point out the way. The disciple must rely on himself. "Brother, thou shalt betake thyself to no external refuge.

[1] But along lines of Indian subjectivity, it may be that the Arahat's perfect desire of release from individuality effects or is such a release.

[2] This outcome of the Blessed One's system was recognized only in India. Not in such guise might Buddhism promulgate itself in other lands. Not all of Asia would appreciate the strenuous intellectual character of the system, nor all of Asia be satisfied with such salvation. Transformed into strange transformations, frequently sensuous and unspiritual, adapted to the different times and countries, "Buddhism" evolved satisfactions of men's need of gods to pray to and of some life to come. Curiously changed in their long journeys were the teachings which were carried across the Himalayas, into the vale of Kashmir, the mountain jungle of Nepal, the snow-land of Thibet, and sowed throughout the Celestial Kingdom, Tartary, Corea, and Japan. For the history of Buddhism in India and of "Northern Buddhism" outside of India, see Kern, *Buddhismus;* Burnouf, *Introduction à l'Histoire de Buddhisme Indien;* Koeppen, *Lamaische Hierarchie;* Vasselief, *Le Bouddhisme;* Schlagintweit, *Buddhism in Thibet; The Lotus of the True Law*, vol. xxi, *Sacred Books of the East.*

Self is the Lord of Self." No hardier thought has the human mind conceived than this of the human being, without a god, working out his own salvation, even though that salvation were but a ceasing to suffer. Buddha's teaching offered salvation only to hearts wearied beyond hope. It announced release from suffering, an ideal of alas, alas, for life! 'T is sorrow! Let us have done with it!

Indian thought and Indian mood as issuing in Buddhism set forth, in lofty and consistent modes, elements of truth. The systems which contained them were warnings for all time that by these paths of abandonment men shall advance neither to God nor to the perfecting of themselves.

What a man thinks and strives for, that he is. This is a spiritual truth when limited to modes of that which desires and thinks, that is, to modes of spiritual being. By indulgence, the evil desire is not slaked, but roused. Man can satisfy himself with nothing transitory or finite; nowhere and never shall he escape the result of his deed: the good deed shall profit him; for the evil deed must he atone. These were the Indian elements of truth.

Man cannot live by bread alone; neither shall he by starvation. There is no virtue in pointless renunciation; and no sure attainment in renunciation misdirected towards an end impossible and unreal. Not human life alone, but all life, is a process of differentiation and development of individuals. Individuality is the basis of human completion, and must fulfil itself through acts and desires, love and attachment, and yearnings manifold, with all the pain connected with the apparently transient state in which the individual lives on earth. And in conceptions of eternal life beyond, unmerged individuality must subsist if there shall be continuance and perfecting of the highest conceivable elements of being. India, in Brahmanism, then with more open eye, in

Buddhism, abandoned as worthless, or as painful, the content of men's lives on earth ; then, scorning individuality as the veriest mode of change and death, it abandoned the existence of the human individual, the basis of all life, the only means whereby that which transcends the human individual may be reached. Man cannot gain God unless man continue to exist himself. Indian thought reaches not conclusions, but—catastrophes. The Absolute All-One,—Brahma and the Ātmā which was It,—was the first leap into the void ; the second was Nirvana.

CHAPTER V.

IRAN.

THE valley of Ferghana, through which runs the Jaxartes when its streams have united, the plateau of Pamir whence flow the chief tributaries of the Oxus, and the mountains and valleys between Ferghana and Pamir were included in the provinces of Sogdiana and Bactriana; and somewhere in these regions, where in Alexander's time survived a spirit brave and free, was the first home of the Iranian race. It was not a land to spoil its dwellers with gentleness. Cold were its winter snows, burning its summer suns. Yet abundant harvests would it yield to toil. Tradition places here Airyana Vaejah, that blessed land to which all people would hasten, had not Ahura Mazda set in each race a love of its own home. Yet the Evil Spirit had made ten months of winter there.[1]

The Home.

In this ancient Aryan land, Aryan and Iranian were once the same. If the race began and multiplied amid the sources of the Jaxartes, it could not extend itself to the east where mountain ranges rose above the line of snow. This people would likely press southwestwardly through the valleys of the Alai range, and follow down tributaries of the Oxus to where the main stream of the river issues from Pamir. It pushed across the Oxus, then followed up the southern tributaries which descend from the northern sides of the western Hindoo Kush where the range is broken and passes lead over the mountains down

[1] *Vendidad*, i.

to India, whither proceeded the portion of the Aryan race that was to become Indian. Other passes lead southwestwardly to the Persian desert. And without crossing the ranges a far path was open to the west, of which also the race availed itself; for a strip of fertile land extends from the Hindoo Kush to the Alburz mountains and the Caspian Sea, leading through the provinces of Media and Atropatene. To the north lie the Turcoman steppes, to the south the Persian desert. Those portions of the race that remained in the old home, or, having reached the Hindoo Kush, passed southwestwardly towards old Persis or westwardly towards Media, may be regarded as the Iranian folk.

The Avesta People.

The *Avesta*, or rather that part of it which the *Gathas* constitute,[1] is the earliest record of this people. Therein they appear as bands of men and women held together by the same faith.[2] Their religious zeal seems not unconnected with change from nomad to agricultural life. For agriculture and the raising of cattle have become sacred duties, and the enemies of the Avesta folk are nomads, godless unbelievers, who harm the cattle and do not till the earth. The Avesta people also call themselves "Aryans," and there comes mention of the "Aryan lands" and "the home of the Aryans,"[3] and also of "non-Aryan peoples."[4] So,

[1] The most available translations of the *Avesta* are those by Darmesteter and Mills in vols. iv, xxiii, and xxxi of the *Sacred Books of the East*, and the later French translation by Darmesteter in vols. 21–23 of *Annales du Musée Guimet*. There is another French translation by de Harlez. The translations of the *Gathas* (*Yasna*, 28–34, 43–51, 53) are not to be relied on. Mills's translation contains much not in the original; and Darmesteter's is vitiated because of his view of the late composition of the *Gathas*. Portions of the *Gathas* are more surely, but somewhat unintelligibly, rendered by Geldner in numbers of Kuhn's *Zeitschrift* and Bezzenberger's *Beiträge*.

[2] See Geiger, *Ostiranische Kultur*, p. 166.

[3] The name survived in Ariana, and the modern name Iran is not unrelated. Herodotus, vii, 62, says that in earlier times the Medes were called Aryans. As the Vedic Indians speak of themselves as Arja, the name Aryan must have existed when Indians and Iranians were one race.

[4] *Yasht*, xviii, 2; xix, 68.

besides the religious, there is with them a race feeling, the sense of Aryan blood; and their enemies were nomads mostly of other race, but with Aryans among them who would not accept the Avesta faith. These nomads were robbers of cattle and men. A place where the earth feels sorest grief is that where "the wife and child of one of the faithful are driven along the way of captivity, the dry and dusty way and lift up a voice of wailing."[1]

Socially and politically the people of the *Avesta* resemble the Vedic Aryans. Lands and cattle were their chief possessions; money they had none. Houses of great and low were simple. Their food was plain; they drank milk, and perhaps freely of fermented liquor. A well-formed race, bodily strength was prized among them; a man should be tall and broad-chested, his eye bright and piercing. These are qualities to mark a king, who should also excel in high insight. Women should be beautiful, tall, with fair skin and shapely bosom, chaste and of good repute.

A prophet arose to this people, Zarathushtra. The record of his faith, the *Zend-Avesta*, was composed during the course of centuries. Much therein regarding him is later priestly formulation. But in the Avesta hymns, the *Gathas*, Zarathushtra is a very real, brave man, with a high thought which he is struggling to make into a people's faith. A prophet's mind is his, a prophet's misgivings, a prophet's trust. One cannot doubt that to this picture of striving manhood there corresponded a great original.

Zarathushtra.

Prophets who establish faiths must needs live what their lips utter. The Buddha is a perfectly enlightened being, serene and sure from the beginning of his teaching: for him there is no further struggle—nor attainment; all is reached. The Iranian prophet is nearer the reality of human life; misgivings and discouragement, contend-

[1] *Vend.*, iii., 11. See Geiger, *Ostiranische Kultur*, pp. 176–193. So up to our times have Turcomans carried off Persians.

ings with them, bringing fuller knowledge of Ahura, extend through the career of prophethood and passionate reform told in the *Gathas*. The life of Zarathushtra, as these heartfelt psalms suggest it, is the very grand, concrete forthsetting of the spirit and principles of the Avesta religion.

It has come to more than one inspired prophet of the foretime, in the course of his prophetic ministry, to see the purpose of his life set in an opening vision of his god and of his call. "And I beheld Jehovah, high and lifted up, heard the seraph voices—holy, holy, holy!" Then ring the words "Whom shall I send?" which overmaster Isaiah's sense of sin and unworthiness. "Send me!" answers the prophet's life.[1] So also answered the life of Zarathushtra. It accords with the sense of revelation and of call that the prophet's life should be throughout responsive to his god, a communion, a seeking of instruction from him, and power and aid. Like Isaiah's, Zarathushtra's life is moulded on his thought of God; and in its seeking always unto him, knowing no other law, no other pattern, the life of Zarathusthtra appears Hebraic rather than Aryan.

There is a Gathic hymn in which, as from a later period of his career, Zarathushtra looks back upon his early visions. The working spirit of his faith is in the prophet's mind: "May men, following the laws of Ahura's Good Thought, work beneficence, and receive the supreme reward here and hereafter; and especially may the teachers of righteousness so be rewarded. Yea, the reward be mine![2] And I will hold thee as mighty and beneficent in the justice to be rendered to the good and to the evil, and in the coming of the might of Good Thought to me."[3] Hereupon the assurance of Ahura's justice-rendering might recalls to the prophet's memory his vision of judgment to be accomplished at the final day: "And I knew Thee as an holy one when I beheld Thee

[1] Isaiah vi. [2] *Yas.*, xliii, 1–3. [3] *Ib.*, 4.

bringing to pass retribution for the wicked, reward for the good, at the world's last change, when Thou, holy spirit Mazda, shalt appear with the power of Right Order (Khshathra) and with Good Thought (Vohu Mano) through whose working men increase in Righteousness (Asha)."[1]

Now the prophet sees again the sharper later vision, which was his call to a career of militant allegiance: "And I knew Thee as an holy one, Ahura Mazda, when Thou didst appear to me with Good Thought, asking, Who art thou? To whom dost thou belong? And I straightway answered, Zarathushtra. A foe will I be to the unbeliever, but a strong help to the righteous, that I may reach heaven. I praise and worship Thee, O Mazda!"[2]

"And I knew Thee as an holy one, O Mazda, when Thou with Good Thought didst appear, and to my questions as to Thy acceptance of my service and my sacrifice, and how I might understand Thy Truth (Asha), didst make answer: Thou shalt see my Asha. Make question as thou wilt."[3]

"And I knew thee as an holy one, Ahura Mazda, when appearing with Good Thought Thy words revealed assaults of men brought on me through my devotion to that which Thou hast declared to be the best. Zarathushtra chooses for himself every holy spirit of thine."[4]

Thus out of the struggles of his career, the prophet realizes the import of its opening visions. They are the lyric note, of which his life was rendering out the story. And the *Gathas* tell this story, yet in a lyric way. For they utter only crisis-notes. It is difficult to connect and set them in the circumstances of their utterance; yet they suggest a period of preparation, a period, as it were, of gathering strength and clearer insight, of cumulating impulse becoming mastering purpose, all leading up to

[1] *Ib.*, 5, 6. [2] *Ib.*, 7, 8. [3] *Ib.*, 9, 10.

[4] *Ib.*, 11, 16. For translation of *Yas.*, xliii, see Geldner in Kuhn's *Zeitschrift*, 1890, p. 316.

the call when the man becomes the prophet. He has been long finding his god: now has his god found him. Ahura's efficient spirit, Good Thought, says to Ahura, the supreme Lord Wisdom, "One man only have I found who will hear Thy instruction and with accordant mind teach men Thy law and declare the faith of Mazda."[1]

The Announcement.

So sounds the prophet call within this man who is but Zarathusthra. In first response from those who might have seemed in direst need of him, there comes a murmur of distrust.[2] Many a sterile word shall he utter to understandings lost through evil.[3] But he is stanch in the faith within him and the assurance of the truth he preaches,—the conflict to the death between the good and evil principle, the triumph of good, and the resurrection of the just. He cries in the assembly, "Hear with your ears, and consider, that we, each for himself, man and woman, may choose against the final day when everyone shall receive the reward of his choice."[4]

Zarathushtra's conviction of the verity of what he preached and of the lordship of Ahura was so intense and eager, so finely felt out to its full conclusions, that he could not but hold other religions false, and seek to uproot them. His religion was a reform; it was also a new spiritual creation. As universally intended[5] as Buddhism, it was as militant as Islam. For militancy lay in its dogma of the conflict of good with the evil, which the good does not convert, but destroys. Zarathushtra adjures his disciples to keep themselves from unbelievers and shut their ears against the lying ignorance of such as would bring death and ruin sheer to house and village. Nay, hew then down with the sword![6] "To him who would deceive the just shall hereafter be groanings, long abode in darkness, noisome food and insult. To such a

[1] *Yas.*, xxix, 7, 8.
[2] *Ib.*, 9.
[3] *Ib.*, xxxi; *cf.* Isaiah vi, 9.
[4] *Ib.*, xxx, 2.
[5] *Cf. ib.*, xxxi, 3; xlvi, 12.
[6] *Ib.*, xxxi, 17, 18.

lot, ye wicked, your works and your religion shall bring you!"[1] While on the righteous shall Ahura and his ministers bestow all blessing.[2]

It could not be but that the prophet of such a faith would soon experience the woes and buffets which his early vision had foretold. He has his followers and supporters, among whom is a king, Vishtaspa; but some of his own family or caste are hostile,[3] and opposing teachers confound the progress of his work: "The false teacher thwarts my doctrine and my life's object through his teachings; he hinders desires for righteousness. This I bewail to thee, Mazda and Asha. And that man thwarts my doctrine who hates the herds and destroys the herbage, and hurls his mace against the righteous. . . . Surely thou wilt do the very best to aid the endeavors of thy faithful one, thou who art stronger than him who threatens my destruction, if I assemble my beloved people to take vengeance on the unbelievers."[4]

The Battle of the Faith.

So it comes to fighting, and sometimes the battle goes against the prophet: "To what land shall I turn, whither carry my prayer? Followers and kinsmen forsake me, my neighbors wish me ill, and the wicked tyrants of the land. How can I advance thy cause, Ahura? I am powerless, stripped of herds and men. I cry to thee. Help me, as a friend a friend. Thy counsel, Lord, I choose."[5] Then, as if addressing men, he speaks: "He who does not move to aid the righteous, works for the Evil One; he shall go to perdition. That one is wicked who succors the wicked; that one is righteous who befriends the righteous. This is thy law, Ahura."[6] And

[1] *Ib.*, 20.

[2] *Ib.*, 21.

[3] This would readily have been the case supposing Zarathushtra to have been a Magian, that is, a member of a priestly caste or tribe, who was introducing innovations.

[4] *Yas.*, xxxii, 9, 10, 16. Geldner's rendering in Kuhn's *Zeitschrift*, 1886.

[5] *Yas.*, xlvi, 1–3.

[6] *Ib.*, 5, 6.

the prophet prays for the overthrow of his evil enemies, and promises paradise to those who aid him.

Towards the end it seems as if the righteous cause had triumphed. These prayers of Zarathushtra have been answered, and he prays that blessings and eternal life may come to such as may thereafter be converted. "And Zarathushtra, he makes offering of his life. He gives to Mazda's spirits the guidance of his acts and words."[1] So is it through his consecrated life. In danger, discouragement, misgiving, he looks to Ahura for aid and enlightenment.[2] He seeks unto no other law, no other wisdom; would conform his life in all respects to Ahura's commands and Ahura's nature; would resemble him and teach others that resemblance,[3]—wherein is righteousness, wherein is belonging to the kingdom of the good, the realm of life, the portion of final resurrection.

Religious Dualism.

The religion which Zarathushtra pressed on men was a dualism which looked forward across the plain of warfare to the final triumph of good over evil, life over death. Its supreme lord of good, Ahura Mazda, Lord Wisdom, with the attendant personifications of his attributes, or rather of human virtues regarded as the creations of Ahura, constituted a conception grand and spiritual. No explanation of it beyond the personality of Zarathushtra has passed the stage of hypothesis. The mode, however, of the apprehension of this religion has no Indo-Germanic parallel; for all is conceived as revelation and subsequent continuous, almost indwelling, enlightenment from God to his prophet. Neither would its ethical conceptions appear to have Indo-Germanic parallel, inasmuch as they remain contained within the nature, the creative power, and the

[1] *Yas.*, xxxiii, 14.

[2] See *Yas.*, xxviii, 6, 7; xxxiii, 7, 8; xxxiv, 12, 13; xlvi, 6; xlviii, 9–11; l, 16.

[3] See *Yas.*, xxxi, 16, 22; xliv, 1, etc., *cf.* xxxiii, 4; xlviii, 3; xlix, 6; l, 6.

ways of Ahura Mazda, and do not tend toward the evolution of a conception of ethical law based on the nature of things, and not dependent on the will and power of a personally conceived god. Consequently, moral wrong, transgression, wickedness, remain, strictly speaking, sin; for the ways and nature of Ahura remain the standard of all righteousness.

The Two Spirits.

"Now shall I preach, and do you give ear and hear, ye who hither press from near and from afar; therefore lay ye all these things to heart as clear, nor let the wicked teacher your second life destroy —the perverted sinner your tongues with his false faith.

"Now shall I preach of the world's two primal spirits, the holier one of which did thus address the evil: 'Neither do our minds, our teachings, nor our concepts, nor our beliefs, nor words, nor do our deeds in sooth, nor yet our consciences nor our souls agree in aught.'"[1]

These two spirits encountered at the first creation, the one bringing life, the other death; and even so will it be to the world's end. The wicked spirit chooses to cause evil, the beneficent spirit chooses to cause good. The demons and their worshippers have not chosen righteousness, but evil.[2] In the end the good spirit shall conquer, and reward with blessedness his righteous ones.[3] There can be no onlookers at this strife; each man must choose his side; he who chooses Mazda must fight the righteous fight against evil conduct and evil men. The righteousness of Zarathushtra had no benevolence towards the enemies of himself and his religion. They were followers of the evil spirit; he dwelt in them. Kindness towards them favored evil,[4] and so was sin in its opposition to the nature of Ahura. But Zarathushtra had no thought of

[1] *Yas.*, xlv, 1, 2 (A. V. W. Jackson's translation); *cf. Yas.*, xxx, 3–6.
[2] *Yas.*, xxx, 4–6.
[3] See *Yas.*, xxx and xlv, 2, etc.
[4] See *Yas.*, xxxi, 14, 15; xxxii, 10; xxxiii, 2, 3; xlv, 11; xlvii, 4.

limiting his faith to a single people; others might accept it and fulfil its righteousness.[1]

Righteousness of Mazdaism; Ahura.

The first demand of Mazdaism is to follow it, protect, and extend it.[2] But Ahura and his ministers were righteous, beneficent, and just. So his religion made like demands on its adherents; perdition awaited the oppressor and the unjust judge,[3] and those who maltreated the cattle.[4] Ahura was the giver of life, the creator of all good; his demands on men included righteousness; nor was he satisfied with the hypocrite's professions, but demanded works.[5]

Probably a worship of natural phenomena prevailed in Iran in Indo-Iranian times. Ahura Mazda likely was once a god of the sky.[6] In the *Gathas* there remains but faint suggestion of his origin.[7] He has become the Lord Wisdom, the creator of mankind and all things good,[8] the source or parent of all personified auxiliary or mediating divine principles. Ahura's activity, creative and beneficent, is that of spirit and intelligence: "Since thou, O Mazda, in the beginning for us our beings and consciences hast formed and our intelligence through thine own mind, since thou madest life clothed with a body, since thou gavest us the works and words whereby one freely may express his belief."[9] Ahura is the creator and fosterer of all righteousness, and the bringer to pass of the reward of righteousness in his followers in the life to come, after the final overthrow of evil. And he is holy, that is, pure of evil, severed from it, the efficient power which works towards severance from it, towards holiness. The man who is holy and works righteousness, for him

[1] *Cf. Yas.*, xlvi, 12.

[2] See *Yas.*, xxviii, 6–8; xlviii, 8; xlix, 5.

[3] *Yas.*, xxxii, 10–14; xlix, 2, 3.

[4] See *Yas.*, xxix; xxxii, 12, 14.

[5] See *Yas.*, xxxi, 10; xxxiv, 9.

[6] See Darmesteter, *Le Dieu Suprême des Indo-Européens*, *Revue des Religions*, 1880; and Darmesteter, *Ormazd and Ahriman*, *passim*.

[7] *E. g. Yas.*, xxx, 5.

[8] See *Yas.*, xxxi, 13.

[9] *Ib.*, 11.

there is no death hereafter, but only for the wicked,[1] those whose lives oppose Ahura's purpose, which is the effectuating of his righteous nature. For such awaits the portion of death;[2] which also is a consequent self-effecting of the nature of evil.

Ahura's nature, character, and ways are revealed in the Amesha-spentas or Amshaspands, the personified spiritual powers through which his purposes are effected. Inasmuch as the Amshaspands are Ahura's creations, they must represent his nature. But the point of departure of the process of personification is humanity or nature—the creation, not the creator. The Amshaspands are personifications of qualities which Ahura has created in mankind and nature. They are thus personifications of created principles of good operative in the creation,[3] and appear as personifications of (1) human virtues and (2) the vital powers of natural life. The first are four in number: Vohu Mano, which signifies "Good Thought" from the intellectual as well as from the moral point of view; Asha Vahista, which signifies "Holiness," or "Perfect Virtue" or "Righteousness"; Khshathra vairya, the power, especially the kingly power, which accomplishes the way of good in social and political order, the genius of good government; Spenta-Armaiti, "Perfect Thought," thought which stands for a right attitude of piety and submission to Ahura. This fourth Amshaspand is feminine, and appears related to an anterior naturalistic conception of an earth spirit. The fifth and sixth, "Health" and "No-death," represent long life and health and material welfare.[4]

The Amshaspands.

[1] *Yas.*, xxix, 5.

[2] *Yas.*, xxx, 8–11.

[3] Consider, *e. g.*, Yas., xxxi, 1; Mazda reigns as Vohu Mano (Good Thought) increases, *i. e.*, in men.

[4] The above explanation of the names of the Amshaspands is mainly Darmesteter's in vol. 1 of his *Avesta* (*Annales du Museé Guimet*, vol. 21), p. 20 *et seq.*

Over against Ahura and the Amshaspands stand the primeval spirit of destruction and his creation of evil demons and all deadly things. But the co-ordination of the evil spirit with Ahura is not forever. In the end evil shall be annihilated, and Ahura come to all-comprehensive exclusive supremacy. Then will there be no power beside him, death having been destroyed.

The Gathic Ideal.

The nature of Ahura and the Amshaspands outlines the Gathic ideal for men. The Mazda worshipper prayed for the good things of this life,[1] and for active and spiritual righteousness which brings weal on earth and happiness in the world to come.[2] "With hands stretched out I pray to fulfil all good works, the first law of Mazda, the good spirit; and for the understanding of Good Thought. . . . I who come to thee, O Mazda, with Good Thought, that thou mayst grant me in the two worlds, that of the body and that of the spirit, the benefits gained by righteousness, by which Ahura places in happiness them that delight him; I who give myself to thee, O Righteousness, and to him who is the first, Good Thought, and to Ahura Mazda, to whom belong Sovereignty not to be overthrown and Good Piety's increase: come at my call for my joy! I who open Paradise, Good Thought effecting it, and the divine rewards for works done in knowledge of Ahura Mazda. As many as I may I seek to teach to seek the good. . . . Come with Good Thought, O Righteousness! give the gifts which last eternally!"[3]

This devoted and spiritual prayer expresses the prophet's desires and the Mazdan ideal. Yet Zarathushtra fell short of Israel's faith. He might not expand his conception of Ahura to the all-comprehensiveness of God, within the unsearchableness of whose purpose is place for all this world's apparent evil. Dualism is a rough rationalistic explanation of the riddle, whose solution only

[1] See *Yas.*, xxxiii, 10; li, 2.

[2] See *Yas.*, xxxiv, 1–4.

[3] *Yas.*, xxviii, 1–6.

Israel could leave to her heart's assurance that Jehovah was sole Lord.

The Prophet and the Later Time.

It sometimes happens that of a race whose capacities of growth and spiritual apprehension are not yet dead, there is born a man with power to discern the reality and spiritual import veiled in the shows of things and the thoughtlessness of custom. The race has reached certain conceptions of man and of his environment which breathes with spirit and divinity. These thoughts are purified from their fetish dross in the prophet's mind, and become possessed of further truth because released of errors. And to this re-creation of his race's thought he adds elements from his own inspirations. New thought has been born. It shall live because of the immortality of truth. Yet its living entails a giving up of self, a loss of its own purity in its leavening work. In the process of its apprehension by the mass of men it is corrupted and reladen with dross.

So was it with the thought of Zarathushtra. He took the conceptions of his race, or rather perhaps of his caste or priestly tribe, and freed them from their imbecilities. Then he builded with them, adding the keystones ever from the inspiration within him. Thus was his system formed, his lofty dualism: the Lord Wisdom and the true Principles of insight and accordance with Ahura, which work his work within the souls of men thereby transformed to soldiery for good. Opposed to these, the dark Evil Spirit interjecting that sufficiency of evil to account for sin and pain and death. But Zarathushtra did not entirely free his mind from prevalent modes of apprehending man's duties of sacrifice[1] and worship; and it is difficult to distinguish between the lower, unspiritual elements which he may have taken over into his religion from the cults about him, and that debasing of his teaching which resulted through its apprehension by the mass

[1] *Cf. Yas.*, l, 9.

of men and by the priestly caste.[1] At all events, whatever lower elements Zarathushtra retained would be held and added to and heaped upon with rite and ceremony. And because his teaching as a whole was too spiritual for popular or priestly apprehension, it was necessary that some definite principle thereof should be taken and materialized, and then formulated in precept and observance suited to the understanding of right conduct by unspiritual men.

Purity.

The principle thus taken was a part expression of Zarathushtra's dualism, indeed a mode in which the universal conflict might be apprehended, which Zarathushtra, not regarding false, may have taken from priestly usages. The *Gathas* contain the precept: purity *(yaozdâo)* is, after birth, the first good for man.[2] Whatever meaning the prophet may have given this word, to the later Avesta religion it became a material conception with ethical or spiritual connotations. In the *Vendidad* it means "cleanliness," freedom from physical impurity,[3] as determined by rules prescribed in that book: "Purity is for man, after birth, the first good; that purity which is in the religion of Mazda, the purity of the man who purifies himself with good thoughts, good words, and good deeds."[4] Impurity or uncleanness lies in the presence of elements of the evil creation—the presence of disease which makes for death, above all, the presence of death itself. The most impure, contagious object is the corpse, which the corpse-demon enters when life is extinct. He fastens on those who touch it, and

[1] There soon comes in the later *Avesta* the magic mystic thoughts regarding sacrifice; that thereby the worshipper strengthens the good against the demon (see *Yasht*, viii, 23, *et seq.*) and gets immortality for himself (see *Yasht*, ix–xi). But these ideas may well have been centuries older than Zarathushtra. He did not condemn divination. *Cf.*, *Yas.*, xxxi, 3; xlvii, 6.

[2] Yas., xlviii, 5.

[3] See Darmesteter, Introduction to vol. ii of his *Avesta* (vol. 22 of *Annales du Musée Guimet*), p. x, *et seq.*

[4] *Vend.*, v, 21.

must be expelled, or rendered powerless by rites.[1] A corpse must not be allowed to defile the holy elements, fire, earth, or water ; hence must not be burned, nor buried, nor cast into the river, but laid on the top of a mountain, with a layer of stones to separate it from the earth.[2] Not all corpses defile, but only those of men and of animals belonging to the good creation of Ahura. Animals created by Angro Mainyu, as the snake or tortoise, were embodied death while they lived; their death is itself purification; to kill them is a holy deed.[3]

The principles of Zarathushtra's Mazdaism were as of course gradually committed to detailed formulation in commands and prohibitions, which, while holding fast to high regard for honesty and truth,[4] assumed peculiar character through certain rules of the religion, especially those relating to impurity and the sacredness of dogs. Evil deeds continued such as made for Angro Mainyu, the Evil Principle, and extended the empire of the demon.[5] Most sins might be expiated by submitting to prescribed penalties, which release the sinner from punishment after death.[6]

Legal Formulation.

Indeed, the Avesta religion based its sanctions mainly on the results of acts to the doer in the life to come. Mightily it held to a resurrection unto heaven or hell; a thought which inclined towards taking plastic form in the late picture[7] of the

The Resurrection.

[1] *Vend.*, v, 27 ; viii, 33, 34.

[2] See *Vend.*, vi, 44, etc. ; viii, 10, etc. It was inexpiable sin to defile the holy elements with dead matter ; but a man does not sin by doing it unknowingly. *Vend.*, v, 1, etc.

[3] *Vend.*, v, 35, etc.

[4] *Vend.*, iv, is devoted to contracts and assaults. Elsewhere it is said : "Break no contract, neither the one thou hast made with a faithless man, nor one made with a just believer.— *Yasht*, x, 2. Desolate is the abode of perjurers and murderers.—*Ib.*, 38.

[5] See the curious later notion of *Vend.*, xviii, 30, *et seq.*

[6] See Darmesteter, Introduction to vol. ii (vol. 22 of *Musée Guimet*), p. xvi, etc. There were inexpiable crimes, *e. g.*, burning a corpse.

[7] *Yasht*, xx, 1, *et seq.*

faithful soul greeted after death by his Religion, in the person of a fair maid advancing towards him 'midst flowers and perfumes; she tells him who she is, speaks of his righteous life, and how it helped the faith: "I—Religion—was lovely, and thou madest me more lovely; I was beautiful, and thou madest me more beautiful; to be desired, and thou madest me more to be desired, and advanced me, by thy good thoughts, good words, and acts."[1]

Zarathushtrianism and the Medes and Persians.

From information given by contemporary inscriptions and by Greek writers, especially Herodotus,[2] it is evident that the religion and customs of the Persians of the fifth century before Chirst present correspondences with the *Avesta*. The God of Darius's Behistun inscription is Aura-Mazda, and Herodotus says that the Persians sacrificed to Jupiter as the circle of the firmament. They appear also to have believed in a resurrection; and there was dualism in their thought of the conflict and alternate reigns of Ormazd and Ahriman, the latter succumbing in the end.[3] The elements, fire, water, and earth, were holy. The Persians did not burn their dead, nor bury them till torn by beasts;[4] their mode of sacrifice was not out of accord with the *Avesta*. And finally in

[1] The soul then advances to Paradise. The experience of the evil soul is in every detail the exact reverse. Certain features of the resurrection life are mentioned in the *Gathas*: there is the Cinvat Bridge, over which a righteous following of the religion of Mazda opens the way,—*Yas.*, xlvi, 10; and there would seem to be reference to a bath of molten fire, out of which righteous souls come unscathed. See *Yas.*, xxx, 11; xxxiv, 4; li, 9.

[2] I, 130–140.

[3] Theopompus.

[4] Perrot (vol. v, p. 632, *Histoire de l'Art dans l'Antiquité*) points out that in the royal Persian rock-cut tombs little attention was paid to the sepulchral vault. It was small and unornamented inside, and not protected with great care,—directly the reverse of the way of an Egyptian tomb. This comports with what Herodotus says; and the *Avesta* does not forbid burning the bones when they have been stripped of flesh. The Sassanian kings were stanch Zoroastrians, and had like tombs. Their purpose was on their exterior face to tell the king's famous deeds, rather than guard his body.

social ethics the correspondence is striking; Herodotus Persians as well as the Avesta folk care supremely for truth, for agriculture, and for the welfare and increase of the family. It is certain that the *Avesta* and the customs of the Achæmenian Persians were not unrelated.[1]

The Medes were a kindred race. Theirs was an earlier and more considerable culture; and their power was at its height while the Persians were a rude mountain people under Median suzerainty. The Magi were the priestly tribe of the Medes, and became the hereditary priesthood of the Persians when the latter had fought the Medes and established political supremacy over them. Apparently wherever Persian religious customs resemble those of the *Avesta*, the resemblance between the customs of the Magi and the *Avesta* is more certain and more definite.[2] And since the Magi are known to have been the authoritative priestly caste among the Persians, the conclusion is not unwarranted that the influence making for this resemblance came from the Magi.[3] The result is not affected by the circumstance that both Persians and Medes doubtless inherited a fund of ancient Aryan religious conceptions, including a number of deities, among whom was Ahura. These considerations may dispose us to accept the definite ancient tradition that Zarathushtra was a Magian.

[1] These matters are clearly presented by Darmesteter in Introduction to vol. iii of his *Avesta*, ch. v.

[2] *E. g.*, Herod., i, 140, says that it was said that the Persians never buried a body till it was torn by a dog or bird of prey, but that there was no doubt of this being customary with the Magi. He then mentions the curious Magian custom of killing ants and snakes and other animals except the dog. The dog is the holiest beast of the *Vendidad*; and snakes belong to the evil creation.

[3] So Herodotus saying that the custom of having the corpse torn by dogs or birds was practised openly by the Magi, but secretly by the Persians, would perhaps indicate that it was longer established with the former, and had pressed itself to observance among the Persians only recently when Herodotus wrote, and against the opposition of still existing prejudices.

There is no longer need to delay over the extreme variance of the traditions as to the time of his birth. Iranian scholars seem now tending to agree upon the seventh century before Christ.[1] Conversely, the intensely earnest, original character of the *Gathas* points close to the prophet for their source. Whatever liturgic use they were put to afterwards, there is no priestcraft nor accumulative legend in their composition. They bespeak thoughts pressing to first utterance; their references to circumstances are the incidental references of truth. Between the origination of these moving psalms in the mind of one of God's great ones, and the Gathic expression of them, there has elapsed no time for sacerdotal formulation; there has occurred no fall from spirit to observance.[2] If not from the lips of Zarathushtra, they sprang from the inspiration of his words, and may have cheered his followers and voiced their zeal to battle for the high new faith.

Time of the Reform.

Though Zarathushtra was a Magian, the religion of the *Gathas* was not the creation of a sacerdotal caste. Not the Roman Church, but Martin Luther, wrought the Reformation. Not an established priesthood, but a reforming, God-inspired priest, created the religion of the *Gathas*. That it was a new spiritual creation, its spirit seeking straight unto its god, is borne witness to by its freedom from dogmatic formulation and its militant enthusiasm; and there is confirmation in the absence of all reference to ancient usage, the mighty authority which would have been invoked had it existed. There is suggestion, indeed, that its reforms were not undirected against the abuses of an hereditary priesthood.[3] At all events, the Gathic religion was a young winged steed which no priesthood had yet bestridden.

[1] See A. V. Williams Jackson, "On the Date of Zoroaster," *Journal of American Oriental Society*, vol. xvi.

[2] Which is palpable in other parts of the *Avesta.*

[3] *Yas.*, xxxi, 10 ; xxxiv, 9.

It would appear that the Magi accepted the new inspired faith. Zarathushtrianism certainly became the religion of Persia, and was ascribed to Zarathushtra; and so the Magi could not have remained the Persian priesthood without being Zarathushtrians. But when did the reform occur? If the new reformed religion had been universally accepted in the time of Herodotus, he likely would have mentioned the name of Zarathushtra. Yet his silence must not be given too much weight, for the fragments of Xanthus of Sardis, who is thought to have lived earlier, speak of Zoroaster as the founder of Magian doctrines;[1] and so afterwards do Plato and Aristotle. One may perhaps conclude that the reformed religion, preached by the prophet himself as early as the time of Cyrus,[2] was established through Persia and Media not later than the end of the fifth century before Christ.

The Persians and their Limitations.

Thus it would seem that the great Aryan prophet offered his religion as a faith for men, and pressed his reforms at a period when the Persian race was coming to its rule. In this race are seen the truthfulness and devoted bravery reflected in the *Gathas*. The religion which the Persians were to hold sprang from the great personality of Zarathushtra. Likewise their rapid mastery of western Asia was due to the genius of one man quite as much as to their own valor; and to another man was due the firm establishment of the Persian Empire. Yet without strong ethical capacities in the Iranian race, the prophet Zarathushtra would never have arisen among them, far less

[1] Xanthus mentions Ζωροάστρου λόγια, and says that the Persians have received from him not to burn their dead or pollute fire.—*Frag. Hist. Græc.* ed. Muller, vol. i, p. 42; and *cf. Frag.* 29.

[2] That Cyrus was at least no intolerantly exclusive worshipper of Ahura Mazda appears from his inscriptions in Babylonian Semitic relating to his conquest of Babylonia—*Records of the Past*, N. S., vol. v, p. 144, etc. Yet, as these inscriptions may have been a part expression of his purpose of reconciling the Babylonians to his rule, their reference to Bel and Merodach would not prove that Cyrus did not worship Ahura Mazda, whose name does not occur in them.

have brought them to accept his teaching. So, without great virtue in the Iranian people of rugged Persis, Cyrus would not have led them to imperial victories, nor Darius Hystaspes have organized the fruits thereof into a stable empire.

The Persians accomplished their destiny along simple lines. Their destiny accomplished made plain their limitations. Before they came under the leadership of Cyrus, they were a rude, brave race of Aryan freemen, though they had been for many years under Median suzerainty. Their valor, directed by the genius of Cyrus, first turned the tables on the Medes, and the position of the two races was reversed, the Persians leading as the Medes had led, only far more potently, because of Cyrus. The era of Aryan supremacy was entered on, and before his death Cyrus was not only the conqueror but the ruler of western Asia, including Asia Minor, with the Ionian cities along its coasts.

After the intervening reign of Cambyses, which added Egypt to the Persian Empire, and the usurpation of the Magian Smerdis (Gaumata), which may have been a revolution in favor of the Medes or of the Magian priesthood, Darius, the son of Hystaspes, of the royal Persian blood, obtained the throne. He was the Augustus who followed Cyrus. With energy and rare skill in the choice of instruments he re-established the empire, and then did more; for he enlarged its boundaries, and so organized the government as a coherent system that it could sustain itself when the king should be a weakling. And from Darius's reign rebellions did not break out as of course on the death of a monarch, as had been the rule from early Assyrian times.

Naturally the Greeks were impressed with the power and splendor of that empire which menaced them with slavery. They were also impressed with the ethical qualities of the Persians, especially their truthfulness, a quality lacking among themselves. This appears in Zenophon's romantic *Cyropædia*, and more instructively in Herodotus. "Next to prowess in arms, the Persians look on having many sons as the chief proof of manly excellence. The boys are taught to ride and draw the bow and speak the truth; the most disgraceful thing in the world, they think, is to tell a lie, and they hold it unlawful to speak of what it is unlawful to do. Noble exploits in Persia are highly honored and bring the doers to greatness. The king does not put his servants to death for a single fault, and in punishing weighs the offender's services against his misdeeds."[1]

The spirit of the *Gathas* confirms these observations; so do the inscriptions of Darius. His way of designating evil is to call it "the lie," and the evil man "the liar." "What I have done, I have done by the grace of Auramazda. He and the other gods came to my aid because I was not wicked, nor a liar, nor a tyrant. I reigned according to the divine law,[2] and committed no violence against the law-abiding man. The man who worked for our house I cherished. The man who sinned, I destroyed. Thou who shalt reign in future times, be a friend to no man that lies, and do no injustice."[3] Then the king records the names not only of the rebels he overthrew, but also of the men who aided him.

Herodotus also observes that no race adopts foreign customs as readily as the Persians, and speaks of their adopting the Median dress, the Egyptian breastplate, and some less innocent matters from the Greeks.[4] This imitative spirit, natural to a lately risen race, appears in the remains of Persian architecture. It would be hard to prove the architecture of any race to have been altogether original, and artistic genius may be shown in adaptation. The architecture of Persian palaces and tombs

[1] Herod., i, 130; iii, 154.

[2] *Avasta.*

[3] Behistun inscription 50–52; see for these inscriptions, *Records of the Past*, i, 109; vii, 85; ix, 65.

[4] I, 130.

is skilful adaptation, under Greek influence,[1] of the architecture of Egypt, Assyria, and Lycia. Many of the borrowed forms were refined and beautified by the Great King's architects, and perhaps for the first time in the East there entered an intellectual sense of architectural proportion; to wit, that the parts of a building should bear to each other a definite proportion, determined perhaps by some unit of measurement.[2]

The Persians were only too ready imitators. The change from a rugged home to possession of the luxury of the older civilizations of western Asia was a greater strain than their character and education could bear. The Greeks called them barbarians, and they were, not only by reason of that which made a barbarian in Greek parlance,—belonging to a non-Hellenic race,—but also because they hopelessly lacked capacity for culture. Quickly they saw the delights of luxury; quickly they grasped them. But they themselves were vitiated. They lost the brave virtues of their home, and gained no civilization from their opportunities. So their wealth became barbaric waste. Of themselves they could evolve no higher culture than they possessed in Persis, nor had they capacity to assimilate aught save the vices of the Greeks.

The contact of force between the Persian and the Greek illustrates another matter. That primitive Indo-Germanic communities were free is borne witness to in Persis as well as India, or among the races of Europe. The Aryan peoples of Asia, however, had a capacity for but a barbarous freedom; they were capable of developing such free institutions as comported with an uncivilized society. As culture or material civilization increased, their manhood and political faculty did not reach to the development or preservation of suitable free institutions; and absolute monarchs arose among a people incapable of self-government. Herodotus' account of the creation

[1] It is not improbable that the architects were Greeks.

[2] See Perrot, *Histoire de l'Art*, etc., vol. v, p. 458 *et seq.* Compare Dieulafoy, *L'Art Antique de la Perse*.

of the Median monarchy by Deices, and of the rise of Cyrus himself,[1] are dramatic statements using Hellenic forms and ideas: they cannot be taken to recount actual facts. But they are enlightening as to the incapacity of Asiatic Aryans for self-government. Because of this incapacity the Persians could not but have Cyrus and his successors as absolute despots, though these despots did indeed accord them privileges over other peoples, and respected certain rights, as that of the heads of the noblest families to approach the king,—a right, however, which was a survival of a more primitive time, and not the germ of any future constitutional freedom.

Not even Cyrus could have understood the inferiority of his valiant Persians to those Lacedæmonians whom Herodotus has him despise because they haggled in the market-place. Still less might Darius, and least of all the foolish Xerxes, understand the power of intelligence and civic freedom whereby pigmy Greece should turn back the onslaught of Asia. Marathon was insufficient teaching. The fact was apprehended, if not understood, when Asia's lord became the fugitive of Salamis.

[1] Herod., i, 96, etc. and i, 125, etc.

CHAPTER VI

GREEK BEGINNINGS.

RACE individuality is a matter of slow evolution of differentiating quality. The process begins at a time indefinitely prior to the appearance of a race in history. At any period the race has a certain character and endowment of faculty, which determine the use it makes of all that offers, but are also affected through every opportunity made use of and acted on by every influence met. Obviously a most important factor is the land where the race makes its home. That sets conditions and offers opportunities. Sloth cannot exist in some lands; lands too rugged keep men rude through hardening circumstances and lack of leisure. Other lands again from situation offer myriad chances to learn and do. But neither the nature nor the situation of a land, nor all it offers in itself or draws from abroad, has ever altogether made one of the great races of the world. Racehood is a problem subtle and complex, beyond our knowledge still.

Hellenic Racehood.

No civilization has ever sprung up in that rough mountain region comprised in the ancient countries of Thrace, Macedonia, and Illyria. Of itself it is too harsh to develop culture, and its dangerous coasts attract no visitors. Harborless Epirus, though farther south, offers the same features. But east of it, Thessaly with mountains has fertile plains and harbors on the great bays which open the land to the Ægæan. Coming from the north, Thessaly is the first land of Greece desirable to dwell in, the first also to make plain how Greece faces towards the east. From Thessaly southwards, on through Doris, Locris, Phocis, Bœotia, Attica, across the isthmus into Peloponnesus, appear more strikingly those propitious qualities which distinguish Greece. No other land is so surrounded, penetrated by the sea, illuminated indeed, for the light-shot colors of those gorgeous waters carry past island-rock and guarding promontory into deep bays, tortuous, narrow, wide, diverse in size and form, only in this alike that none is dark. Back from the sea, Greece is benign variety. Mountains and lowlands intersect; sometimes the mountain character predominates, sometimes the narrow hollows broaden into plains. It was a land of mountain fastnesses and lovely valleys, fertile and well-watered, kept so through human industry.[1] There, not far apart, grew earth's most different fruits; the mountain oak looked down upon the olive some thousand feet below. Likewise in close neighborhood grew up divers small peoples; for Greece was cut and barricaded into parts, wherein each clan could well preserve its independence, and satisfy its needs from the variety of soil. No locality was fitted by nature to hold rule over the whole. The land was one to evoke much from its dwellers; its mountains would keep them free in bravery and strength, its valleys teach them gentleness, while the sea would bring knowledge and incite to enterprise. That land might have made much of men bringing thither poor endowments; but the people who were to become the Hellenic race were not ungifted while they yet stood at the portals of Greece.

The Greeks were an Indo-Germanic race, and must at some time have left the ancient Aryan home. They may have entered Europe by routes to the north of the Black

[1] Greece never was a spontaneously fertile land like Egypt. It required the toil of its inhabitants, to which, however, its response was generous. Says Demaratos, the exiled Spartan king to Xerxes: *τῇ Ἑλλάδι πενίη μὲν αἰεί κοτε σύντροφός ἐστι.*—Herod. vii, 102. Nowadays, because Greece through its misfortunes is almost treeless, there is lack of water.

Sea. Crossing the Danube, they may have moved south-westerly through a country which would hardly tempt men to stay, till they saw the Adriatic. Turned by the sea, they may have passed south through Epirus, in the heart of which, at Dodona, on a little lake, their descendants were to establish perhaps the most ancient of Hellenic shrines. From Epirus they would overspread the Thessalian plains, then wander southward, and on into Peloponnesus. The Cyclades are pleasant islands, forming stepping-stones from Greece to Asia Minor. The stretches of water between them were not such as to hinder even rude navigators from crossing; and these islands have been inhabited from most ancient times. Their early dwellers may not have come from Greece, but, on the contrary, from Lydia or Caria, and yet may have been Aryans too. For at an early period there were Aryans in Western Asia Minor. Herodotus was probably right in saying that the Phrygians came from Thrace: why was it not a natural course for peoples who had crossed the Danube and entered Thrace, to cross the Hellespont? It is likely that many such crossings occurred, some in early, some in much later times. Troy was an ancient city, and there is no reason to think its people were not Aryans, though we may hardly call them Greeks. Perhaps the point of veriest interest is this: when did Aryan peoples, dwelling in the Greek peninsula or Asia Minor or in the Ægæan islands, develop such distinctively Hellenic traits that they may be called Greeks? The fundamental archæological fact of the matter is that throughout the entire Ægæan region, continental as well as insular, are found remains of buildings and a mass of rude objects, brick, stone, clay, and copper, which give no indication that the early inhabitants of all these lands were not kindred peoples. On the contrary, throughout this entire region, from Troy to Cyprus, throughout the Cyclades and in the eastern parts of European Greece, these objects present such resemblances as to indicate a common intercourse, but no intercourse with the world outside, to the east or south.[1] Herein, however, lies no clear evidence of kinship. The products of such barbarous handicraft are much the same the world over. Barbarous dexterity is insufficient to fashion material in correspondence with what the race would express, and as children do not fully show their inborn differences of taste and faculty, so distinguishing race-traits evince themselves but vaguely till the race, wakened from its childhood, begins to choose with more conscious discrimination. Differences in the faculties of barbarous races are often disguised in potentialities not yet actually distinguishable.

The makers and users of these rude articles then probably were Aryans; the articles show nothing distinctively Hellenic, yet there is reason to suppose that they belonged to people some of whom were becoming the Hellenic race. For these rude unidentified productions are lower stages of a later artistic activity which begins to show itself Greek. These better art productions are found in widely separated places from Troy to Egypt. But their chief place of origin apparently was the mainland of Greece, and indeed those little kingdoms the names of whose chief towns appear in Homer. A great fund of these better art productions has been taken from the tombs and ruined palaces of the princely fortress towns of Argolis—"golden Mycenæ" and "walled Tiryns." There is nothing to indicate, however, that they were not the work of men whose forefathers made and used the rudest utensils found by Ægæan shores. It would seem to have been a matter of progress and awakening. At all events, in Hellas, if not in Asia Minor,[2] as early

[1] See Meyer, *Geschichte des Alterthums*, vol. ii, § 77, *et seq*. The greatest fund of these objects is from Troy.

[2] The most recent discoveries in Troy place the Homeric Ilion on the same level of culture with Mycenæ. See Dörpfeld, "Die Neuen Ausgrabungen in Troja," *Mittheilungen des Archäologischen Inst.*, 1893, p. 199; *ib.*, 1894, p. 380.

as the fifteenth century before Christ a people was evincing itself Greek, and was making quick progress in civilization under enlightenment drawn from intercourse with more advanced but inferior races.

Sources of Civilization; Egypt and Babylonia.

For the ancient world, Egypt and Babylonia were the primary sources of knowledge and suggestion. Of the beginnings of civilization in these two countries nothing is or ever has been known, even by the peoples dwelling in them at the earliest times of which record remains. But since neither Babylonia nor Egypt, during all the periods of which there is some knowledge, shows clear advancc beyond the civilization reached thirty centuries before Christ, the passing length of years of prior growth may be imagined.

From these earliest times comes evidence, if not of direct intercourse between the two, at least of undertakings in war or traffic reaching out from either country through the lands between them, and so deviously in the direction of each other. If this evidence be uncertain because scanty, it gathers bulk with the passage of the centuries, and in the cuniform letters of the fifteenth century found at Tell el Amarna in Egypt is ample record of intercourse back and forth from Egypt to Babylon and Assyria. A number of these letters from Egyptian governors of cities along the coasts of Syria, show that the cuniform writing was used in those intermediate lands, a fact of as yet unexhausted import, but accounted for by even earlier records, which it tends to confirm, that Babylonian or Mesopotamian kings had conquered and held Syria some centuries before, when Asiatic Hyksos were conquering Egypt. The historical record is abundant of the converse later fact, that after the Hyksos had been expelled, Thothmes III in the sixteenth century conquered all lands to the borders of Mesopotamia.

Such then is the early situation; Babylonia and Egypt, the two primal possessors of art and knowledge and political power, extending their force and influence outwards through intermediate lands, and towards each other, in the varied intercourse of war and peace.

Hittites.

The intermediate lands also had their peoples. From the fifteenth century for several hundred years, the people important from their numbers, wide extension, and military power, were the Cheta (the Chatti of Assyrian monuments, the Hittites of the Bible). They dwelt, or from time to time extended themselves, through Syria, and far into Asia Minor. Judging from the remains of their architecture and sculpture, such civilization as they possessed came from Babylonia or Assyria rather than from Egypt. Much of the force of the original was lost in the crude Chetan work, which bettered nothing and originated little, but dulled and brutalized what it borrowed. The Cheta seem to have been a poorly endowed race, yet from their position they could not fail to play at least the inert mediary part of bringing elements of Mesopotamian civilization to where they might be turned to suggestion by less civilized but more capable peoples of Aryan stock, who were spread through the north and west of Asia Minor, and might thence carry their increased fund of knowledge to Cyprus, Crete, the Cyclades, and Greece.[1]

But in the awakening of the Hellenic spirit to consciousness of itself and what it sought, the part played by the Cheta was slight compared with that of another people who, not through their position, but through their bold tireless traffickings, carried the art of Egypt and Mesopotamia, vulgarized in insignificant commodities, to Mediterranean coast lands and islands from Gades to the Hellespont. No one knows whence the Phœnicians came. From the first they appear as sea-gulls rearing their young upon the cliffs, but living more

Phœnicians.

[1] Little can definitely be said about the Cheta which will not be set aside when their inscriptions are understood. Their monuments are gathered in Perrot and Chipiez, *Histoire de l'Art*, etc., vol. iv, and *cf.* Humann-Puchstein, *Reisen in Klein Asien*, etc.

upon the water. They were not a numerous people. Phœnicia is but a coast; and by the sea lie all its cities. Sidon was the first chief town, and may have been at the height of its activity in the sixteenth century, when Thothmes III had established for a time Egyptian rule over Syria. Doubtless the Phœnicians readily acknowledged Egyptian suzerainty, and at this early period set their future policy of recognizing the overlordship of whatever monarch should be most powerful on the eastern Mediterranean shores, provided only he would leave the Phœnician cities free, and furnish business for their ships. The Egyptians were no sea-loving people; but their power and wealth were great. That Sidon should guard her head at home within the shadow of Egyptian power, and furnish ships and sailors for whatever enterprise the Egyptian monarch had at heart, on the Mediterranean or the Red Sea, was an arrangement of plain mutual benefit.

After a period in the course of which the Phœnicians founded Citium in Cyprus, commercial supremacy passed from Sidon to Tyre.[1] There resulted no change in Phœnician life or policy, which was merely to traffic in the most lucrative regions, or retire elsewhere when a more powerful race took to the sea and drove them off by force or competition. The Phœnicians founded few large cities and refrained from grasping territorial power. Their numbers were small, and trading stations answered their needs. Did they found towns or trading stations on the mainland of Greece? They frequently sailed thither, and Greek tradition bears plenary testimony to their influence. A strong tradition ascribes the foundation of Thebes to a Phœnician, Cadmus; but if Thebes was a Phœnician foundation, those sea-traders selected such an inland site as they never chose elsewhere.[2] At all events, the Phœnicians carried on incessant traffic with the mainland of

[1] See Lenormant-Babelon, *Histoire Ancienne de l'Orient*, vol. vi, p. 474, *et seq.*

[2] *Cf.* Meyer, *Gesch. Alterthums*, vol. ii, § 95.

Greece and the Ægæan islands, till the Greeks, stimulated perhaps by what they learned from the foreigners, drove them from those waters; and the Ægæan, from a Phœnician, became a Greek sea.

There exist remains of Phœnician cities, and some few inscriptions; while articles which the Phœnicians made and traded in are still found scattered through Mediterranean lands and islands.[1] But the race could not portray itself as a Greek could portray it; and the most luminous picture of Phœnician doings is from Homer. In the *Odyssey*,[2] the swineherd Eumæus tells Odysseus how he came to be a serf in Ithaca: "There is an island called Syria, as you may have heard, over above Ortygia where are the turning places of the Sun.[3] It is not very thickly peopled, but a good land, rich in herds and flocks and wine and corn. No death is there nor sickness for mortals; but when people grow old, silver-bowed Apollo comes and slays them with his painless arrows. In the island there are two cities, and all the land is divided between them, and my father was king over them both—Ctesius, the son of Ormenus, a man like to the immortals. Thither came the Phœnicians, famous sailors, cheats, bringing countless gauds in their black ship. Now in my father's house was a Phœnician woman, tall and handsome, and skilled in handiwork; her the cunning Phœnicians beguiled, and one of them made love to her as she was washing clothes by the hollow ship, for that always catches the mind of womankind. He asked her who she was and whence she came, and she told him her father's home: 'From Sidon rich in bronze I am, and the daughter of rich Arybas; but Taphians, pirates, seized me coming in from the fields, brought me hither, and sold

[1] See Perrot and Chipiez, *Histoire de l'Art*, etc., vol. iii, for an exhaustive account of Phœnician art.

[2] *Od.*, xv, 404–484.

[3] *I. e.*, where the sun turns back from the west. Syria is represented as a western island.

me into the house of my master for a goodly price.' Said the man: 'Then would you now return with us, and view again the lofty home of your father and mother, and see them, for they still live and are said to be rich?' And the woman answered: 'This may be, if you sailors will take oath to bring me home unharmed.' All made oath, and she continued: 'Be quiet now, and let none of you speak to me, meeting me in the street or at the well, lest some one tell the old man at home, and he bind me in fetters and devise death for you. But keep the matter in mind and hurry your business, and when your ship is freighted, send word to me at the house, and I will bring such gold as I can lay hands on, and something besides will I willingly give for my passage. I am nurse to my master's child, a cunning little boy, who runs about after me. I will bring him to the ship, and he will fetch you a good price when you sell him among distant people.' Speaking thus, she went away to the house, but they stayed a year in our land and got together much wealth in their hollow ship. When all was ready they sent a messenger to tell the woman. And there came a crafty man to my father's house with a gold and amber chain. Now my mother and her maidens were handling the chain in the hall, and looking at it, and talking over the price. But he nodded to the woman and went to the ship, and she taking my hand led me forth. In the front part of the house she found the cups and tables of those of my father's followers, who had been eating. They had gone forth to the session and the place of parley of the people. So she snatched three goblets and hid them in her bosom and carried them away, I foolishly following. Then the sun set and all the ways were darkened, and quickly we reached the harbor, where was the swift ship of the Phœnicians. And they went aboard, taking us up with them, and set sail, for Zeus sent a wind. Six days and nights we sailed, but on the seventh Artemis the Archeress smote the woman with her shaft. So they cast her overboard to be a prey for seals and fishes, but I was left afflicted. And wind and wave bore us to Ithaca, where Lærtes bought me; and thus did my eyes see this land."

Such were Phœnician ways. Thrifty, energetic, sensual, cruel, was this people of traffickers and kidnappers. Their religion was distinguished by sensual debauchery and human sacrifices. Their art was slovenly and ignoble imitation of the arts of Egypt and Mesopotamia, and throughout its course shows no organic development. They had no care for beauty; but they had the clear-sighted instinct of gain, and knew what things to imitate and trade with; and they became clever manufacturers of what other peoples wanted, or might be induced to want. In their own country and elsewhere when building for themselves, they made skilful use of natural situation, and where they might they hewed and adjusted their walls from cliff and hillside. Thus they got stability and defensive strength, the objects which they aimed at. Their boldness and cupidity made them strong defenders of their independence and their wealth. A king, to gain their submission, must be powerful, and keep his hands off, and his armed presence without Phœnician walls. With rare skill and bravery has Tyre resisted more than one omnipotent besieger.

The Alphabet.

Between the Babylonian and Egyptian civilizations, which had reached their zenith, and the gifted but semi-barbarous Aryan peoples of the Grecian mainland and Archipelago, who should thereafter show themselves Hellenic, the Phœnicians were universal intermediaries. They distributed their multifarious wares, the products of their imitative handicraft. Then, as it were, they presented themselves and their derived and borrowed thoughts. They worshipped many partly transformed divinities whose originals had dwelt in Mesopotamia. Astarte had been Ishtar;—in Cyprus, at least, she was to become Aphrodite;[1] and the

[1] See Meyer, *Gesch. Alterthums*, vol. ii, § 91.

many eastern thoughts which the Phœnicians had embodied in Baal-Melkart may have passed into the deeds and attributes of Heracles. But best, and perhaps last gift, they gave the Greeks an alphabet. Here again the part of the Phœnicians was not originative, but very intelligently adaptive. Egyptian hieroglyphics and their cursive hieratic simplification consisted in part of ideographs, in part of signs which stood for syllables, and in part of signs which stood for elemental vowel or consonantal sounds. The last were, properly speaking, alphabetic signs, or letters. To designate them the Egyptians used figures of objects whose names as spoken began with the initial sound which the alphabetic sign should represent.[1]

In borrowing from the Egyptians a mode of writing convenient to record perhaps their trading transactions, the Phœnicians took neither the ideographs nor the syllabic signs; but only such of the alphabetic signs as represented consonants; and from these they formed twenty-two letters corresponding to consonantal sounds. These Phœnician consonants might by no means express distinctly all that the Egyptians could express by their elaborate compound system of ideographs, syllables, and vowel as well as consonantal sounds. But the writing would be clear enough for the needs of traffic; and the men who had devised it had done something of transcendent importance in the progress of universal civilization, and something which in a process of adaptation would come almost inevitably, but might never have been reached in the way of original invention. The Egyptian language bore no resemblance to the Phœnician, a Semitic tongue closely allied with Hebrew. Egyptian writing had been invented to express the Egyptian language. Consequently, in borrowing and adapting

[1] The letter *L*, for example, was the figure of a lion ; the Egyptian word for lion (*labo*) beginning with the initial sound of *L*. See Ph. Berger, *Histoire de l'Écriture*, p. 97.

Egyptian written signs, the Phœnicians could select only those expressions of elemental consonant sounds which the Phœnician language had in common with the Egyptian. And inasmuch as the two languages were entirely different from each other, signs which could express elemental sounds common to them both, would, for the most part, be suitable to express elemental sounds common to all human tongues.

In devising visible means of communicating thought, the primitive unassisted invention is the ideograph. A mode of writing originated by a race may advance towards an ultimate analysis of vocal sounds, as did the Egyptian in using alphabetic signs. Yet there would come no occasion to lay aside its compound system of ideographic and syllabic signs suitable to that language, though to none other. But the Phœnicians, in adopting from the Egyptian writing a system suited to their own language, would of necessity leave all that was peculiar, and take what was universal in the Egyptian system; though as matter of fact they did not feel the need of taking all that was universal (*i. e.*, the vowel signs). Thus were fulfilled the two conditions antecedent to the formation of an alphabet suitable to all tongues: first, that a system of writing should originate and advance to at least a part expression of elemental vocal sounds; and secondly, that another race should form from it a system of writing adapted to its own quite different tongue. The derived system will of necessity consist of signs expressive of elemental sounds which are the same in all languages.[1]

[1] There is another illustration of this matter. The cuniform writing as used by Babylonians and Assyrians did not advance beyond ideographs and syllabic signs. The Persians formed the cuniform writing which they used in inscriptions from the Babylonian. The Babylonian cuniform had no alphabetic signs; its syllabic signs were not suitable to the Persian tongue. So the Persians took a certain number of ideographs, whence they devised thirty-six alphabetic characters (vowels and consonants), to render the articulation of their own speech. Except in inscriptions the Persians used the Aramaic alphabet. See Ph. Berger *Histoire de l'Écriture*, etc., p. 78, etc. and 214 etc.

Thus was derived and formed the Phœnician alphabet, the basis of all alphabets in present use. It was not complete, for it contained only consonants. Not later than the tenth century it came to the knowledge of the Greeks;[1] and was likely first used by them for purposes of trade, as the Phœnicians used it,[2] and not till some time afterwards either in public inscriptions or for literary compositions.[3] In the meanwhile the Greeks made the letters more symmetrical, and, passing through an intermediate manner of writing alternately from right to left, then left to right (boustrophedon), they changed the direction of writing and the facing of the letters, so that all should read from left to right.[4] This was convenient and artistic—Greek. But it was nothing to the main Greek alphabetic invention of a full set of vowel signs, whereby they completed the alphabet, and rendered it more definitely expressive, and fit to visualize the sonorousness of speech.[5]

Mycenæan Civilization.

From contact with other peoples a weak race may pass from sight, its distinguishing traits effaced, itself perhaps enslaved. A stronger race turns alien skill and proffered knowledge to opportunity to reach a greater selfhood, and gathers strength resisting alien force. Vigorous races advantage themselves in different ways from foreign contact. The Hebrew gained

[1] See Larfeld in J. Muller's *Handbuch der Klassischen Alterthums-Wissensschaft*, 2d ed., vol. i, p. 495, *et seq.*

[2] See Meyer, *Gesch. Alterthums*, vol. ii, § 253.

[3] The earliest extant Greek inscriptions are hardly earlier than 700 B.C. But the fact that the Greek alphabet is nearly developed in them—already possesses vowels—indicates some centuries of previous acquaintance with writing on the part of Greeks.

[4] See Ph. Berger, *Histoire de l'Écriture dans l'Antiquité*, p. 128, etc.

[5] Arthur J. Evans's *Cretan Pictographs and Præ-Phœnician Script* goes to prove that the "Mycenæan" people were acquainted with an ideographic, and possibly linear, mode of writing. The fact remains, nevertheless, that the Greeks did form their alphabet from the Phœnician ; and the probability is unshaken that the Phœnician alphabet was in the main constructed through a process of adaptation rather than original invention.

moral force and clear self-consciousness repelling other peoples' degradations. The Greek became himself by accepting art and knowledge from abroad, transforming all he took. The transformation of the foreign thought, the foreign handicraft, to what it was not, a new art gaining form, Greek genius conquering its foreign lessons, Hellenic race individuality becoming clearer, Hellenic faculty, character, spirit, unfolding—this is what is disclosed by the happy treasure-trove from Mycenæ and other places where the glad Greek child stretched forth its hands to gather life.

The objects constituting the remains of this civilization are not Egyptian, not Babylonian or Assyrian, not Chetan, not Phœnician. The tombs, the palaces, the fortress-walls, of which ruins remain, are bedded in the soil of Greece. The decorations and sculpture, the arms, the vases, the cut stones, the goldsmith's work, were executed by men whose home was nowhere else. It is an interesting fact, difficult to explain, that few foreign articles, and perhaps none of Phœnician workmanship, have been found in Tiryns or Mycenæ.[1]

Since the men of Tiryns, Mycenæ, Orchomenus, left no inscriptions—none at least which have been read,—their character and civilization must be judged from their presentation of themselves in art.[2] It behoved these cities or rather citadels to be defensible, a consideration determining their sites. They were surrounded by thick walls built mostly of large, roughly shaped stones set in

[1] Meyer, *Gesch. des Alterthums*, ii, § 114.

[2] The authorities here are first of all the excavations of Dr. Schliemann, and the collections of objects taken from them, to be found at Athens and elsewhere. Secondly, Dr. Schliemann's publications (*Mycene*, *Tiryns*); Schuchardt's book on the *Schliemann Excavations;* the publications of Dr. Dörpfeld; Furthwængler and Loesche's *Mykenische Vasen*. The data are exhaustively collected and lucidly set forth in vol. vi of Perrot's *Histoire de l'Art*, etc.; admirable is its summary of the characteristics of Mycenæan art, ch. ix, § 9, his indebtedness to which the present writer would acknowledge. Perhaps the most beautiful reproductions of objects of Mycenæan art are contained in the Ἐφημερίς Ἀρχαιολογική, published at Athens.

clay and rubble. Near a gateway the stones were hewn into rectangular blocks and laid in regular layers, and thus the ends of the wall were made stable to resist the lateral pressure of parts more roughly built. The walls contained galleries and casements. They represented an effective mode of using the stone of the country for fortification, practicable for a people with whom iron was a rarity. Other representative architectural remains are the dome-shaped tombs at Mycenæ and elsewhere, and the palace of Tiryns. The most famous of the former has long been called the Treasury of Atreus. In the Tiryns palace, wood was freely used. These constructions, the tombs as well as the palace, evince in their plan and decoration that care for symmetry and proportion which later should distinguish classic architecture. But the decoration, despite its grace and regularity of design, is not fully Greek, for it lacks that illuminating pertinence of theme and motive whereby classic Greek architectural decoration emphasizes the character and makes clear the import of the building. These older people disliked to leave on wall or architrave or column any space unfilled with design or carving. But their designs, not being expressive of the purpose of the building, produce an effect of thoughtless barbarous profusion. These buildings had not reached the grand simplicity of classic construction.

From the crude execution of the limestone mortuary steles, this people would seem to have had no foreign instruction in the field of larger sculpture. At all events, it was an art in which they were unpractised. What some of their artists could execute in fresco may be seen in the fragment from the Tiryns palace, where a lithe human figure, springing on a galloping bull, shows in living line the superiority of man's skilled agility to the strength of the ponderous brute. Probably there were many paintings of like excellence. A yet superior artistic skill appears in some of the small cut signet stones[1] and

[1] See, *e. g.*, the one given by Perrot, vol. vi (*Histoire de l'Art*, etc.), plate xvi, 12, from Vaphio.

in the design and workmanship of the products of the goldsmith's art, easily chief among the witnesses of Mycenæan love of all things beautiful. Graceful and lovely are the diadems, the earrings, brooches, bracelets of gold. Most plainly, however, does the artist's genius bespeak itself Hellenic in scenes of life and struggle inlaid on Mycenæan sword-blades or raised in high relief on the gold cups of Vaphio. On one blade are the blossoms of flowers like lilies, bending, unfolded;[1] on another, cats are hunting ducks by a river where lotus grows[2]—a scene which may have been suggested by some Egyptian model. But the cats, the ducks, the lotus, here are drawn as in life —not as in Egypt. The most famous blade of all shows a lion hunt. Two lions flee towards the end of the blade, but the third springs on a prostrate hunter, over whom his comrades aim their spears and arrows at the lion rushing on. On this blade appears a new thing in art, a unity and centring of interest by the arrangement of the figures, not as in the Egyptian battle-pieces, by making the Pharaoh monstrous and all others in the picture pigmies.

This art, both in its crude efforts and its more advanced accomplishment, in so far as it succeeded in presenting any subject, rendered it with the diversity and unconventionality which exist in life. The rendering of life is reached most largely in the Vaphio cups. On one of these, while two wild bulls are caught in the net, a third dashes his captors to the ground; the bulls on the second cup are tamed; a man drives one off, urging it along and directing it by a rope tied to the hind leg. The cups are masterpieces of the goldsmith's art. Faults there are of drawing; but the scenes are diversified, spontaneous, living, and show artistic qualities which came to Greece from no other land of earth.

Though Mycenæan pottery did not reach the level of the goldsmith's art, it shows itself the product of the same race by its original and diversified manner of repre-

[1] Perrot, plate xix.

[2] Perrot, plate xvii, 1.

senting natural objects, plants, polyps, fishes, birds. Even the goldsmith's work showed faults in drawing the human figure with wasp-like waist, faults original and peculiar, which the artist would have avoided had he copied more his foreign models, and been less himself. Vase-drawings of the human figure are utterly crude, yet preserve the same faults as the goldsmith's work. And being thus related to other work of the same race and time, the Mycenæan pottery, by its use of geometrical patterns as well as by its graceful forms, relates itself to later products of the Greek potter's wheel.

The goldsmith reproduced the human visage in relief as on the Vaphio cups, or outlined in profile, or in the features of the masks which were to resemble the dead whose faces they covered in the tomb. One and all these visages are clear in their negation of any other race-hood than Hellenic. They resemble, though they cannot be said to have fully attained, the classic Greek countenance.

This art called Mycenæan takes joy in the beauty of the many forms which life and natural growth suggest. It copies the flower which is not useful, but simply beautiful; it delights in myriad curves and spirals; for vases and wall decoration, it chooses nothing more frequently than themes derived from the weird tentacles of the polyp. Scenes of conflict are frequent, sieges, combats between man and man, between man and beast. These scenes are true to life in this, that the conflict is not easy; the victor is not victor as of course and effortless; rather is the struggle grim, painful, the end not certain. These men saw life truly. And in the conflict scenes wherein, it may be with sweat and danger, the man masters the bull or slays the lion, there seems almost discernible that which was to be a glorious motive in Greek art, the presentation of intelligence conquering the brute. Wide is the range of motive and interest shown in "Mycenæan" art, from mortal conflict to the drawing of a flower, or faces in quiet profile; and it is real, not ceremonial interest that is shown. For its own beauty is the flower drawn. Not out of pompousness, but for the human struggle in it, is the conflict reproduced just as it occurs. There is in this art a spirit of life, a sense of truth, a sense of reality and of proportion, a love of beauty, a breadth of interest, all of which make up a clear, mute prophecy of Greece.

Attacks on Egypt and on Troy.

Testimony from Egypt in recent years is making clear that the peoples who from somewhere had come to the Ægæan lands did not leave undisturbed the older civilizations of the southern coasts of the Mediterranean. Passing southward along the western shores of Asia Minor, and then eastward, the island of Cyprus would not long remain unvisited, and thence it were not a far journey to Phœnicia. The Asiatic coast once reached, if the adventurous bands were not turned back, or lured to settle in Philistia, news of rich plunder towards the Nile could not fail to tempt them farther. Or indeed from the Cyclades and Greece itself, passing by the way of Crete, it was an easy voyage to Egypt. Such voyages at all events occurred. The decline of Sidon may have been due to these naval incursions from the north; perhaps the Sidonians had imparted the art of building ships and sailing on the sea to these people quick at learning. And it is not improbable that the Philistines who oppressed Israel had come in ships from Cyprus and the farther north. In the thirteenth century Meneptah II, and after him Ramses III, had to defend Egypt against a united attack of these Ægæan peoples, and loudly the Pharaohs laud their victories over the invaders.[1]

The names of the defeated enemies are told, and seem to be the names of peoples who, if not Greek, were at least from out the region which was becoming the Grecian world. The warriors are drawn with rounded and also

[1] See Brugsch, *Egypt under the Pharaohs* (1891), p. 311, etc.

feathered or plumed helms; their features are not Semitic nor African, and if not clearly Greek, at least not clearly un-Hellenic. This is not the first appearance of such peoples on Egyptian monuments: long-sworded Shardanes, who formed the foreign body-guard of Ramses II, would seem to have come from over the sea, and to have been an Aryan people.[1] A later king, Psammetechos I,[2] employed Greek mercenaries, and established them at Naukratis. Further, Mycenæan pottery has been found in Egypt mingled with eighteenth dynasty remains.[3]

These facts from Egypt are met by finding at Mycenæ and at Rhodes articles with the name of Amenophis III of the eighteenth dynasty, and of Ti, his queen.[4] There can be no doubt that Mycenæ and her sister cities flourished in the fifteenth century. Their civilization was the growth of centuries preceding, and lasted till the Dorians destroyed it. But before then, whatever part, direct or indirect, or none at all, the men of Mycenæ and their kin had taken in attacks on Egypt and Phœnicia, they had besieged and burned a city by the Hellespont, doing a deed of ever widening fame. This people, beauty-loving, caring for so much of life, who dwelt in Lacedæmon, Argolis, Attica, Bœotia, Thessaly, and many islands of the Grecian seas,[5] wrote no name on their monuments; their domed and shafted tombs, their citadels and palaces, are unlettered, mute.[6] But while the memory of

[1] *Cf.* Meyer, *Gesch. des Alterthums*, ii, § 134–137.

[2] 665 B.C.

[3] Egyptian influence in Mycenæan art is perhaps to be ascribed rather to direct intercourse with Egypt than to Phœnician intervention.

[4] About 1440–1400 B.C. See Meyer, *Gesch. des Alt.*, ii, §§ 82, 129. *Cf.* Petrie, "Egyptian Basis of Greek History," *Journal of Hellenic Studies*, xi, p. 271, etc.; *ib.*, "Notes on Antiquities of Mycenæ," *ib.*, xii, p. 199, etc. Perrot, *Histoire*, etc., vol. vi, ch. xii.

[5] See Schuchardt, *Schliemann Excavations*, p. 315, and xxix of Leaf's Introduction. *Cf.* A. J. Evans, "A Mykenæan Treasure from Ægina," *Journal of Hellenic Studies*, vol. xiii, 1893, p. 195.

[6] Yet see Evans's *Cretan Pictographs*, etc.

them was strong, nay, rather while they still themselves enjoyed the life of earth, songs honored and preserved the name of the Achæans. Not for want of the most splendid of earth's voices should they be voiceless.

The remains of this civilization present palpable variances from the customs of the Homeric epics. At Mycenæ the dead were buried and perhaps crudely embalmed; in the epics it is usual to burn the body on a pyre.[1] Possibly Egyptian influence was stronger at Mycenæ than when the epics were composed in their present form; or the burial of the dead may simply represent common primitive notions of ensuring a continuance of life after death. There are also apparent variances between the Homeric and the Mycenæan dress, and a more perplexing divergence lies in the fact that the lords of Mycenæ seem to care not at all for the products of foreign art, while in Homer splendid objects, when not the work of Hephaestus, are made by Phœnicians. On the other hand, definite points of coincidence establish the identity of the Mycenæans with the Homeric Achæans: the places prominent in Homer correspond with the localities where "Mycenæan" remains have been found; the Homeric epithets are most apposite, "great-walled" (τειχιόσσαν) Tiryns, Mycenæ "abounding in gold" (πολυχρύσος); the ruins of Orchomenus accord with its Homeric repute for wealth; and the remains of the palace at Tiryns explain and illustrate the palace of Alkinous in the *Odyssey*. These and other coincidences in matters of broad fact and close detail easily overcome special divergences, which are indeed explained by the uncontroverted view that much in the epics is the composition of bards living in the Æolian and Ionian settlements of Asia Minor, after the Dorian conquest of Peloponnesus.

The Achæans.

At a period not far from the traditional date, 1104 B.C.

[1] *Cf.* Leaf in Introduction to Schuchardt's *Schliemann Excavations*, p xxv, etc.; also Helbig, *Die Homerische Epos*, etc.

rude mountain tribes of Dorians descended upon their Achæan kin. The Dorian conquest was not accomplished in one generation. Long struggles for supremacy are indicated by the traditional repulses of the Heraclidæ. In the end, however, the Achæans, fallen perhaps from their ancient valor, had to yield to Dorian strength; and one result was an increased migration to the islands of the Ægæan and the coast of Asia Minor, where probably there were already flourishing Achæan settlements, formed by the extension of Achæan peoples before the Dorian invasion had furnished further motive for leaving their native land.[1] For the purposes of this migration and the Grecian settlement of the coast of Asia Minor, those Greeks who from Thessaly crossed to Lesbos and the adjacent coast are known as Æolians; those are to be called Ionians who from farther south, from Attica—whither they had been pressed together by the Dorian invasion, says the tradition—passed to the Cyclades, and crossed to the western southern coast of Asia Minor. Smyrna was the border settlement, and there, where met Æolian and Ionian speech and story, tradition fitly placed the birth of Homer.

The settlement of the coast and neighboring islands did not take place without conflicts with peoples already there, in race perhaps akin to the new-comers from the west. These Greeks, who were conquering a broader Troad, would never lose the memory of the mighty Achæan achievement, the wide power of Agamemnon, and the glory of Achilles. Of what should their song be but of these ancestral deeds mirrored in their own? And as they looked back to their fatherland, lovingly perhaps, their thoughts would turn to famed Returns of the heroes, the most famous, striving, loving Return of all, that of great Odysseus. The Dorian invasion, which rudely broke the brilliant life of European Greece, would but accelerate the growth of Greece in Asia, where the Achæan—the

[1] *Cf.*, Meyer, *Gesch. des Alt.*, ii, § 138–141.

Æolian-Ionian—genius should finally reach full expression in the completion and perfecting of the treasury of song brought from Æolis and Mycenæ.

Whatever palaces and minor things material were produced by the art of the Mycenæan time would, unless destroyed, remain exactly as they were made by men in whom Greek character and faculties were but nascent. It was otherwise with the songs that told their deeds. Not as a scene inlaid upon a sword-blade, fixed while the blade endure, might these be kept, but only in the formative memories of men, which hold the past indeed, but as a gathering reflex of the present. The present moulds the past to its ideals; and so song grows. From all that circumstances threw in their path were these Achæans, generation after generation, building their lives, building themselves, selecting with clearer discrimination what conformed to a gradually developing Hellenic character. These songs were not formal sacred chants stiffening to magic formulæ with forgotten meaning. They were songs of life, and could not but be continually moulded by the tastes and discriminations, the selecting and discriminating memories, of men who in each succeeding generation were becoming more positively and completely Greek. By the ninth century how much more had the race lived and endured and learned; how much more had it laid aside of what was not it; how much more distinctly Hellenic had it become. All of which would be continually mirrored in these living, ever-growing songs. Finally the great bard Homer—be he one or many—who sings these songs at last and composes them to what they are, is perfect Greek, and the Hellenic genius, in him become its perfect self, completes the structure of the epic past.

Homer's presentation of that past was more Hellenic than that past had been; and yet neither in substance, nor in form or spirit, was it a severed new creation, but a final perfect utterance of rougher notes heard long before in Æolis and Mycenæ—an unfolding of the spirit of

Mycenæan art. That art had shown life true and real, seeing the reality of death and pain, the uncertainty of the straining conflict. This first view comes to clearer vision and finds its greatened epic counterpart in the manifold verities of the poems and the "equal" conflicts round the walls of Troy. *Μῆνιν ἄειδε θέα*—sing, goddess, of the anger of Peleus's son; *Ἄνδρα μοι ἔννεπε Μοῦσα*—tell me, O Muse, of the man of many wiles who suffered much! So the epics open; such the real and human themes which they shall expand. But intimations of like veritable human interest in the man, his strength, his faculty, his skill, murmur in Mycenæan art. By superior mind and skill the bulls are mastered, as Odysseus masters Polyphemus. And as the man of Mycenæ would have all things ornamented to the full, though his inchoate Hellenic spirit does not make the ornament germane and expressive, likewise Homer speaks of nothing great, garment or shield or man, without adorning it with beautifying epithet, which also further tells its character—for Homer is full Greek. Love of beauty is becoming conscious of itself in Mycenæan art; in the epics it is clear and universal, holding all life.

CHAPTER VII.

HOMER.

ALTHOUGH not mature, the Greek spirit has become distinctively itself in Homer. Thenceforth, in a continuous course it raises and develops the qualities which it has reached, bringing them to manifold yet related expression in conduct and philosophy, literature and art. With intelligence and insight, with comprehensive human vision, and with unique capacity for joy, the Greek desired the utmost, the best, the most veritable elements of life. He desired it all intensely, eagerly, strenuously, for his deepest thoughtfulness was not morbid; he did not feel distaste for life because of its limitations; no yearning for the impossible turned him from endeavor for the utmost that might be had. His was complete acceptance of life, with ever finer discrimination in selection.

The Greek Genius.

Desire for the thronging contents of physical and intellectual life appears in the *Iliad* and *Odyssey*. The full and many-sided natures of the Homeric heroes contain wondrous many of the feelings and desires which make life's contents still. The finer modes of intellectual discrimination are not yet evident, as they will become; but there is already clear appreciation which weighs and balances the elements of life.

The conscious and intelligent desire for the utmost of life involves such balancing of its contents, in order that the less may be surrendered for the greater when all may not be had. The function of intelligence is to weigh and estimate, adjust desire to the object's worth. It apprehends proportions. Greek intelligence shows itself in palpable endeavor to adjust and proportion life. Greek mind is great, inasmuch as it discloses itself so plainly as proportioning intelligence. A faculty and habit of estimating, balancing, proportioning all things involves continual reasoning, as well as reasonableness, openness to conviction by the force of argument. Very striking is the part which reason plays with Greeks. Reason rather than emotion appears to lead them ever, whether aright or astray. Homer's passionate heroes never cease to reason; sustained reasoning fills Greek dramas; the speeches in Thucydides are arguments addressed to the reason of the hearers; there is in them little passionate appeal. Greek reasoning thoughtfulness never, till times of decadence, turned to hesitation. Coupled with fearless acceptance of life's conditions, it did not clog, it guided action. What Pericles says of the Athenians applies only in a less degree to all the Greeks: "We have a peculiar power of thinking before we act, and of acting too, whereas other men are courageous from ignorance, but hesitate upon reflection."[1] The habitual acting under the conscious guidance of reason gives a tone of selfishness to Greek ethics. Yet, no other race except Rome so greatened individual selfishness into patriotism, which with the Greeks was also fortified by reason. "In my judgment," says Pericles, heartening the Athenians during the plague, "it would be better for individuals themselves that the citizens should suffer and the state flourish than that the citizens should flourish and the state suffer. A private man, however successful in his own dealings, if his country perish, is involved in her destruction; but if he be an unprosperous citizen of a prosperous city, he is much more likely to recover. Seeing then that states can bear the misfortunes of individuals, but individuals

[1] Pericles's funeral speech, Thucydides, ii, 40, Jowett's translation; *cf.*, Aristotle, *Politics*, vii, 7.

cannot bear the misfortunes of the state, let us all stand by our country, and not do what you are doing now, who, because you are stunned by your private calamities, are letting go the common hope of safety, and condemning not only me who advised, but yourselves who consented to the war."[1] Yet many Greeks did care more for their party than for the whole city, and never foreign enemy could hate as could the exile of the same blood, whose love of city was fused into desire to get her again within his grasp. Alcibiades, most universal of traitors, spoke common sentiments when as an exile he told the Spartans: "I love Athens, not in so far as I am wronged by her, but in so far as I once enjoyed the privileges of a citizen. The country which I am attacking is no longer mine, but a lost country which I am seeking to regain. He is the true patriot, not who, when unjustly exiled, abstains from attacking his country, but who in the warmth of his affection seeks to recover her without regard to the means."[2]

Life is the exercise of faculty; and in exercise of faculty is joy. To many races life might be pleasant, might be dumbly satisfying, and might have its fierce exultings; but the Greek, through his finer, more intelligent, more highly human energy and eagerness, felt joyousness, and knew it as a principle of life,—life's *raison d'être* of happiness. Normally was life glad; the clear Greek consciousness of this might be intensified to pain at life's untoward interruptions, incident to mortality. "Be young, dear soul of mine; quickly shall there be other men, and I be black earth!" might sing Mimnermus.[3] So comes the cutting pain which the Greek could never quite dispel from life, but over which the Hellenic spirit endeavors in many modes to make good the principle of joyousness—joyousness in what life offers. Fleeting, dashed with the

[1] Thucydides, ii, 60. Jowett's translation.

[2] Thucydides, vi, 92, Jowett's translation.

[3] Mackail, *Selections from the Greek Anthology*, p. 267.

sadness of their transience, are life's sweet instinctive pleasures. But it has deeper joy springing from happy or successful exercise of man's noble faculties, the worth of which reason confirms. Such joy lay in the high strenuous deed accomplished, bringing broad satisfaction from its nobleness and assurance of glory; or such joy lay in energy of mind. Greek intellect, strong and active, seeking to proportion life, could not but apply itself to the acquisition of the knowledge requisite; it also sought that larger knowledge which might prove life's far criterion, and which was in itself a highest mode of life. As something to be loved and got for its own sake the Greeks sought knowledge—philosophized. And this search for various knowledge, for farthest, deepest knowledge of all life, in which Greeks sought to satisfy the cravings of the soul, was one phase of Greek intelligent endeavor after life's most veritable elements, which lie in what is nearest to the seeker man, in that which is most really part of him. And again, such striving for life's utmost could not but issue in effort to heighten each human capacity and faculty. This meant to greaten man and make of him the utmost. The Greek sought to complete himself. In conduct and in that idealizing reflex of life which is literature and art, he sought to display heightened human traits and show the man enlarged—more closely kin to the kin race of gods.

And for life thus considered, reasoned on, proportioned, understood, felt, joyed in, and completed, greatened to its fullest bound, there was a final thought which crowned and compassed all,—the thought of beauty. Beauty was one and manifold; life's perfectness, and therein one; and yet approached in many ways, and therein manifold, and comprehensive of all life. Love of the beautiful, the full and proportioned perfect, its myriad forms appealing to the sense and to the mind, was the high Greek emotion; therein lay the farthest yearning of the Greek spirit, that which made it Greek.

Greek love of beauty was cognate with Greek love of knowledge, since it also sprang from the Greek intellect regulating, wishing to see proportioned, fit, symmetrical and harmonious, the many objects precious in Greek eyes. It was a love seeking in its object unity, form, measure, harmony, fitness, adaptation to ends, power and glory. Under the guise of beauty the Greeks loved life, essential life, not its incidents, but life itself, proportioned, harmonious, victorious, as it were—the very fulfilment and consummation of human being. And thus the love of beauty closely entwined itself with joyousness which is the perfect energy of unimpeded function — therefore completing and strength-giving, therefore beautiful.

These were elements of the Greek conception and love of beauty—a thought and love which had its further mysteries hardly to be declared, but to be sympathized with, felt, and so realized. Akin to it, and sprung from gifts difficult to analyze, was the Greek creative imagination, that artist faculty so potent in them that their thoughts stood forth bodied with fitting and completed forms, or moved in concrete instances of human action typical of wide truth. The Greek observed closely and saw veritably, and gathered knowledge and experience of fact; on all of which he reasoned well. Then the all-compelling, compassing, more than inductive, visualizing, form-giving imagination transformed the content of experience to living modes of poetry and art, wherein was farthest verity and the necessary truth of that which lives.

Greek Intellect and Imagination.

The Homeric epics were the first-fruits of clear Greek apprehension of the facts of life and the Greek formative imagination, whose creations would have been fiction had they not been art. Throughout the poems the working of these two faculties is evident and distinguishable. Homer's physical knowledge is small, and that little is mixed with error. But as a fact appears to him he clearly thinks it, nor confuses it in contradictions. Fair and open is his apprehension of the general facts of life, quite clear is his consciousness as to what he does not know. He reasons wisely, never mistaking wish for its fulfilment, but basing his judgment on his observation. He has also the potent and resistless imagination of the race, which will endure nothing vague or abstract, but must visualize its thoughts and understandings in its creations. The clearness of Homeric apprehension of life issues in truthfulness of imagination. A chief example is the Homeric pantheon.

Exemplified in the Homeric Pantheon.

At stages of mental growth corresponding to the Homeric, other peoples in animistic mode have conceived natural phenomena as endowed with will and motive not unlike the human. But Homer's artistic imagination has dramatized his gods, made each a complete personality with a distinct character, and most consistently has the Homeric imagination builded its creations out of observation. Homer had observed nothing essentially different and superior to human nature. In his gods human life is freed from such limitations as it might lay aside and still remain itself. Strikingly true to human nature are the gods. Homer consistently withholds from them perfection; they are neither omniscient nor omnipotent. No person is so. When the poet says, "the gods can do anything," "the gods know all,"[1] he means that they can do much impossible for men, and know much to men unknown. He puts them at times in ignoble situations, subjects them to discomfiture and pain, and blinds even Zeus with folly.[2] Olympian divinity is humanity enlarged along the lines of artistic truth. Truly the gods know lust and fear and hatred, grief and joy, are jealous, envious, and revengeful; and they know themselves to be so ready with deceit and guile that no wise divinity trusts another except under oath. Like men also they

[1] *Od.*, iv, 379, 468 ; x, 306.

[2] *Il.*, xix, 95, etc.

are placable, and sometimes pity misery; they acknowledge ties of gratitude and friendship, know parental love and filial; but conjugal love, beyond what may lurk in temporary lust, is far to seek in the Homeric Olympus. So in speaking and acting, in their manner of yoking their horses, clothing or arming themselves, fashioning implements and taking their rest, they act like men and women; and Olympian society and governance, with its feasting and song, its council of the gods over which Zeus presides like Agamemnon on earth, is a true heightened likeness of human affairs.[1]

The frailties of the gods were those most natural to men; and they had the qualities which men admired. In the possession of all good things they were so fortunate, so excellent, that men might term them blessed.[2] In stature they exceeded men, and they were fairer; their strength was greater and their power of voice, so their knowledge and their wisdom. They possessed superhuman means of moving where they wished and of doing what they would; they were free from old age and death. Yet divine strength was not different from human, only there was more of it. Men nourish their lives on meat and wine and the fruits of the earth; the gods maintain theirs on ambrosia and nectar. The conditions of their deathlessness are similar to those on which depend the continuance of mortal life. Ares was once like to perish when he had been bound in chains by monstrous mortals.[3]

The relations of the gods to men were influenced by feelings prevailing among human beings. The gods would treat well those who treat them well. Says Athene to her father, "Did not Odysseus rejoice thee with his sacrifices in the wide Trojan plain? then why wast thou so wroth with him, Zeus!"[4] Ill-luck to such as neglect the gods! Artemis, forgotten in sacrifice, sends the Calydonian boar, living to be a plague, in its death to

[1] Compare such passages as *Il.*, v, 720, etc.; *ib.*, 838; xviii, 370, etc., and *ib.*, 408.

[2] *Μάκαρες θεοί*, the epics, *passim*.

[3] *Il.*, v, 385.

[4] *Od.*, i, 60.

breed murder and feud.[1] Teucer, the great archer, forgetful of Apollo, fails to win the prize.[2] Mercilessly do the gods destroy those who contemn them, or boastfully compare themselves with the deathless ones,—witness mute Niobe turned to an enduring monument of a goddess' wrath.[3] Hard is the anger of a god;[4] woe to mortals who strive with them, though with first success, for the gods bide their revenges; "not long-lived is he who fights with immortals, nor shall his children prattle on the knees of him coming from war and dread battle."[5] Prayers and sacrifices are the means of obtaining from the gods what is desired and the resources of those who have incurred divine anger. "The gods themselves may be bent, and them with the odor of sacrifice and with grateful vows, with libations and the smoke of meat-offerings men supplicating turn, so oft as any one transgresses and errs."[6]

Zeus and the Other Gods.

Mightiest and wisest of the gods[7] was Zeus whose plans endure,[8] whose will no other god could baffle.[9] He is stronger than the other gods combined.[10] He alone never descends among warring Greeks and Trojans, but sends his messengers and dreams, while he sits on Olympus or the peaks of Ida rejoicing in his glory.[11] Since he is matchless in knowledge and strength, his promises come to pass, when affirmed with an Olympus-shaking nod of the dark brows.[12]

[1] *Il.*, ix, 532.

[2] *Il.*, xxiii, 863.

[3] *Il.*, xxiv, 602; see *Il.*, ii, 595; v, 406; *Od.*, viii, 226.

[4] *Il.*, v, 178.

[5] *Il.*, v, 407.

[6] *Il.*, ix, 494. The conception of the gods as partisan allies is clear in Homer. So speaks Paris to Helen after his duel with Menelaus: "Woman, upbraid me not with thy harsh reproaches. Now indeed Menelaus has conquered, with Athene. Another time I may him, for there are also gods with us."—*Il.*, iii, 438.

[7] *Il.*, xiii, 631.

[8] *Il.*, xxiv, 88.

[9] *Od.*, v, 104.

[10] *Il.*, viii, 17; xxi, 193.

[11] *Il.*, viii, 51.

[12] *Il.*, i, 524.

Zeus knows gratitude, at times he is moved to pity,[1] and prayer he may answer; but little gratuitous benevolence is looked for from him. Is not wisdom largely guile, whereby one accomplishes ends and overcomes enemies? Whose guile shall equal that of wisest Zeus? Without compunction he sends a lying dream to Agamemnon,[2] and again he sends Athene to make the Trojans violate an oath.[3] When he is angry he is harsh,[4] threatens to hurl to Tartarus any god disobeying him;[5] again, he threatens to flog Hera, who always thwarts and angers him, and reminds her how once he hung her up with anvils hanging from her feet.[6] Of the gods, Apollo and Athene are most dear to him, but he cares little for them all; seated on Olympus, he laughs with delight, seeing them join battle among themselves.[7] But even from the standpoint of the accomplishment of one's own pleasure, Zeus is not perfect. Though his will cannot be baffled, it may be pestered, and he too must grieve at the death of his son Sarpedon;[8] his wisdom is not complete, very far is he from omniscience, he may be deceived.

The wife and sister of Zeus, and therefore the most powerful of the goddesses, is Hera, the self-willed queen, the violent partisan of the Greeks, the unappeasable hater of Troy. She is chief actor in two of the episodes[9] which have made men think that Homer was a mocker of his gods, whereas he was an artist. No gracious divinity was Hera the queen, but she had beauty and strength and wily wisdom to work her will; so she was an admirable figure in the eyes of Homeric Greeks, even in her rage as she snatches Artemis' bow and beats her with it.[10]

A beautiful figure is Phœbus the bright, Apollo born in light,[11] the best of the gods,[12] even in Homer god of

[1] *Il.*, xix, 340; *Il.*, xxii, 167.
[2] *Il.*, ii, 6.
[3] *Il.*, iv, 69.
[4] See *Il.*, viii, 470.
[5] *Il.*, viii, 13.
[6] *Il.*, xv, 17.
[7] *Il.*, xxi, 389.
[8] *Il.*, xvi, 431.
[9] *Il.*, i, 530–610; *Il.*, xiv, 153, etc.
[10] *Il.*, xxi, 479.

[11] The only connection in the epics between Apollo and the sun lies in the name Φοῖβος, and such an epithet as λυκηγενής, born in light. Helius is the Sun god in the epics.

[12] *Il.*, xix, 413.

prophecy and song;[1] his is the lyre which sounds before the gods when the sweet-voiced Muses sing in turn,[2] his are the gentle darts, bringers of peaceful death to men.[3] Apollo is always in harmony with Zeus; "dear Phœbus," the latter calls him; and he never comes in direct conflict with another god. On the day when the gods fight in the Trojan plain, Poseidon says to him, "Phœbus, why hold we aloof from each other? It is not seemly, since the others have begun;—the more shame if we return to Olympus without a fight."[4] Him answered the lord, far-shooting Apollo: "Earth-shaker, thou wouldst not call me wise if I fought with thee because of miserable mortals, who, like leaves, now are quick with life, then perish inanimate." So saying he turned away, for he shrank from the combat out of respect for his father's brother.

Athene is the daughter of Zeus,[5] and dear to him not on that account alone, but because through her wisdom she obeys him; only once she starts with Hera to help the Greeks against his commands. Yet she has no affection for Zeus, and when his words displease her she is seized with fierce wrath; but sits silently brooding her purposes.[6] In the *Iliad* she is intelligence in arms, never blind raging force, like Ares. In the *Odyssey* she is the ready counsellor, in resources and wiles surpassing other divinities, as Odysseus does other mortals. In both epics she is goddess of fine art and handicraft, endowing men and women with skill,[7] or herself fashioning articles of female apparel;[8] and already she has a temple at Athens.[9]

The remaining divinities represent less intellectual traits of mankind. There is Poseidon, the Earth-shaker, brother of Zeus. Jealous and envious, in the *Iliad* he complains to Zeus of the wall the Greeks have built with-

[1] *Il.*, i, 72, 603; *Od.*, viii, 79, 488.
[2] *Il.*, i, 603.
[3] *Il.*, xxiv, 759.
[4] *Il.* xxi, 435.
[5] *Il.*, iv, 515.
[6] *Il.*, iv, 20; *Il.*, viii, 457.
[7] *Il.*, v, 59; *Od.*, viii, 492; vi, 232; vii, 110; xx, 72.
[8] *Il.*, xiv, 178; v, 733; ix, 390.
[9] *Il.*, ii, 537; *cf.* *Od.*, vii, 78.

out a hecatomb to the gods, which will make men forget the wall built by himself and Apollo for Laomedon;[1] in the *Odyssey* he shows little beyond violent rancor.[2] Then there is mad Ares, with his shout equal to the cry of ten thousand men. He is stupid, adulterous, the personification of rage, unrestrained, yet impotent. He is the all too-frequent companion of laughing, loving, golden Aphrodite, goddess of womanly beauty and of love. When Aphrodite, inexpert in war, is wounded by Diomede, she flies to borrow the horses of her dear brother Ares to escape to Olympus;[3] and Ares, when overwhelmed by the stone thrown by Athene, is helped from the field by Aphrodite till she too feels the wrath of the war goddess.[4] In the *Odyssey* Aphrodite is the wife of Hephaestus; and there Ares and the frail goddess form the centre of a scene of exquisite humor.[5] The kindest and saddest of divinities is Achilles' mother, Thetis of the silver feet, daughter of the Old Man of the Sea. She it was unwilling who was forced to wed a mortal,[6] and bear to her grief a glorious short-lived son. Kind deeds has she done for other gods; in the *Iliad* she is motherhood in tears. There also hover in the epics shadowy forms, the Erinyes, wanderers in mist and darkness, avengers bringing the remorse, ill-luck, and punishment which come on earth to murderers, swearers of false oaths, maltreators of parents, or despisers of supplicants; the Muses, and the Charites, spirits of beauty and loveliness; Atè, Folly, who entangles men, walks over their heads and takes away their wits; the Litæ, Prayers of repentance, who halting and with downcast eyes follow after fleet Atè to heal the harm.[7]

The Homeric gods are creations in perfect truth to human nature, and perfect individualities. In part because of their very clear plastic definiteness, will the

[1] *Il.*, vii, 442; *cf. Od.*, v, 118.
[2] *Od.*, i, 20, 68.
[3] *Il.*, v, 357.
[4] *Il.*, xxi, 416.
[5] *Od.*, viii, 26, etc. The lay of Demodocus.
[6] *Il.*, xviii, 432.
[7] *Il.*, ix, 502.

serious Greek thought, searching for truth, sever its sense of divine and natural law from such divinities. Even in the epics, though no god does any act inconsistent with his character, there come expressions showing that ethical thought is rising above this inimitably drawn pantheon. Especially in references to Zeus, or to "the gods" collectively, there is a tendency to ascribe higher ethical traits to them.[1]

Existence after Death.

Where facts are to be observed, Homer observes them, and does not frame his judgment to his wish. For example, hatred of death does not lead his views as to life after death beyond his opinions regarding the nature of man. Of the body, he knew much; knew many of its parts, and formed erroneous but not self-contradictory conceptions of their functions. The body was the palpable part of man, himself in fact —Achilles' wrath sent many spirits of heroes to Hades, and gave *themselves* as a prey to dogs and vultures.[2] Homer had hardly conceived of mind as an immaterial principle—but quick was the flight of thought. Hera speeds from the peaks of Ida as darts the mind (νοός) of one who, having travelled much, thinks in his heart, "if I were here or there."[3]

At death the breath, or spirit, the ψυχή, left the man and became his shade, while he himself was dissolved by corruption, or burned by fire; the knowing, loving, hating, acting man perished, nought surviving but the shadowy, strengthless image. The gods freed a few mortals from death. Menelaus, because he had Helen to wife, they carried to the Elysian plain at the bounds of the earth "where life is easiest; no snow is there, nor storm, but always Oceanus sends the west wind to blow cool on men;"[4] and a loftier immortality was given Heracles, whose shade Odysseus sees in Hades, but "he himself rejoices with the gods at their banquets, and has Hebe of the lovely feet to wife."[5]

[1] See *Od.*, xiv, 83 and *Il.*, iv, 160.

[2] *Il.*, i, 3. [3] *Il.*, xv, 8; *cf.* *Od.*, vii, 36. [4] *Od.*, iv, 561. [5] *Od.*, xi, 601.

So when the hero falls, there he lies; and the ψυχή "flying from his body goes to Hades bewailing its fate, leaving strength and youth."[1] The fluttering thing cannot even pass the hateful gates of the "abodes fearful, dank,"[2] until funeral rites are performed. Patroclus' shade comes in the night to Achilles: "'Thou sleepest, and hast forgotten me, Achilles. Bury me quickly that I may pass the gates of Hades; the shades drive me away, the phantoms of men outworn, nor suffer me to join them beyond the river. So I do but wander up to the wide-gated house of Hades. And now give me thy hand. I beseech thee with tears; for never again shall I come back from Hades after ye have burned me on the pyre.' 'Why, dear one, hast thou come hither, and why bid me do these things? Surely all thou askest will I perform. But stand nearer; for a little let us throw our arms about each other, and take our fill of wailing.' So saying, Achilles reached out his hands, but grasped nothing; for like smoke the shade was gone beneath the ground with a faint cry. And Achilles sprang up, and smote his hands together in grief, 'Alas! so there exists even in Hades a breath (ψυχή), and a semblance, but nothing to it! For all night long has the shade of wretched Patroclus stood over me, wailing and making moan, and marvellously like to himself.'"[3]

The shades were fluttering images of men outworn. Not only body and its strength were lacking; strength of mind and intelligence were gone. Unreal and senseless were the thoughts of shades—forgetful shades who must be given blood to drink before they can recognize Odys-

[1] *Il.*, xvi, 856; xxii, 362. [2] *Il.*, xx, 65.

[3] *Il.*, xxiii, 69, etc. Funeral rites were the due of the dead (*Il.*, xvi, 457), which the living performed from affection or dread lest the unquiet shade draw on them the anger of the gods (*Od.*, xi, 73). Their clear purpose was that the shade might enter Hades where it would have dolorous companionship. But it may be inferred from the rites that they had the further purpose of fitting out the shade for existence in Hades; for the arms and things most dear to the dead man were burned with him, and in Hades the shade might use them.

seus at the mouth of their dark pit. A certain wavering memory and thought have they, enough to tantalize, not enough to enable them to hold comfortable converse of their past lives—"their utterance was like the twittering of bats."[1] Only the shade of the prophet Teiresias had strength and intelligence, for "Persephone gives him mind even when dead and he alone has understanding."[2] Small chance for reward and punishment among such shadows! Desolate was the fate of the pious and the impious, hero and coward. Minos sits awarding shadowy dooms,[3]—what mattered they to the phantoms! Three arrogant mortals, who had contemned the gods, were saved by them for infernal punishment.[4] But crimes against men met their retribution, if at all, on earth, where valor and prudence also had their reward.

Thus Homeric views of existence after death outran but little primitive logical inferences from life's data. The two most clearly seeing of ancient peoples, the Hebrews and the Greeks, were slow to reach any fuller conception of a future life. Only the Greeks did not restrain their plastic imagination, must even here visualize their dark conceptions. "Then," says Odysseus, "I saw the shade of Heracles, and about him was the clamor of the dead as of birds, flying on all sides scared; but he like black night held his naked bow and an arrow on the string, glancing fiercely as about to shoot."[5]

Thoughts on Life.

Homer's eager Achæans had begun to think on life. They knew it was short, and hoped for little after it, so it sometimes seemed a slight thing. "Why dost thou ask my race?" says Glaucus[6] to Diomede, "even as the generations of leaves are the generations of men. The wind scatters the leaves

[1] *Od.*, xxiv, 6.
[2] *Od.*, x, 492.
[3] *Od.*, xi, 568.
[4] *Od.*, xi, 575, Tityus, Tantalus, and Sisyphus.
[5] *Od.*, xi, 605.
[6] *Il.*, vi, 146. Young Glaucus more than any other character in the *Iliad* is tinged with melancholy; he was descended from one whom the gods' hatred drove crazed to wander apart from men.

upon the ground, and in the spring the forest buds and puts forth others. So one generation of men blooms, anon it passes away." The epics often touch on life's brevity, and often comes the thought of inevitable death besetting men in myriad shapes.[1] Men are ill-fated;[2] "there is nothing more wretched than man among all things that breathe and creep upon the earth," says Zeus.[3] And besides the woe of its brevity, life was grievous in other respects. The tone of the *Odyssey* is given in two frequently recurring lines, "thence we sailed on afflicted in heart, glad to escape death, having lost our dear comrades."[4] The gods devise evil,[5] nor does Zeus accomplish the thoughts of man.[6] After many wanderings, Menelaus is safe at home with Helen; but he has not great joy in his possessions,—his brother Agamemnon had been murdered![7] Human lots were but the sweepings of celestial mansions. Those men are fortunate into whose lives comes joy as well as sorrow. Yet the Achæans loved life eagerly, never doubting the worth of its prizes. It was short, more the pity; but how filled with joys and griefs, well worth shunning or striving for while life lasted. The great sorrow was death when it came. Others might tire of life because short and disappointing, but in Homer none are tired except the dead—*οἱ κάμοντες*; all are eager, feeling grief, yet knowing not its weariness; hating death, yet not embittered with life because of it.

Homer's was not a contemplative age. The wisdom of the epics is taught by the action of the heroes, the current of the story, and the outcome of it all. Some clear ethical utterances are there fitting the occasion, and a few general reflections are found—a man does not excel in everything—love catches womankind.[8] Much more may

[1] *Il.*, xii, 326.
[2] *Δυστήνοι*, a frequent epithet.
[3] *Il.*, xvii, 446.
[4] *Od.*, ix, 62; x, 133.
[5] *Od.*, i, 234.
[6] *Il.*, xviii, 328.
[7] *Od.*, iv, 90.
[8] *Il.*, xxiii, 670; *Od.*, xv, 421; *cf. Il.*, xiii, 729; *Od.*, viii, 167.

be learned from the flashing light which makes up Achilles' life, or the noble picture of Odysseus, more complex, more slowly drawn. Only in the idea of fate the experience and knowledge of the age were combined in a judgment upon life of universal application.

Homeric Idea of Fate.

Nature and life offer to men's notice certain ordinary courses in the occurrence of phenomena, whence rise notions of usual results from given circumstances, of consequent regularly following its antecedent, cause regularly operative in effect. The normal courses of things had been observed by the Greeks, though they provided everything in nature with a guiding spirit. The actions of men depended immediately upon the doers' wills, yet also generally followed usual courses. Human beings were born, grew up, had a share of sorrow, a taste of happiness, became decrepit with advancing years, and most inevitably died. In general, human affairs followed courses warranting prediction. If a stronger host went against a weaker one, though each had its heroes and its aiding deities, probably the stronger host would win. If an eager, valiant, overweening youth went to a distant war, probably he would gain fame, and probably, though dear to the gods, his life would be short; if an older man, valiant and strong, sagacious and cunning, went to the same war, it was likely that he would survive, likely even that he would see his home and prudent wife again.

Such events, in accordance with probabilities, seemed to come from the nature and relations of things. But if the gods could affect human actions, and were also thought the mainspring of action in the world about man, why did natural phenomena as well as the actions of men follow usual courses? Each human being was an individual living out his own life; each god was a superhuman individual subject to Zeus, yet in large part doing his own will. But all natural objects, brutes, and human beings had certain characteristics, natures, tendencies;

the general outcome was the observed course of affairs. And as human wills and actions followed usual courses, it was conceived that the wills and actions of the little more than human gods would also follow usual courses, harmonizing with the inherent natures and tendencies of men and gods and things.

Moreover, if the action of individuals or of independent causes seemed arbitrary, there was an element of the inevitable contained in effects. Helius might threaten to mount the heavens no more; but if he did, it was inevitable that light for gods and men should issue from him. So the hero might stay his hand, or some god might turn his spear; but if the spear did strike, and was stopped by no sufficient armor, it would pierce. The elements of the inevitable might consist in results arising from the relations of men and things, or might inhere in their natures, as it inhered in the nature of man to die, of a stone to fall. Events whose necessity came from the inherent nature of things and men were certain; those which inevitably sprang from contacts and relations could be prevented only by preventing such from taking place. Then finally men could act only in certain modes, and though gods could act in other and further modes, even they could not act in any mode. And as matter of fact, affairs went on in usual courses in accord with antecedent probabilities, which in their turn were inferences from former regular courses of events.

These universal elements of the inevitable or probable constitute the fundamentals of the Homeric conception of fate as an all-pervading and ordinarily resistless power inherent in circumstances and in the natures of men and things and gods, a power essentially blind, brute, and implacable, and though almighty, yet from lack of consciousness, spontaneity, and intelligence, utterly helpless to be or act otherwise than as it does,—a necessity for all, a necessity unto itself. It was the early Greek phase of the Indo-Germanic tendency to discern potency outside the will and power of personally conceived divinity.

It was a natural growth of the conception, that fate should be conceived not only as inevitable, but ascertainable—by the gods at least—and declarable in advance.[1] Then one step more and the fate of the individual is conceived as determined and known from his birth, or before it. And with epic consistency the fate of each man harmonizes with his character. Then the conception drew to itself two connotations: First, human lives are hard, and the one sure event in them is death. So fate came to carry the idea of death as the most inevitable, fated, fatal event in life. Secondly, men become accustomed to the usual courses of events around them, become used to the relations and effects of things in life. What is usual tends to gain acquiescence and approval. The idea of fate was the broad expression of the usual and the inevitable, and thus acquired the connotation of proper. Therefore to disturb the course of fate was improper, to act against fate was wrong. The gods, who are wiser than men, are watchful over fate; knowing that which is to come, and which ought to come, they help bring it about.

Homer uses five words to express fate and the personal lot of man,—*μοῖρα, μόρος, αἶσα, κὴρ* and *πότμος*. Excepting the two first, these are neither identical in meaning nor from the same root. But they are sometimes used interchangeably, that is, some one of them in a sense more peculiar to another.[2] *Πότμος* and *κὴρ* carry

[1] We might err in speaking of it as pre-ordained, for that would imply an antecedent cause, which Homer neither asserts nor denies. With him fate is simply there, and has been there from former times.

[2] These different words indicate the complex origin of the Homeric idea of fate. *Μοῖρα* (*μόρος*) is from the same root with *μείρομαι*, to apportion or receive as a portion: *αἶσα* is from the same root with *ἴσος*, like, equal. *Πότμος* is from the root *πετ*, found in *πίπτω*, to fall, and in *πέτομαι*, to fly (perhaps also, to fall. *Od.*, xii, 203), and so might mean the personal lot which falls out when the helmet is shaken (*Il.*, vii, 183). It has an evil meaning, carrying the signification of "death." A man meets "death" and *πότμος*, or simply meets *πότμος*, as we say "meets his fate." See *Il.*, ii, 359; vi, 412; xv, 495; xx, 337; *cf. Od.*, xvii, 131 and *Il.*, xviii, 96. *Κὴρ* is from the same root with *κείρω*, to cut off, and in meaning is always

the notion of death, the most universal fact that touches man. *Κήρ*, however, is the usual word for man's personal lot, which, wind as it may, always ends in death. "My mother," says Achilles, "Thetis of the silver feet, said that one of two diverse fates (*διχθαδίας κῆρας*) would bring me to my death: if abiding here I fight about the city of the Trojans, my return is cut off, though my fame shall be imperishable; but if I fare homewards to my dear native land, my great fame perishes, but my life shall be long."[1]

Homer's usual words to express destiny are *μοῖρα* (*μόρος*) and *αἶσα*.[2] Both may mean portion or part, due portion, then that portion established or apportioned by fate, then fate itself, destiny; and both may carry the thought of "right." These meanings may be followed in the epics.[3]

connected with death, indeed usually means the death allotted to each mortal. In many places in the *Iliad* a prudent warrior, by retreating or dodging a spear-cast, escapes *κήρ*. See *e. g. Il.*, xiv, 462; *cf. Il.*, iii, 6, and *Il.*, xxiv, 82. *Κήρ* is often joined with adjectives meaning evil or deadly, *e. g. Il.*, iii, 454; and *Il.*, xii, 326 speaks of *κῆρες θανάτοιο μυρίαι*, the myriad dooms of death, which no mortal can escape.

[1] *Il.*, ix, 410.

[2] *Μοῖρα* = *κήρ* (personal fated death) in *Od.*, *Il.* 100. So in *Od.*, xvii, 326, *μοῖρα θανάτοιο* seizes the dog Argos. It is frequently joined with adjectives of evil significance, *e. g.*, *ὀλοή* or *κακή*. The deadly signification of *αἶσα* appears in the phrase *αἴσιμον ἦμαρ*, the fated day. *Il.*, xxi, 100.

[3] *Μοῖρα*, *e. g.*, means a part or portion, then due portion, as one's proper share of booty, or meat at a feast. See in succession *Od.*, iv, 97; *Il.*, xvi, 68; *Od.*, xi, 534; iii, 40; xvii, 258; xx, 171 and 260. Penelope tells Odysseus, "men may not stay awake always, for the immortals have set a time (*μοῖραν*) for everything," *Od.*, xix, 591. Polyphemus milks his ewes in due order (*κατὰ μοῖραν*), *Od.*, ix, 245, 309, 342; the Trojans flee from the Greek camp not *κατὰ μοῖραν*, *Il.*, xvi. 367; *cf. Il.*, xii, 225. The Greeks listen respectfully (*κατὰ μοῖραν*) while Agamemnon takes his oath, *Il.*, xix, 250. To speak *κατὰ μοῖραν* is to say what is proper or just (*Il.*, i, 286), or as when Menelaus is asked to interpret an omen he pauses in order that he may answer aright, *κατὰ μοῖραν*, *Od.*, xv, 170. And finally Odysseus referring to Polyphemus' violation of the rights of suppliants, and his bloody meal, tells him that he has acted not *κατὰ μοῖραν*, *i. e.*, unrighteously, *Od.*, ix, 352.

It is doubtful whether fate is personified by Homer except as a manner of poetical speech.[1] With him it is merely a unification of all the inherent forces of things into a universal impersonal power. No prayer is ever addressed to it, nor is it ever said to doubt or hesitate or consider, as do all men and gods. Neither does it ever act with a motive.[2]

Destiny is over all, and the lot of each man is "spun for him" at birth;[3] Hector bids his wife not to grieve, "for no man against fate shall hurl me to Hades, and I think no man escapes fate, coward or brave."[4] Such thoughts seem to compass every event, leaving nothing to chance or arbitrary will. But Homer's idea of fate merely reflects the apparent course of events. A human lot hangs apparently on three matters—will, chance, and, lastly, there are events necessarily fated, like decrepitude and death. The conclusions of a more advanced time may exclude one or more of these factors. Not so Homer. Frequently events are on the point of turning out against fate, and twice unfated events occur.[5]

When Agamemnon, to try the host, proposes to give up the war, and the men rise with a shout and rush to the ships, a return against fate would have happened had not

[1] *Κήρ* is poetically personified in one of the scenes on Achilles' shield, *Il.*, xviii, 535.

[2] The various terms meaning fate are sometimes the subjects of active verbs. *Ὀλοὴ μοῖρα* causes Hector to remain without the walls, *Il.*, xxii, 5; *μοῖρα κραταιή* urges Tlepolemus against Sarpedon, *Il.*, v, 629. See also *Il.*, v, 613; xiii, 602; xxi, 83; and compare *Il.*, xix, 87, 410; xvi, 849; xxiv, 49, 209; and *Od.*, vii, 197 with *Il.*, xx, 127. *Θάνατος* was poetically personified quite as much as fate, *e. g. Il.*, v, 83; xvi, 334, 580. We still say "death overtook him." There are clear instances of poetical personification in Homer, where no personality is really attributed. Thus the arrow leaps eager or raging to fly, *Il.*, iv, 125.

[3] *Od.*, vii, 197; *Il.*, xx, 127; xxiv, 210.

[4] *Il.*, vi, 487. *Cf. Il.*, xviii, 117.

[5] The phrases are *ὑπέρ μοῖραν*, *ὑπέρ αἶσαν*; more common is the compound *ὑπέρμορον*.

Hera sent Athene to prevent it.[1] In the sixteenth book of the *Iliad*, the "sons of the Achæans would have taken high-gated Troy by the hands of Patroclus," had not Apollo forced him back from the wall, striking with his immortal hands the shining shield of the hero: "Back, Zeus-born Patroclus! it is not fated that Troy shall fall beneath thy spear, nor beneath the spear of Achilles, a far better man than thou."[2] In these instances the course of fate was only threatened; but in the same sixteenth book Patroclus kills Hector's charioteer, and the even conflict sways to and fro about the body till, as the sun is setting, the Achæans prevail over the Trojans against fate.[3]

All these were occurrences affecting multitudes. Sometimes an unfated event threatens or falls upon an individual. In the twentieth book of the *Iliad*, Apollo has roused Æneas to stay the slaughtering career of Achilles; the heroes meet, and Æneas is like to be slain. At this point Poseidon tells Hera that it were shameful for Æneas, whose gifts were always pleasing to the gods, to die deceived by Apollo; and he adds: "It is fated (μόριμον) for him to escape, that the race of Dardanus perish not."[4] So Poseidon sheds a mist over Achilles' eyes, snatches up Æneas and sets him again on the earth, far off at the edge of the battle, saying: "Æneas, what one of the gods is urging thee infatuate thus to contend with the son of Peleus, who is mightier than thou and dearer to the gods? Rather give way whenever thou meetest him, lest against fate thou enter the house of Hades. But when Achilles has met death, then emboldened do thou fight amongst the foremost, for none other of the Achæans shall slay thee."[5] In another instance

[1] *Il.*, ii, 155; the word ἐτύχθη is used, which strictly denotes happening by chance.

[2] *Il.*, xvi, 698. See also *Il.*, xvii, 319; xx, 29; xxi, 515.

[3] *Il.*, xvi, 780 (ὑπὲρ αἶσαν).

[4] *Il.*, xx, 302.

[5] *Il.*, xx, 332, *cf. Od.*, v, 436.

the act contrary to fate is accomplished. Near the opening of the *Odyssey*[1] Zeus exclaims to the gods about him: "Forsooth, how mortals blame the gods! For they say that evils come from us, but they even of themselves have sorrows beyond (or contrary to) what is fated, just as now Ægisthus contrary to fate married the wife of Atrides, and slew him on his return, knowing the utter destruction [it would bring], since, having sent Hermes, we warned him not to kill the man nor marry his wife; for vengeance should come from Orestes when he should reach manhood. So Hermes spoke, but prevailed not on the mind of Ægisthus, though advising him for his good. And now he has paid atonement in full measure." Finally, in certain other instances, a man might have escaped his fate, but did not. Ajax Oileus, cast upon the rock, would have escaped his fate,[2] though hated by Athene, had he not let fall a proud word, saying that, despite the gods, he had escaped the gulf of the sea; then Poseidon smote the rock, and Ajax perished in the brine. Likewise had Patroclus regarded Achilles' behest not to pursue the Trojans, he would have escaped the evil fate of black death; "but always the mind (νοός) of Zeus is stronger than the mind of men."[3]

The Gods and Fate.

The Olympians did not create the world and mankind. Accordingly Homer did not think of Zeus as having in all respects absolute power over beings which were not his creations. But the power of Zeus is tremendous to shape events. Its limitations lie in the qualities which inhere in things and constitute their natures, and in what is thereby necessitated. He did not create these qualities and he cannot change them, although he can often direct or hem in their effects. It is inherent in the nature of man to die; within the range of fate nothing is more fated than death. Homer broadly states that "the gods cannot ward off death common to all, even from a man who is dear, when the destroying

[1] *Od.*, i, 32. [2] *Od.*, iv, 499, ἔφυγε κῆρα. [3] *Il.*, xvi, 385.

fate of death takes him down."[1] Yet Zeus, seized with pity at the sight of his son Sarpedon about to join battle with Patroclus, exclaims to Hera: "Alas me! that Sarpedon, dearest to me of men, is doomed to be overcome by Patroclus! And my heart within me is divided, whether snatching him up safe from tearful battle I will set him down in rich Lycia, or whether I will now overcome him by the hands of the son of Menœtius." Hera answers: "Dread son of Saturn, what word hast thou spoken! a mortal man long ago doomed by fate wouldst thou wish to loose from death? Do it. But we other gods will not approve."[2]

Just as human energy or lust might carry events against fate, much more might Zeus. But there is no suggestion that the gods can turn the courses of fate and make it operate in some changed way. The gods are wise, they respect the inherent nature of things and the fated order of events; and since the ultimate reason in Homer why every god and man refrains from carrying out his desire is the fear of evil to come upon himself, the inference, if somewhat far, is not unjustified that the gods respect fate lest by acting contrary to it they overthrow themselves along with the established order.

Gods may have other—partisan—reasons for upholding the course of fate. They usually interfere to prevent violations of it which would favor the side they hate. Had not Hera and Athene prevented the return of the Greeks, Troy, so hated by these goddesses, would have remained undestroyed. Apollo upholds fate by preventing the Greeks from capturing before its time the city dear to him. Poseidon's rescue of Æneas is more disinterested, for Poseidon was hostile to Troy, and saves Æneas because of the many sacrifices of that staid warrior, and also lest it anger Zeus, whose regard for fate is broad and impartisan.[3]

Fate is more inevitable in so far as dependent exclu-

[1] *Od.*, iii, 236.

[2] *Il.*, xvi, 431–433. See also *Il.*, xxii, 168.

[3] See *Il.*, xx, 30.

sively on the innate nature of things which Zeus did not create. He is the ruler over all. Though innate qualities are beyond his power, the mutual relations and effects of men and things are within it. Universal is the tendency of all things, men as well, to act according to their natures. This tendency, which constitutes the less inevitable element of fate, coincides, so far as mortals see, with the will of Zeus who wisely recognizes it. Consequently, fate sometimes appears a power above Zeus, and again subject to his will, or one and the same with it.

It is said that Zeus knows all things, what is allotted and what is not allotted for mortals.[1] But he does not foreknow everything that is to happen, for he doubts as to what he shall do,[2] and one feels that the series of events making up the *Iliad* were not foreknown to Zeus. The *βουλή*, the will or plan of Zeus, was being accomplished from the time when first Atrides and Achilles parted, having quarrelled;[3] but he had not conceived this plan before Thetis came a suppliant and begged him to avenge her son.

The *βουλὴ Διός* was accomplished,[4]—a will, however, no way contrary to fate. Achilles says, "I deem I have been honored by the decree of Zeus,"[5] *Διός αἶσα*, a phrase showing how fate and Zeus's will are so at one that fate may sometimes be regarded as coming from him. This frequent phrase always refers to matters within the province of Zeus to regulate.[6] So speaks Odysseus over the slain wooers, *μοῖρα θεῶν* overthrew them, and their

[1] *Od.*, xx, 76.

[2] *Il.*, ii, 3, he considers how he shall fulfil his promise to Thetis. *Il.*, i, 520, Zeus sends Thetis off secretly lest Hera find out; but Hera does find out, which Zeus cannot have foreknown.

[3] *Il.*, i, 5.

[4] The phrase *Διός νόημα*, *Il.*, xvii, 409, seems equivalent in meaning.

[5] *Il.*, ix, 908.

[6] Thus in *Od.*, ix, 52, the evil *αἶσα* of Zeus was that the Cicones should put to flight Odysseus and his men; in *Od.*, xi, 61 it is the evil *δαίμονος αἶσα*, which together with wine causes the death of Elpenor, who falls from the roof when drunk. In *Il.*, xvii, 321, again, through the *Διός αἶσαν* the Greeks get the better of the Trojans.

evil deeds;[1] and he says to the shade of Ajax, Zeus is to blame, he laid thy doom on thee.[2] Lycaon tells Achilles, *μοῖρα ὀλοή* has placed me again in thy hands, I must be hated by Zeus.[3] And in answer to Achilles, Xanthus, the immortal steed, tells him that on that day they will bear him safe, though near him is the day of destruction, —neither are we to blame, but a great god and strong fate.[4]

And how does Zeus himself speak of fate? In the fifth book of the *Odyssey* he sends Hermes to announce to Calypso the "firm decree (*νημερτέα βουλήν*) the return of Odysseus, how he is to come to his home with no escort of gods or men; but, suffering hardship on a raft, on the twentieth day shall he arrive at the land of the Phæacians, who shall send him with much treasure to his dear fatherland; for in this manner is it fate for him (*οἱ μοῖρα*) to see his friends and come to his lofty house."[5] Here the "firm decree"—presumably of Zeus—is in contents identical with what is fate for Odysseus; the two correspond, yet may not have the same source.[6] Again is the full accord between fate and the will of Zeus seen in the passage where Zeus holds up the scales to announce that the moment for Hector's death is come. In the eager chase, pursuer and pursued have sped three times around Troy, "but when for the fourth time they reached

[1] *Od.*, xxii, 413; see *Od.*, xi, 292.

[2] *Od.*, xi, 560.

[3] *Il.*, xxi, 83.

[4] *Il.*, xix, 408. The god referred to is Apollo, but Apollo directed by Zeus. So the gods devise a man's doom for him, *Od.*, iii, 242; compare *Od.*, xxii, 14, when Odysseus prepares death and *κῆρα* for the wooers. In *Il.*, xxii, 365, Achilles says he will accept his *κῆρα* whenever Zeus and the other gods bring it about.

[5] *Od.*, v, 30. For this use of *οἱ μοῖρα* see also *Il.*, vii, 52; xv, 117; xxiii, 80; *Od.*, iv, 475.

[6] Compare the phrase *σοὶ θέσφατόν*, which means "it is a degree of god for thee," which for men is equivalent to "it is fated for thee."—*Od.*, iv, 561; x, 473. See Nägelsbach, *Homerische Theologie*, 127; and *cf. Il.*, viii, 477. Throughout one is reminded of the relation of the Vedic *rita* to Varuna; see *ante*, chap. iii.

the springs, then did the Father poise the golden scales and place therein two lots of long-grievous death, the one of Achilles, the other of Hector, tamer-of-horses, and taking hold at the middle he lifted the scales; and fell Hector's fated day and went to Hades, and Phœbus Apollo left him."[1] The fall of Hector's fated day announces the course of fate, and Zeus merely holds the balance aloft, influencing neither scale. Hector's fated day falls by the force of fate, by the power of the course and tendency of things,—his hour was come. On the other hand, it is not to ascertain whether Hector is then to be slain by Achilles that Zeus lifts the scales. The death of Hector is already resolved on by Zeus, and Athene has been sent to bring it to pass.[2] And to this resolve of Zeus is the hero's death directly due, just as much as to the course of fate. The lifting of the scales announces the fated hour and shows the accord between fate and the will of Zeus. These two are here as always in perfect harmony: fate the huge force, the overwhelming dumb tendency of events, and Zeus's will guiding on events along the course of fate.[3]

It is evident that the Homeric view of fate meant no benumbing fatalism. In a solemn moment, Hector might pause and regard fate as all powerful, yet he uses the thought only to comfort his wife. At times mortals feel powerless to control the event. Telemachus, feeling his impotence to drive off the wooers, hopelessly tells his affairs to the disguised Odysseus, adding, "but now these things [*i. e.*, the outcome] lie on the knees of the gods."[4] Here Telemachus seems to give up. But the same phrase is used by warriors about to join in desperate battle, and then means "I will do my best, the gods may direct the

[1] *Il.*, xxii, 208.

[2] See *Il.*, xxii, 166.

[3] In *Il.*, viii, 69, Zeus also holds up the scales to show forth the fate of the battle, and the Greek lot falls; Zeus thunders and the Greeks flee, as in outline Zeus had previously determined on.

[4] *Od.*, xvi, 129.

event."[1] Something may be read between the lines of a passage in the fourth book of the *Iliad*. Menelaus has overcome Paris in the duel, and demand has been made on the Trojans to fulfil the oaths and give up Helen. The truce still continues, and the hosts lie expectant. Now the gods hold council in Olympus, and the outcome is that Zeus sends Athene to make the Trojans break the oath. She darts from Olympus, and like a flaming meteor drops between the hosts. "And wonder seized them looking on, horse-taming Trojans and well-greaved Achæans; and thus would one say to his fellow, 'Either again there will be evil war and furious strife, or else Zeus is about to establish friendship between the sides, even he who is the director of the war of men!'"[2] So looking on this ball of fire, not recognizing a goddess, men felt that something was about to take place, and that they could not control what it should be. Men are helpless, whispers the passage. Yet no reference is made to fate; it is Zeus who is so powerful that men have little hand in guiding their destinies.

Homeric Ethics.

Homer and Hesiod made the gods.[3] The highest Greek revelation was the inspiration of the Muse. It is characteristic of the race from the beginning that it did not regard its knowledge or its rules of conduct as revealed by God. In Homer the gods constantly communicate with mankind, love and hate them with varied feeling ranging through the whole scale of human affection, lust, and hate; frequently the gods appear to mortals and command or warn them. But Zeus promulgates no code of righteousness; he commands or forbids specific acts. And it is clear that such dramatic presentations of the gods, which sprang from the Greek artist soul, afforded no standard of human right-

[1] *Il.*, xvii, 514; xx, 435. In other places the phrase carries no other idea than that future events are in the hands of the gods. See *Od.*, i, 267, 400.

[2] *Il.*, iv., 79.

[3] See Herod., ii, 53.

eousness, or criterion of human sin. These gods were nature's children with all the frailties natural to men. And as for the righteousness of their governance, why, Zeus once sent Athene down from heaven to make the Trojans break an oath rendered inviolate by sacrifice to Zeus himself.

Wherein then did the Greeks find the source and sanction of their rules of conduct—often broken? Even in that which they saw, perceived, and knew. Directly, luminously, in ways open to the tests of reason, they fashioned rules of conduct from their store of experience. In the data of their ethics they included all their knowledge of man and his environment, and their judgments upon life; herein entered their dismal views as to the outworn semblances which twittered out inane existence in the underworld, existence far too blank to hold reward or punishment ; herein entered their thoughts of the results of acts on earth, and also those farthest generalizations upon life which made up the thought of fate; herein entered those more plastic expressions of the powers which aid or thwart men's lives—those living, human, natural gods. These gods were part of life and not above it; yet, since they were rulers of the world, it was impossible not to think that they stood for more than their own whims, even for those further active principles of retribution which, as the Greeks learned from life, awaited the ill-considered, overweening acts of men. Nothing is more displeasing to the gods than the insolent pride through which men ignore their mortality, and wantonly act out their cruel wills—till retribution comes.[1] "For the blessed gods do not love cruel deeds, but they honor justice and equitable acts in men."[2] Odysseus, disguised in rags, says to Amphinomus, the least evil of the wooers, warning him to remove from among them: "Of all that earth nourishes, nothing is feebler than man, who, so long as the gods give him might and sustain his

[1] This is the quality of ὕβρις which marks the wooers. [2] *Od.*, xiv, 83.

strength of limb, thinks ill will never come upon him. But when the blessed gods bring on him woes, then he has to bear them with enduring heart. For I too might have been prosperous among men, but I did many infatuate deeds, letting my strength do its pleasure, and relying on my father and brothers. Therefore let no man do evil, but let him possess in silence the gifts of the gods whatever they may give."[1]

He then who is wise will reverence the gods in twofold mode; will not forget propitiatory offerings to their human moods, pleasing them thus as men please men; and will refrain from acts which revert upon the doers' heads. These Greeks knew life, understood mortal impotence, and realized the need to supplement it through propitiation of the higher powers. "Pray, stranger, to Lord Poseidon, for thou hast chanced on his feast, coming hither, and when thou hast poured to him and prayed, as is right, hand the goblet of sweet wine to thy companion to pour therefrom; for I think he too prays to the deathless gods, and all men need the gods."[2]

Right conduct therefore was the fruit of wisdom,[3] human at source, often aided by divine suggestion. Wrong conduct was the fruit of folly. The wise man respects the gods, finds out their wishes and obeys; and he deals aright with men:—the foolish man does otherwise. Wrongdoing was blamed; it brought retribution from gods or men; and in its evil results to the doer lay the proof, if not the essence, of its being wrong. Wrong was folly; says Agamemnon to Nestor of his wrong to Achilles: "You have rightly named my folly; I was a fool, nor do I deny it."[4]

Inasmuch as the Homeric Achæans were most eager in their desires, and saw the sanction of their acts in the good or evil results to the doer, they admired nothing so much as success, that far success which, without tripping, wins and holds the thing desired. And it is this quality

[1] *Od.*, xviii, 130.
[2] *Od.*, iii, 43.
[3] *Cf. Od.*, xviii, 228.
[4] *Il.*, ix, 115; *cf. Il.*, xix, 86.

of success that from Homer onwards gradually gathers round itself a divineness, and sanctifies the man's life if it abide with him to the end. With Homer, quite consistently, human excellence lay within the compass of the two heroic virtues, *ἀρετή* and *πινυτή*: the first, physical strength and valor; the second, that mental insight and capacity, that *prudentia*, which combines cunning and wisdom as to men, and wisdom and respect as to the gods. Under all circumstances the possessor of *πινυτή* will see what is best to do, therefore will not err, will not do wrong. He will know how rightly to treat his friends, how by guile to overthrow his enemies, and how duly to respect and obey the gods. It was thought to follow, as of course, that this excellent understanding would find fitting expression in words,—indeed was it clearly distinct from the faculty of speech?—and that as its possessor knew good counsels so would he be eloquent.

Thus the Homeric Achæans, being Greeks, reasoned on life and fashioned its ideals. *Ἀρετή* was the physical energy of valorous desire; *πινυτή* the clear intelligence which reached mortality's far ends. Eagerness to gain these ends became in the Achæan soul a burning shame of acts which tripped the man pressing along the path of far success, or spotted the fair fame which the Greek was ever to love more than life. The heroic passion is to do mighty deeds of warfare or adventure, and so win fame and wealth. But around it, in the epics, circles a play of trait and motive, love and sympathy, which completes the fair contents of mortal life. In Homer the genius of the Greek race shows its early cherishings of all that should enlarge the life of man.

The Epic Round of Human Trait.

So a full round of human interest comes to expression in the *Iliad* and *Odyssey*. It is all fresh and youthful; but it is the youth of a full man. In simple mode, Homer's men and women are moved by many human sympathies and feelings; quick their joy, quick their tears; another's sorrow wakes remembrance in the friendly heart of like sorrows of its own. Terrific is the pathos of the scenes of utter heart-break, as that of Hector's death and Andromache's fearful hasting to the wall—to see his body dragged at Achilles' wheels. Lovely and subtle is the pathos of the scenes of mingled feeling—the *δακρύοεν γελάσασα* of Andromache receiving her child back from Hector's arms—or that scene of mingled joy and woe when in the halls of Circe the loathsome swine-forms drop from Odysseus' comrades, and they embrace their rescuer, loudly lamenting, till even the goddess is moved to pity;[1]—or that picture of great, unknown Odysseus sitting at the Phæacian banquet, while Demodocus sings of the fierce quarrel between Odysseus and Achilles, which had been foretold in the days when the woe was about to roll upon the Trojans and Danaans. "Such was the song the famous minstrel sang; but Odysseus, with his mighty hands, pulled his cloak over his head, for he was ashamed to weep before the Phæacians. And whenever the divine minstrel paused, Odysseus would uncover his head and taking a goblet pour a libation to the gods. But when the song began again, he would cover his head and moan."[2] This bard himself, blind Demodocus, shows life's compensations, he whom "the Muse loved exceedingly, and gave him good and ill, for she took away his sight and gave him sweet song."

The quick social nature of the Achæans showed itself in the glad hospitality extended to all strangers—and no wanderers more welcome than "the tribe of minstrels,"[3] who sang at feasts the famous deeds of men;—the gods fashioned the fall of Troy that it might be a theme of song for future men.[4] But others sang besides the bards—Achilles quells his heart singing to his lyre of the deeds of heroes.[5] And apart from minstrelsy, sweet is joy of simple human intercourse between understanding men.

[1] *Od.*, x, 388.
[2] *Od.*, viii, 62.
[3] *Od.*, viii, 479.
[4] *Od.*, viii, 579; *cf. Od.*, ix, 5; xvii, 270.
[5] *Il.*, ix, 186.

Odysseus and trusty swineherd Eumæus are supping in Eumæus' hut; Odysseus asks Eumæus' story, how he came to wander from his country, whether his city had been sacked, or wherefore. Eumæus answers: "Friend, since you ask me these things, sit now quietly, and be glad and drink your wine. The nights are long, and there is both time to sleep and time to listen for those who like. The others who wish may go forth and sleep till dawn, when let them break their fast and follow the master's swine. But we two will drink and eat and enjoy the story of each other's troubles, recalling them; for afterwards a man gets pleasure from his trials, one who has suffered much and wandered far." [1]

Among such people there were trusty comrades and dear friends. The essence of comradeship is mutual confidence and common occupation; friendship adds the finer element of love. The two Ajaces represent comradeship. In the dark hours when, 'midst the adverse battle, such of the Greek leaders as remain unwounded are holding off the Trojans from slain Patroclus, the greater Ajax tells Menelaus with Meriones to bear away the body, while we two, the Ajaces, "in your rear will fight the Trojans and divine Hector, having the same mind and one name, as heretofore we have often withstood the sharp fight standing by each other." [2]

Men and women in the epics love their children. Forever glowing is Hector's caress and warrior prayer that his son's fame surpass his own.[3] Achilles, at the sight and words of Priam, weeps for his absent father; and in Hades the feeble shade of him once mighty asks to learn of that same aged father, longs for life and strength again to ward off dangers from his dear head; asks also of his son Tlepolemus, is he valiant, famous? And when told

[1] *Od.*, xv, 390.

[2] *Il.*, xvii, 718. "As in this glorious and well-foughten field, we held together in our chivalry."—Shak., *Henry V.*

[3] *Il.*, vi, 476.

of Tlepolemus' brave deeds, off strides the shade rejoicing.[1] And does not Odysseus love Telemachus, and he love and almost worship that great father, whom at first he thinks some god! The poet pictures him sitting silent amidst the taunts of the wooers, watching his father, expecting the signal.[2]

Yet not for veneration for their fathers would the Greeks close their eyes to facts. In the *Iliad* Agamemnon foolishly reproaches Diomede with being an unworthy son of a valiant father, and Diomede's follower answers: "We boast ourselves to be far better men than our fathers. We took seven-gated Thebes, though we led a smaller host against a stronger wall, trusting in the omens of the gods and the help of Zeus; but they perished in their impiousness. Do not, therefore, ascribe equal honor to our fathers."[3]

As Telemachus, respectful, modest in speech, abashed at the thought of addressing the venerable Nestor, is the youth of the epics, Nausicaa is the maiden. The poet has given her the sweetest modesty and innocence. At the river, like Artemis among her wood-nymphs, is she fair among her fellow-maids. Odysseus, seeing her, exclaims: "Thrice happy are her parents—if she be really mortal—beholding her so fair entering the dance, but most blessed he who shall prevail with wooing gifts and lead her to his home!" Of Odysseus, on whom Athene sheds grace, Nausicaa muses softly, as he sits on the shore. Then while her maidens give him food, she yokes the mules and speaks to him: "Rouse thee now, stranger, to go to the city, so that I may send thee to my father's house, where thou wilt see the noblest of the Phæacians. And do as I tell thee, for thou seemest not indiscreet. While we are passing through the fields, do thou walk with the attendants behind the wagon.

[1] *Od.*, xi, 538.

[2] *Od.*, xx, 385.

[3] *Il.*, iv, 405. Their fathers had attacked Thebes against the warnings of the gods.

But when we come to the city I would avoid the ungracious speech of men, who might say,—who is this goodly stranger with Nausicaa? where did she find him? Now he will be her husband. Verily she regards not the noble youths of the Phæacians who woo her.—And indeed I would blame another girl who conversed before marriage with men without her parents' knowledge." The poet gives a last glimpse of Nausicaa; she is standing by the door-post in the hall of the palace, and sees coming from the bath anointed and fairly clad the great stranger who has shown himself so courteous, wise, and strong of arm. Her eyes wonder at him as she speaks: "Hail, guest! and when thou art in thy fatherland sometime think of me, for first unto me thou owest the ransom of thy life."[1]

The epics know well the tender love between a man and wife. Noble is Hector's love for Andromache; and through what terrors, and away from what sweet lures does Odysseus strain towards his home! What were his yearnings? To see his old father and mother, should they still linger on earth; stronger may have been the wish to see his son, and the longing which is child of manifold remembrance, to look once more upon the land of his youth; and yet above all he yearned to hold his dear wife in his arms. Calypso would keep him on her island, make him her husband, give him immortality; she tells him of the trials of his voyage, the dangers of his return, and adds that she boasts herself to be no less fair than that wife of his whom he longs all the days to see:—what says the hero to her? "Goddess, be not angry with me. And I know that wise Penelope is less fair than thou, for she is a mortal, and thou an immortal ever young. Yet all the days I long to journey homewards and see the day of my return. And if some god shall wreck me in the sea I will endure, possessing my soul steadfast in evil, for I have already suffered much from waves and war, and let this be added thereto."[2] The same hero thus tells

[1] *Od.*, viii, 457. *Od.*, vi, contains the tale of Nausicaa. [2] *Od.*, v, 214.

Nausicaa his thought of wedded life: "May the gods give thee thy desire, husband and home and concord therein; for nothing is stronger or better than a man and wife who dwell together in unison,—a sight to make their enemies grieve and their friends rejoice, but most of all they know their happy lot themselves." [1]

And how is it with the wife? Does not Penelope love and remember and hope? With what devices does she put off her stormy, cruel wooers, hoping, intending never to marry one of them. And Odysseus twenty years away! Yet she remembers all, the clothes he wore when he set out for evil Ilium; night and day she pines and weeps, and her tears pour forth at the sight of the bow—of anything which once was his.

The Thought of Beauty.

Intercourse was marked by courtesy of manner, showing high regard between men. Rarely does a Homeric personage address another without some title of respect, and courteous terms are used even of enemies. Ajax and Achilles speak of the great Trojan hero as divine Hector. Charming is the courtesy with which a chief receives whoever may come to his abode. Achilles greets the trembling heralds with, "Hail, Heralds, messengers of Zeus and men! Come near. I do not blame you, but Agamemnon, who has sent you for the girl Briseis." [2] And still nobler is the courtesy with which the bereaved hero treats the suppliant Priam.[3] This formal epic courtesy of intercourse not only marks the high consciousness of the personal worth of heroes, but is a phase of that which is with Homer the broadest thought and loveliest desire, the thought of beauty, of beauty intellectual and physical, gratifying the mind or the eye or ear. Conceptions of intellectual and moral beauty were the reflex of Homeric far-sighted views of life as to what was fitting, right, or proper, as to what was broadly well for man; the reflex, too, of Homer's mind and love of knowledge.

[1] *Od.*, vi, 180. [2] *Il.*, i, 334. [3] See *post*.

Homer's mental power, performing its perfect function, and so conforming itself to the mould of intellectual beauty, manifests itself in the structure of the epics, in their plan and arrangement, their artistic form and splendid movement, and in the fitness of their episodes.

The use of the word καλός, whose primary meaning is "beautiful," shows the wide associations and extensions of the thought of beauty, even in these earliest times. Καλόν in the epics is used in the sense of fittingly, properly, becomingly; says Odysseus to the Phæacian who would taunt him into taking part in the sports, "thou dost not speak καλόν.[1] Again it is said it is not becoming (καλόν) to boast loudly;[2] and Penelope declares that it is not fitting (καλόν) nor just (δίκαιον) for the wooers to ill-treat a guest of Telemachus.[3] Poseidon challenges Apollo to combat, but says, "Begin thou; it is not fitting (καλόν) for me to begin: I am older and know more than thou."[4] Again Poseidon tells certain of the Achæan chiefs that it is not proper (καλόν) for them longer to shun the battle.[5] Priam, meeting Hermes in the night and hearing from him about Hector's body, asks, "Who art thou that tellest me so fairly about my son?"[6] And in other places the word means "well."[7] Naturally it often means charming or delightful: "Nor [at the banquet of the gods] was there lacking the lovely (περικαλλέος) lyre which Apollo had, nor the Muses, who sang in turn with a beautiful voice."[8] And Odysseus says that it is most delightful (κάλλιστον) to hear songs, feasting at a banquet.[9]

[1] *Od.*, viii, 166; *cf. Od.*, xvii, 381.
[2] *Od.*, xvii, 19; *cf. Od.*, xviii, 287.
[3] *Od.*, xxi, 312; see *Od.* xx, 294.
[4] *Il.*, xxi, 440.
[5] *Il.*, xiii, 166; *cf. Il.*, vi, 326; viii, 400; ix, 615.
[6] *Il.*, xxiv, 388.
[7] See *Od.*, xv, 10; xvii, 397, 460, 483; *cf. Od.*, xiv, 253, 299.
[8] *Il.*, i, 604; *cf. Il.*, xviii, 570; *Od.*, x, 227.
[9] *Od.*, ix, 11; see *Od.*, i, 370; ix, 3.

The primary meaning of the word is "fair to see." Transition to it is made by a passage wherein the poet shows the intimate connection between the idea of what is hideous to behold and what is shocking mentally and morally. From the walls of Troy, Priam is entreating Hector not to await Achilles; he speaks of his many good sons already slain, and how much more will be the grief of all if Hector falls. Then he implores Hector to pity him entering on the path of old age, whose life Zeus is making so hard, with the slaughter of sons and the dragging away captive of daughters and the casting down on the earth of little children: "And perhaps I shall last of all be torn by dogs before my doors, when the spear has taken my life. It befits a young man killed in battle to be gashed with the spear, and all is seemly (καλά) for him when dead, whatever may come to him. But when dogs defile the gray head and beard of an old man slain, that is indeed the thing most pitiable that comes to wretched mortals."[1] What could be uglier than the naked body of an old man, gashed and torn? What could be more shocking, too, to every moral and intellectual feeling?

Everything prized by him would the Homeric Achæan have beautiful: his horses and chariot, his garments and his arms. The splendid detailed description of Achilles' shield shows how the poet loved a beautiful object. And in human beings nothing was more prized, more loved, than beauty. Athene pours grace (χάρις) over Odysseus, makes him taller and fairer, that he may find favor in Phæacian eyes.[2] Beauty (κάλλος) is a gift from the gods;[3] and how they loved it in mortals Ganymede might tell, snatched up by Zeus for his beauty, and lovely Clitus, whom the Dawn carried away to live among the im-

[1] *Il.*, xxii, 37.

[2] *Od.*, vi, 235; vii, 19; see *Od.*, ii, 12; xvii, 63; xxiii, 162.

[3] *Ibid.* and see *Il.*, vi, 156; *Od.*, vi, 18; *Od.*, viii, 457; *Od.*, xviii, 192; *Od.*, xvi, 211.

mortals.[1] Other good qualities join with it, as, of course, "large and beautiful," "tall and fair," "tall, fair, and accomplished,"—thus does the poet speak of his heroes and his women.[2] Achilles was most beautiful as well as mightiest of the Achæans.[3] And nothing in Paris so shocks the noble Hector as that his brother should be so splendid of form and so unvaliant.[4] In the night scene in Achilles' tent, stricken Priam perforce marvels at the beauty of the slayer of his son; stricken Achilles admires the noble dignity of the father of his dear one's slayer.

But it is of chilling interest to note how the Homeric Greeks could sometimes sever their admiration for beauty of form from kind feeling towards the possessor; how they could admire and hate. The Achæans throng around to marvel at the splendid form of dead Hector, "nor did any one draw near that did not wound him."[5]

Only Helen is so fair that no one of the Achæans or Trojans blames her, and the poet never. Fate and her divine beauty justify Helen. Erring perhaps, fate-driven, is she, rather than sinning of her own free will. Ever goes she clothed in beauty, ever are her thoughts most beautiful; she is divine of women, whether we see her on the wall of Troy when the cracked voices of old men declare it no wonder Greeks and Trojans fight for such a woman, whether we see her at her loom weaving in a mighty web the deeds of heroes, or verily even when she ascends the couch of him with whom she had fled home, husband, child. Could Helen resist fate? Ah, no! *Would* she? The poet does not say; only we know her beauty and her grace, her words and movements. Who

[1] *Il.*, xx, 235; *Od.*, xv, 251. *Od.*, vi, 42, describes Olympus, the abode of the gods, in a way showing how much lovely localities were prized by the old Greeks, although they had no sentimentality as to nature.

[2] *Od.*, xiii, 287; xv, 418; x, 396.

[3] See *Il.*, 673. So in *Il.*, xiii, 432, is κάλλος naturally joined with ἔργα. Compare the phrase ἠΰς τε μέγας τε, *Od.*, ix, 508.

[4] *Il.*, iii, 39.

[5] *Il.*, xxii, 369.

moves us more than Helen, the unhappy cause of all the woe? Whose lament for Hector is so touching? Not wifely Andromache's. And lovely are her self-reproaches, in which mingles a pity for herself and Paris, "on whom Zeus has placed such an evil fate that we shall be a theme of song to men in times to come."[1] Yet she feels her shame quite as much as the hard will of the gods that put it on her; and the shame which she has brought on her brothers. Looking from the wall, she does not see them. "Either they did not follow from loved Lacedæmon, or they did follow in their sea-sailing ships, but now will not mingle in the battle of men, dreading the shame and the many reproaches which are mine." So she spoke; but them the life-giving earth had, even in Lacedæmon, their dear fatherland.[2]

The Greatness of Man.

Another final Hellenic thought presents itself through the range of epic story,—that of the greatness of the heroic man despite his mortality. The epics heighten every human quality, by no means the moral qualities alone or even pre-eminently. They greaten manhood altogether. Humanity is beheld glorified, not by circumstances or capacities unhuman, but in the greatness of human trait. No hero is ever lifted out of his essential humanity. Of this essential humanity the gods are but the reflex; and consequently, not the gods, but Achilles and Odysseus, are the crowning glories of epic creation. In them, heroic ideals are incarnate. Yet the two heroes are very real. Nowhere exist characters defined in stronger line. Achilles is swift and radiant human force; in his glowing heart molten passions surge and swell, burst forth in fiery words, transform the hero to a raging bane; and when the rage is past, Achilles is again a gracious demi-god. Odysseus is courageous intelligence and enduring strength, which win success and fame, gain their end as does the force of Achilles, and without giving up life therefor. The Greek

[1] *Il.*, vi, 357.

[2] *Il.*, iii, 236.

race loved Achilles as a son of promise who was too young to die; not less did they regard Odysseus, whom they more instinctively imitated. For Achilles was what the Greeks wondered at; Odysseus was what they admired and were.

Achilles.

As one reads and feels the Greek epic, a unique impression is produced by Achilles, this marvellous being, so vehement, passionate, wrathful, tender in love of friend, convulsive in grief, cruel in revenge, then graciously pitying. In every bodily quality he surpasses the other heroes; no one else can wield the Pelean spear; no other man alone can lift the bar of Achilles' door. But for his swiftness and grace, he might be colossal; but colossal he is not, only tall and goodly, fairest of men. Likewise in every passion, spiritual quality, and mental trait that is his, Achilles is great. Patroclus is the dear friend of the hero, that is his role, that is his character; he is an accessory and a foil to Achilles, waits expectant on his moods, does his behests, acts only for his glory, except when carried along by his own impetuous valor. And yet, notwithstanding that Patroclus' personality has its centre and its bounds in this devotion, Achilles' love for Patroclus was greater, was an affection reaching beyond anything the lesser man Patroclus was capable of. This is but a single illustration in the topic of Achilles' grandeur; for he is fierce in his wrath, strong also in self-restraint, lofty in his indignation, in sorrow exceeding the comprehensions of other men, a very torrent of avenging hate, and sublime in his gracious moods. In nothing is he small; his greatness is beautiful in its completeness.

Glory is a continuing, mighty motive with Achilles. It was born with him and made his boyhood swift and eager, led him to choose warfare around mighty Troy rather than a dullard's lengthened years. Easily was he first in deeds among the Achæans until the outrage put upon him by Agamemnon ; then anger thrusts glory from his mind. For a time this anger is dominant, holding him in inactivity which he whiles away singing the famous deeds of men ; and under the dulling influence of anger he thinks of loathsome Hades, and questions whether it were not better to sail home to Phthia, comfort himself with a wife, and live those long years once promised him. The imminent destruction of the fleet moves him to send Patroclus to his death. Then grief and avenging hate bury anger out of sight, overwhelm the horror of an early death; and Achilles chooses revenge and death, as before glory and death had been his choice. Again the glory motive comes. If he breathes revenge, mightily is his heart set on fame ; and with him glory and the love of fame forbade his being infamous in any way. Greek is he to the core, Greek in his calm fearlessness which rational confidence inspires, Greek in his self-restraint and his obedience to the gods, Greek in his love and hate, and Greek in his mercy at the end, sprung from an understanding of the pitiableness of men. As from the height of larger personality the heart-stricken hero comforts Priam. It is night ; Achilles sits in his tent ; two comrades are removing the remains of the evening meal. Suddenly Priam enters, passes by the two, clasps Achilles' knees, and kisses the hands which have slain so many of his sons. Wonder seizes them while the old man speaks: " Think of thy father, godlike Achilles, who with me is entering on the dreary path of old age. Perhaps neighboring chiefs are pressing hard upon him, and there is none to ward off the war. Yet he, hearing of thee as yet alive, rejoices in the hope of seeing his loved son some day return from Troy. But I am all bereft, for of my bravest sons, not one is left. Fifty had I when came the sons of the Achæans. Most of them fierce conflict has laid low ; there was one who protected the city, and now thou hast slain him as he fought for his country, even Hector. For him am I come to the ships of the Achæans, bringing thee a ransom. Reverence the gods, Achilles, and pity me, as thou rememberest thy father. I am more pitiable. I have endured as no other earthly mortal has, to lift up my hands to the slayer of my son." [1]

Achilles gently pushed him back, and both wept aloud, —Achilles for his father and Patroclus, Priam for his son. Then he sprang forward and raised the old man in pity of his gray hair: "Ah, hapless! Many ills hast thou endured. How didst thou dare to come to the ships of the Achæans alone, and meet the eyes of him who has slain many and the brave ones among thy sons? Iron is thy heart! But sit, and our sorrows will we let rest in our breasts, grieved as we are. No help will come from chill lament; for the gods have made it the lot of wretched mortals to live in affliction while they are without sorrow. Two jars stand on the floor of Zeus filled with evil gifts, and another with blessings. He to whom Zeus gives a mingled lot, at one time encounters evil, at another, good. But him to whom Zeus gives of the evil kind, he makes a wretch of; hunger drives him over the broad earth, and he wanders honored neither by gods nor mortals. Thus the gods gave splendid gifts to Peleus from his birth; for he excelled all in fortune, and was king of the Myrmidons, and though mortal, had a goddess for a wife. But even to him did god allot evil, for no race of mighty sons was born in his palace, only one son, who was to bring no joy. For I do not tend him now as he grows old, but am here at Troy, bringing sorrow to thee and thy children. And thou, old man, heretofore have we heard thou wert fortunate, that thou didst surpass in wealth and sons all throughout Lesbos, Phrygia, and by the boundless Hellespont. But then the heavenly ones brought bane to thee, that always is there battle and the slaughter of men about thy city. Endure, nor make such unappeasable lament. Grief for thy brave son is unavailing. Thou canst not raise him up." [2]

[1] *Il.*, xxiv, 485.

[2] *Il.*, xxiv, 518.

Priam's thoughts are with his son: "Bid me not to sit, O Zeus-born, while Hector lies uncared for by the tents, but release him now, that I may see him with my eyes, and do thou receive the ransom."

Whereat Achilles, moved, replied: "Trouble me no more, old man. I mean to release Hector; for there came a messenger from Zeus, even the mother who bore me. And I know, O Priam, that one of the gods has brought thee to the ships of the Achæans. So vex not my soul in its grief, lest I respect thee not though a suppliant, and transgress the commands of Zeus."[1]

So he spoke, and the old man feared; and Achilles sprang forth through the door, and took the precious ransom from the wagon, except two robes which he left to cover the body. Then he bade the maid-servants wash the body away from Priam's sight, lest seeing his son the old man should not restrain his wrath, and anger Achilles to kill him. When the body was washed and anointed, Achilles lifted it upon the wagon, calling with a moan on his dear comrade: "Be not angered at me, Patroclus, if thou dost hear in Hades that I have given up noble Hector to his father; for not unworthy is the ransom, which I will duly share with thee."[2] And he went back into the tent, sat down, and spoke to Priam: "Thy son is released, old man, as thou hast wished, and lies on a bier. Thou shalt see him in the morning when carrying him away. Now let us have a thought of food. For even fair-haired Niobe bethought her of food, although her twelve children had perished in her halls, six daughters and six sons in their prime. Apollo angered with Niobe slew the sons, and archeress Artemis the daughters, because Niobe compared herself with Leto, saying she had borne only two children and herself many. And the two destroyed the many. Nine days they lay in their gore, for there was none to bury them, as Zeus turned the folk to stone; on the tenth the heav-

[1] *Il.*, xxiv, 560.

[2] *Il.*, xxiv, 591.

enly gods buried them, and Niobe bethought her of food when she was weary with weeping. So let us also think of eating, noble old man. Hereafter shalt thou mourn thy son carrying him to Ilion."[1]

Achilles and his comrades prepared the meal, and when desire for meat and drink was satisfied, then Priam marvelled at Achilles, to see how great and fair he was, for his face was like the gods, and Achilles marvelled at Priam, beholding his noble aspect and hearing his voice. When they had gazed for a while on one another, Priam asked for a couch, for he had neither slept nor tasted food since Hector's death. Achilles had a fair bed spread for him beyond the inner room; then said: "Lie thou there without, dear old man, lest some of the Achæan chiefs, who are always coming to consult, find thee here and tell Agamemnon, and there be delay in giving up the dead. But tell me how many days wouldst thou have for Hector's burial, so that I may keep back the host."[2] Priam answered: "If indeed thou art willing that I should perform the rites for Hector, thou dost a welcome deed for me, Achilles. For as thou knowest we are pent within the city, and the wood is far on the mountain. Nine days would we mourn, and bury him on the tenth, on the eleventh raise his mound. On the twelfth we will fight again, if needs be."

"These things shall be as thou biddest, aged Priam; and for the time thou sayest I will hold back the battle."[3] So he spoke and clasped the old man's hand that he might have no fear. And Priam and his herald slept by the entrance, but Achilles in the inner room, and by his side lay fair-haired Briseis.

So by mercy, culminating in an act of kindness unbesought, the wild heart of Achilles finds a calm,—an act of kindness done by a hero looking in the face of his own death. Many tears have fallen at the story of the woes of Priam, and the hard death of Hector, the hero who

[1] *Il.*, xxiv, 599. [2] *Il.*, xxiv, 651. [3] *Il.*, xxiv, 669.

loved his wife and country and fell for them. There is subtler pathos in the fate of Achilles, which the poet does not bring to pass, though holding it ever in view. The life of the hero, to his knowledge fated to be short, is all unhappy, despite the glory of it. Toils are there in it, and enough; his reward is outrage; and his indignation brings on him the sorrow for which he is to find no solace. Far from home is he, and soon to die; bereaved will be aged Peleus, bereaved in the thought is Achilles; dead is the friend he cherished. Who can comfort him? Who can fitly sympathize? None of his good friends in the Achæan host comprehends him and his great grief, yet withal, in his loftiness he comforts Priam, as he can; for his nature is greater than Priam's. Priam understands it not, else would he not have pressed again for Hector's body. Achilles comforts Priam; but who is to comfort Achilles?[1]

Odysseus.

The *Odyssey* is the glorification of a man representing heroic intelligence; it celebrates mind and wiles and steadfastness. Yet the hero has a heroic body, wherewith he may excel others in valor and strength. Odysseus represents every virtue which to Homer's mind intelligence implies—piety towards the gods, proper and just dealing towards men, and strong affection for such objects—wife and child and parents—

[1] The *Odyssey* gives a glimpse of the hero's shade in Hades, coming up through the murkiness accompanied by the shade of Patroclus and other heroes. Odysseus, to whom the shades appear, cries Achilles hail, in that the Argives honored him while living as a god, and that he now rules the dead. Achilles answers, speaking largely as in life, that he would rather be the thrall of a poor farmer upon earth than king of all the dead. Then he asks whether his son has distinguished himself, and of his father, and thinks how, were he but alive, he would defend him, should need be. Odysseus can tell him nothing of Peleus, but praises the valor of Achilles' son at Troy, and tells his deeds. Hearing this, the shade moves away with great strides, rejoiced that his son is illustrious. *Od.*, xi, 467–540. Other shades moan in Hades. Achilles makes no lament; he is still the mighty semblance of a mighty self, and the only shade that is glad at anything in Hades. In *Od.*, xxiv, 93, the shade of Agamemnon congratulates the shade of Achilles on his enduring fame.

as a right-minded man cherishes. His intelligence consists of knowledge of what is wise and right to do, readiness of mind, fertility of device. He is ever the ready man, good at word and deed;[1] he is ever the perfectly courageous man who keeps his presence of mind. And he is steadfast, will neither be turned aside nor discouraged.

A man of large experience, versed in all the knowledge of the world was he,—"Tell me, Muse, of the man, the ready one, who wandered afar after he had destroyed the mighty citadel of Troy, and saw the habitations of diverse men and learned to know their minds; much did he suffer on the deep, striving to win his life and the return of his comrades."[2] This man had known the perils of war, the perils of the deep, perils among savage men, more than other men had he suffered: "Alkinous," says he, "have no such thought; for neither in form nor feature am I like the immortals who possess the wide heaven, but to mortal men who die. Whomsoever ye know who has suffered most grievously, to him do I liken myself in sorrows."[3] He had experienced what of good or ill the world had to offer; he had learned what it had to teach; would tell it all too, this most companionable hero.[4]

Odysseus' character is complex, but consistent throughout, and the Odysseus of the *Iliad* is the Odysseus of the *Odyssey*. In the *Iliad* it is to the ready man that Athene comes seeking some one to check the rush of the Achæans to their ships;[5] it is he who chastises Thersites and with apt words turns the people's minds to the war.[6] His speeches are the most skilful and persuasive in the *Iliad*,[7] though in fiery directness below those of Achilles or Diomede. He is also a man of wiles.[8] Diomede selects him for a companion on the perilous night espial, and cunning is his conduct to the Trojan spy.[9] He is also a

[1] *Od.*, ii, 272.
[2] *Od.*, i, 1.
[3] *Od.*, vii, 208.
[4] So Menelaus says, *Od.*, iv, 104.
[5] *Il.*, ii, 165.
[6] *Il.*, ii, 240–330.
[7] See *Il.*, iii, 216.
[8] *Il.*, iii, 200.
[9] *Il.*, x, 240, etc.

busy man, careful, always attending to some matter. Priam in the truce, watching the Achæans from the wall of Troy, sees Odysseus not at rest, but moving about inspecting the ranks.[1] He is always valiant in battle, not a humble or submissive man; quickly he resents Agamemnon's unjust reproach;[2] and ready enough is he to oppose and chide the monarch proposing to abandon the war.[3] In the games, by skill and cunning he foils the greater strength of Ajax wrestling,[4] and ever mindful of his friend Athene wins the foot-race through her aid.[5]

The *Odyssey* gives the fuller picture of the man; therein is he seen tried in every emergency, and the iron strength of his character appears, and its height and goodness. As he is strong, steadfast for his own purpose, so is he faithful and valorous for his comrades, until they perish by their impious folly.[6] Through the perils of the Return was Odysseus just to them, no one lacked his share of food and booty,[7] even as he had been a just king in Ithaca, kind as a father, before they all set out for Troy.[8] Trusty swine-herd Eumæus loves and reveres him so that he shuns to call his name in his absence, but speaks of him as the "loved one."[9]

Odysseus' large experience has taught him caution; he distrusts others frankly, without bitterness. Calypso comes to him as he sits on the shore, bids him not to grieve, and says that she will do the wish of his heart, and send him away to his fatherland on a raft. He answers quickly: "Another thought is in thy mind, goddess, when thou dost bid me on a raft attempt the great gulf of the sea, which not even ships pass over. Nor would I embark—thou misliking it—without thy oath not to plan evil against me."[10] Neither are his eyes to be blinded by the flash of heavenly divinity. Athene comes to him in

[1] *Il.*, iii, 196.
[2] *Il.*, iv, 349.
[3] *Il.*, xiv, 82.
[4] *Il.*, xxiii, 725.
[5] *Il.*, xxiii, 755.
[6] See *Od.*, x, 135; xii, 112, 225.
[7] *Od.*, ix, 42, 549.
[8] *Od.*, ii, 234; iv, 690.
[9] *Od.*, xiv, 147.
[10] *Od.*, v, 171; *cf. ib.*, 355.

Ithaca when he first awakens on his native shore; after a little she takes her true form, and smiling, with compliments for his shrewd fabricated tales, she adds in gentle reproach, "Yet thou knewest not me, Pallas Athene, who am always at thy side in perils and made thee dear to all the Phæacians." Odysseus answers: "Hard is it for a mortal, though a wise one, to know thee, goddess, in thy many shapes. This I know, that thou wast good to me of old, so long as we sons of Achæans warred about Troy. But after we had sacked the city and set sail, and some god had scattered the Achæans, then I never saw thee, child of Zeus, nor did I perceive thee coming aboard my ship to ward off trouble from me."[1] But when Athene tells him she will now be his helper, he trusts her gratefully, and is ready to fight hundreds, alone with her aid. And yet the only bitter words that pass his lips are those in which he answers when she has said now she will go to Lacedæmon to fetch Telemachus, whom she sent thither for tidings of his father: "Why then, didst thou not tell him, thou who knowest all things? was it that he too might suffer sorrows wandering on the barren sea, and eat the bread of strangers?"[2]

Odysseus' nerve is iron. In the hollow horse he restrains the chiefs from making outcry when they hear the voice of Helen.[3] Reaching Ithaca, he keeps his own counsel, finds out who are faithful to him—whether his own wife is still faithful—and, except to Telemachus, discloses nothing till the event is ripe. The trusty Eumæus in his swine-herd hut tells the beggar monarch of all his loving respect for his long-absent king, and the waning hope of his return. Not even to him does Odysseus open his heart. Yet the hero-spirit flashes from the rags. When Telemachus has told of shameful wooers' doings, out speaks Odysseus: "How is it thou dost stand these shames, being such as thou art? do the people hate thee? do thy kin hold off? Were I the son of Odysseus, might

[1] *Od.*, xiii, 312. [2] *Od.*, xiii, 416. [3] *Od.*, iv, 280.

my head be cut off if I made not myself a bane to them all; and if by numbers they overcame me single-handed, then would I die, slain in my palace, rather than behold strangers insulted, maid-servants vilely treated, wine spilled, and food devoured—all vainly."[1] Ragged in his palace, he can bear the insults of the wooers; one of them strikes him with a stool; Odysseus stands unmoved, shaking his head, musing evil.[2] That night, lying by his palace door, he sees the shameless maid-servants going to the insolent wooers with sly laughter—shall he slay them? and his heart growls within him. Yet he smites his breast: "Endure, heart! A shamefuller thing hast thou borne, on that day when Cyclops was devouring thy brave comrades. Then didst thou endure till thy cunning brought thee from the cave where thou thoughtest to die."[3] Day comes, and the infatuate revelling goes on. A wooer throws an ox's hoof at the beggar; the beggar moves his head to avoid it, and smiles.[4] At last the hour is at hand, the bow is brought, Odysseus discovers himself to the two faithful herdsmen, and he tells them bid the women make fast the doors, and not look in if they hear a din and groaning in the hall.[5]

Odysseus is also a shrewd and thrifty Greek, he awaits Cyclops in his cave to behold the giant and see whether he will give him gifts of hospitality.[6] He tells Alkinous that, longing as he is for home, he would wait a year for splendid gifts such as the king and his nobles might give him;[7] awakening in Ithaca, ignorant where he is, first of all he counts these gifts and bestows them safely;[8] and even with the still white heat of vengeance in his breast, in rags in his palace, he is pleased when the wooers give his wife gifts of the wooing which was not to be accomplished.[9]

Zeus says Odysseus excels all others in wisdom (*νοόν*)

[1] *Od.*, xvi, 91.
[2] *Od.*, xvii, 462.
[3] *Od.*, xx, 18.
[4] *Od.*, xx, 300.
[5] *Od.*, xxi, 235.
[6] *Od.*, ix, 229.
[7] *Od.*, xi, 356.
[8] *Od.*, xiii, 200.
[9] *Od.*, xviii, 281.

and in sacrificing to the gods.[1] That is to say, he was a pious, god-fearing man. There is no higher word in the epics than that with which he checks the old nurse's shrill rejoicing at the death of the wooers: "In thy soul, old woman, be glad, and restrain thyself, nor cry aloud. It is not right to exult over slain men. These the fate of the gods overcame and their deeds. For they honored no one of mortal men, neither high nor low, who came to them. Wherefore through their wicked folly have they met a shameful death."[2]

Throughout the tale one marks Odysseus' love of adventure, and his eagerness to see and learn. To see and learn was one motive leading him to the Cyclops' cave, where, indeed, he learned bitter things; and wherever he comes he will learn what manner of men may be there.[3] So will he, bound to the mast, hear the deadly Siren peril. Borne from where they sit 'midst whitening bones, over the hushed sea, the clear song rises: "Oh! come hither, far-famed Odysseus, great glory of the Achæans; stay thy ship and hear our voices. For none has ever driven past in his black ship till he has heard from our lips the sweet lay; but having had the joy of it, he sails on, and knowing more. For we know all that in the wide Troy-land Argives and Trojans underwent at the will of the gods; and we know whatever happens on the teeming earth."[4] So the straining hero tugs at his bonds, that he may hear this lay and know more.

And, after all, when this mighty knowledge-and adventure-loving wanderer has reached his home, when he has sprung upon his threshold bow in hand, intent to slay and slay in fierce revenge, when he has slain, and has stridden like a lion over the corpses, seeking if perchance one might still breathe, and when he has once more felt around him the arms of his wife, has seen his father, and at last has become fixed on the throne of sea-girt Ithaca,

[1] *Od.*, i, 66; *cf. Od.*, xiii, 297.
[2] *Od.*, xxii, 411.
[3] See *e. g. Od.*, ix, 172.
[4] *Od.*, xii, 184.

is he then for all his latter days quietly to sit and eat and sleep? Such were an inconsequent fate. After all these struggles and accomplishments, he is again to set forth bearing on his shoulder an oar, and with it wander on till he come to a people ignorant of the sea and its ships, who shall take the oar on his strong shoulder for a winnowing-fan; there shall he fix it in the earth and sacrifice to Poseidon. Then he shall return to his home and offer a hecatomb to the immortal gods. When this pious adventure is all accomplished he may rest. And a gentle death shall come to him from the sea and slay him when overburdened with a smooth old age, and all the people shall be blest about him.[1]

[1] *Od.*, xi, 121. This sacrifice to Poseidon and extension of his cult was to reconcile him to Odysseus for the blinding of Polyphemus.

CHAPTER VIII.

GREEK PRINCIPLES OF LIFE.

EAGERLY the Achæans desired the full contents of life; they would excel in valor, overcome their foes, get the fame thereof, and therewithal goodly possessions and fair women. He was the hero who attained success, only far-sightedly, not with the insolence of disregard which reaped return of evil in the end. The longing for it all, and the full fame thereof, the lasting praise of fellow-men, roused in the hero-heart a sense of shame of each untoward act. So would he respect such rights of others as he recognized, be courteous, cognizant of others' merit, guest-reverencing, jealous of the favor of the gods, in comradeship good at need, in friendship devoted unto death, in enmity a bane to hateful men. Helpful to all these ends were valor, iron endurance, cunning, sagacity, and all such knowledge as brought wisdom and preserved from folly. And the heroes burned to hear song of famous deeds, those the memory of which still throbbed. Beyond this, Greek nature was already instinct with wish to find out and to learn. Knowledge is becoming an element of life; and already throbs that creative artist soul which cannot but love loveliness, figure what it loves, and hold it to be true for reason of its beauty.

Unfolding of the Greek Spirit.

Hellenic qualities, ardent in the epics, become clearer, more spiritual, and are builded to a perfectness mature and all-proportioned in the life, the literature and art, and the philosophy of classic Greece. Throughout appears the all-compassing vision, the acquisitive and proportioning mind, and that imagination, creative, plastic, ethical, which in the drama enacts furthest mortal truth, and in sculpture makes visible the perfect human form, holding soul as the flower holds life, and in philosophy discloses intellectual conceptions visualized, and set as beacons on the heights of reason.

Μηδὲν ἄγαν.

With the Greeks, so long as lasted the great days of Greece, life was a whole whereof all things that might enter it were elements, indispensable to life's completeness, but so distinct as to admit of proportioning in relationship. This relationship of proportion carries as a consequence a universal principle of Greek life and thought, one stated in many forms. It lies in the avoidance of the extreme, self-control so guided by reason as to avoid excess—temperance, measure, proportion, fitness. This principle inhered in the Greek conception of beauty, and moulded Greek ideals of conduct. It was the outcome of the many-sided Greek nature combined with Greek insight into the proportionate worth of things. Homer does not state it broadly, for the *Iliad* and *Odyssey* are from a time not given to generalizing. But the course of the epics points to it, and it appears in Homer's horror of *ἄτη* and *ὕβρις*, folly brought by the insolence of pride, sure to meet overthrow. The wicked, ill-starred wooers of Penelope are always insolent, *ὕβριν ἔχοντες*. After Homer, the idea found general expression in the phrase *μηδὲν ἄγαν*—nothing too much; then in the word, *σωφροσύνη*,—wise temperance. Hesiod bids men preserve moderation; the half is better than the whole.[1] Theognis applies the principle to feelings—do not be stirred too much by good or evil; it is the part of man to bear all.[2] Take measure of thyself, says Pindar.[3] Pegasus threw Bellerophon seeking to soar to heaven.[4] Desire moderate things,[5] not such as befit only the immor-

[1] *Erga*, 692, 720.
[2] Theognis, 657.
[3] *Pyth.*, ii, 34.
[4] *Isthm.*, vi, 44.
[5] *Ib.*, v, 71.

tals,[1] and set God above all.[2] Is not he the supreme ordainer, hence of gravest importance to man? So one must duly weigh advantages; some gains may not be worth while.[3] There is danger in too great prosperity, lest it beget pride, which surely brings ruin. Upon him who is puffed up the gods send folly, and he perishes.[4] The moderate lot is to be preferred.[5] Thoughts like these pervaded all Greek life as principles of action which Greeks should follow. They showed themselves in love of harmony, proportion, beauty, in desires for the best that life offered; yet nothing too much, nothing too costly, nothing entailing too great ill; but a weighing of all things.

The Deed of Fame.

To all peoples come moods in which life is but a slight, flitting thing. Some races, like the Hindoo, are overpowered by a sense of life's shortness, and cease to see anything in mortal life worthy of endeavor. Happily, the Greeks were eager, and in their full desire for the all-proportioned most of life, they loved perfection, loved men and objects beautiful or noble in themselves. The fact that man had few years to live did not make against the absolute worth of noble achievement. Greek philosophy recognized this principle, while with men whose lives were eager action, the enduring element of their achievement, so far as concerned themselves, was the fame of it; and that was felt to be enough by all Greek heroes from Achilles to Timoleon.[6] It is evident that men feeling the transcendent worth of mortal achievement could not be fatalists. Yet, to the Greeks of classic times, fate was even more inviolable than with Homer. It continued to hold the broadest Greek generalizations upon human life; and, as with

[1] *Pyth.*, iii, 59–62; *cf. Nem.*, xi, 13, and Euripides, *Alcestis*, 799.
[2] *Pyth.*, v, 25.
[3] *Nem.*, xi, 47.
[4] See Æsch., *Persæ*, 804, 817.
[5] Æsch., *Agam.*, 456.
[6] See Pindar, *passim*, and *Pyth.*, viii, 92; also Simonides of Keos, iv.

Homer, through these more mature periods, Greek ethical thought remains inseverable from the rational knowledge on which it is based.

Fate and Zeus.

Thoughts of fate pervaded all Greek literature and influenced Greek life. The literature contains no single expression conveying an adequate notion of the conception; and often expressions of the same writer are inconsistent.[1] Life is no simple matter; no human formula applies to all its phases. Fate, the motive power of events, or the movement itself, evades formulation. There are also, of course, through Greek literature such general exclamations as are common with all peoples,—expressions of unhappiness or despair,—Me miserum!—Oh, my unhappy lot! Alas, cruel fate! *ἰω! ἰω! μοῖρα! μοῖρα!*[2] or expressions of the inevitableness of what is to come, of what is fated,[3] such phrases as "Nothing is stronger than necessity."[4]

Whether fate was above the gods, or the gods—rather more and more Zeus—above fate, was not determined by the lyric and dramatic poets more definitely than by Homer. From many phrases fate would seem to be over all; from many others, Zeus would seem the supreme ordainer, acting through fate as an instrument. The general result is that Zeus and fate ordinarily move together, and either one or the other may be regarded as the ordainer of events. Pindar speaks of Zeus guiding the *δαίμων* of those he loves,[5] and the phrase, *μοῖρα*

[1] The Greeks had moods, like other men. Archilochus, *Frag.*, 15, speaks of toil and painstaking doing all for mortals, and in the next *Fragment* imputes all events to chance and fate.

[2] Æsch., *Prom.*, 713.

[3] *E.g.*, *τὸ μέλλον ἥξει.* Æsch., *Agam.*, 1211; *cf.* Æsch., *Choëph.*, 95; Eurip., *Andromache*, 1204.

[4] Eurip., *Alcestis*, 962; *cf.* *ἀναγκῇ δ'οὐχὶ δυσμαχητέον*, Soph., *Antig.*, 1106, which Mr. Jebb renders, We must not wage a vain war with destiny! The words signifying fate retain nearly the same meaning as in Homer. *Μοίραι* in the plural are more frequently spoken of than in the epics. See Soph. *Antig.*, 987; Æsch., *Eumen.*, 920; Pind., *Pyth.*, iv, 145; Kallinos, 9.

[5] *Pyth.*, v, 122.

θεῶν or αἶσα Διός is frequent as in Homer.[1] Theognis uses μοῖρα or Zeus or θεοί almost equivalently in speaking of the powers controlling men's lots.[2] And the complete accord, for men practical identification, of fate and Zeus appears from such a phrase as τὸ μόρσιμον Διόθεν πεπρωμένον,—destiny ordained of Zeus.[3] Yet many phrases make fate or necessity superior to the gods. Even God cannot escape what is fated, said the Delphic oracle.[4]

Ethical Development of the Thought of Fate.

But the question thus crudely put, whether Zeus was above fate or fate above him, cannot be answered from Greek literature; neither one nor the other was true simply. A solution may be had, however, by considering the ethical as well as the physical side of the development of the idea of fate after Homer's time.

Pindar, in the seventh Isthmian ode, speaks of the oracle told by Themis, how it was fated that Thetis should have a son mightier than his father; so Zeus and Poseidon refrained from the marriage each had desired. Here fate would have been stronger than Zeus, had he, by doing a certain act, brought himself within its operation. By refraining from the marriage, Zeus might keep his throne. The whole story is not yet told, for the

[1] See Solon, *Frag.*, 4, and 13, 30; Pindar, *Ol.*, ii, 23, *Ol.*, ix, 4, 5; *Pyth.*, v, 5.

[2] Theognis, 133, 149, 157, 171, 1033; *cf.* Æsch., *Agam.*, 886; Æsch., *Persæ*, 102, 893; Æsch., *Sup.*, 657; Soph., *Œd. Col.*, 421. Soph., *Frag.*, 786; Eurip., *Androm.*, 1268; Eurip., *Elek.*, 1248; Eurip., *Orestes*, 79; Æsch., *Choëph.*, 298.

[3] Pind., *Nem.*, iv, 61; *cf. Nem.*, vi, 16, and references in the last note. Plato has the phrase θεῖα μοῖρα, *Apol.*, xxii, or θεοῦ μοῖρα, *Rep.*, 492 *e*. These phrases with Plato refer to providential agency and facts which occur through divine action. See note 20 to page 176 of Zeller's *Plato*.

[4] Herod., i, 91. "Art is weaker than necessity. Who steers necessity? The Fates and mindful Erinyes. Is Zeus weaker than these? He cannot escape what is fated."—Æsch., *Prom.*, 519. *Cf.* Simonides, 5, 21; Soph., *Frag.*, 236. Parmenides uses ἀναγκή in the sense of μοῖρα, lines 91 and 98. See Ritter and Preller, *Hist. Phil. Græcæ*, 96, 101 B, 101 D, 141 A, 121 b, 149 Bb.

reason lay far back in the curse of Cronus on the son who had overthrown him.[1] So this fate had its origin in a curse, and was entailed on Zeus for impiety towards his father. It was still conditioned on some further act, then unknown to Zeus, but lying like a sunken rock in his path. Likewise, in regard to men, the moral nature of fate, the part identity of fate with right, with Themis, gradually becomes clearer, until fate, with Zeus, becomes the great awarder of punishment. The original pointing of man's destiny is in his own hands; only the consequences of his act, his future acts and sufferings, are fated.[2] Fate does not take the absolute initiative, but is always, or has been once on a time, conditioned on something within the power of the man or his ancestors. Ἄτη brought by great prosperity, may lead the man to do the fatal act; fate itself comes into operation afterwards.

The Accursed Act; Houses of Laius and Atreus.

The family being a unit in ancient times, succeeding generations were involved in the crimes of ancestors, so as to inherit and effectuate a curse,[3] which had been called forth by some deed of the person cursed, and might be conditioned on some further act. No curse is uttered against innocence, nor is there any suggestion that it would be operative. A curse may be regarded as the imprecation by the injured person of what might be the fit and fated consequences of the wrong. The effect of a curse may be followed in the two houses of Laius and Atreus.

The story of the house of Laius is variously given, but the central strain is this. Laius had been warned by the Delphic oracle that he should have a son who should kill

[1] See Æsch., *Prom.*, 932.

[2] This of course resembles Brahman and Buddhist doctrines, the power of the act in entailing consequences. Indeed, these thoughts only express universal truth, open to the observation of all mankind: the consequences abide for all wrong-doers.—Æsch., *Eumenides*, 511–515.

[3] See Solon, 13, 30; Eurip., *Her. Fur.*, 1261; *cf.* the Biblical "Visiting the sins of the fathers," etc.—Ex. xx, 5.

him; and his son Œdipus brought the oracle to pass, and, having slain Laius, unknowingly wedded Jocasta, his own mother. By her he had two sons and two daughters, and then the matter came to light. Jocasta hanged herself, and Œdipus put out his eyes. Thereafter his sons imprisoned him; and he cursed them that they might divide their heritage with the sword. To avoid the curse, they agreed to rule alternate years; but when the time came, at the first year's end, for Eteocles to give the rule over to Polyneices, he refused; and Polyneices, having obtained aid from Argos, assaulted Thebes, but only to perish at his brother's hand, whom he also slew.

This outline of crime and hate requires supplementing. Why should such an oracular curse have been pronounced over Laius, that he should have a child only to perish at its hands, or incur the great ill of leaving no issue? There was a reason, though the reason which has come down may not be as old as the original myth.[1] Laius, the son of Labdicus, and great-grandson of Cecrops, carried off Chrysippus, the son of Pelops, and was the first among men to practise the custom which among gods Zeus initiated with Ganymede. For this, Pelops invoked on him the curse that he might never have a child, or if he should that the child might slay him. The Erinyes enter into the carrying out of the curse in its secondary stages, but not yet, for apparently they act only as blood avengers or at the call of a parent who has been dealt with impiously.[2] Afterwards, Laius, being very long childless, sent to Delphi, and received an oracle that he should have a son who should slay him. The oracle was not in the nature of a

[1] For the incidents about to be mentioned, see generally the preface of Aristophanes the Grammarian to Euripides' *Phœnicians*. The crime of Laius is referred to by Plato, *Laws*, 836 C. It is not referred to in Æschylus, Sophocles, or Euripides, but was not pertinent to their extant dramas. The earliest version of the story of Œdipus, *Odyssey*, xi, 271, etc., does not mention the crime of Laius. There is nothing in the epics suggesting the existence of this kind of immorality.

[2] See *Il.*, xi, 454.

warning to beget no children, but simply that he should be a father, and die by his son's hand.[1] The wrong to Pelops had been done, and the curse was already hanging over him, sure to fall, yet still conditioned on his begetting a child, an act which apparently he might abstain from. He did for a time abstain from intercourse with his wife, until he forgot the oracle, or drunken desire overcame him, and Œdipus, his fateful son,[2] saw the light. Still endeavoring to escape the oracle, he pierced the babe's feet with golden rings, and exposed it on Mount Cithæron. But Œdipus was preserved, and afterwards hearing an oracle that he should kill his father and marry his mother, he fled from Corinth, where dwelt those whom he thought his parents. While making his way to Thebes, he met and killed Laius. Then, having solved the riddle of the Sphinx, he entered Thebes, where he was made king and given to wife his own mother Jocasta. Thus Œdipus is trebly polluted, born under a curse, then slaying his father, and marrying his mother. Now, according to the *Odyssey*, the Erinyes enter, for Jocasta hanged herself, "bequeathing to him many ills, even as many as a mother's Erinyes might bring to pass."[3] Pindar has it otherwise. Laius meeting death at the hands of his son, "the swift Erinyes beheld it, and slew his (Œdipus') sons each with the other's sword."[4] This is the vengeance on the patricide.

The dramatic version is different. In that the sons do impious wrong to their self-blinded father, by imprisoning him (Æschylus)[5] or (Sophocles) by driving him from

[1] Æsch., *Septem.*, 743, makes this oracle a warning against begetting children,—a divergence here.—*Cf.* Soph., *Œd. T.*, 712.

[2] *Μόρσιμος υἱός*, Pindar, *Ol.*, ii, 35.

[3] *Od.*, xi, 719.

[4] *Ol.*, ii, 35.

[5] This is what is said in the preface of The *Seven against Thebes*, *εγκατακλείουσιν οἰκίσκῳ αὐτον*. Compare, however, *Seven against Thebes*, 783.

the state; and for this he curses them.[1] Hence there are two curses working themselves out on the sons of Œdipus, the original curse on the race, and the curse from Œdipus. Each infatuate act (ἄτη) brings a new curse or deepens the effect of the old one, which the first infatuate act (πρώταρχος ἄτη)[2] occasioned. If the sons of Œdipus had not ill-used their father, perhaps they might have escaped; yet they could not have escaped their racehood. And if Eteocles had not unjustly refused to give up the kingship to his brother at the end of the year, perhaps there might have been no strife between them; or perhaps he was doomed through the curse to be thus unjust. As it is, when Polyneices has invaded the land, Eteocles yields to his fate: "Since God so hurries on the business, let the whole race of Laius, hateful to Phœbus, drift with the breeze upon Cocytus' wave. . . . Abandoned by the gods, why longer fawn upon the doom of death?"[3] As he rushes forth, the chorus moralizes: "I fear the destroying goddess, the Erinyes, lest she accomplish the wrathful curse of their father. But the bane urges on these things."[4] And they mutter over the old crime of Laius, when warned by Apollo that, dying childless, he should save the state; nevertheless, he begot in Œdipus doom for himself.[5] The working out of the curse on the two sons in Sophocles' *Œdipus Coloneus* differs only in detail from the version of the *Seven against Thebes*. Œdipus curses them for having cast him out.[6] Never-

[1] According to the Cyclic poem of the *Thebaid*, Œdipus cursed his sons for disobediently setting on his table the wine-cups of Laius, "and the Erinyes failed not to hear." See Dr. Jebb's introduction to his *Œdipus Tyrannus*, p. 16.

[2] Æsch., *Agam.*, 1163.

[3] Æsch., *Sept.*, 686, 699.

[4] *Ib.*, 717.

[5] *Ib.*, 739, etc.

[6] But the curse is pronounced at a later period, when Polyneices comes to Colonus to seek his father's aid, knowing the oracle that the side favored by Œdipus would win. See *Œd. Col.*, 421, etc.; but *cf. ib.*, 1375.

theless, with Sophocles, more entirely than with Æschylus, the doom of the two sons is dependent on the curse from their father, and less intimately connected with the accursedness of the race.[1] Still, after the sons have slain each other, the hard lot of the house is referred to in the *Antigone*, how there is no help for the house of Labdicus, which some god casts down from generation to generation. Antigone herself had not been cursed by Œdipus; she had only acted with loving courage, but she also belonged to the curse-stricken house.[2]

Likewise, with the house of Atreus, it is the curse-born *δαίμων* which causes all the woe,[3] though the *δαίμων* was but the agent of Zeus.[4] A curse lay on this house; yet it is not so prominently the working of this curse that causes the ruin, as the very nature of the crimes committed, which avenge themselves in new-begotten crime.[5] Cries Cassandra, as Agamemnon's murder is on the verge, "I scent the track of crimes done long ago. That harsh chorus never leaves this house, but bolder, having drunk men's blood, that revelling band abides of sister Erinyes, not to be cast out. One strain they sing, that primal impious act, loathing that brother's couch so cruel found to its defiler."[6] A brother's bed defiled, the defiler's children slain and fed to him,—should not this engender evil in a house forever? Besides, there were murders, incests many in the race sprung from Tantalus, himself punished by the gods for evil deeds. So was the race fostered on all crimes. What escape could there be

[1] A usual advance to individual discrimination in the award of punishment; *cf.* Jeremiah xxxi, 29, and Theognis, 731, etc.

[2] *Antigone*, 584, 593, 860. The *Antigone* was written before the *Œdipus Coloneus*, and in the latter play perhaps Sophocles was more deeply influenced by the later moral doctrine of the subject's responsibility solely for his own wrong-doing, and perhaps only for crimes done knowingly.

[3] *Agam.*, 1444, etc.

[4] *Agam.*, 1461.

[5] Still Thyestes had cursed the whole race of Atreus.—*Agam.*, 1578.

[6] *Agam.*, 1155, etc., and see *ib.*, 1185, etc.

for any scion of it? Ancient outrage breeds other outrage sporting in human ills, and so on and on.[1] And when Paris came to Menelaus' house, and took away Helen, and the two brothers assembled all Greece to recover her, and bring untold woes,—not on Ilium alone; and when the war had worn on, and the murmurs for Greeks slain at Troy because of private feud had been rising many years, were these not to do the work of a people's curse on those two headstrong kings?[2] And to have slain guiltless Iphigenia in order that guilty Helen might be brought back, was not this a crime fitted to bring its own retribution, even though in foresight Agamemnon bound his daughter's mouth, that dying she might utter no curse against the deed-cursed race?[3] And Clytemnestra with Ægisthus conspired against Agamemnon and slew him. The chorus of old men hardly know how to bewail the murdered chief, who pays the penalty of his own and of ancestral deeds, as is the law of Zeus.[4] So the evil genius of the house causes the woe,[5] working out the old curse in new crimes, and their evil consequences to the doers, among whom is now Clytemnestra, who shall also atone. It was from adulterous hate, as well as desire of vengeance for the sacrifice of Iphigenia, that Clytemnestra killed Agamemnon. But as to Orestes, the command of Apollo laid on him the sacred duty to avenge his father. So the curse ends here. He is pursued by his mother's Erinyes, but is absolved from blame and freed from their pursuit in the end.

An effective curse must be occasioned by a wrong done,

[1] *Agam.*, 738. In *Agam.*, 1194, Cassandra speaks of the murder of Agamemnon as about to take place in vengeance for those children whose spectral forms she saw holding their hearts and entrails, on which their father fed.

[2] *Agam.*, 442.

[3] *Agam.*, 227.

[4] *Agam.*, 1530.

[5] *Agam.*, 1444. An idea that Clytemnestra eagerly takes up as freeing her from guilt.—*Ib.*, 1451.

whereupon the curse uttered[1] becomes as fate to the wrong-doer, and his family it may be,—becomes the δαίμων, the evil spirit, or the particular doom of the house. Above all, it is retributive. So is the fate of man generally conditional upon his nature and especially upon his deeds. All men are mortal, that is, fated to die—an instance of fate dependent on the nature of man or his inherent limitations.[2] There are also special individual lots or fates dependent, in the first place, on some voluntary act of the individual or his ancestors, as has been seen. But that a crime is fated does not absolve the doer. Says Clytemnestra, asking Orestes for life, "Fate, my child, was the cause of these things." Replies Orestes, sardonically, "And Fate prepared this doom for thee."[3] Again he tells his mother, "My father's fate, your deed, prescribes this fate for thee."[4]

Retributive Nature of Fate.

The course of a man's life may be placid and fortunate, in which case it is likely he has led a good life and is loved by the gods.[5] A man's evil fate takes its start from his ἄτη or ὕβρις, causing him to commit wrong or crime. The Greeks generally felt that too great prosperity might incur the envy of the gods and bring the

[1] While we comprehend the ethical notions surrounding the conception of a curse, the power of the curse itself, the deadly spoken word, is very remote from us. It is related to all beliefs in spells and incantations, the power of which consisted in the words themselves, and was dissipated by deviation from the formula. The prayer of the wronged may be equivalent to a curse in working destruction or vengeance. See Æsch., *Choëph.*, 455.

[2] Thus Pindar says men are an ἔθνος ταχυπότμον, *Ol.*, i, 66. So it might be the nature of other beings,—*i.e.*, fated for them—not to die. See Æsch., *Prom.*, 772, 954.

[3] *Choëph.*, 896.

[4] *Choëph.*, 913 See also *Agam.*, 1482, where the chorus admit that the δαίμων of the house had been at work, yet no one will absolve Clytemnestra. *Cf.* Soph., *Aias*, 925; Soph., *Frag.*, 842.

[5] Zeus guides the δαίμων of those he loves. Pind., *Pyth.*, v, 124; Pind., *Ol.*, ii, 39, speaks of μοῖρα holding the happy πότμος of a race, and in *Pyth.*, v, 17 and 26, μοῖρα and αἶσα are both used in a good sense.

possessor ruin.[1] This, however, was but the belief of those who failed to see the intervening link: prosperity brings *ἄτη*, and that brings overthrow. Says Æschylus: "It is an old saw that great prosperity does not die childless, but brings insatiable woe on a race. I hold differently; for it is the impious act that bears more evil deeds[2] like to the parent stock. The fate of righteous houses is blessed with fair children."[3] Yet Æschylus knew the danger that prosperity would cause insolence and crime, and thus he elsewhere lets his chorus speak: "Be man's life free from misery with enough to satisfy the wise; for wealth is no protection to a man when he has spurned the altar of right. A wretched impulse drives him on, the irresistible, far-scheming child of folly."[4] Wrong-doing brings ill on the doer. Solon expresses the broad doctrine—a man atones for evil deeds sooner or later, or if not, then his children atone.[5] These dramas of the houses of Laius and Atreus are dramatic embodiments of the ethical truth that no man can elude the retributive consequences of his acts, or even the result of his nature and racehood. The consequence or denouement works itself out in the form of immediate or final calamity; or when the person has himself wittingly committed crime, it works itself out in further crimes, which at last entangle him in ruin.

This conception of the retributive nature of fate connects it with the Erinyes, who are sisters of the *μοίραι*,[6] or even identified with them[7] As far back as Hesiod, the *μοίραι* and *κῆρες* pursue with vengeance the trans-

[1] Herod., iii, 40; *ib.*, vii, 10, 46.

[2] Involuntary crimes may be a punishment for previous crimes. Soph., *Œd. Col.*, 965, etc.

[3] *Agam.*, 727, etc.

[4] *Agam.*, 370, etc, ; *ib.*, 1302.

[5] Solon, 13, 30. So the Trojans atone for Paris's crime, which they upheld. *Agam.*, 353, etc. See *Eum.*, 511–515.

[6] *Eumenides*, 920.

[7] *Eumenides*, 165. In Eurip., *Elektra*, 1252, the Erinyes are called *κῆρες*.

gressions of gods and men.[1] Æschylus says, the dark Erinyes execute sure vengeance,[2] and Sophocles says, "the Erinyes of the gods are in wait to ensnare Creon in the crimes which he has committed."[3] But it is not with justice of a retributive nature only that fate is connected. Hesiod makes the three Fates the daughters of Themis by Zeus, who gave them the greatest honor, that they distribute good and evil to mortals.[4] So from their birth are the *μοίραι* connected with right and wrong. Æschylus calls them *ὀρθονόμοι*, "justly awarding,"[5] and Pindar suggests their ethical nature, saying they stand apart to hide their shame at enmity among kin.[6] Conversely, there is the idea of fate in some of the uses of the word *θέμις*. It was *θέμις* that after Achilles' death no one should take Troy but his son.[7] To live without ills is *θέμις* only for the gods.[8] In these instances *θέμις* could be rendered "fated," and the intimate relation of the two ideas appears in the phrase, *μόρσιμα οὔτε φύγειν θέμις*, "It is not right to shun what is fated."[9]

The Erinyes; Expiation.

The nature of the Erinyes, or Eumenides, throws light on the Greek idea of expiation. The chorus of Eumenides in Æschylus' play say of themselves: "We are the eternal children of night, and called curses under the earth."[10] "All-pervading destiny assigned us the lot to pursue murderers of kindred till the earth covers them, and dying they are not freed from us."[11] Towards the end of the same drama[12] Athene says, "They manage all things hu-

[1] *Theogony*, 220.
[2] *Agam.*, 448.
[3] *Antigone*, 1075.
[4] *Theogony*, 904.
[5] *Eumen.*, 921.
[6] *Pyth.*, iv, 145.
[7] Soph., *Philok.*, 340; *cf. Autig.*, 880.
[8] Soph., *Frag.*, 861.
[9] Eurip., *Heraclidæ*, 615. The righteousness of fate's retributions is indicated by a phrase like this: *οὐδενί μοιριδία τίσις ἔρχεται ὧν προπάθῃ το τίνειν*. *Œd. Col.*, 228, which Jebb translates, "No man is visited by fate if he requite deeds which were first done to himself."
[10] *Eumen.*, 394.
[11] *Eumen.*, 320.
[12] *Eumen.*, 890.

man, and he who has not found them hostile (has not offended them) knows not why a sudden blow strikes him; but it is on account of his ancestors' crimes." The Erinyes are avenging goddesses. Athene herself, fearing their bane, by wise words propitiates them towards her people, and wins them to dwell propitious and honored under Mars's Hill. They were true Greek personifications of the powers that punish, and were a conception which became spiritual with the progress of ethical thought gradually laying stress on the intent with which an act is done, making that the test of crime. Far older than the notion of a human conscience, they may at an early period have been conceived to execute punishment through the mental self-torturings of the criminal. In time, however, they were almost transformed into human consciences. Thus the Eumenides of Æschylus become the visions of a fevered imagination with Euripides. Orestes—the same Orestes, but how different!—is frenzied with a sense of what he has done. Menelaus asks him what disease is destroying him, and he answers, "Conscience, because I know that I have done dreadful deeds."[1]

Punishment; Intent.

A related phase of ethical development may be traced in the broadening of the idea of punishment. Even down to Æschylus' time, punishment was vengeance—that is, something concerning only a person injured by the crime. Æschylus does not feel that some one must punish Clytemnestra and Ægisthus; rather, Orestes must avenge the murder of his father. Otherwise, the Erinyes of a father unavenged will pursue him.[2] On the other hand, if he slay his mother, her Erinyes will pursue him, as they do in the two last plays of the trilogy. In time the idea of punishment broadened with the spiritualizing of the Erinyes. They ceased to be the curses hurled by the individual dead because he was wronged, and became the

[1] Eurip., *Orestes*, 396.

[2] See *Choëph.*, 260–297.

conscience of the wrong-doer, stinging him because he had committed a crime. Thus the idea of wrong outgrew mere thought of injury to the individual alone, and the thought came that, apart from the demand of vengeance by the wronged, the wrong-doer ought to be punished. A person might be injured irrespective of the intent of the wrong-doer; and justifiable intent or absence of intent would be no plea to his demand for vengeance. Otherwise as to the general sense that a man who has done an injury ought to be punished, and here was the path by which advanced the thought that intent was the criterion of guilt, with which thought the conception of expiation came to be connected.

In Æschylus, Clytemnestra's Erinyes pursue Orestes. Vengeance is sought; in the end he is delivered from them and absolved from guilt because matricide in vengeance for a father's death was justifiable, it being a greater crime to kill a husband than to kill a mother.[1] Here the old and the new are combined, the old idea of vengeance for wrong suffered, and the new idea of a deed justifiable, or the reverse, on general ethical principles. Sophocles shows clear ethical advance: "There is no guilt in involuntary wrong;"[2] "for those who err unwittingly, anger is softened."[3] The *Œdipus Coloneus* is a drama of expiation, and in it Œdipus exculpates himself on the ground that crimes unwittingly commited are not blameworthy. "My acts have been sufferings rather than deeds,"[4] says he. "Bloodshed, incest, misery,—all this thy lips have launched against me, all this that I have borne, woe is me! by no choice of mine! For such was the pleasure of the gods, wroth, haply, with the race from of old. Take me alone, and thou couldst find no sin to upbraid withal, in quittance whereof I was driven to sin thus against myself and against my kin. Tell me now, if by voice of oracle some divine doom was coming

[1] See *Eumen.*, 203, etc.
[2] Soph., *Frag.*, 599.
[3] Soph., *Trach.*, 727.
[4] *Œd. Col.*, 266.

on my sire, that he should die by a son's hand, how couldst thou justly reproach me therewith, who was then unborn, whom no sire had yet begotten, no mother's womb conceived? And if, when born to woe, as I was born, I met my sire in strife and slew him, all ignorant of what I was doing and to whom, how couldst thou justly blame the unknowing deed?"[1]

Œdipus asserts that he had himself committed no former crime, as punishment for which he should have been driven, even unwittingly, to commit other heinous crimes; and he completes his defence by saying, whatever he did, he did not willing it. When a man errs, however, life and the consequences of the wrong may not ask as to intent, and retribution often follows on the act itself. Œdipus has unwittingly done frightful deeds. Life will not wholly remit their penalties. His subsequent life is to be one long expiation, with the result that he die at peace with God, yet himself unforgiving towards his own sons, who had wronged him knowingly. His curses on them still echo while the story of his "passing" is told. There is no forgiveness taught for intentional crime, nor any notion that enemies should be forgiven. Yet the *Antigone* contains the idea that repentance is always well.[2] Teiresias tells Creon, to err is human, but he who turns to repentance may not be unblest.

Phases of Greek Ethical Development.

These, then, were phases of Greek ethical development: a broadening of the conception of vengeance to that of punishment, a growth of the idea of expiation out of that of reparation to the person injured, a recognition of the injustice of entailing a curse on children for the crimes of parents, and a clearer thought that crimes unwittingly committed might

[1] *Œd. Col.*, 965, etc., Jebb's translation. Œdipus is on the verge of the problem how to reconcile God's foreknowledge with human freedom of will.

[2] Soph., *Antig.*, 1023, etc. A further note of the growing spiritualization of Greek ethics is found in Sophocles' conviction that prayer is more important than rites, *Œd. Col.*, 485; and he conceives that a god may understand even unuttered prayers.—*Elektra*, 657; *cf. Frag.*, 854.

be expiated, finally that they were not crimes at all.[1] So blamelessness or guilt should depend on the intent of the doer of the deed. This principle, however, did not see the ethical criterion solely in the intent accompanying an act, but rather included the general sum of personal intentions, motives, and tendencies constituting self, fully recognizing the responsibility of the human being for his character and all acts springing from it. The Greeks asserted this responsibility, not to be evaded, of the human individual for himself, and they recognized differences of character and faculty in men as facts of which reasonable ethics should not complain but take account. So Pindar, a great ethical poet, sang in many notes, how that the mightiest factor of a man's achievement was his inborn nature (*φυά*), the inborn virtue of a scion of noble stock;[2] that is, as it were, the divine favoring fate within him.[3] Says Heraclitus finally, *ἦθος ἀνθρώπῳ δαίμων*,—Character is a man's genius.

Ἀνάγκη

So, then, a man's lot is in part conditional upon his acts, and fate avenges, punishes. But the ethical moment is not the sole factor in destiny. Human life lies not altogether within the pale of ethical considerations. Mortality binds it with necessity—*ἀνάγκη*. This is also fate, and never ceases to be fate. So fate never became entirely ethical, but always stood for those limitations on humanity proceeding from man's mortal nature and circumstances out of his control.

and the Gods.

From the early epic representations of the gods, wherein theogonic function had been transformed to all manner of human immorality, the higher modes of later Greek poetry, as well as Greek philosophy, each in its own way, should clear itself, and more readily because of the plastic excellence of these

[1] Says Demosthenes, *De Corona*, 338, "Men bestow anger and punishment on those who do wrong knowingly, pardon on those who err unwittingly."

[2] See *Ol.*, ii, 94; ix, 100; xiii, 13.

[3] See *Ol.*, ix, 28, 110.

early artist creations. Nevertheless, certain fundamental conceptions did not cease to be a wellnigh determining factor in all modes of Hellenic thinking, artistic as well as philosophic. These appear first in the Homeric limitations of the functions and power of the gods, supplemented by the Homeric idea of fate. Homer's gods did not create the universe, and in everything there was the brute force over which the gods had scant control. Here were thoughts which should maintain themselves as the physically necessary, unethical elements of fate, till, through Greek philosophy, they should be shaped to conceptions of natural law. To the Greeks their gods might never represent all the powers outside of man and stronger than him; events might not be brought completely within divine governance. As thoughts of the gods, finally of Zeus almost single and supreme, were purified, they might maintain themselves in correspondence with lofty ethical ideas; the gods might become the upholders of all righteousness, and identify themselves with the ethical side of fate. But fate's brute, necessary modes endured despite the gods, admitting no ethical solvent. They were rigid facts, data which human conduct, to be reasonable, fully ethical, must take account of.

Thoughts of the Gods and Thoughts of Life.

Since the functions of Greek gods never broadened to control all life, Greek thought constantly varies, now bringing more of life, now less, and again nothing, it may be, within the scope of deity's control. The poets hold the gods personified, and tend to see most of life lying in divine hands. The philosophers take from the gods distinct individuality, anon all personality, and tend to see law everywhere and over all. Greek ideals of life, in their ethical development and spiritualization, may be followed in the poets' thoughts of the gods and human conduct. It will be plainly noticeable how the Greek ideal of conduct and the best good for man comes with increasing clearness to inhere in the man himself, not in his circumstances,—another phase, indeed, of Greek spiritualization.

Even in the Homeric hymns, the gods have begun to lay aside human frailty.[1] The hymn to Ares shows far loftier thought of that god than the epics, and another hymn tells how Hephæstus with Athene taught mortals to live like civilized beings, not in caves like beasts.[2] With Hesiod, times are changed. No longer is sung the splendor of great and cruel deeds, but justice and temperance and industry. The *Theogonia*, with all the horrible necessities of its myths of monstrous engenderings, presents the picture of progress from chaos to divine rule. In the *Erga* there is already the idea of punishment, not personal vengeance, from God; and Zeus has become a just awarder of rewards and punishments to men,—Zeus, who implanted justice in men, while he ordained that fishes, birds, and beasts should devour each other.[3] Hesiod disapproves evil strife, yet approves another kind of contention for mortals,—emulation, one neighbor trying to outdo another in wealth.[4] He has many maxims of homely prudence: Take thought for the winter. Have thine own wagon; when thou needest to borrow, it may be refused. He advises work: Hunger attends the idle; labor is no shame, but idleness,[5] and—for Zeus is just—wealth obtained by force and fraud prospers not,[6] and a man devising ill for another fashions it for himself.[7] Hesiod is still far from prizing toil as a discipline and means of improvement; better if one could live without it, like the blessed beings of the Golden Age, when the earth brought forth of her free will.[8] On the whole, he counsels moderation.[9]

Bravest of the lyric poets, Tyrtæus sings the praise of valor. He praises not mere size and strength, but cour-

[1] Hardly in the hymn to Hermes!

[2] Hymns viii and xx.

[3] See *Erga*, 239, 267, 276–281.

[4] *Erga*, 11.

[5] *Erga*, 302, 311.

[6] *Erga*, 320, 352.

[7] *Erga*, 265.

[8] *Erga*, 109, etc.

[9] *Erga*, 694, 720; *cf. Erga*, 40, 41.

age and readiness to die for one's country.[1] The lyric poets do not sustain this strong note. Many of them lived in the all too happy islands of Ionia, where the spirit of civic freedom might not maintain itself as in Hellas. Soon comes Mimnermus, bewailing the shortness of life,[2] yet he has moral ideas, and cares for truth.[3] Sage Solon is more wholesome in his esteem of heaven-bestowed prosperity and good repute. He wishes to be dear to his friends, terrible to his enemies, and possessed of riches rightly acquired; for god-given wealth abides, but ἄτη soon mingles with what comes through evil deeds, and sharply the anger of Zeus descends on the evil-doer, or his children atone.[4] The abstract worth of justice is now coming to be appreciated.[5] Much attributed to Theognis shows a growing complexity of life.[6] He has many clear-headed worldly precepts, often is pessimistic, and finds fault with the apparent course of things: Who can honor the gods, seeing the evil prosper?[7] And he shows small hope of anything after death.[8] Simonides Iambograph has also dreariness enough. Life is short, and death ends the matter, say many of the lyric poets; but Simonides of Keos presents another immortality, as he sings the fame and fair fortune of those who died at Thermopylæ and Platea.[9]

To conquer in the contest drives away care, says Pin-

[1] Tyrtæus, 12, 1; *ib.*, 10, 1, are the well-known lines:

> Τεθνάμεναι γὰρ καλὸν ἐπὶ προμάχοισι πεσόντα
> ἄνδρ' ἀγαθὸν περι ῇ πατρίδι μαρνάμενον.

[2] Mimnermus, 1, 10; 2, 5; 5.
[3] *Ib.*, 8.
[4] Solon, 13, 1, etc.
[5] See Phocylides, 17.
[6] *Cf.* Κύρνε, φίλους κατὰ πάντας ἐπίστρεφε ποικίλον ἦθος, ὀργὴν συμμίσγων ἥντιν ἕκαστος ἔχει, Theognis, 213.
[7] Theognis, 743; see *ib.*, 425; but *cf.* *ib.*, 687.
[8] Κείσομαι ὥστε λίθος, Theog., 568. See *ib.*, 973, 1047.
[9] Simonides of Keos, 4; and Mackail, *Greek Anthology*, p. 140.

dar;[1] he who has achieved does not think of death.[2]

Pindar.

Victory in the games loves song, the fittest follower of crowns and valiant deeds,[3] which hide ye not in silence.[4] The report living after a man reveals his life to the poets;[5] but one who has achieved, if his deeds are unsung, goes to Hades having breathed vainly and gained short joy.[6] What is man? A shadow dream, a thing of a day; yet god-given glory may make his life serene.[7] Fame compensates for life's shortness; mortal achievement is of absolute worth despite mortality. The Greeks of Pindar's time hardly conceived of anything as fine which was unknown to fame.

Clearly the Greeks viewed achievement, saw wherein it consisted and its difficulties. Well they knew what endeavor was needed to excel among Greeks, and how hard to gain was all wise skilfulness.[8] So was valorous endeavor one noble element of the fair deed. The deified incarnation of this was Heracles, the hero-god,[9] leader in the commonalty of toil. Sluggish capacities, faculty and strength which court not dangers, have no honor.[10] The poet praises toil, which, to be perfect, must attain success. "We win in the games, as in battle, as in life, by the favor of God, ourselves not lacking in valor."[11] The favor of God gives and sanctifies success, itself the proof of merit; for God favors only the worthy. Who will do, must suffer;[12] no happiness comes without toil;[13] delight follows the swifter for it.[14] Pindar did not look on the toil itself as joyful: toil was toil.[15] The victory brought

[1] *Ol.*, ii, 56.

[2] *Ol.*, viii, 72.

[3] *Nem.*, iii, 7.

[4] *Nem.*, ix, 6.

[5] *Pyth.*, i, 92.

[6] *Ol.*, x, 100. The dead beneath the earth hear of the glory of their descendants.—*Pyth.*, v, 100.

[7] *Pyth.*, viii, 92.

[8] *Σοφίαι μεν αἰπειναί*, *Ol.*, ix, 107.

[9] *Ἥρως θεός*, *Nem.*, iii, 22.

[10] *Ακίνδυνοι ἀρέται*, *Ol.*, vi, 9.

[11] *Ol.*, viii, 68; *cf. Ol.*, ix, 118.

[12] *Nem.*, iv, 31.

[13] *Pyth.*, xii, 28.

[14] *Nem.*, vii, 74.

[15] *Cf. Nem.*, x, 24. See *Nem.*, viii, 50; *Pyth.*, x, 42. Nevertheless Pindar is on the way toward Æschylus' "from suffering, knowledge."

forgetfulness of the pain. "Best physician for labors undergone is noble cheer; and songs, cunning daughters of the Muses, charm with their touch."[1]

Valor and good counsel are two virtues;[2] but the might and wisdom and eloquence of mortals come from the gods:[3] boast not; it is all Zeus.[4] And let no man be insolent, but always desire things fit for his mortality.[5] Pindar loved splendor,—the splendor of marble columns and the splendid feast, and too the splendor of the hero-past. Naturally he prized a further factor in a man's success,—his inheritance of virtue from good ancestors: The man sprung from the common herd shall hardly rival the noble-born.[6]

Pindar was indeed Greek, seeing mortality's limitations, and deeply feeling the greatness of man, kin to the gods, sprung from the same earth-mother, a thing of naught, ignorant of his destiny, but with some likeness to the greatness of mind and nature of the immortals.[7] Let man recognize what is great; above all, reverence the gods, thinking no ill things of them;[8] then honor himself in right prizing of his nature, in right understanding of his faculties, in right endeavor after the noble, fitting deed, seizing the moment. Small help in excuse, daughter of late-considering after-thought.[9] Rightly Pindar knows that wealth is a good only to the wise: Be thy life simple, such as the wise praise,[10] and hope that god-given glory will crown it all. After death, there is one below to punish the evil; but those who have kept troth and their

[1] *Nem.*, iv, 1.

[2] See *Pyth.*, ii, 63.

[3] *Pyth.*, i, 41; *Isth.*, iii, 4.

[4] *Isth.*, iv, 49. See *Pyth.*, v, 25; *Nem.*, vi, 28.

[5] See *Pyth.*, iii, 59–62; *Ol.*, ix, 30; *Ol.*, viii, 68; *Pyth.*, ii, 34; *Pyth.*, v, 122; *Pyth.*, viii, 73; *Isth.*, iv, 9; *Isth.*, vi, 44.

[6] *Ol.*, ii, 94; *Ol.*, vii, 91; *Ol.*, ix, 107; *Nem.*, i, 25; *Nem.*, iii, 40.

[7] See *Nem.*, vi, 1.

[8] See *Ol.*, ix, 40.

[9] *Pyth.*, v, 27; ix, 84.

[10] *Nem.*, viii, 36–40; *Frag.*, 235.

hands free from unjust deeds lead tearless lives in the golden islands.[1] Thus, considering both man's mortal life and what he might be beyond the grave, clearly of supreme import with Pindar was the man himself, disclosing his own nature in strenuous endeavor or sloth or insolence, and, according to his worth or worthlessness, aided or cast down by divine fortune.

Æschylus.

In Æschylus the growing ethical ideals of Greece came to expression in glorifying the qualities of Zeus, whose nature, except perhaps in the *Prometheus Bound*, contains the highest conceptions so far reached. As a poet, Æschylus would be held in the necessity laid by the Greek creative imagination on its possessors of beholding qualities and attributes embodied in great personalities and concrete facts. Wherefore his broadest ethics and profoundest thought must be included in the personalities of his gods, and move those dramas which wrought out their catastrophes under divine directing. Otherwise the artist impulse of this Titan mind would be sore hampered by the admonishings of its rational intelligence that these things were not well. The dramas of Æschylus are not thus hampered; they may be taken to contain the farthest reach of Æschylean thought, with all its moral questionings. But there is also in them, at least in the *Prometheus Bound*, a following of certain not ignoble theogonic myths which probably presented themselves as verities to the poet's mind. Such a complete poet, profound as was his thought, might not be altogether a philosopher. The artist imagination cannot but hold as felt and seen realities much that the more predominantly scientific mind subjects to sceptical analysis.

To Æschylus, Zeus could not but have form; his nature must be made of human qualities, though here the thoughtful poet would discriminate against human frailty. Æschylus thought of the gods generally as having had

[1] *Ol.*, ii, 56, etc.

beginning, and so of Zeus as having once been young and newly come to power. Was not Zeus then less wise and moderate and merciful? Young Omnipotence on the throne of his deposed progenitor, still stormful from fierce overthrow of Titans, might harshly punish the first disobedience of a subject. Being men, we sympathize with Prometheus, whose crime was excessive love for mankind. But the drama of *Prometheus Bound* does not pronounce Zeus unjust. Seeing the chained Titan, the chorus of nymphs exclaim at the tyrannical (ἀθέτως) rule of Zeus with his new-made laws,[1] but, on second thought, they ask Prometheus, "Dost thou not see thou hast erred?"[2] For themselves, they fear the power of Zeus, and pray never to come in conflict with his will.[3]

It was an ancient thought, not commonly gainsaid before the time of Æschylus, that the all-powerful ruler must be right, having the supreme justification of power and impunity. With reference to God, this principle was to tax the minds of men in many lands. In Israel the vivid questions of Job's agony were to wither to the dulled hopes of the Preacher. The ethics of man's lot lie within this problem, the problem of all pain. It is implicit in the Promethean drama, nor does the poet solve it. Zeus might be harsh; but he was supreme. Æschylus saw, therefore, no criterion by which he might be adjudged criminal. There was, moreover, another element compromising to Prometheus' case. We may be silent before the Titan's grandeur, his far vision, his scorn in pain. But he is a rebel: "I hate all the gods, all those who, having had good from me, use me ill unjustly."[4] This is almost a cry against the supreme in life. Prometheus did what seemed humanely right in benefiting mankind. But he must expiate his benefits —other great benefactors of men have done so,—for they were conferred in accordance with the law of the supreme, that, in order to benefit, one must give, himself it may be;

[1] *Prom.*, 156. [2] *Prom.*, 266. [3] *Prom.*, 535. [4] *Prom.*, 996.

this is the law of sacrifice for all attainment. Moreover, the punishment of Prometheus is partly representative of fate, in whose action there was always the element of inherent necessity, to which Plato still saw the axis of the universe fastened.[1] Though Greeks might fail to bring all life within the compass of ethical principles, a drama like the *Prometheus* is mute recognition that it is futile to consider morality apart from life's necessary limitations, which are indeed the data and environment of moral law.

But, aside from broader considerations, it is still to be remembered that the Zeus of the *Prometheus* is a theogonic Zeus fashioned to a myth. In the poet's mind he may not have represented the full moral governance of the universe. Besides which, Zeus does not state his side in the drama, the second of a trilogy. The third may have reconciled the Titan to his mighty opposite, and finally justified the supreme lord.

Other dramas of Æschylus are almost monotheistic. From the first chorus of the *Suppliants* it is clear how high above the world is Zeus, whose will is hard to discern, whose ways are dark, who hurls mortals from their towering hopes, and without exerting his strength; toilless are the workings of the divine.[2] Such the power of Zeus, lord of endless time,[3] whose mind is an abyss,[4] and his goodness equals it; he is the guardian of suffering mortals, the awarder of evil to the evil, good to the good:[5] "King of kings, of blessed ones most blessed, most mighty bringer to pass, hear and grant our prayer; ward off the wanton outrage, so hateful to thee."[6] In the *Agamemnon* the chorus of old men, feeling the burden and the sense of coming ill, can think of lightening

[1] *Rep.*, 616.

[2] *Suppliants*, 82–92.

[3] *Sup.*, 567.

[4] *Sup.*, 1043.

[5] *Sup.*, 376, 397.

[6] *Sup.*, 518, *cf. Sup.*, 586–593. "What without thee is accomplished for mortals?" *Sup.*, 802; *Agam.*, 1463.

their minds only in an appeal to Zeus, the one being fit to aid.[1]

The function of Zeus, as the awarder of evil to evil-doers, included both the idea of vengeance, which had its counterpart on earth in the natural law of retaliation,[2] and also the idea of punishment—who does wrong *ought* to be punished.[3] This had its counterpart in the law forming the basis of Æschylean ethics: the doer shall suffer the like of his deeds, evil for evil, blood for blood.[4] But men not wholly wise or just, how shall they learn? From suffering.[5] "He is wise who sings in praise of Zeus, Zeus who leads mortals to be wise, whose law it is that suffering shall teach. Mindfulness of woes past drops on the heart in sleep and makes men wise against their will."[6] Not only does Zeus punish, but it is his way that his punishments—men's sufferings—shall teach.[7] This wholesomeness of punishment for the wrong-doer himself is the crown of Æschylean ethics; it brings the gleam of hope to punishment, which is vengeance broadened by the thought of universal right. This is not far from Plato's thought that it is better for an evil man to be punished than escape.[8]

Æschylean wisdom is summed up in the great chorus of the *Eumenides:* "Let awe remain to watch the heart; wisdom through suffering profits. Who if thoughtless of consequences would revere justice? Sanction thou neither the unrestrained life, nor the life of a slave: God gives might to the golden mean. Pride is the child of impiety; but from health of soul comes fair fortune. Revere the altar of justice, nor spurn it with godless foot, thine eyes set on gain; for punishment is at hand, and a fitting outcome awaits each man. He who of his free will

[1] *Agam.*, 156.

[2] Choëph., 115, 392.

[3] See *ante*.

[4] *Agam.*, 1540, see *ib.*, 747.

[5] *Agam.*, 170, 241.

[6] *Agam.*, 168–174.

[7] Δίκα, Justice, has also the office to teach men through their sufferings. —*Agam.*, 241.

[8] Plato's *Georgias.*

is just shall not be unblessed or utterly destroyed. But the sail of the unjust shall be riven, and God mocks the rash man who thought himself secure. Wrecked on the reef of justice he perishes."[1] Notice the sequence of thought: fear may be well; suffering profits; who would restrain himself were it not for consequences? Follow the mean, which is self-restraint and temperance; be just, for the unjust perishes unawares, and the just man shall at least not be utterly comfortless. Æschylus connects the mean with the thought, from suffering, wisdom, which finds its sanction in that which it implies, the more than justice, the benevolence, of Zeus.

Sophocles.

Æschylus had set forth in language unapproachable the grandeur of Zeus and his justice; showing, too, how the finest ethical idea so far conceived—from suffering, wisdom—was Zeus's law. Sophocles laid more exclusive stress on the intent with which an act was done, and brought out the idea of expiation. More definitely than Æschylus, he asserts the identity of divine law with the highest principles of human conduct. "May destiny find me unfailing in every word and deed sanctioned by those laws sublime, born in the ether, whose father is the Sky. No mortal parent was theirs, nor shall oblivion ever lay them to sleep. A divine power is in them that grows not old."[2] The *Antigone* is the drama of the conflict between laws human and divine, nor is the issue left uncertain. Antigone stands before Creon, whose command she has set at naught by covering the corpse of Polyneices.

"*Creon.* Thou there, with the eyes fastened on the earth, dost thou confess or deny having done this?

Antigone. I admit I did it. I do not deny.

Creon. Knewest thou our edict forbidding this thing?

Antigone. I knew: how could I not?

Creon. And yet thou durst transgress the law?

Antigone. Yes; for Zeus did not proclaim it, nor jus-

[1] *Eumenides*, 491–535. [2] *Œd. Tyr.*, 863–871.

tice, dweller with the gods below; for they have laid down laws for men. Nor could I think that thine, an edict of mortal, could override the unwritten fixed laws of the gods. They are not of to-day nor yesterday, but live always, and no one knows when they began. I would not, through fear of any man's resolve, incur the judgment of the gods for their breach."[1]

In obedience to these divine laws Antigone covers her brother's body; and she dies for her act, as human beings may suffer for their obedience to the laws of God in defiance of the laws of man. Such acts are revolutionary. As she is passing to her living tomb, the chorus of Theban elders cannot but say: "From the summit of thy topping boldness, my child, thou hast fallen heavily upon the pedestal of justice. Thou art paying for some deed of thy fathers."[2] The old men feel there is something questionable in Antigone's deed, and revert to the curse in the family as a makeshift explanation of her conduct and its consequences. Antigone transgressed the king's law; and who is to declare the law of God? Sophocles did not touch this question, merely assuming tacitly that the divine law might be known from oracles and the utterances of seers, its most general and unqualified precepts being felt in the conscience of every one. But the drama leaves the conviction that the best human conduct is that conforming to the laws of God, which, in case of conflict, prevail over the ordinances of man, and woe unto him who does not know them, these inexorable laws! The chorus at the last speak a lesson of the *Antigone:* Wisdom has the chief part in happiness, and reverence towards the gods must be inviolate; great words of proud

[1] *Antigone*, 441–460.

[2] *Antigone*, 853.

[3] The deities may be pitiless against those who have offended them. At the beginning of the *Aias*, Odysseus is moved at the sight of his crazed enemy, feeling his own humanity and chance of overthrow. But Athene's face is set against Aias, and she has no pity.—Soph., *Aias*, 123, etc.

men bring their punishment of heavy blows, and in old age teach the chastened to be wise.[1]

Things go hard with mortals; the gods rule, and so they are to blame; why not cry out against them? is that not just, when fortune is insolent?[2]

Euripides.

This is the radicalism of Euripides, who will not reverence the gods when his moral reason disapproves man's fortune and their acts. Amphitryon says to Zeus: "I, a mortal, surpass thee in virtue, though thou art the great god; for I have acted better than thou."[3] Here Pindar would have seen blasphemy, and Æschylus, inconsequence, and the more reverent wisdom of the same and later times, held that such lines were impious. But Euripides, seeing that life is hard, blames it lightly on the gods, whom he half disbelieves in.[4] Yet he has the remnants of the good morality which thought success to be the child of endeavor;[5] only one never feels sure that he is speaking heartily in such strains; he rolls his morals out so easily: "There are three virtues which thou shouldst revere: honor the gods, and those who nourished thee, and the laws common to Greece."[6] Euripides had a great faculty of speaking in the characters of his *dramatis personæ;* with weakened ethical convictions, he could the more easily put himself in another's place. He has still the belief of the older dramatists, that crime and injustice do not prosper; and who can put it better than Euripides? *βραχεῖα τέρψις ἡδονῆς κακῆς.*[7] Yet any

[1] *Antig.*, 1347–1352.

[2] Euripides, *Suppl.*, 552.

[3] Eurip., *Hercules Furens*, 342.

[4] Euripides' bitter sayings about the gods are scattered through his works; see *Fragments*, 294, 893; *Troades*, 469; *Hercules Furens*, 1319. But *cf. ib.*, 1345; these sayings accord with his saws on life's hardness,—*e. g.*, *οἴμοι: τί δ' οἴμοι; θνητά τοι πεπόνθαμεν.* *Frag.*, 302, from the lost *Bellerophontes*, a true Euripidean note. See also *Frag.*, 662.

[5] *Frag.*, 477, *πονός γαρ, ὥς λέγουσιν, εὐκλείας πατήρ.* Notice the *ὥς λέγουσιν.* See also *Frag.*, 366, 239, 242.

[6] *Frag.*, 219.

[7] *Frag.*, 364; *cf. Frag.*, 305.

one can utter moral saws, and the finer, truer morality of the older dramatists is seen rather in the soundness which inheres in the structure of their plays and the outcome of each drama or trilogy, which is to such Euripidean utterances as living a good life is to preaching it. Euripides must have felt that he understood all the thoughts of his predecessors. His was an intellect that saw the highest and subtlest principles; hardly a pre-Christian maxim or precept which he did not consider and express.[1] Whether he felt them, who knows? Not Euripides!

Comparing Æschylus with Euripides, it is noticeable that the spiritualization of ethical principles is completed, and there is no longer doubt that intent is the criterion of innocence or guilt. This spiritualization shows itself also in the delineation of passion. Nothing can exceed Clytemnestra's hatred of Agamemnon: "And a third blow—thank-offering to the gods below—as he lay, I gave him. He gasped; from the wound his blood gushed over me, a shower as gladdening as the rain of Zeus to the bursting blade of corn."[2] As an expression of bloody physical hate, this passage is unequalled; yet Medea's hatred of Jason is to Clytemnestra's as mind to body. She has slain hers and Jason's children, and has murdered Jason's new bride, her own supplanter. She stands in the sun-chariot, with the two dead children at her feet, Jason below, weeping, pleading to bury them, or even to touch them. Says Medea, "Go home and bury your wife." Answers Jason, "I go bereaved of my children." And this last thrust from Medea: "You do not grieve yet. Wait for old age!"[3] This is intellectual hatred, but as intense as the glad blood-bath of Clytemnestra.

With this complete spiritualization, this intellectuality and thoughtfulness, has come scepticism, hesitation, and sophistic moralizing. "The mind is a god in each of us."[4] So be it, Euripides, and a god that speaks with a

[1] See *e.g. Frags.*, 642, 198, 926, 746, and indeed his works *passim*.

[2] *Agam.*, 1356, etc. [3] *Medea*, 1394. [4] *Frag.*, 1007.

queer divergency. "We know the good, and do not work it out, from laziness, or setting some pleasure first."[1] This is the weak divergence of intelligence from desire, which comes with waning moral strength. "The tongue swore, but the heart remained unbound."[2] More divergence and spiritualization. But here at last is what Euripides really feels: "One has opinions; but the truth we have not, child."[3]

Conduct; Public Men.

These thoughts on life and ethical principles suggest the conduct which the lives of the best Greeks exemplified. The elements of right conduct were intelligence supported by a courageous will, the intelligence showing itself in a fair view of the circumstances making up the man's environment, in a correct judgment as to what was possible for him, in a choice of the very best or greatest or noblest attainable by him, in the avoidance of excess, in never setting great store on things unworthy of great pains, in abstaining from those acts which the ethical standards of his time declared wrong, and in keeping the mind balanced in the midst of success, and so avoiding insolence and folly. The courageous will was needful to enable the man, among the vicissitudes of life, to do in all dangers what his intelligence told him was best, to die for his country, if needs be.

These qualities are shown by a statesman of the best type, like Pericles.[4] He chose for himself the highest pursuits, knowing himself capable; he kept his mind set on them, never decoyed by any lure; his conduct showed perfect self-control and courage, consisting in a knowledge of what is to be feared and what not, and in acting accordingly. That he was correct in judging himself fit to be a leader of the state, is shown by the fitness of all his measures for the good of Athens. He estimated her

[1] *Hippolytus*, 380. [2] *Ibid.*, 612. [3] *Frag.*, 18.

[4] So, in a different way, does Socrates' life exhibit them all, and very perfectly.

power and resources accurately, and perfectly he judged her character and its possibilities; likewise as to her external relations and the measures proper for her, his judgment was perfect. Never was a crisis more perfectly understood than the approach of the Peloponnesian war was by him. That war was sure to come, and so he said; Athens was sure to win, if she would follow the course he planned for her. The event proved him right, Athens losing only because, after his death, she abandoned his policy. And even now the ruins of the Parthenon bear witness that Pericles' statesmanship included the whole well-being of the state.

Many Greek statesmen, although possessing great intelligence and marvellous faculty of devising means, came to grievous ends because in success their love of glory was turned to vanity, and they failed to keep their poise; they were guilty of ὕβρις and ἄτη; or they sinned against the principle of μηδὲν ἄγαν, giving too much—their good repute—for worthless gains. An instance of this less perfect type is Themistocles; gifted with as keen intelligence as ever mortal man, in great success his character failed him. So he fell, nor had the courage to remain nobly fallen, mindful of his country, and holding to the noble selfishness called patriotism, which might have restored him to Athens and preserved his glory; but he must needs, in his vanity and eagerness of self, become a traitor to all that had made him Themistocles. Other examples of this less perfect type are Miltiades, who also lost his poise; Alcibiades, who never had poise or honesty of purpose, and whose vanity doomed him from his youth; or Pausanias and other Spartans, who could not refuse bribes.

Greek Freedom.

Evidently it was essential to all Greek careers, indeed to all admirable and characteristic Greek action, as well as to the development of the underlying principles and views of life, that the individual should have power to shape his life according to his will,—that he should be free. The thought of freedom is not to be dissociated from any mode of Greek life, private or public. It was an element, not only of Greek citizenship, but of Greek manhood. The life of the Greek man in his individual interests and family relationships was unimpeded by rigid complexities of ceremonial observance. The capable man knew enough of life and its rules of right and wrong to regulate his conduct; the wise father could lead his household in matters of daily right relationship to superhuman powers. There grew up in Greece no numerous class of priests, necessary intermediaries between men and gods, and so authoritative regulators of men's daily lives. The Greek ordered his life in his relations to the divine as well as human, an ordering which, if free, was careful and strenuous. In his civic relationships, likewise, should the Greek be free, strenuously self-ordered. And in great Greek days citizens put more on themselves than any tyrant ever imposed on subjects. But these self-orderings and impositions of tasks upon themselves should all be along the lines of conduct, achievement, attainment, self-perfecting development approved by Greek intelligence and prompted by the full compass of Greek desire.

The Greek State; Aristotle's Views.

The Greek city-state itself, the *πόλις*, might be regarded either as government or as the sum total of the lives and interests of its citizens. But however regarded, the qualities and principles of conduct admired in a state were the same as those admired in an individual. Indeed under the latter aspect, as Plato, Aristotle, or Pericles sought ever to regard the state, it was the citizen writ large. "For those who believe that a good life in the case of an individual depends upon wealth, agree in considering that the state also as a whole is happy if it is wealthy; those who hold a life of tyranny in most honor for individuals, will all say that the state which has the largest number of subjects is the happiest; and one who recognizes in virtue the source of an individual's happiness, will assert that the more virtuous state also is the happier."[1]

Seen from the outside, a Greek city-state was an autonomous community, walled in, and surrounded by an area of appertinent country. Athens, the largest of them, was originally formed from the consolidation of several small neighbor communities. Sparta was itself smaller than Athens, but had a large area of land—Laconia—which was occupied by a subject population. The governments of these city-states are usually classed under heads of Monarchy, Aristocracy, and Democracy. Any of these forms might contain what Greek sentiment approved. And they differed from their "perversions" by possessing universally admired qualities which the latter lacked,—intelligence, reverence, self-restraint, temperance, the outcome of which in a government is adjustment of function to capacity, and law-abidingness, or what Socrates calls justice.[2] Monarchy was the oldest. Sanctioned by Homer, it existed in Sparta through historic times. The carefully limited dual monarchy of Sparta was perhaps more widely respected than any other government in Greece. A tyranny differed from a monarchy in that it began in seizure of what the tyrant had no right to,—supreme power. Then, in contrast to the rightly ruling king, the tyrant sought not his subjects' good; but was unrestrained, irreverent of right, guilty of ὕβρις, the insolence of outrage; to kill him canonized the slayer. Aristocracies were next in order of origin; Aristotle calls their perversions Oligarchies. Here again there was nothing in the form which prevented the government from containing much approved by Grecian sentiment. A government of this form might be time-honored, like that of the Bacchiadæ at Corinth; it might refrain from outrage, might be law-abiding. More frequently an oligarchy was a many-headed tyrant, licentious, evil-minded to the many. Finally a democracy

[1] Arist., *Politics*, vii, 2.

[2] Xen., *Memorabilia*, iv, 4.

might be also good or bad, reverent or shameless. At Athens democracy came gradually. Aristocratic elements were perhaps predominant even under Solon's laws. The democracy is completed under Pericles, and after his time suffered with the state's decline.[1] The Athenian democracy fascinated Greece, and probably few can follow its course without thinking that on the whole it held more elements admirable from an Hellenic point of view than any other Greek government. It came to embody the early Solonian precept that no citizen should be unconcerned in the state's political welfare. For Solon had enacted that when there were civic disturbances, whoever did not take up arms for one side or the other should be disfranchised and have no part in the city.[2] And perhaps more temperately than any other Grecian city, yet with unfaltering bravery and resolution, Athens fulfilled the old saying of Heraclitus: "The people must fight for its laws as for its walls."

Thus the righteousness of a Greek city-state, viewed as government, lay in the observance of law and the maintenance of justice. From the side of the citizen, it meant immunity from despotic robbery and outrage, the preservation of what the customs and thought of the Greek communities recognized as his rights; and within the compass of these rights, it meant liberty.

As in Greece it could not but be recognized as misfortune to be debarred from the exercise of that portion of human faculty and freedom which employs itself in political government, the matter of the form of government could raise the question of lawfulness and justice from the point of view of the right of every citizen to participate therein. This becomes clearer when the state is regarded not merely as the governing function in the community, but as the community itself, viewed as an organism wherein the citizens are members, an organism,

[1] *Cf.* Aristotle's *Constitution of Athens.*

[2] Aristotle's *Ib.*, viii.

therefore, that includes and is the totality of the purposes and attainments which their lives may compass. The right of the citizen to participate in the government of the state is then a right to participate in the control and freedom, the higher life, of this supreme and comprehensive organism. The evolution of Athenian democracy presents the most luminous illustration of this principle, a principle, however, which Aristotle thought should remain subject to limitations set by the citizens' fitness to participate in the government. The state, says he, "is an association of households and families in well-being with a view to a complete and independent existence . . . in a life of felicity and nobleness. The object of the political association is not merely a common life but noble action. And from this it follows that they who contribute most to the association, as so conceived, possess a larger interest in the state than they who are equal or superior in personal liberty, or birth, or wealth, but inferior in political virtue."[1] But democrats "hold that justice is equality; and so it is, but not for all the world, but only for equals," while oligarchs hold that "inequality is justice; and so it is, but only for unequals. Both put out of sight one side of the relation. . . . The oligarchs, if they are superior in a particular point, viz., in money, assume themselves to be superior altogether; while the democrats, if they are equal in a particular point, viz., in personal liberty, assume themselves to be equal altogether."[2] Each party represents but a partial justice. Were the state an association for increasing the multitude of possessions, the oligarchs would be right. Thereupon he points out the fallacy in the view that inferiority in one respect, wealth for instance, implies inferiority in all respects, and renders a man unfit to share in the government,[3] and he argues conversely that not

[1] *Politics*, iii, 9, Weldon's translation.

[2] *Ib.*, iii, 9; see also v, 1.

[3] *Ib.*, iii, 13.

every superiority entitles its possessor to a larger share in the government.[1]

With Aristotle, ethics, the well-being of the individual, leads up to politics, the well-being of the state: "We have seen that in all sciences and arts the end proposed is some good, that in the supreme of all sciences and arts, *i.e.*, the political faculty, the end is pre-eminently the highest good, and that justice, or in other words, the interest of the community, is the highest good."[2] He thought every form of government perverted which did not aim at the well-being of the entire community, but sought only to benefit an individual or a class; tyranny—a perversion of kingship—is for the benefit of the tyrant; oligarchy—a perversion of aristocracy—for the benefit of the rich; democracy—a perversion of the polity—for the benefit of the poor.[3] He always had in mind an ideal polity, consisting in a right mingling of aristocratic and democratic elements, making a mean between the two.[4] Love of the mean follows him through his political discussions, in which he regards the middle class as most fortunate, and as the class which should hold the balance of power between the poor and the rich.[5] He speaks of the occasional advisability of getting rid of pre-eminent individuals—as Periander sagely cut off the tallest heads—even in governments which are not perversions. No painter, says he, admits anything, however beautiful in itself, out of proportion

[1] *Politics*, iii, 12.

[2] *Ib.*, iii, 12, Weldon's translation; see also *Nich. Ethics*, i, 1. Though Aristotle was not a man of affairs, a grasp of political matters was given him by his knowledge and his aptitude for systematizing. While not always free from prejudices, he could be impartial. Not conservative himself, he saw the value of conservatism and the import of initial changes. "There is no parallel in altering an art and altering a law. For all the potency of a law to receive obedience depends upon habit, and habit can only be formed by lapse of time."—*Politics*, ii, 8. On the other hand, he remarks, it is not what is ancient, but what is good, that the world wants.—*Ib.*

[3] *Ib.*, iii, 7. [4] See *Ib.*, iv, 9, 11; v, 9. [5] *Ib.*, iv, 11.

to the rest of his picture.[1] In discussing political matters, Aristotle seems to be drawn by the exigencies of the subject from his idea that a life of contemplation is the best. Such a life it were futile to expect from a community.[2] Yet although when laying stress, as he needs must, on virtue as the chief good for a state, he lets the contemplative life pass from his view, he ever and again returns to the thought that the highest life is the speculative, and finds truth in this thought for states as well as individuals.[3]

Like the individual, then, of which it is the greater counterpart, the state cannot have happiness without the qualities on which it depends,—valor, justice, prudence, and temperance—nor the highest happiness without philosophy.[4] So speaks Aristotle. It was no peculiar view of his that the well-being of the state and of the individual are the same. The ideal conduct for the state was the same as for the citizen, and when success and glory came to states, it was through the same qualities that made the statesman great. In the various Greek city-commonwealths these qualities existed in different degrees, some communities possessing more of one good quality, others more of another, and through the same besetting sins which ruined statesmen, came the fall of states. Athens is ever the example; she had the intelligence and she had the courage, she set her heart on herself and her glory as worthy of all hazard and exertion. Therefore she overcame at Marathon; therefore, giving up her city, she saved herself and Greece, and all of us to-day, it may be, from pernicious Asia; therefore she would never join with Persia to enslave Greece; therefore she rose to empire, and crowned herself with garlands of great

[1] *Politics*, iii, 13. Yet, after all, Aristotle returns to his logic as to the rightful grounds of political authority, and asserts that an individual overwhelmingly pre-eminent in virtue ought to rule.—*Ib.*

[2] The best life for the state "is one which possesses virtue furnished with external advantages to such a degree as to be capable of actions according to virtue."—*Ib.*, viii, 1.

[3] *Ib.*, vii, 3.

[4] *Ib.*, vii, 1.

deeds and fame, and made her city beautiful. And after this, ready enough was she to fight that she might hold her empire and her glory. But Athens failed to keep her poise; she aspired to conquests beyond her strength, she too was guilty of ἄτη and ὕβρις.

Civic Liberty.

The racial superiority of Aryan peoples of Europe over their Asiatic kin markedly appears in their capacity for developing the free institutions of self-government, after emerging from early rude intolerance of restraint. No Asiatics made this advance. As Vedic Indians or Persians laid aside their first mountain bravery, they laid their liberty aside. Their strength of character, their power of civic self-ordering, did not reach to the complicated exigencies of civilized life. In Europe, peoples of kindred stock have passed out of savagery and thence under primitive kingships. At this stage, with Asiatic Aryans, the limitations on the king's power make impotent surrender to absolute monarchy. With Greeks and Romans, like early limitations gather strength, and positively assert themselves as rights of other members of the community to participate in its direction. Thenceforth the irresponsible rule of a monarch is held a thing unreasonable, monstrous, and unjust. "That is not a city which belongs to one man."[1]

In Greece, this was primarily a matter of rational, strenuous self-assertion of the individual—of the mass of individuals constituting the city-state. First, the better few assert themselves against the single king; then comes the self-assertion, often bloody, of wider circles of individuals against the grasping oligarchs. Along with this primary mode of the struggle goes endeavor to remove the arbitrary element from authority, and in its place compel ruling individuals or bodies, in the use of their powers, to follow not their good pleasure or peculiar lust, but that which had been formulated as right and recognized as law, whether declared in the form of codes or existing in the

[1] Soph., *Antig.*, 735.

definite consciousness of the community. This endeavor, if successful, issues in constitutional government administering law. Such a government is the highest expression of consensual civic freedom; and the liberty of the citizen consists in maintaining it, holding it to unfailing correspondence with the varying needs and advancing life of the community, and in obeying it. Civic liberty did not absolve from duties, but imposed them: "Stranger, tell the Lacedæmonians that here, obedient to their laws, we lie." This immortal epitaph is a consummate expression of Greek liberty.

That the Greek city-states were enabled to evolve these modes of self-government and maintain liberty, was due to Greek rational intelligence ordering the full compass of Greek desires, and to the strength of those desires ordered thus, and thus transformed into the energy of character which, through the great days of Greece, empowered Greeks to do the dictates of their reason. In lowly mode this strength of character showed itself in laying aside the luxuriant flowing eastern garb, and turning to a hardier, more athletic dress. First this change was made in Sparta, when her citizens imposed on themselves the terrific Lycurgan *régime* of life;[1] then were like changes made at Athens, as her spirit rose and chastened itself. So throughout Greece such reforms accorded with the intelligent strength of mind with which the Greek set about purposefully to perfect his physique. In mode sublime this same energy was shown in the sacrifice of hearth and home whereby Athens guarded her trust of liberty from the Persian.

Honor, Temperance, Beauty.

The relation of duty on the part of the citizen towards his city was a matter of this strength of character directed by intelligence. It is well summed by such a word as *αἰδώς*, which is a twofold sentiment, reverence for all things to be desired and revered, and shame at all things shortsighted, evil, shameful, unreasonable, and so cowardly. It was

[1] Thucyd., i, 6.

the Greek honor, a reflex of the sum of ethical approvals become instinctive in the strong character which they had moulded.[1] It was a sentiment of intelligence, a child of forethought, as Pindar most Greekly calls it, *προμαθέος αἰδώς* which puts valor in men.[2]

Education should accustom Greek youths to *αἰδώς*,[3] as a habit of the soul, whereby habitually and instinctively they might shun base things, and obey the dictates of reverence. This principle touched all parts of life; but especially from its inculcation should youths gain devotion to the city and courage to die for it. Despite much intractable individuality and selfishness among the Greeks, and the frequent partisan hatred which narrowed Greek souls, nevertheless, till times of decadence, all-mastering was the sentiment of standing steadfast unto death for that higher unity of interest, the city, which held the citizen and all his interests within its greater worth.[4]

"They fled from dishonor," says Pericles over the fallen Athenians, "but on the battle-field their feet stood fast."[5] And the dominant note of the great funeral oration is honor, glory, and the undying fame won by enlightened and courageous discharge of duty to the state. Athens's bitter enemies had said of her citizens: "Their

[1] Thus it appears in Homer. "Why, Glaucus," says Sarpedon, "is high honor paid to thee and me in Syria, and all look on us as gods? and for what do we hold a great and fair demesne by the banks of Xanthus? Wherefore now foremost among the Lycians must we withstand the burning fight, so that they may say, not inglorious are these kings of ours who rule in Lycia and eat fat sheep and drink sweet wine."—*Iliad*, xii, 13. With a like sense of *noblesse s'oblige* Odysseus feels that he must rescue his vanished comrades on Circe's island.

[2] *Ol.*, vii, 44.

[3] *Cf.* Hermann, *Handbuch*, vol. iv., § 34.

[4] The absorbing interest of the Greek in his city showed itself in his loving adornment of it with fair buildings, while throughout all the great days of Greece private dwellings remained slight and unadorned. Indeed the home-life seems meagre compared with civic life. Greeks lived in the market-place, in the law-courts and political assemblies, in the gymnasia, and later in the schools of philosophy.

[5] Thucydides, ii, 42; *cf.* Thucyd., i, 144.

bodies they devote to their country as though they belonged to other men; their true self is their mind, which is most truly their own when employed in her service."[1] Love of the state is the most enlightened love of self. "I would have you day by day fix your eyes upon the greatness of Athens, until you become filled with the love of her; and when you are impressed with the spectacle of her glory, reflect that this empire has been acquired by men who knew their duty and had the courage to do it, who in the hour of conflict had the fear of dishonor always present to them, and who, if ever they failed in an enterprise, would not allow their virtues to be lost to their country, but freely gave their lives to her as the fairest offering which they could present at her feast. The sacrifice which they collectively made was individually repaid to them; for they received again each one for himself a praise which grows not old and the noblest of all sepulchres. I speak not of that in which their remains are laid, but of that in which their glory survives, and is proclaimed always and on every fitting occasion both in word and deed. For the whole world is the sepulchre of famous men."[2]

Shame was the spur, fame the goal. Achilles in his boyhood made great deeds his play,[3] and in his manhood gave his life for fame. Says Pindar, *οἴκοθεν μάτευε*,[4] "seek at home," look to your virtues and accomplishments; these, which are yourself,—nothing else,—shall give you glory. Greeks cared much for wealth; wise Greeks saw there could come much good from it, when the possessor had also wisdom. Yet wealth was recognized as but an accessory and possession. Possessions might satisfy a barbarian,[5] give him glory, but not a

[1] Thucyd., i, 70. Speech of Corinthian envoys at Sparta.

[2] Thucyd., ii, 43. These extracts from Thucydides are from Jowett's translation.

[3] Pind., *Nem.*, iii, 43.

[4] *Ib.*, iii, 31.

[5] Great was Persian wonder that Greeks strove for olive crowns.—Herod. viii, 26.

Greek. Glory and fame came to Greeks from deeds done, not from things possessed.[1] Fame was the crown of toil, making men immortal. "To all men equally cometh the wave of death; and falleth on the fameless and the famed; howbeit honor ariseth for them whose fair story God increaseth to befriend them when dead."[2] He whose heart is set on valor, giving up wealth and toiling therefor and doing noble deeds, deserves the meed of praise and fame;[3] meet for such deeds is divine song,[4] which adds to fame, itself beautiful, the element of formal beauty.

The spiritual splendor, fame, is brought by success, the fitting outcome of endeavor. It was not natural with a Greek to think of merit without thinking of it as completed by success. Success made beautiful the man's endeavor; it came from the union of virtue with good fortune: "When a man hastens, God joins him,"[5] a principle of Homer as well as Æschylus. It is possible to feel the beauty of a career like Timoleon's, of complete divine success, and the perfectness of it. Feeling its beauty, if we think how the Greeks regarded such success as the stamp of divine recognition of excellence, we shall understand how it called forth their reverence.

To the Greeks of the best Greek days, all sides of life and modes of viewing it were so correlated in the bonds of reason that the several virtues and excellences appear as aspects of each other; they were different phases of the same rationally sanctioned principles which based themselves upon intelligent, comprehensive, all-proportioning consideration of life. In manner brave and open-

[1] See Pindar, *Pyth.*, viii, 85–100.

[2] Pind., *Nem.*, vii, 30, Myer's translation. So god-given glory may bless man who is but a shadow-dream.—*Pyth.*, viii, 92.

[3] Pind., *Isth.*, i, 43; iii, 7

[4] Pind., *Nem.*, ix, 6.

[5] Æsch., *Pers.*, 738. Demosthenes, ii Olynthiac, expresses the same thought; a man who is inert cannot expect his friends, much less the gods, to help him.

eyed, Greek ethics would take account of all life's facts. With reference to life's full content, Greek principles of conduct slowly shape themselves. These, followed strenuously, become elements of character and issue in the sense of *αἰδώς*, and this *αἰδώς* is begotten of intelligence and so relates itself to the proportioning principle of conduct—nothing too much—and of the best the most. Then these same principles, as man's inner nature, represent the condition of a mind sane and safe, moderate, proportioning, *σώφρων* (*σῶς* and *φρήν*), whose is the quality of *σωφροσύνη*, moderation, temperance, self-restraint, that which lusts for nothing overmuch.

Σωφροσύνη,[1] as well as *αἰδώς*, was an aim in the education of youth. To aid the youth to subject his body to his mind, give him temperance and self-control, and finely harmonize his complex being, mathematics, music, harmony, and rhythm were taught.[2] Plato and Aristotle thought music had great influence in moulding character, and found in it encouragement to duty, incitement to fight and die therefor, or calm influence, toning and attuning the character, freeing it from all excess, and bringing it into a state of rhythmical, harmonious, beautiful activity.[3] Says Plato: "Rhythm and harmony sink into the recesses of the soul, and make the man graceful, if rightly trained therein; but if not, the reverse. He who has been duly nurtured in these matters will have the keenest eye for defects, whether failures of art or misgrowths of nature; and, feeling a just disdain for them, will admire beautiful objects and gladly receive them into his soul, and nourish himself on them and grow to be fair and good; and, reach-

[1] Plato in the *Charmides* makes this word elude a round of definitions.

[2] A musical education would include a knowledge of *ῥυθμός*, measured time, and *ἁρμονία*; it would include playing on the lyre, singing, and keeping step as in a chorus.—Plato, *Alcib.*, i, 108 d.

[3] Plato, *Rep.*, iii, 398-403; Aristotle, *Pol.*, viii, chaps. v–viii. Of the modes of melody or music, they approved most of all the Dorian; and disapproved the Lydian, as tending towards voluptuousness. *Cf.* D. B Monro, *Modes of Ancient Music*, p. 7, etc.

ing the age when reason comes to men, will welcome her as akin to himself, because he has been thus nurtured. Men never become truly musical until they know the essential forms (or ideas) of temperance and courage and liberality and munificence and all akin to these, and their opposites. Surely, then, what fairer spectacle can there be to him who has an eye to see, than that of a man who, with beauty of soul, combines beauty of form corresponding and harmonizing with the beauty within, because having share in the same pattern? He who is truly musical will love only such men, and will not love him in whom there is dissonance."[1]

The principle of *αἰδώς* holds many of life's weightier matters; but life's lighter, subtler, lovelier phases escape its loftiness. Σωφροσύνη is somewhat negative, keeping men from excess. And these principles are not altogether final, inasmuch as neither holds the thought of the all-complete perfection which gives joy. There was, however, applicable to conduct a thought final, positive, and all-inclusive; all-inclusive, in that it compassed whatever *αἰδώς* held and all the joy-inspiring loveliness which did not clearly come within its scope; positive, in that, while of a surety it forbade excess, it meant also fulness, the presence of everything which should be there; and it was final in that it held perfection. This was the thought of beauty. In the works of poets, artists, and philosophers this crowning Hellenic thought appears enlarged, enlightened, its elements clear and distinguishable. It also lived beyond these works. No act of life but presented itself to the Greek consciousness as beautiful or ugly. This thought was the stamp of what was Greek; herein Homer's Achæans prove themselves Hellenes; and in times of degeneracy, by failing to keep the thought of beauty inclusive of all life, those who were Greek by race belied their racehood, fell from the large pattern of their heritage.

[1] **Plato, *Rep.*, iii, 401 e–402 e; *cf.* Timæus, 87 c.**

Wide was the ethical significance carried in the epics by the word καλός;[1] in later literature its meaning ranged from beautiful to the eye or ear to "right."[2] Applied to conduct, it meant honorable, that which conformed to αἰδώς, and it might carry the notion of being best for the doer too. This twofold significance appears in words spoken by Antigone, καλόν μοι τοῦτο ποιούσῃ θάνειν;[3] "it will be well for me to die doing this," for "I shall rest a loved one with him I loved, sinless in my breach of human law; duties more enduring than to the living I owe to those below, where I shall be forever."[4] This incidental meaning of ultimate advantage, is often absent. Neoptolemus says: I had rather fail, doing nobly (καλῶς), than conquer dishonorably (κακῶς).[5] θέμις, the eternal right, is the Beautiful (τὸ καλόν), with the divine sanction added. "Thou art Polyneices' sire," says Antigone to Œdipus, "and though he may have wronged thee, it is not θέμις for thee to wrong him."[6] This word may contain the idea of what is fated,[7] and thus what is θέμις and καλόν is brought into relation with the moral order, a breach of which is surely avenged by fate.

Many years before Plato, had Sappho cried: "He who is beautiful to look upon is good; and who is good will

[1] See *ante*, p. 185.

[2] The word has also idiomatic meanings; *e.g.*, νῦν γὰρ ἐν καλῷ φρόνειν, "be wise in time," Soph., *Elek.*, 384, *cf. Œd. T.*, 78; see also Soph., *Elek.*, 662; Soph., *Frag.*, 849, and θεοῖς καλά, pleasing to the gods.—Soph., *Antig.*, 925.

[3] Soph., *Antig.*, 72. The words refer to the burial of her brother Polyneices.

[4] *Cf. Antig.*, 557. Elektra (Soph., *Elektra*, 237) asks how could it be καλόν for her to forget the dead. It would be neither honorable nor for one's good, for the dead avenge themselves.

[5] Soph., *Philok.*, 94; *cf.* Soph., *Aias*, 1349. So in Euripides' famous phrase, τὸ καλὸν σφαλερόν,—*Iph. in Aulis*, 21, *i.e.*, perilous honor.

[6] Soph., *Œd. Col.*, 1189, *cf. ib.*, 1031, where Œdipus would kiss th cheek of his preserver Theseus, but hardly thinks it θέμις for one polluted. In Soph., *Elek.*, 565, it is said that it would not be θέμις for polluted Clytemnestra to have direct word from Artemis.

[7] See Soph., *Philok.*, 346, and *ante*.

soon be beautiful."[1] The Lesbian trusted beauty. The perfect Attic mind of Sophocles knew the disproportionate nature of crime, and evil's ugliness; lies are not *καλόν*;[2] and so Euripides says, virtue is man's greatest beauty.[3] Leonidas thought it would not have been fitting for him to leave Thermopylæ—*οὐ καλῶς ἔχειν*;[4] and when Mardonius sent Alexander—not the Great—of Macedon to lure Athens from the cause of Hellas, there was perfect beauty in the answer of the Athenians, standing in the ruins of their city, that never would they join with Persians to enslave Greeks.[5]

[1] *Frag.*, 101.
[2] Soph., *Frag.*, 325.
[3] Eurip., *Frag.*, 1017.
[4] Herod., vii, 220.
[5] *Ib.*, viii, 140–144.

CHAPTER IX.

GREEK ART AND POETRY.

OF necessity Greek principles of conduct must be set forth and illustrated from Greek poetry and art. But not alone as sources of information, or incidentally, do these two bear witness to Greek traits, and to the desires and loves, the admirations and ideals, of the Hellenic race. For in themselves Greek poetry and art afford ideal exemplifications of all these matters, exemplifications free from the shortcomings of life's actual opportunities, and formed and fashioned that they might be perfect and have the beauty which perfection is. The exemplification is twofold, in substance and in form. The first lies in the subject chosen, the elements of life which the poem or statue shall set forth; let them be large, and in their action unimpeded, undiminished by untoward accident. The second lies in the manner of accomplishment, the formal beauty of the work of art.

Exemplification of Greek Ideals in Poetry and Art.

The subjects of Greek art and poetry are from the fund of fact and knowledge, ethical principles, and views of life, which the Greeks had gathered with experience. They relate to the compass of Greek desires—the manifold content of human life. The choice of subject also would show how the Greek desired the most of life, and with discrimination desired the best of it. Herein would also enter Greek proportioning intelligence seeking to set forth the subject chosen, and the very best and most of its essential qualities, not other lesser or irrelevant matters. So there appear in these creations largeness and unity, the qualities of the subject greatened to sublimity, and shown inevitably to be seen, unbefogged by other things. This last quality of definite unity would spring from the clearness of the Greek perception, the purity of outline of all images reflected in the Greek consciousness, and from the corresponding lucidity of Greek intellect, which kept all its concepts free of inconsistency, sharply distinguished from their contraries. Finally, the Greek visualizing, grasping, and fast-holding artistic imagination sees and shapes the content of Greek experience in concrete personality and action.

Because to high intelligence the Greeks united supreme creative artist-faculty, they recognized and illustrated in their works the broad identity of the principles underlying excellent accomplishment in all fine art, principles which, in their application to poetry, sculpture, painting, architecture, are subject only to such special variances as are imposed by the different means and material which each art employs. Well knew the Greek, knew with his mind and realized with his imagination instinctively, that the principles of artistic unity apply to all the arts; he knew that all the arts might rightly strive to set forth life's best and highest, the noblest qualities of man in grand delineations; he knew how, in all the arts, effects are heightened by contrast and proportion; and how all arts, in setting life forth, follow life. A result is that, in Greek marbles, greatened human qualities unite in ideal personalities, even as like qualities are made manifest in the character and action of Æschylus' or Sophocles' *dramatis personæ*, or appear reflected in the arduous and high accomplishment of those on whom the odes of Pindar flash a golden fame.

Pindar makes the man's fair deed show forth the greatness of the man, and exhibit human faculty heightened to sublimity and beauty; he encircles the man with a setting of his fair deeds, and each deed greatened in its pain and difficulty. No hero wins easily; strong are opponents, hard is success, and the way beset with destiny. He must be wise and strenuous who attains. Great, therefore, is the hero who is crowned: onlookers take him for a god. Or again, Pindar heightens life by setting forth the burning eagerness with which men seek its prizes; he shows how fair it is and worthy to be loved. And over all, he hangs the halo of success, divine in that it comes not without God aiding, and the man straining too.

The Greatness of Man; Pindar, the Dramatists, and Phidias.

Pindar's art evokes the hero's greatness from his deeds. Æschylus manifests man's greatness in dramatic modes. He heightens passion in its acts, shows hate's almost sublimity in Clytemnestra; he heightens the qualities of his characters by showing their acts—acts which are truly theirs—fraught with the consequences of them, and linked by fate to acts which went before; then he shows the doers of the acts uplifted through the majesty of the ethical principles which encircle them with fate's control, and displays each act commented on by furthest choric wisdom. How great the greatness of the fate-encompassed will that wrought these deeds! How great the consequential import of the man's first reddening of his hand in crime when he was free! Nor is this greatness lessened by the dark mysteriousness of answering fate, when the consequences of the doer's acts smother his vision and becloud his mind. So in grim grandeur move Æschylus' creations; and likewise, though not so Titanic, but with fuller round of human attributes, Sophocles shows completed men and women. Both poets keep proportion true, and make sublime use of contrast,—contrast of before and after the catastrophe—and admit no elements distracting, unessential.

With like intelligence, following like artistic laws, and with like all-grasping imagination, which fashions farthest life to concrete form, Phidian sculpture works; only it sets forth life full and quiescent, as suits marble. In these marble forms, life's elements are united in clear personalities, even as Sophocles or Æschylus or Pindar embodied life's inevitable laws, life's fatal bounds, life's grandeur, height and depth and glory, in Œdipean calamities and the fate-fraught deeds of Atreus's house, or in a song of glorious achievement at Olympia. And in their artist works, sculptor and poet, in modes adapted to their respective arts, but following principles essentially the same, strive for that perfection which is beauty.

The Love of Beauty.

It is common knowledge how severed, how lacking in solidarity, was the Hellenic race politically, and how bitter were its numerous envies, hates, and jealousies. Yet it always felt itself the Hellenic race, and the rest of the world barbarians. It were hard to analyze this deep and broad sentiment; but we see some of the spiritual factors which bound together all the Greeks, those who dwelt in Asia Minor, Magna Græcia, and the many islands of the Mediterranean, as well as the dwellers in Hellas. There was the common speech, and the poetry, epic and lyric poems, and afterwards the dramas; then there were the games, in which all Greeks and none else competed. But deeper than all these, or rather that of which these were manifestations, were common Hellenic traits of character, like ways of looking upon life, like thoughts, like tastes, like loves,—the love of fame, the love of knowledge, over all the love of beauty, of which last the orator Isocrates speaks in his *Helen*: "She was gifted above all others with beauty, the first of all things in majesty and honor and divineness. Nothing devoid of beauty is prized; the admiration of virtue itself comes to this, that, of all manifestations of life, virtue is the most beautiful. The supremacy of beauty over all things can be seen from our own dispositions towards it and them. Other things we seek merely to attain, as we have need of them; but beautiful things inspire us with love, love which is as much stronger than wish as its object is better. The beautiful inspire us with good-will at first sight; to them alone, as to the gods, we are never tired of doing homage, delighting to be their slaves rather than the rulers of others. Care for that gift is to us so perfectly a religion that we hold the profaners of it in themselves more dishonored than sinners against others, while we honor for all time those who have guarded the glory of their own youth in the chasteness of an inviolable shrine." [1]

From the beginning, the love of beauty was instinct in the race. As the centuries brought clearer racehood, finer feelings, and maturer thought, the sense of beauty became an intellectual conception, while it intensified as well to strong emotion. Out of this last are run Sappho's molten lyrics, nor was it unfelt by philosophers. All are thrilled when the fair Charmides enters,[2] or the beautiful youth in Xenophon's *Symposium*. Others besides Greeks feel emotion, often not of the highest, at the sight of beauty in human beings; but the Greeks above other races were moved to a higher passion, overmastering, inspiring. In the *Phædrus*,[3] Plato, having mentioned the inspired madness of prophets, speaks of the madness inspired by the Muses, which, seizing a tender and virgin soul, fills it with frenzy to adorn great deeds and marshal them in verse. Without this rage, no one need knock at the Muses' door, says he, as he says in his *Symposium* that only those poets who are inspired by love reach immortality. Both are the same,—divine rage inspired by the Muses, or the overwhelming yearning after things noble. Then, in the *Phædrus*, Plato continues, dilating on the dwelling-places of the soul before it fell to earth, and all the beauties there: " And when the soul in man has flashes of remembrance of the beauty wherein it once abode, then, like a bird, it would fain fly upwards, careless of things here; whereupon the man will seem possessed.

[1] Translation condensed from Jebb's *Attic Orators*.

[2] Plato, *Charmides*.

[3] *Phædrus*, 244, etc.

This mad yearning for absolute beauty is the best of all frenzies; and only he possessed with it shall be called a lover. . . . That man whose soul has long fallen from its true abode or has become foul, when he sees a beautiful being, feels no reverence, but like a beast would satiate his lust; but he who in a lovely face or form sees traces of the beauty whence he came, first shivers, thinking of the terrors which came on him when he fell to earth; then gazing, he is filled with awe, so that, did he not fear to be thought a madman, he would sacrifice to his beloved as to the image of a god. Soon a revulsion seizes him and a warmth, till the sweat pours from his body."

Plato's Eros.

Thus in the *Phædrus,* with profusion of detail and poetic imagery, as was his wont, Plato expresses the intensity of the supersensual passion for beauty. But it is in the *Symposium* that this poet-philosopher follows the passion to its utmost reaches, separating the lower, narrower phases, ordering and enlightening and universalizing it with reason, till love, which in its heart of hearts is love of beauty, becomes the spiritual motive which shall wing all human yearnings unto that Supreme Good which is Beauty Absolute. Eros is the motive leading men on, the principle of human striving; Eros is desire, yearning for that which is not had, or yearning for the continued possession of that which is ours. Thus it might include all human motives and desires, the causes of all human actions. But as these desires are directed by a loftier knowledge, bringing a purer spirituality, they attach themselves to objects more worthy of attainment. So is Eros a desire, a motive of action, a longing for passionate enjoyment, having much dross, often bringing but questionable advantage. Let knowledge come, and winnow out the chaff, that the soul may love only the best. This and much more is poetically suggested by the succession of discourses on love in the *Symposium.*

Phædrus begins and praises Love as a mighty god, and eldest of the gods. Love makes men dare for their beloved, giving courage to Alcestis, a woman, making cowards heroes, and heroes more heroic. The next speaker, Pausanias, attempts to distinguish. We should not praise Love thus unqualifiedly, for there are two Loves, the heavenly and the common. The common Love has no discrimination, desires only to gain an end, careless of gaining nobly, and thus works good and evil. But those inspired by the higher Love love that which is most intelligent and noblest in their beloved, and desire his good. Eryximachus, the physician, follows, recognizing the separation of the two Loves, and seeing this separation between healthy and diseased desire extend throughout all nature. Then Aristophanes describes the passion of love by a humorous myth. The mortal race had originally a different form from the present,—a round body, two faces, four arms, and four legs, in every respect the double of the present human form. Because of their overweening strength and insolence, Zeus cut them in two, so that each had but one face, two arms, and two legs; and Apollo stitched up their wounds. Ever since then, the parted mortal halves desire nothing so much as each other, would fain become one again. This desire is love, and if each one had his true love again, the race would be happy. All praise then to that god, Love, who leads us back to our own nature, giving us to hope that, if pious, he will restore us to our original state and bless us.

The Symposium

The poet Agathon then gives his inspired encomium. Love is the fairest, best, and most blessed of the gods, ever young and tender, nestling in the souls of men. He can neither do nor suffer wrong from god or man; for, if he suffers, he suffers not by force, nor does he act by force; for all men serve him freely. Then he is temperate; for temperance is the ruler of pleasure and desire, and no pleasure masters Love. As to courage, has he not conquered the God of War; so, conquering the bravest, he must himself be the bravest. He is also most excellent in wisdom; for he is a poet, being the source of poetry in others. He is skilled in all art; only those artists whom love inspires have the light of fame. Medicine, archery, and divination were discovered by Apollo guided by Love and Desire, and to Love are due the Muses' melody, Athene's weaving, Zeus's empire over gods and men. Love orders the empire of the gods, the love of beauty, for there is no love of deformity. Before then the gods did dreadful deeds under the rule of Necessity. Since the birth of Love, and from love of the beautiful, has sprung every good in heaven and earth. He fills men with affection; makes them to meet at feasts, sacrifices, and dances, giving kindness and friendship, banishing enmity, the joy of the good, the admiration of the wise, the wonder of the gods, desired by those who have no part in him, and precious to those who have the better part in him; parent of delicacy, luxury, desire, fondness, softness, grace; regardful of the good, regardless of the evil; in every word, work, wish, fear,—pilot, comrade, helper, savior; glory of gods and men, leader best and brightest.

When Agathon ceased, there was no praise to add; his poet's vision saw the entire realm of love in its spirituality, its universality, in its beauty. He felt Love the Inspirer to be love of the beautiful. But Socrates must scrutinize all this before setting on it the seal of philosophy. He first perplexes Agathon with a little sophistry. Love cannot be beautiful and good, for Love is a desire of the good, and nothing desires what it has.[1] Yet Love is not foul, because not fair, but a mean between the two, just as right opinion, which is incapable of giving a reason, is a mean between knowledge and ignorance. Love is a great spirit (δαιμών), intermediate between the

[1] Socrates, in general accord with his Platonic characteristics, gives his view of love in the form of a discourse by the wise woman, Diotima.

mortal and the divine. He is the interpreter between gods and men, and the go-between, for God mingles not with men. His father was Plenty, the son of Discretion; his mother Poverty. And partly because he is naturally a lover of beauty, and partly because he was born on Aphrodite's birthday, he is her attendant. His fortunes follow his parentage; he is poor, hard-featured; homeless he lies on the earth, always in want. Also, like his father, he is forever plotting against the fair and good; bold, enterprising, strong, a hunter of men, weaving intrigues, full of resources, a pursuer of wisdom, a philosopher. No god is a philosopher or seeker after wisdom, for he is wise already; nor do the ignorant seek wisdom, for they do not know their want of it. But those who, like Love, are a mean between the two, are philosophers or seekers of wisdom. For wisdom is a most beautiful thing, and Love is of the beautiful; therefore is Love also a philosopher, or lover of wisdom, and so a mean between the wise and the ignorant.

Love, then, is love of the beautiful or the good, desire to possess it in order that the lover may be happy (*εὐδαίμων*), which is a final end. All men desire their happiness, yet not all are called lovers, just as all makers are not called poets, but only those concerned with music and metre. Desire of good and happiness is but love great and subtle; and lovers love the good, the everlasting possession of it; this is love.

Love is birth in beauty, birth of body or of soul. Beauty is the destiny presiding at birth. Love is not love of the beautiful only, but of generation and birth in beauty. For generation to the mortal is a kind of immortality; and so Love is love of immortality. All beasts will die for their offspring, which is their immortal part. So are men most strongly moved by a love of an immortality of fame. They whose bodies only are creative beget children to preserve their memory. But creative souls bear wisdom and virtue. Such creators are the poets and all true artists. What man, thinking of Homer and Hesiod, would not rather have their children than human ones, or would not rather have such children as Lycurgus or Solon left behind them? Such men have been parents of virtue, and temples have been raised in their honor because of their children, such as were never raised in honor of any one for the sake of human children.

These are the lesser mysteries of Love. He who would proceed aright in the quest of the more deeply hidden, must in his youth visit beautiful bodily forms (*σώματα*), and first love one such form only, out of which to create beautiful thoughts. He will soon perceive that the beauty of one form is akin to the beauty of another, and then that beauty of form is everywhere one and the same, whereupon he will cease to love any single form excessively, and become a lover of all beautiful forms. In the next stage, he will perceive a more honorable beauty in souls than in outward form, so that if a beautiful soul have but little comeliness, he will be content to love and tend her, and bring forth thoughts which will make youths better, until he is brought to see beauty in institutions and laws, and to know that the beauty of them all is of one kin, and that bodily beauty is a trifle; and after this he will seek till he see beauty in the sciences, not like a slave in love with the beauty of any one youth or man or institution, but, nearing and beholding the broad sea of beauty, he will create many noble thoughts in bounteous love of wisdom; and there will he greaten till he see some single science, which is the science of beauty. Let us consider it. He who has learned to see things beautiful in due order, when he comes to the goal will suddenly see a nature of wondrous beauty, which is everlasting, neither becoming nor perishing, nor waxing nor waning, not fair in one respect and foul in another, nor at one time or in one relation or at one place fair, then again foul, nor fair to some and foul to others; neither fair in the likeness of a face or hands or any part of the body, neither any form of speech or knowledge, or existing in another being, as in an animal, or in earth or heaven; but beauty, simple, absolute, and eternal, in which all perishing beauties share, itself becoming neither more nor less, nor suffering (πάσχειν) thereby. When any one, through true love, rising above perishing beauties, begins to see that beauty, he is not far from the goal. And this it is to go, or by another to be led, aright to the things of love, to use the lower beauties as steps to mount on for the sake of that other beauty, going from one to two, and from two to all fair forms, and from fair forms to fair practices, and from fair practices to fair knowledges, and from these knowledges attaining to the knowledge which is of beauty absolute, in which communion he shall bring forth and nourish, not images of virtue, but real virtues, and become dear to God, and be immortal if mortal may. In the attainment of this, no man shall find a higher helper than Love.[1]

Such is the Platonic Socrates' discourse on love and beauty. Love is the impulse; beauty is the motive; the complete activity is love of the beautiful.[2] Speaking more closely, Plato's conception of beauty may be thus outlined. Measure and symmetry everywhere pass into beauty and virtue.[3] Plato, like other Greeks, was repelled by the unformed or unlimited. Without measure, there is no proportion, no beauty, no justice, no good.[4] Great and small exist not only in relation to each other, but also in relation to the ideal standard or mean. All arts are on the watch against excess or defect as real evils, and the

[1] After Socrates ceased, Alcibiades, rushing in, drunken, gives in a wonderful picture of Socrates himself an artistic instance of spiritual love and beauty, which in the abstract Socrates has been describing. The above condensation owes some obligations to Professor Jowett's translation.

[2] Perhaps we may see what Plato means in saying that the beautiful is difficult (χαλεπὰ τὲ καλά, a proverb), *Rep.*, 435 c; and that the many cannot be philosophers because unable to understand absolute beauty.—*Rep.*, 493 e.

[3] *Philebus*, 64 e.

[4] *Crito*, 48 c; *Rep.*, 506 a. There is proportion in truth, *Rep.*, 486 d.

beauty of every work of art is due to the observance of measure.[1] The very existence of art depends on there being a mean or standard of measure.[2] Again, says Plato: " Everything that is good is fair, and the fair is not without measure, and the animal who is fair may be deemed to have measure. Now we perceive little symmetries and comprehend them, but for the lordliest and greatest we have no understanding; for, as regards health and disease, virtue and vice, there is no symmetry or want of symmetry greater than that of the soul to the body. When a weaker or lesser frame carries a great and mighty soul, or when the reverse occurs, then the whole animal is not fair, for it is unsymmetrical; but the very opposite will be the fairest and loveliest of all sights to him who is able to see." [3]

Elements of the Greek Conception of Beauty.

Beauty is no one thing; it lies not in the possession of one quality, but of many. It is not merely " the mean," not merely measure, proportion, or fitness. Neither is it merely adaptation to a purpose—utility. On the other hand, a beautiful thing need not possess all qualities, only it must lack nothing, which means that it must have all essential to itself. Beauty is perfection, perfection in good things which make for life. Whatever is entirely excellent is beautiful, provided it have no vile associa-

[1] *Statesman*, 284 a.

[2] *Statesman*, 284 d.

[3] *Timæus*, 87 c. Socrates had found the good (ἀγαθόν) as well as the beautiful (καλόν) to be relative to some object. The two with him were much the same, and both comprehended in the useful (τὸ εὔχρηστον). Fitness for some use was the main element of the Socratic conception of beauty, at least as defined in the *Memorabilia;* see Xen., *Mem.*, iii, viii, and iv, vi. Plato certainly saw the Good in all beauty and did not distinguish between the two. Rather, he says, that acting well (εὐ) and beautifully (καλῶς) and justly (δικαίως) is the same.—*Crito*, 48 c. Aristotle, as he separated virtue from knowledge, so he did not identify the good and the beautiful. Yet, although drawing distinctions, Aristotle recognizes that the same qualities which make a thing good make it beautiful; beauty lies in the mean, in avoidance of extremes—in moderate and measured magni tude and in order.—*Poetics*, vii, 4.

tion, no association with matters essentially deficient, base, evil, deadly. At the very least, the preponderance of association must be with life and things noble. A surgeon's knife may be finely formed, and of use in removing tumors, and so related to healing, yet has such intimate association with hurtful things that it cannot be beautiful. But a sword means valor, freedom, and defence of right, and though it may also deal wounds and death, such death may make for life, may be beautiful, since there are matters worth dying for.

Beauty abstains from everything impertinent. A beautiful object must have only what is germane, what is organic, what makes for the perfection of it as a whole. Everything beyond is superfluity, which means detraction, robbery of interest from the object itself, dishonoring that object by filching attention to things intrusive.

And how can beauty be except it be itself? How can a beautiful thing be something else? If it pretend to be what it is not, what becomes of its essential nature, of its measure, its proportion, its utility, its fitness? A thing is never fit for what it pretends to be and is not. Pretence can never be beautiful. Quite different is the pleasure Aristotle finds in likeness wrought through works of art or poetry, epic and dramatic, which is not pretence. The statue does not pretend to be a living being, but a representation of one. The epic is but a vivid description, the drama but a living representation. None of them is pretence at being other than it is. A statue becomes pretence when made of wood so painted that it pretends to be marble, which is different from coloring the marble or wood so as the better to represent clothing or flesh, wherein also there was no pretence. So an epic poem or a drama becomes pretence when impertinent embellishments are foisted into it.

The conception of κόσμος also entered into the Greek thought of beauty. This meant order and also ornament, and was finally applied by the Pythagoreans to the grand order, the universe, as opposed to the chaos out of which it came. The κόσμος, says Plato, meaning the universe, is more beautiful than anything in it.[1] Another element of beauty was harmony, which was almost beyond order; it was a rhythmic, beautiful order. Ἁρμονία originally signified joining or fastening, putting well and securely together. Afterwards it was applied to musical matters, first by the Pythagoreans, who spoke of the celestial harmony of the spheres, and called the soul a harmony.[2] Heraclitus gives the word deep meaning: συντελεῖ ἅπαντα ὁ θεὸς πρὸς ἁρμονίαν τῶν ὅλων,[3] God orders all for the harmony—the proper subordinated and ordered welfare—of the whole. But the lightest, finest element of beauty was χάρις, grace, charm. This means ease, the absence of strain and over-exertion. A beautiful object which possesses grace is not only beautiful, but is so easily, pleasurably to itself and all beholders. Similar is the indefinable grace of style of Plato or Lysias, a charm consisting in the perfect facility with which they express themselves aright. This is χάρις in writing, like the grace of a marble Hermes.

Beauty inheres in the beautiful object;[4] it is not a matter of surrounding or of incident. That an object or a human being is placed in an interesting situation does not give it beauty. The beautiful object is and can be such only in itself. Circumstances cannot give beauty; they may form the matter of beautiful conduct, yet even then the beauty consists intrinsically in the knowledge, virtue, or will of the actor. The highest Greek thought always expresses clearly some ideal of human life, human being and its intrinsic qualities, as distinct from incident and accompaniment. The best Greek would know or be, rather than possess or be surrounded by. " Knowledge,

[1] The *Timæus*.

[2] Ritter and Preller, *Historia Philosophiæ*, 68 B and 71.

[3] Heraclitus, *Frag.*, 61 ; Ritter and Preller, *Hist. Phil.*, 37.

[4] By the term " object " is to be understood something forming a whole in itself, not something which is merely part of a whole, like a stone in a building.

rather than the realms of the Great King!" exclaims Democritus. And the true art and literature of Greece set above all else the goodness, the beauty, the perfect faculty, the perfect being, of the man himself.

This delineation of pure life, this seeing the supreme interest in the object itself, and not in its incidents or situation, was inseverable from the endeavor of Greek art and poetry to realize the perfect, an endeavor which will often best advance itself by excluding the peculiar. Peculiarity is usually aberration, its exclusion a first step toward perfection. In this way Polyclitus deduced the canon of the human form, shown in his *Doryphorus*. This canon held the normal human form, seeking a closer adherence to nature's truth than she herself attains. Art like that of Polyclitus is the reverse of realism; yet it seeks mainly physical perfection; it does not seek to emphasize the body's loftier qualities, which express man's intellectual nature. On the other hand, while the works of Phidias or Sophocles preserve fidelity to normal humanity, they present its higher qualities most prominently. Both Sophocles and Phidias, respectively following the modes of dramatic poetry and plastic art, sought the normal, the perfect, sought to exclude imperfection; but in their art all else was subservient to intellectual import and that physical perfection which is appropriate thereto. They sought perfection in intellectual and spiritual qualities appropriate to man and unshared by brutes.

The Universal in the Concrete.

Thus Greek art attains the universal by seeking the complete excellence of life. The normal is the typical; the higher the type, the more it tends to constitute a universal ideal. Phidian sculpture embodies elemental life, pure life in enduring traits, then normal life, which is beauty through the exclusion of the peculiar, the imperfect, the grotesque;[1] nor does it attempt to express subtle

[1] Sie (Beauty) muss unbezeichnend sein.—Winckelmann, *Werke*, vol. vii, p. 76.

thoughts or particular sentiments arising from some special circumstance. Likewise the great Greek dramas admit no sentiment lacking in universality, because dependent on trivial or narrow circumstances; no sentiment to which the common heart of man would not respond. From this broad base, the art of Phidias and the great dramatists rises to the ideal by making all things animal yield prominence to what is noble and distinctly human, thus setting forth what it were universally well that men and women should become.

These creations, notwithstanding the universality of the qualities which they embodied, were not vague types, but complete and distinct personalities. A dramatic poet fuses universal elements of human lot and human nature into individual personality in many ways. Abstract human qualities become constituent traits of an individual when united, as it were, in single definite relationship to an environment of actual life. Personality is constituted of a sum of human traits existing in identity of relationship to all else in the universe, and made into a living unity through the inscrutable enfolding action of a single will. Again inscrutably, this personality has passions and desires. The individual's thoughts may be abstract, impersonal, hardly connected with himself. Not so with passion and desire, which are intimate and personal desiderative elements of the individual personality. They always immediately and distinctly imply that wherein they are rooted, from which they proceed, an individual. Emotionalized with desire, the individual's thoughts cease to be impersonal; become his sentiments, part of his spirit. The personages of a drama may be constituted of universal human quality. The poet makes their personalities clear through placing them in definite situations respecting other men and definite facts, and then setting forth the reciprocal action of their character and surroundings, thereby causing each man to display himself in doing and suffering. A supreme dramatic artist will effect this without impairing the elemental universality of his creations. They will be typical and yet individual, as are the personages of the great Greek dramas.

Sculpture is less suited than the drama to setting forth action and situation, or expressing vivid passion. When seeking that perfection which is beauty, sculpture may achieve definite personality by a distinctive combination of human qualities in marble forms, which may be placed indeed in definite situations, and given such action as will render their qualities clear without detracting from their universality by the impairments of specialization. In a statue of Athene, Phidias combines and shows in their perfection those qualities which were hers, her power, her intellect and spirit, and her maidenhood. Similarly Hermes or Ares had their attributes, which should be grandly shown in their statues. Each statue would present a distinct personality because embodying different qualities, a distinctness which would not be impaired by the perfectness of all the qualities entering each statue. Creations of ideal art are not vague when they embody truthfully principles of form and being deducible from actual life; which is to say, so long as art works along the lines of nature's truth, and does not seek impossible combinations of inconsistent qualities. The greatest Greek artists and poets conceived the perfect in clearly outlined form, completely visualized it in their souls, saw it. It was not vague to them, but natural and real. Their creations correspond, and possess that highest artistic individuality arising from the original and imaginative, completed and harmonious combination of great and universal qualities into perfect unities of human form and character. The great Greek artist beheld his creations as they could not but be, as he could not but see them,—clearly, definitely, completely, inevitably. The creations of his vision took their forms according to their qualities. The artist did not proceed in the reverse way, trying to fashion form, with nothing in it.

Many-realmed and irresistible was the Greek imagination. The Greek mind tended always to visualize its thoughts, and behold its most spiritual conceptions in the guise of form. The spiritual is not conceived by the archaic thought of any race. But the Greek habit of regarding the spiritual as form, remained after spiritual conceptions were purified from material elements. This tendency was cognate with the Greek dislike of the indefinite, unlimited, unformed, which carried the idea of unrestraint,—as from chaos had sprung the impious monstrosities who fought against the gods. So this tendency appeared wherever ethical considerations entered, and made the Greeks conceive the virtues as in some way contained in form. Plato's theory of ideas is an example of the Greek way of visualizing thought, before subjecting it to rational analysis. A Greek saw before he reasoned; and in the end reasoned more clearly through the vivid perception of what he reasoned about.

Definition of Art from Greek Stand-points.

One need but cast these thoughts into closer form to obtain what shall be a definition of art from the point of view of the loftiest Greek endeavor and attainment. Art (*ἡ τέχνη*), says Aristotle, is a way of making (or creating) according to the reason, or rationale of truth, *i. e.*, of actual fact.[1] Substantially following this remark, it may be said that fine art—broadly speaking, sculpture, painting, poetry, and music—is creation in accordance with nature's general truths, those general principles and types which the mind forms in comparing, combining, selecting from, and excluding objects presented to the sense. A true work of art, be it a statue, a painting, or a drama, embodies or sets forth in concrete combination principles of general truth and validity more truly than can any actual facts or objects, which always present peculiarities or aberrations.

The Greeks had no distinct conception of that faculty with which they were pre-eminently gifted—imagination;

[1] *Ἕξις μετὰ λόγου ἀληθοῦς ποιητική*, *Nich.*, *Ethics*, vi, 4.

which is the faculty of the mind that combines[1] and brings to form universals. Imagination creates a concrete embodiment for the general types and classes of facts, be they facts of simple bodily existence or facts of action or conduct. Thus it is the faculty which, working diversely according to the nature of the art—sculpture, painting, or poetry,—embodies general truths of human being in the great personality of a gold and ivory Zeus, or general laws of human conduct and its consequences in a drama or an epic, or, as it were, imagination's finest function, brings to lyric form the subtle moods of men. In fine, imagination is the artistic faculty, which embodies the type in the individual, the general in the concrete, and makes the universal real. The artist's function is not only truly to conceive the general principles and types, but also to combine and present them in concrete instances.[2] And art may be defined as the expression of the typical, the general, the universally significant, in the form of the concrete or individual.

Whatever does not come within the tenor of this definition is not, and never has been, recognized as art,—as art creative. For example, in the portrayal of an actually living man, if the sculptor or painter endeavor merely to copy what he sees in the face at any given time, his best result can be but a mere photograph of a passing facial phase. The true portrait-artist generalizes from out the multitude of fleeting expressions the subject's veritable being, and expresses that in the portrait.[3] Even here, though within narrow limits, is call for generaliza-

[1] It is only in combination that universals can be rendered concrete ; no human being can consist of but one quality ; no life can consist of but one type of fact.

[2] The artist, of course, is not always conscious of this process. He, in common with other men, or, in a greater degree, as he may be pre-eminently gifted, holds in his mind a mass of general truths. His imagination sets them in concrete instances ; and his thought may come as a flash or in the guise of feeling.

[3] *Cf.* Aristotle, *Poetics*, xv, 11.

tion and imagination, is scope for art. Again, passing from sculpture and painting to literature, that will not be art which does not embody general truths in modes of the concrete. Mere narrative of actual fact, physical or mental, while it may be history or science, is not art;[1] nor is the mere statement of general truths, though that may make a didactic or philosophic discourse. The general truths must be combined and embodied in concrete reality, in the form, for instance, of some story of human conduct and its consequences; that will then be art, and true art if the general principles be true and brought to fitting expression. The sister arts are distinguished from each other through the means used by each, sculpture making use of stone and bronze, painting making use of canvas and color, poetry making use of melodious diction, and music making use of sound. Further, the means used by each art bring special limitations as well as facilities, and in a general way assign to each its own province and make it there supreme. But though the means used distinguish one art from another, means cannot make art art, and though a sculptor cannot express himself without stone and chisel, nor a poet except through melodious diction, there is much carving which is not art, and verse which is not poetry.

Traits of Greek Architecture.

Architecture differs from sculpture, painting, and poetry in that primarily it is not art, but handicraft having an immediately useful end in view. A great building's general form, resulting from its plan and the mode in which the architectural elements are conformed thereto, will reflect the genius of the race or time, and may impress the beholder and affect his mood. This is true of a Greek temple or a Gothic cathedral. But in itself construction, architectural form, cannot speak to men definitely; cannot, as a poem or a group of sculpture, present the clear

[1] *Cf.* Aristotle, *Poetics*, ix.

embodiment of definite principles of human life.[1] This may be artistically accomplished only through the building's sculptural and pictorial adornments. The architectural excellence, the structural beauty, of a building intended for some noble purpose, will largely depend on the building's general fitness for that purpose, which is to be made artistically apparent in such of the building's sculptures and paintings as present definite imaginative expression of its builders' knowledge and views of life. Thus, as completed in adornments which set forth its purpose in artistic illustration and commentary, a great building like the Parthenon or the Rheims cathedral, may rightly tell the furthest truths reached by the time; and in its fittingness to form the setting of the story, as well as serve what other ends it is intended for, it may partake of such noble beauty as cannot belong to any palace ministering to private luxury.

But buildings may possess germane structural beauty, as did Greek temples, even irrespective of their sculpture and colored decoration. Architecturally regarded, the palpable characteristics of a Greek temple were order, symmetry, and then proportion. The last consisted in preserving such relations of size and number throughout the building's parts as should constitute it an organic whole, to which nothing might be added without impairment. The more important sculptural adornments occupied certain definite spaces, the pediment, the metopes, the frieze. Each figure naturally conformed to the limits of its allotted position; the predominant lines of the sculptured groups harmonized formally with the architectural lines defining the spaces occupied by them; and spiritually each group was complete, accomplishing its theme within the space it filled. Apparently the Greeks did not extend their care for order to the relative situation of a number of buildings. No order can be seen in the

[1] Accordingly Aristotle does not place architecture among the fine arts; it was not "imitative," see *post*.

arrangement of the buildings on the Acropolis of Athens. A temple was erected on a sacred spot; to erect it elsewhere would be to ignore its purpose; doubtless following some tradition the Parthenon was erected where it is, and the Erechtheum where it is; neither site was chosen with reference to the other, or to anything save the sacredness of the site itself. But there results no lessening of the beauty of the temples, for that was intrinsic, independent of surroundings. A temple was so complete and perfect in itself that its situation relative to other buildings could not impair its beauty.

Greek temples were truthful. There was no pretence in the material used, there was no deceptive covering of joints. Probably the Greeks did not conceive this principle consciously as an artistic canon; rather their instinct for real excellence, not the make-belief thereof, bound them to truth in construction, and they felt no temptation to conceal and deceive in their architecture. Yet Greek artistic love of truth came to conscious expression in certain architectural forms suggesting the designer's intent that a thing should not only show what it is, but through its appearance suggest its function. For example, the function of a column, to uphold, is emphasized by flutings, which indicate the direction of the support the column gives; and much of the impressiveness of the Doric temple lies in the massive columns suggesting by their slight swell (entasis) and spreading echinus the weight of the superstructure they uphold so firmly. Thus the column got organic beauty, befitting itself and in structural harmony with the rest of the building. The entasis, moreover, by preventing stiffness and all idea of strain, imparted grace, suggesting that the column performed its function easily; and the echinus, in conjunction with the square plinth of the capital, formed an agreeable transition from the round form and upright lines of the column to the square and horizontal architrave; all of which imparted beauty strictly structural and organic.

The architectural knowledge of Greek builders becomes more astonishing the better it is known. There are certain discrepancies between sight alone and the testimony of careful measurement in regard to the lines and proportions of large buildings. Lines really straight may appear to sag, columns really upright appear to be pressed outward. The purpose of a temple is to be viewed, not measured; and in its construction allowance must be made for the illusions of the eye. Consequently the lines of the Parthenon's architrave and stylobate curve upwards slightly, and no column is exactly upright, but the lines are drawn and every column is so erected that to the eye all may be perfect.

But the Parthenon discloses subtler motives for the avoidance of an absolute regularity never found in living objects and suggestive of stiffness and lack of animation. With all its order and strict outline, the Parthenon makes no such impression, which seems to have been avoided by the use of slight curves throughout, instead of perfectly straight lines, and by refraining from absolute equality between co-ordinate parts. The intercolumnar spaces vary, so does the height of the columns, the breadth of the plinths, of the triglyphs, and of the metopes. These deviations are too slight to be perceived by the eye, but their result is beheld in a quality of life imparted to the whole structure. And before the builders left a temple, it received a marvellous and loving finish, whereby was shown solicitude for utmost perfection in the construction of such buildings as should stand for Greek reverence for what the Greeks revered.

The Record of Progress in Greek Sculpture.

Fragmentary as is the record which lies in the remains of early Greek sculpture and decoration, it illustrates Greek intelligence and faculty. Greece garnered much from older civilizations, nor hesitated to make use of all suggestions. In art she used foreign models, gradually transforming whatever she adopted. And the early history of Greek art presents the interesting spectacle of Greek genius not once, but twice, conquering its foreign lessons. First, the victory is almost reached by Mycenæan art, the art of a people itself as yet hardly Greek. Thereafter came the age of Dorian invasion, when European Greece fell back in civilization. Her art had to begin again. Once more she makes use of foreign models and instruction, and, transforming all she takes, she again and more completely brings out her art victoriously Hellenic.[1]

Thus the Greek intelligence adopts what is needed, and with discrimination fashions it anew, continuously progressive. It is, however, the Greek sculpture in the round of the seventh and sixth centuries that most strikingly shows the definite intelligent progressiveness of the Greek artistic genius; even such a progressiveness as the ancient world before Greece cannot show. Egyptian sculpture of the Old Empire had many excellences, which were certainly not reached in a night; rather were they the growth of untold centuries, as to which we are ignorant. But after that time, Egyptian sculpture shows conventionalizing rather than progress, a hardening to a few definite forms. Likewise the earliest examples of Mesopotamian sculpture imply a previous progress to such excellence of workmanship as they display. But thereafter no marked and vital progress is apparent.[2] Much fuller is the record of Assyrian sculpture; but it also shows slight progress.

Early examples of Greek sculpture in the round come from the Cyclades and Asia Minor, as well as from the mainland of European Greece; and crude is their art. They are not earlier than the seventh century. But the comparatively few large pieces which remain show unmistakably how each successive decade intelligently improves upon the conception and performance of its predecessor.

[1] Here the illustrations are mainly in decorative and relief work. See M. Collignon, *Histoire de la Sculpture Grecque*, vol. i, livre i, ch. iii and iv; and H. Brunn, *Griechische Kunstgeschichte*, Buch i, cap. iii.

[2] To be sure the record is most scanty.

Each later statue seems to lay some archaism aside, some imperfection, some element of failure to represent man truly.[1] Two centuries of advance along the way of intelligent and artistic discrimination and improvement, and Phidias will appear. After the supreme achievement of the great masters of the fifth century, Greek sculpture makes no further catholic advance, and in the succeeding still great times of Scopas and Praxiteles begins to indicate the modes in which it will decline. But the modes, through which it was to decline from Phidian greatness, are themselves for a while modes of special advance in the subtler delineation of human characteristic and emotion. Even in its decay, within its lowering scope, Greek genius is still fertile and partially progressive.[2]

The Beauty Sought.

The beauty which the Greek sought in sculpture—like that in architecture—was the beauty of intrinsic, essential being, the beauty of pure and gracious life;[3] and happy were the Greeks, happy are we through them, that sculpture is the art of arts to express this. Its capabilities and limitations coincide with the delineation of essential life. It is unfit to express such interest as may arise from situation or accident; quite unsuited to the trivialities of *genre* and circumstance. Nor will it express life's perplexities; the action must be simple, with its interest definitely centred, undispersed in detail. Nor can the sculptor turn this way and that, under conflicting motives. In great sculpture one motive must overwhelmingly predominate. The highest ideals of Greek sculpture were undisturbed by considerations beyond the plastic delineation of noble

[1] See again this story of early Greek sculpture, so far as we know it, lucidly told in Collignon's *Histoire de la Sculpture Grecque*, vol. i, livre ii.

[2] See *post*, chap. xi.

[3] By "pure" life is meant life in its essential qualities, unaffected by transient incident or special circumstances. Yet it is unlikely that the Greeks were conscious of seeking pure life in art; rather this was a result of their intelligence which looked naturally for what was essential in the matter in hand, and was not tempted aside by irrelevant detail.

life. Not a question of trivial detail, of unessential circumstance, perplexed the artist's mind centred with the intensity of genius on the attainment of one great thing. That artist's mind, moreover, was so set on the intrinsic qualities of his subject that he cared not even for their display in action under the incitement of special circumstances. He would represent the qualities themselves in their normal poise. In Phidian art there is no display or striving for effect. Its sublimest creations do not act up to the full extent of their powers. In the Parthenon frieze the gods sit easy and undisturbed, their powers quiescent, only indicated by divinity of form and feature. Likewise the faces of the youths on horseback are calm and controlled, well within their limits of expression. Yet a comparison of these youths with the divinities well shows how Greek sculpture at its highest could, without sacrifice of individuality, delineate life broadly and typically. The forms and features of the divinities are typical of their class; besides their distinguishing traits, each god and goddess shows ease, freedom from anxiousness, sense of superiority over mortals, easy fellowship among themselves, leisure and entire repose, perfect serenity, power with confidence therein, and immortality; all of these being qualities universally attributed to the gods. Very different are the youths; they are beautiful, they show life's flower; we have never seen such lovely forms together. Yet they have no trait of divinity. Thoughtfulness for the solemn festival broods on each countenance. Blessed youths are they, yet very thoughtful of what they are taking part in. And while every divine form in the frieze is incarnate deathlessness, there is no youth in all the pressing throng over whose bier we might not think ourselves shedding hot tears.[1]

The living bronzes of Myron, his athletes and his animals, almost breathed, so instinct and filled with life were

[1] Illustration of like differences may be seen by comparing the *Meleager* of the Vatican with the *Hermes* of the Vatican and the *Apollo Belvedere.*

they, so living through and through in every limb and muscle. But theirs was vital force, not spirituality; neither was there spirituality in the more reposeful and formally harmonious athletes of Polyclitus. The sculptures of Phidias were spiritual and ideal. Yet it were mistaken to seek in them the expression of subtle thought or emotion. It is life in purity and quietude that fills their features; spirituality and intellect are there, also in still repose, not specially directed to the thought of this or that.[1] Theirs is pure existence simple and undirected, unconditioned on circumstances or environment; it represents the equilibrium and poise of life, which is disturbed when the mind and vital forces are called to action, but toward which they tend again, as the sea to calm. Such sculpture represents perfect human traits in their normal, enduring mode, thus bringing to expression the subject's true personality; for all states of action or suffering are transient in proportion to their intensity, and are lacking in complete representative truth as they depart from the subject's normal poise and bring a portion of his attributes into a prominence merely accidental.

Phidian Qualities.

The idealism of such art broadened into universality. Like tragedy, it freed the beholder's mind from narrow thoughts of self and its anxieties; it was an uplifting joy; it was an education in beauty and an admonition to temperance, reverence, and piety. Great was the ethical impressiveness of these sculptured forms; a quality which issued from the greatness of personality which they embodied, this greatness itself arising from the imaginative,

[1] It is after all to be borne in mind that we know nothing of the faces of statues which were the work of Phidias himself. We know him through his influence, as in the frieze and pedimental groups of the Parthenon, whether he designed any of the extant figures or not. If, however, Furtwängler's interesting opinions (*Meisterwerke der Griechischen Plastik*, pp. 4, etc.) are correct, and we still have a close copy of a Phidian work, the *Athene Lemnia*, it will be plain that the countenances of the statues of Phidias were sublimely noble and intellectual—idealizing highest mental qualities.

creative union in each statue of elemental qualities of life in grand proportions. Quintilian says—and how did a Roman know it?—that the Olympian Zeus of Phidias added something to religion, so nearly did the majesty of the work equal the divinity of the god.[1] In plastic art the act or object represented must be beautiful to the mind in order that the visible form may be wholly beautiful to the eye. Otherwise there will be inconsistency or deficiency. The joy of the eye in the lines of beautiful form will be lessened by a sense of ethical error or hideousness, by a sense of evil or death. Beauty is perfection in good things; Phidian art eternalized in form the perfection of the best, and so reached the sublime.

Phidian art makes clear that a condition of quiescence is best adapted to set forth great personalities in their completeness. A topic might, however, require figures in action, as that of the Parthenon metopes representing the conflict between Lapiths and Centaurs. Even here the countenances of the Lapiths, who stood for civilization as they defended sacred right against savage force, remain unmoved and beautiful, showing the poise and self-control of the defenders of the high cause. Passion is permitted only in the faces of the Centaurs; and why not? They had no noble character, to express which their features should be held in repose; savagery, passion, disproportion, was their nature. And it may be said generally, whenever noble Greek sculpture seeks to set forth the great achievement of some lofty character—the conquests of Apollo, the victories of Heracles—it represents the god or hero quiescent after his accomplishment, indicating symbolically the accomplished act, and showing the powers of the god or hero in the divine or heroic form: the deed is done, the arrows of Apollo have been shot, Heracles sits with the apples in his hand.

Other art of Phidias's time was less sublime. The

[1] Quint., *Inst. Orat.*, xii, 10, 9.

Argive Myron moulded athletes whose excellence lay mainly in their physique, in their physical strength and faculty. If the climax of the existence of such beings lay in some feat of strength and dexterity, showing them at their climax would sufficiently express their being and at the same time show their achievement. To have shown Zeus hurling thunderbolts at giants would have expressed but a small part of his enskied divinity. To have shown Heracles struggling with the Nemean lion would not have expressed the full personality of that hierarch of toil. But the culmination of a discus-thrower's being might lie in that very discus-whirl which Myron immortalized in bronze; and hence Myron is not to be criticised for moulding the very act, for therein he omitted no great faculty of his subject.[1]

The Athlete and the God.

The discus-thrower of Myron, considered in connection with the repose of Phidias's sublimer creations, suggests this principle observed during the best times of Greek art: to represent in violent action athletic beings when the act was the true subject of the sculpture, or when that act so stood for the sum and climax of the subject's personality and attainment that to represent him in the act would suppress none of his essential qualities.[2] The decorative sculpture of a temple might also represent a god or goddess, or a divine hero, in action, when another statue belonging to the same temple set forth the subject's personality completely.

The unity of a statue or painting or group of statues,

[1] So in regard to matters intellectual and spiritual, some human traits are of higher worth in a personality than others. The one climax of noble feeling, which some poor creature once experienced in a moment of high enthusiasm, may be the matter best worth recording, though it be the matter most transient in his life.

[2] One reverts here to Lessing's well-known utterance that a transient act should not be expressed in sculpture. Manifestly this criticism does not comport with many admirable productions of Greek art, not with the *Laocoön* itself, from which he named his book.

as of a literary composition, results primarily from the artist having some matter to express in form or words, and possessing a vision and intelligence clear and single for *it*, that is to say, for what is essential thereto. The peoples of the earth before the Greeks had little of this intelligence or artist's vision. If the first architect of an Egyptian temple had in his mind any design clear and single, it was hardly strong within him and was not felt at all by after-builders. The result at last is that the temple, one cannot say "when completed," but when its final bulk is reached, wanders, lacks unity of conception and proportion, is not organic; quite different from Greek temples which had all these qualities. Again, Assyrian relief sculpture was panoramic, and its purpose was to narrate. Yet its story has no proportion, no emphasis of what is important, no subordination of what is unessential.[1] One recalls the sculptural narrative of the overthrow of Teuman, the Elamite king: without the accompanying inscription, it would be impossible to distinguish him in the elaborate monotony of the slab. But from the beginning there was unity of composition in Greek design. Instance the bronze sword-blade from Mycenæ with its inlaid lion hunt.[2] The peril constitutes the centre of interest in the composition, from which the eye of the beholder does not wander any more than did the mind of the artist while his hand was forming the design.

Unity and Symmetry.

In relief sculpture the Greek artist disliked leaving empty space, which partook of the nature of the indefinite. At first he filled with irrelevant work the space not occupied by his main figures.[3] Soon Greek aversion to all not germane to the main subject of the composition

[1] Far less has it the slightest element of artistic creativeness, of true art, which means the embodiment of the universal.

[2] See *ante*, chapter vi.

[3] This is seen in the scroll-work of Mycenæan decoration (see *ante*, ch. vi), and again when Greek art starts afresh, in the so-called geometrical style of the very early Dipylon vase.

began to assert itself, and the artist learned to fill his whole space with adjuncts appropriate to the main design.

The matter and technique of archaic sculpture hardly admitted the subtler elements of unity, which were evoked by the perfected art of the fifth century,—unity in mood and tone, constituting a harmony, and implying rhythm and symmetry of form and grouping. The simplest symmetry is mere balance, avoirdupois adjustment, the symmetry of inorganic, lifeless objects. Through their balance they retain their positions. Disturb it, and they fall. Such was the lifeless symmetry of Egyptian and archaic Greek statues. In order that an object appear alive, it must show capacity for movement and living strength to sustain it in various positions. The more finished artist avoids positions suggestive of inorganic equilibrium: his statues will have the symmetry of life, adjustable to any position the living being may assume.

Similar remarks apply to a group of statues forming a single composition. The Greek always made such groups symmetrical, but such symmetry might be mere balance or the symmetry of life. The figures from the pediment of the temple of Athene at Ægina illustrate the archaic symmetry of composition, although each figure in itself has much of the symmetry of life. The grouping suggests such symmetry as might have been needed had the middle of the pediment rested on a fulcrum, and so required for its balance the same number of figures on each side of the centre, with every figure on one side counterpoised by a figure on the other, corresponding in size, position, and distance from the centre. This is not the symmetry of living groups. For instance, in the Parthenon pediments, where the symmetry of life is reached, the figures, instead of equilibrium, suggest harmony, congruity of thought or interest, and as it were a balance of life on the two sides.

Both the Æginetan and Parthenon pediments have unity of composition, which in the pediment of the

Ægina temple is somewhat mechanical. The subject of the composition is the fight over the body of a warrior fallen at the centre of the pediment. Directly towards this point all the figures on both sides aim their spears or arrows. The eye of the beholder will not wander, but the effect is stiff. One may say, not only that such a regular and appointed combat never took place, a remark inapplicable to sculpture showing idealistic tendencies, but also that any such combat is inconceivable as taking place among living combatants, every one of whom is a freely moving being, incapable of geometrical regularity of action. The artist had not reached the power of idealizing along the lines of verity, and his result was an impossibility. Very different is the unity of composition in the east pediment of the Parthenon, the subject of which was Athene's bursting into being from the head of Zeus. The interest culminates in the centre, where stood the three actors, Athene, Zeus, and Hephæstus, who struck the blow which freed her. Grouped immediately on either side were the heavenly gods, who are wonderstruck at the sight of the goddess. But the goddess's birth is of import to others besides, who are represented or symbolized in the composition as afar from the birth scene. The transition is made by female figures darting forth from the centre to announce the great event. Nowhere is there mechanical equilibrium, but everywhere diversity of attitude and grouping; even diversity of interest, for the attention of the distant figures is not yet aroused. The supreme unity of the composition is from the spectator's point of view.[1] He beholds the event and the astonishment of those who saw it; he sees the darting messengers, and as his eye passes to the quiet forms farthest from the centre, he feels the mighty import of Athene's birth for them and all the world. As in all

[1] So it is, for instance, in Raphael's *Transfiguration*. The spectator's thought supplies the unity, and is thereby itself rendered active, imaginative, creative.

greatest sculpture, more is suggested than is told, and the spectator's feelings are roused to expectancy, rather than let flag by the sight of something entirely done and past.[1]

The greatest Greek statues, the chryselephantine works of Phidias, have perished. Coins, ugly statuettes, and old descriptions give an idea of them, but hardly enable us to judge of their excellence. We know, however, that the unanimous esthetic sense of the most artistic race pronounced them supreme among works of art. The ruins of the Parthenon and of its sculptured decorations remain. From them, or rather from it, for they all form an organic whole, may be learned what nobility of motive, fulness of thought and life and beauty Greeks could embody in a single creation of the combined arts of architecture and sculpture.[2]

The Parthenon.

The Parthenon was a temple of the Doric order, yet showing traces of the Ionic style, as for example in containing a continuous frieze within, instead of metopes.[3] Its length was two hundred and twenty-five, its breadth one hundred Attic feet, giving the proportion of nine to four. Beyond this, there is no certainty as to the mutual commeasurability of its different parts. The consummate architectural knowledge and skill by which stiffness was

[1] The reconstruction and interpretation of the east pediment has been the subject of endless discussion. One of the last schemes is offered by Furtwängler, *Meisterwerke der Griechischen Plastik*, pp. 243, etc. He returns to the idea that the *Fates* were really meant for the Fates (Moiræ). The *Iris* is not Iris, but Hebe perhaps; the *Theseus* is Kephalus, the beautiful hunter. This is all hypothesis, of course, and no one knows whom the figures represent. One thing is clear, however, that some of the figures are represented as still ignorant of the event. In the *west* pediment of the Parthenon the figures tend, rather than point, towards the centre. There is diversity; and the unity is not brought out mechanically, as in the Ægina pediment.

[2] Here again, though it is known that the Parthenon was colored, it is best, for certainty's sake, to be silent over that part of its ornamentation.

[3] As in the somewhat older Doric temple of Poseidon at Pæstum.

avoided and veritable life given it, have been already spoken of. As a building it gave the impression of perfect proportion and perfect order and completeness, with no superfluity. Then the entire building and every part of it possessed grace,—no strain or overloading, but each part fulfilling its function with perfect ease, and the whole giving the impression of confident and enduring strength.

The architectural congruity is carried out in the manner in which the sculptural decorations harmonize throughout in conception and technique. Unity of composition, which has been spoken of with reference to the statues of the east pediment, appears in the other sculptures adapted to different positions and architectural requirements. Some of the metopes show traces of the archaic struggle with difficulties of material; but for the most part each metope is complete in itself, with its principal motives and lines finding a climax and centre within the sculpture. Beyond this, the metopes on the four sides of the building form groups devoted each to a single topic.

A frieze, on account of its shape, is adapted to represent a continuous matter. It cannot well have a centre towards which the rest tends, or even a centre of supreme interest to which all else is accessory. It must rather, to vary the threatening monotony of its long line, show rising and falling waves of interest, quiet here to rest the spectator, vivid action there to excite his interest, and through all a rhythm of movement [1] and a harmony of composition excluding everything which by disproportionate interest or size might detract from what precedes and follows. The Parthenon frieze effects this rise and fall of interest by the succession of groups taking part in the Panathenaic procession which forms its subject. We see stately maidens moving quietly, eager horses and their riders, magistrates and on-lookers, till

[1] Rhythm is *τῆς κινησέως ταξις*,—the composition or ordering of the movement.—Plato, *Laws*, 665 a.

our eye finally rests with the seated gods. No one could see the whole frieze at once, but successive portions of it, as he walked beneath it. Hence it was fitting that the whole frieze should not present the same moment of time, but give the idea of a procession making ready, starting, and in motion, a plan which readily affords a rise and fall of interest. Some of the youths are not yet mounted; ahead of them are others on horses starting at slow pace, preceded by yet others in rapid gallop. Waves of rhythm appear in the rise and fall of the horses' limbs and bodies, while their heads, and still more the heads of the riders, remain more nearly on a line. This last conformity to the shape of a frieze gives a general tone of control and order to the squadron, and excludes all fear of the eager horses mastering their riders,—a spirit of control indeed comparable to the calm and peace of Socrates at the end of the *Phædo*, which, like a noble dominant, controls the grief of his disciples.

All this makes rhythmic movement, while the well-nigh rhythmic grouping of the seated gods may be seen by following the detail of the pose of each succeeding divinity. The frieze extended around the four walls of the inner temple, with which circumstance corresponded a general division of the procession in four parts, connected by a figure at each corner indicating by his action that he is marshalling the figures following him with reference to those ahead, beyond the corner. So the composition led the visitor towards the head of the procession, where sat the on-looking gods. Light reached the frieze from below rather than from above, and from below the spectator viewed it. Towards the bottom the figures were carved in lower relief, that they might not shade the upper portions. The height of the frieze was near three feet, its length near five hundred; yet was every group and figure in it so suited to the requirements of these dimensions and to all that came before and followed, as to offer no unpleasant suggestion of being carved to fit.

Likewise each group sculptured in the metopes adequately occupied its circumscribed area. But perhaps the highest art in constructing figures to meet architectural requirements was in the groups which fill the triangular pediments so naturally and gracefully that one would not think to see them change their positions even if the sloping gables of the roof were lifted.

Such was the external or structural perfection of the sculptures of the Parthenon, which was shown in the composition of each group and its suitability to its position. Further, each figure shows breadth of treatment, avoidance of small line and belittling detail, and general nobility of execution. Each figure shows the grandeur of Greek ideal sculpture, no peculiarity or shortcoming of form, but everywhere the combination of great and universal traits in noble personalities. And beyond this, there was breadth of general conception. Some of the sculptures have as subjects myths and matters of supreme local interest, but there is no narrow treatment; rather, everything stands forth in its significance, not for Athens alone, but for all mankind.

These formal unities and perfections were but material means to the supreme motive and thought, the glory of Athene and her chosen people. The Attic conception of Athene gave the inspiration. She was the goddess of the land, the giver of the olive, the bestower of handicraft, the inspirer of polity, the helper in all achievement;[1] and, above all, it was she who represented and embodied in divine personality the virtues of the race, its energy, its toil, its wisdom, its self-control, and finer spiritual discernments. The Parthenon was to symbolize and embody these qualities, and signify the glory which the possession of them brought to Athens. Its structure

[1] Of all gods and goddesses, Athene is the universal helper in heroic action,—helping Heracles, Theseus, Achilles, Odysseus. This suggests the high part which the Greeks conceived intelligence to play in all great deeds.

should in all respects conform to this purpose; the statues and sculptured adornments of the building should set forth and carry out this purpose, and there should be nothing out of harmony. Accordingly there may be discerned, beyond the structural and formal unity of the building and its parts, two further modes of unity fulfilled: one epic or dramatic, that the whole building set forth one topic; the other lyric, that all accord in tone and mood and thought.

Within the temple stood the great statue of Athene the virgin, beautiful, unmoved by passion, unswerving from high purpose, victorious and giving victory to hers; nurse of the race too, and bestower of handicraft on Pandora, first-made of women, as the sculptures on Athene's shield and the statue's base told. This statue was at once an image of the goddess, a symbol and suggestion of what the sculptures of the pediments, the metopes, and the frieze should explain and amplify. On the east pediment, Athene bursts into full and potent being; on the west pediment, she conquers Poseidon, striving for the Attic land, and symbolizes by her olive gift the good fosterer she will ever be. But no mere local god shall be the patron of imperial Athens, Persia's conqueror and the "eye of Greece." As Athene was the helper of Athenian achievement, which was the achievement of the highest race, so had she ever been the helper in all heroic acts, in all deeds and accomplishment which had made for civilization and for good. The sculptures of the metopes pass beyond the bounds of Attica, find their topics in broad Athenian and Hellenic achievement, wherein Athene aided; pass even beyond the heaven-assisted deeds of men to the primordial conflict wherein divine intelligence asserted itself over brute strength, the Olympian overthrow of earth-born giants, most of all Zeus's and Athene's victory, and symbolic of all victories to come of mind and order and civilization over their evil opposites. This was the subject of the metopes on the eastern side, the first and earliest, the morning side. The rest of the metopes showed those victories of men which came by Athene's aid. On the south, bestial centaurs are conquered by Lapiths, Theseus aiding; on the west, wild Amazons are overthrown, another victory for Theseus and his Athenians and for civilization; and on the north, perhaps the conquest of Troy symbolized the overthrow of the Persians by the Greeks, pre-eminently by the Athenians, and all through Athene's aid. With the frieze we turn to Athens's inner self, the peace and festal honor of Athene. Its unbroken line shows Athens's victorious present and her glory, the wisdom of her elders, the strength and beauty of her youths, and her graceful maidens. By Athene's help she has attained, and now, through sacrifice and honor to her goddess and the other deathless gods, she crowns her own fair deeds. She has reached god-given leisure for noble and happy life.

Greek Tragedy; Aristotle's Poetics.

Aristotle's *Poetics* is ill-written, but profoundly suggestive. Its critical formulations are most enlightening as to all things Greek, for they proceed from Greek standpoints, and outline the poetic, even the artistic, accomplishment of the race. And since Greek art within its sphere was very truth and excellence, Aristotle's analysis and formulation of certain of its qualities present some canons of artistic criticism of universal validity. In holding art to be the presentation of the universal in forms of the concrete,[1] Aristotle was stating in most general terms what the Hellenic genius had actually wrought in poetry and sculpture. It is instructive to follow him as he focuses his critical reflections upon the drama, and observe how readily his remarks find illustration in extant Greek plays.

Before Æschylus, drama was drama, that is to say, *action*, as well as speech. Words, music, mimetic dance

[1] See *ante*.

and gesture, together made the play. Consequently Athenian tragedy had its origin in mimetic representation as well as in the dithyrambic recital accompanying it. The plays of Æschylus, as they exist in written form, are not the full dramatic story. Dialogue and chorus were filled out with important action. An Æschylean trilogy was to be seen as well as heard. With Sophocles, and still more with Euripides, the drama becomes more completely literary. Henceforth, though the setting remain an element, a play is to be heard, or even read, rather than seen. But this origin of the Greek drama[1] is not without its bearing on Aristotle's view of tragedy.

"Tragedy is the imitation[2] of an action weighty and complete, of definite magnitude, in language made beautiful[3] in modes suitable to the different parts, by persons acting, and not through narrative, effecting through pity and fear the purging of such emotions."[4] This definition outlines Aristotle's views of the nature and effect of tragedy, and suggests his conception of dramatic unity. A drama should be an organic whole, unencumbered with superfluity, unimpaired by anything impertinent or incongruous. This fundamental principle of all artistic composition applies with peculiar strictness to the drama,

[1] Wherein it does not differ from the dramas of other lands and times; the pantomime is at first the important part.

[2] The ordinary meaning of the term "imitation" is not clearly the same as that of Aristotle's use of the word μιμήσις, for the term is usually applied only to the reproduction of matters of concrete fact actually existent. But such were matters for history, not poetry, to imitate (*Poetics*, ix). Poetry should imitate the type, but indeed must first create it. So Aristotle's phrase, as he applies it to tragedy, is closely related to his definition of art in *Nich Ethics* (see *ante*, p. 266). But the matter has often been exhaustively discussed (see the dissertation in Twining's *Aristotle's Treatise on Poetry* and Butcher's *Aristotle's Theory of Poetry and Fine Art*). As to the modes in which poetry imitates or creates, Aristotle has chiefly two in view, narrative and impersonation, the latter being the dramatic mode, the former the epic, though Aristotle praises Homer for speaking so much in the persons of his heroes, and so making his epics imitate in a dramatic manner.

[3] Literally "sweetened," ἡδυσμένῳ.

[4] *Poetics*, vi, 2.

which is the presentation of an action complete and of a definite and proper magnitude. The action must be complete, that is to say, must be a whole, having (1) a beginning which implies no necessary antecedent, but is itself a natural antecedent of something to come; (2) a middle, which requires other matters to precede and follow; and (3) an end, which naturally follows upon something else, but implies nothing following it. Then the action must be of a certain magnitude in order to be beautiful; for nothing is beautiful which is either so large or so small as to be unsuited to ready apprehension.[1] More especially the action must be of such magnitude as can, under the conditions of dramatic representation, readily be grasped by an audience; it cannot be as extensive as that which might fill an epic. On the other hand, it must be large enough to hold serious matter and lead up naturally to the catastrophe wherein it ends. So much for the formal qualities of the action. The more essential qualities of those weighty actions which are "tragic," will appear in noticing the different elements of a tragedy, and receive final comment from consideration of what should be the effect of the play.

The Plot.

Since tragedy is the imitation or presentation of an action, its most important element is that which performs the chief part of the imitation; and this is the plot or story (μῦθος), which indeed *is* the imitation—the dramatic presentation—of the action,[2] corresponding with the action point by point, and subject to the same requirements of unity, completeness, and magnitude.[3] Says Aristotle: "Tragedy is not an imitation of men, but of action and life. Hence its purpose is not imitation or representation of character, but lies in the story and its incidents, and the structure of the plot."[4]

[1] *Poetics*, vi, 9, etc. [2] *Ib.*, vii. [3] *Ib.*, vi, 6.

[4] Hence it is the plot of a drama that, like the action which is to be dramatized, does not admit into its structure such episodes as might not disturb the looser unity of an epic.

This critical view accords with the intrinsic nature of the greatest Greek dramas. One has but to read the *Œdipus Tyrannus* to feel that its chief end is not to express sentiments, delineate emotion, or even to set forth character. The dramatized story, the plot, the unfolding of incidents, the unexpected, unavoidable discovery, the dreadful catastrophe, holds the reader as it held the audience; and what it all sets forth is not character, nor passion, but life in its dark tangle of all that thwarts or fashions, raises men or casts them down. Herein truly is human character a mighty factor; but it is not all, and the drama sets forth all, even life's full complex of action, wherein character is but part of destiny. A Greek drama is an instance of the action, nay, the conduct, of life's forces; and the μῦθος outbulks in importance all other dramatic elements.

An action fashioned, wrought out, and commented upon, creatively presented in a drama, is become a concrete instance of the working of life's universal factors. The actions and utterances of the chorus are evoked naturally and inevitably by the course of the drama, in which the chorus also should be involved.[1] Their utterances point the drama's universality, relate its events to universal laws of life, and display the fortunes of the actors set in the moral laws which bring them to their issue. This is the dramatic function of the chorus.[2] But the true drama, that is to say, the action itself, displays its universality in its own consistent consequence of event, wherein life's laws display themselves. This consistency is displayed externally in deeds which accord not only with the doer's situation, but with his character, the other determining factor in his fortune.[3] More spiritually

[1] The chorus, *e.g.*, in the *Agamemnon* or the *Œdipus*, is concerned in the action of the piece more closely than as a mere sympathetic spectator.

[2] The choral utterances of the *Œdipus* and *Agamemnon* strikingly perform this function. See *e.g.* the *Œdipus*, 863, *et seq.*

[3] This consistency makes a drama just, with such justness as is shown in the dramas of Æschylus and Sophocles, as well as in the epics. Notice the

this consistency appears, as the effect of fortune upon character is seen in the changed man. The chorus in the *Agamemnon* sings of the divine law whereby men, through suffering, are led to knowledge without their willing it.[1] Sophocles' dramas embody this way of the divine. In Œdipus, even in the more stubborn-minded Creon of the *Antigone*, is shown the poet's beautiful artistic apprehension of the humbling and enlightening effect of calamity on a not ignoble man. Thus the Greeks dramatized this depth of truth, human and divine, even showing how through suffering man is brought nearer God.[2]

It is part of Aristotle's definition, that tragedy imitates or sets forth an action through persons acting it out,[3] and not through narrative. Greek taste did not permit horrors to be enacted on the stage, and the necessity of informing the audience of these events, and of others which it was not practicable to present, put the dramatists to the makeshift of the messenger—the ἄγγελος—so frequent in Greek plays. Here Aristotle's critical requirement that the drama should be wrought out through action, and not by narrative, was infringed, and most flagrantly by Euripides. The messenger-device meant incomplete dramatic presentation, it was undra-

Agamemnon, the summit of all tragedy. Therein life is just. Nothing unmerited happens; every one in the drama has sinned. The chorus knows not whether to sympathize with Agamemnon, yet knows well to condemn Clytemnestra. The reader of the play does not ask why Cassandra gave no warning, but rather feels the weight of destiny that sealed her lips. She could not speak, even if she clearly knew what was to happen. But did she know? In her, prophecy is a dark and overwhelming foreboding, which stifles utterance, then frenzies to hardly articulate speech. She foresaw her own fate too; she was not guiltless; had she not deceived Apollo? She moves us strongly, but with no wish to save her. She is so tragic, so held by doom, that her only proper action is to forebode her death and die. Finally, it was meet that the murderers should boast their foolish day, before they too went their way appeasing fate.

[1] *Agamemnon*, 184, etc.

[2] This in the *Œdipus Coloneus*; compare Wolsey in Shakespeare's *Henry VIII*—"I feel my heart new opened," etc.

[3] *Δρώντων*, *Poetics*, vi, 2.

matic and a flaw in the construction of the plot. It was sometimes avoided by making the narrative of what had taken place off the stage a part of the essential action of the drama; Clytemnestra's announcement to the Argive Elders of her murder of Agamemnon is very drama, being a part of the catastrophe.

It goes without saying that the structure of the plot should be artistically and imaginatively probable. Says Aristotle, touching the veriest trait of Greek artistic genius, the dramatist should *see* his plot, keep its scenes before his eyes; then he will be unlikely to fall into inconsistencies or improbabilities which a spectator of the play would notice.[1] Each succeeding incident must be the proper, nay, the inevitable, outcome of what has gone before, though coming in a striking and unexpected manner, like the admirable revolution (περιπετεῖα) and discovery (ἀναγνώρισις) which come in the *Œdipus Tyrannus.*[2] The catastrophe must rise as of necessity from out the operation of the laws of life embodied in the drama.[3]

Ethos; Human Freedom and Love's Bondage.

The elements of a tragedy next in importance after the plot are what Aristotle calls ἦθος (sometimes in the plural, τὰ ἤθη) and διάνοια. His definitions of these two matters are not clear, perhaps from failure adequately to express his meaning and also because his analysis was incomplete. But there is most suggestive significance in what he says. Ἦθος, as here used by Aristotle, is usually

[1] *Poetics*, xvii.

[2] A revolution is a change to the reverse of what was expected ; *i.e.*, any event where the agent's action has produced an effect the opposite of his intention. A discovery is a change from the unknown to the known, taking place between those whose fortunes form the catastrophe of the piece. A beautiful revolution and discovery is contained in the story of Joseph and his brethren—as Twining remarks.

[3] For instance, Aristotle says the best kind of discovery is not that from a visible sign or feature suddenly recognized, nor one invented or adventitious, nor even the discovery springing from inference, but that which arises out of the action of the piece, ἐξ αὐτῶν τῶν πραγμάτων, as in the *Œdipus*. *Poetics*, xvi and xi.

rendered character, and διάνοια primarily means thought, viewed in its activity or energizing, not as quiescent capacity, which is νοῦς (mind).

It were well to follow his explanations of the terms. Since tragedy is the imitation of an action, there must be persons to carry the action on; and these *dramatis personæ* are what they are by virtue of their ἦθος and διάνοια, which determine likewise the nature of their acts. More especially ἦθος signifies the man's underlying determinant qualities, which make him such a person as he is; while διάνοια is that intelligent faculty through which, in speaking, he sets forth his sentiments and opinions as circumstances require. Through the latter, accordingly, he effects whatever is to be accomplished by speech, demonstrates or refutes, rouses in others feelings of pity, fear, anger, and such like, and shows a matter's importance or insignificance.[1] As for the ἤθη of the *dramatis personæ*, the underlying qualities of character, they should be good, that is, should show goodness of motive; they should be appropriate—a man may be drawn valorous, but not a woman. Moreover, they should be natural, and each character drawn consistently throughout, even in its inconsistencies.[2] And further, since tragedy is the imitation of what is above the common level, the poet should follow the example of good portrait-painters, who veritably reproduce the distinctive form and features of the subject, yet make them more beautiful. So in making *dramatis personæ* hot-tempered, easy-minded, or with other such like traits, the poet, while making them of such a temper, should make them noble, like Homer's Achilles for example.[3]

From the above it is clear that by ἦθος Aristotle intended the abiding elements of personality or character.

[1] *Poetics*, vi, 5, 6, 16; xix, 1, 2.

[2] *Ib.*, xv, 1–5. An illustration of a character consistent in its inconsistencies is Cloten in Shakespeare's *Cymbeline*.

[3] xv, 8.

There lies, moreover, in his words the further implication that qualities of character, to constitute ἦθος proper to poetry and art, must be large, strong, and comprehensive, must represent good motives; and in Greek eyes good motives were such as were not narrow, not shortsighted, not ignoble, but took account of life in its height and breadth. In such a broad sense as this, dramatic ἦθος must be *ethical;* it implies καλοκἀγαθία in a human personality. Aristotle suggests his farthest meaning just at the point where his analysis stops incomplete. The problem of the freedom of the human will did not present itself to the Greeks in that ultimate and inner form in which it has perplexed men's minds for the last eighteen centuries. One reason why the Greeks did not perceive the problem, but simply recognized man's will as free, however unable he might be to effect it, was that in general they noticed only the physical, and the more occasional spiritual restrictions on human action. These came from fate and the will of the gods, powers broad and all-encompassing and which took account of wickedness; but yet were forces from without. For the Greeks never had a conception of an omnipotent and omniscient personal God whose original pre-ordainments might—perhaps must—encompass and control the apparent self-directings of the human will. From his unconsciousness of this problem Aristotle speaks somewhat unanalytically when he makes the deeply significant remark that ἦθος is that which manifests deliberate choice,—that which shows what sort of things a man chooses or shuns in matters requiring a decision.[1] Thus it becomes the sum of human quality regarded as self-determining and selective; it is the expression of man's personality in inner choice, in free determination. Hence only he has ἦθος whose self-determining qualities of character are strong enough to preserve his freedom of choice; he whom passion flings hither and thither has it not. We shall hardly go beyond

[1] *Poetics*, vi, 17 ; *cf.* xv, 1.

Aristotle's meaning if we find ἦθος to signify such large combination of human traits in a personality as make it great, strong, and impressive; as make it good through the goodness, to wit, the reach and compass and proportioning self-adjustment of its motives; as make it human in the highest sense, because they hold it free, choosing its course of conduct, not swayed by passion.

It is now plain what Aristotle means by saying the tragedies of most of the recent composers are ἀήθεις,—without ἦθος. Likewise, among painters, there is the same difference between Polygnotos and Zeuxis; the former is a good delineator of ἦθος, the latter's work has none.[1] That Aristotle drew in his mind the same distinction between Sophocles and Euripides may be inferred from his approval of the former dramatist's remark that he made men as they ought to be; Euripides made them as they were.[2] Moreover, it is easy to see that Sophocles' *dramatis personæ* have ἦθος while those of Euripides have not. A flawless character were not fit for tragedy;[3] a character may have flaws and yet possess ἦθος. Such is the case with Sophocles' Œdipus; possibly he was overweening in self-reliance, certainly he was carried away by his imperious temper, wherein lay the beginning of his ruin. But he is good, his motives are good, they are broad, such as those of a beneficent ruler should be; his wrath in the drama has its source partly in his thought of what is due him because he is what he is. Throughout the time of the play, even as he had been before, he is masterful and energetic; his acts anticipate others' suggestions. At the end, when ruin, utter, horrible, has fallen on him, his strength of character endures, his vision is still clear, he sees himself as others must see him,—as a pollution. "Let me be cast out!" he cries. In the *Œdipus Coloneus*, from a realization of himself and the motives of his conduct, that is, out from his own character, he gathers final calm; and from a view of the relation

[1] *Poetics*, vi, 11. [2] *Ib.*, xxv, 6. [3] See *post*.

of his character to his fortunes, he gains a sense of consecration to some purpose over him, and he is satisfied.

The *ἦθος*, the perfect beauty, of Antigone is clear. The weaker sister Ismene is a foil to Antigone's greatness; yet even she does not narrow her dissuading arguments to small personal motive; she argues from what she would regard as right.[1] But Antigone's greatness is such that she sees the matter absolutely—she will honor her brother's corpse: "Well is it for me to die doing this!"[2] This is Antigone, the note that tells her very self. Thereafter, when brought before Creon, the whole thought of her great justification[3] is of the divine laws of righteousness. Quietly she looks upon herself with reference to these laws, not to her desires. Creon tells her she will be hateful to the brother who slew Polynices and was slain by him. Antigone rises above this argument—"I loved them both, but joined not in their hates."[4] As she passes to her tomb her womanhood feels her fate sadly, almost hopelessly, but so fittingly, so beautifully always,[5] and so true: "Behold, princes of Thebes, the last daughter of the house of your kings, and what I suffer and from whom! because I revere what must be revered."[6]

Antigone's conduct in this last drama of her unhappy house was but one part of what she was. Many other and further deeds she might have done; further capacities were hers of loving and revering. What a wife she could have been, and what a mother! what strength of love and duty was in her, untold by the story![7] Her love is love free born; its strength works free with all the laws of righteousness which it honors so duteously. Love with Euripides is passion's slave, which galls itself against the laws of righteousness.

[1] See *e.g. Antigone*, 49, etc.

[2] *Ib.*, 72.

[3] *Ib.*, 450, etc.; *ante*, p. 228.

[4] *Ib.*, 523; *cf. ib.*, 559, 560.

[5] See *ib.*, 824, etc.

[6] *Ib.*, 940.

[7] Antigone is frequently spoken of as statuesque, and rightly in at least this respect, that, like Phidian statues, her actions are well within her capacities.

It is even so. With Euripides there has come spiritual bondage. Passion's slaves are neither great nor free. Quick rise the waves of shallow waters. Passion had not so violently moved the men and women of Euripides had they been stronger men and women, greater, better, more self-controlled, more clearly seeing, more righteous. In heightening passion, he thus lowers character, and narrows motives down to self and self's loves and hates. Medea, in his great drama of hate, has no thought beyond her sufferings and her hatred, no slightest consideration of things broader, ethical. Even the chorus seems scarcely to relate Medea's situation and conduct to broad laws of life, but concerns itself with the personal hard lots of women—touching, but not sublime. What another sort of passion's slave is Phædra in the *Hippolytus*, every one knows, or readily can see by reading the play. Again, the *Ion* is a lovely piece in many ways; it concludes happily, but with no good or broad motive having once worked in it. One turns at last to the lovely pathos of the *Alcestis*, to find what? That she is just the reverse of Medea in every way; instead of personal hatred, here is personal love, and very lovely love, of husband and children; but how much less in compass than Antigone's! In Alcestis' speech with Admetus it is always personal matters that she recalls, how much more she has done for him than he for her, for instance. Then she bespeaks his kindness to their children with utmost sweetest pathos. And when she has passed for the moment to her tomb, it is solely from the point of view of personal regret that Admetus bewails his lot and counts Alcestis dead as better off than he.[1]

Euripides was the progenitor of the love-motive in literature, the motive of passionate love between a man and woman with all its pangs. But as treated by this great delineator of passion and his Hellenistic successors,[2] love might move to pity, even to fear; it would

[1] *Alcestis*, 935, etc.

[2] See chap. xi, *post*.

seldom rouse admiration, for it was seldom admirable, or noble, or broad, or finely, highly human; it lacked *ἦθος*, was not ethical, at most might be unethically pathetic. The reason is clear. That cannot be distinctively and highly human which is not free. And this love in Euripides and later Greek literature stands for no free human choice on the part of either man or woman. It may bring tumultuous joy, likely will bring affliction. But it is always something put on mortals by Eros or Aphrodite, a thing with which men and women are smitten, no part of their will, no part of their highest, distinctively human, self-determining character.

This passionate slave-thing, love, lacks *ἦθος*—is unethical—from another point of view, in that it can consider but itself, takes no account of life's full contents, is a shortsighted, haphazard, unproportioning thing in man. The nobility of Greek tragedy lies in its presentation of the greatness of humanity inwardly free, however thwarted or cast down by mightier forces; nay, human greatness is shown forth through the dark power of hidden fate which casts it down. Love's passion was treason from within, a Delilah bondage of human greatness unto its own destruction.

Music and Diction.

Besides the tragic elements just now spoken of, Aristotle finds three others needful to tragedy: the scenic setting of the piece (*ὄψις*) the music (*μελοποιία, μέλος*), and the diction (*λέξις*).[1] With Aristotle music had educational and ethical import: "melodies contain in themselves representations of moral qualities."[2] As for diction, its excellence lay in perspicuity and in its being neither below nor above the dignity of the subject.[3] Consequently the diction of tragedy, to be suited to the dignity of weighty actions, should be noble; the virtue of such style is to be clear without being mean. The poet must avoid that superabundance of metaphor which obscures, and yet make

[1] *Poetics*, vi, 7. [2] *Politics*, viii, 5; *cf. ib.*, viii, 6, 7. [3] *Rhet.*, iii, 2; iii, 17.

use of language sufficiently figurative, novel, and distinguished, to preserve his style from the commonplace.[1] Thus will his diction be fitting and beautiful. In all of these respects Homer's style is perfect.[2]

Effect of Tragedy; the Tragic Character.

The effect of tragedy—its proper effect though not its conscious end—is through pity and fear to purge the soul of such emotions. The word κάθαρσις[3] used by Aristotle, is a metaphor apparently taken from medicine, and signifies primarily the expulsion from the human soul of pity and fear regarded as hurtful things. Aristotle's thought, however, here incompletely expressed, must be gathered from the relation of this remark to the rest of his views on tragedy.[4] The thought of purging implies expulsion of what is detrimental. It is to be inferred that tragedy will purge of evil things, not of what is good. Nothing is more evil than to be a slave, an inner, spiritual slave; for the quality of being free is essential to human virtue. Passions produce just this inward slavery, for they nullify the will. Hence it were well that the soul should be purged of fear and pity regarded as emotions which sway where reason and man's self-determining will should rule. Tragedy exhibits the principles of things pitiable and dreadful, exhibits dreadful and pitiable acts and conditions in their universal aspects, and thereby instructs the soul, widens its vision, experiences it in things of fear and pity, so enables it to apprehend and know, whereby it shall not suddenly be made a slave in ignorance. So shall the man be calm and free in presence of the like. But again, tragedy purges the soul of such emotions considered as hurtful, painful, and disturbing elements. It draws the feelings forth, relieves the man of them, and gives him calm. That a great tragedy has

[1] *Poetics*, xxii. [2] *Ib.*, xxiv, 1, 2. [3] *Ib.*, vi, 2; *cf. Politics*, v, 7.

[4] *Cf.* the discussion of the matter in Butcher's *Aristotle's Theory of Art and Poetry*, ch. vi. In *Il.*, xxiv, Achilles tells the stricken Priam the story of Niobe, and the passionate scene ends in perfect peace (*ante*, pp. 190–193) — an epic forerunner of the Aristotelian catharsis.

this effect is proved by experience, which we may know as well as Aristotle. Moreover, a Greek tragedy usually closes in quiet tones with such incident, or comment of the chorus, as is fitted to lower the excited feelings of the spectators and divert their minds to a consideration of other matters than the tragic event seen in its sheer fearfulness.

Finally, in a sense intermediate between these two conceptions of the tragic purge, it can be said that the sight of things dreadful and pitiable purifies the fears and pities of the soul from sentimentality, connection with objects trivial or unworthy; also from too exclusively egotistic direction, taking them beyond the bounds of the individual and particular, affording view of what is universal and typical in such matters; and thus, freeing them from the extremes of extravagance and apathy, it induces the mean and increases the philosophic virtue of the soul.

But that things should be truly dreadful and pitiable, having this right tragic effect upon the soul, it is necessary that they should be such and bear such relationship to life, that their presentation will not affect the soul perversely. The action dramatized must be such, have such consistency throughout, and eventuate in such result, that it will altogether square with life's truest, broadest laws. It must not be inconsequent, untruly related to those principles which hold life's height and depth, and so control. In this broad sense the tragedy must not be unethical; for it must be a true and veritable instance of life's broad, controlling, fateful forces; thus will it present life in its farthest verity and power.

So may we see how Aristotle's view of what is rightly dreadful and pitiable, and of the character and fortune best suited for tragedy, reflect broad Hellenic judgments upon life, life not in its accidents but in its ultimate necessities of law. These shall be represented in the hero of the tragedy. He must not be a perfectly good man, not an absolutely flawless character; there must be some flaw to which destiny may attach its tendrils. For, that ruin should come upon an absolutely flawless man, flawless in himself and in his ties of blood which also tell, did not accord with Greek judgment as to what was normal, as to what was fit. Hence, says Aristotle, such a spectacle upon the stage is senseless and abominable;[1] it is too out of relation to the ways of life—life's universal ways, not its accidents—to present itself rightly as dreadful and pitiable; it has no lesson, no effect; the spectator's soul is simply shocked. Again, a bad man passing from evil to good fortune is not a fit subject for tragedy. That were most untragic (ἀτραγῳδότατον), it rouses neither pity nor fear, nor is it fit to see.[2] Conversely, the downfall of an utterly bad man does not fulfil the conditions of tragedy. It satisfies our humane sentiments;[3] but rouses no pity, since we feel that the misfortune was deserved; and it rouses no dread, since it does not touch us; we feel dread only of what might happen to such as we ourselves are. The proper tragic personage is the man between these two moral extremes, neither flawless nor wicked; one whose downfall is occasioned through some fault.[4]

These short paragraphs of the *Poetics* are far from exhausting tragic possibilities; indeed they hardly take account of all the noblest works of Greek tragedy, as, for instance, the *Antigone* of Sophocles; and yet that tragic heroine accords with Aristotle's furthest views of tragic fitness. Her fate presents truly the relationship of such a personality to the ways, the laws, of life. Given an Antigone in like circumstances, and she must do as did this perfect flower of pagan womanhood, and meet a fate like hers. The veritable tragic spectacle is that of human downfall, wrought out, not through wickedness nor yet blamelessly, which last in tragedy means inconsequen-

[1] Μιαρόν, a pollution.
[2] Φιλάνθρωπον.
[3] *I.e.*, it is φιλάνθρωπον.
[4] *Poetics.* xiii, 2, 3.

tially; but wrought out by virtue of the veritable action of all the factors, intrinsic human quality and extrinsic circumstances, in mutual interaction and inevitable issue.[1]

We notice finally that Aristotle's definition of tragedy includes no mention of the beautiful as a tragic or artistic end. This is simply Greek. All things of weight and perfect excellence were beautiful, as of course; else lacked they excellence.

[1] The element of the terrible must not be lacking to a tragedy; hence a "happy ending" is not a proper tragic ending. And Aristotle commends Euripides for the unhappy ending of his plays. Such plays presented on the stage produce the most tragic effect, and in this respect, that is in the tragically moving ending of his plays, Euripides shows himself most tragic of poets, faultily as he manages other matters.—*Poetics*, xiii, 6.

CHAPTER X.

GREEK PHILOSOPHY.

THE desire of knowledge, and the faculty of knowing, and distinguishing between the known and unknown, were peculiarly characteristic of the Greek race. Most ancient peoples did not perceive and know with sufficient clearness to distinguish what they saw from what they did not see, and what they knew from all the rest whereof they were ignorant. In the mental stores of Egypt and Babylonia, chaff never ceased to be as good as grain; and India saw and knew all things through the mist of her desires. Greek knowledge was destined to know itself. Because of its ever clearer recognition of its sources, its modes and means, its evidence and bounds, it was to show the same unique and definite progress through reasoning selection and discrimination, which Greek art discloses alone among the arts of ancient peoples.

The Greek Desire for Knowledge.

The desire to know has various motives. Any savage wants to know how to capture his prey and kill his enemies. And the anxiety to keep in safe relationship to everything having power to hurt or benefit, is a sufficient motive for the lore of sorcerer and priest and seer. With the Greeks appears a desire to know, having no immediate practical reason, nor motive beyond the satisfaction which the knowledge gives. This is a trait of Odysseus in the *Odyssey*, and is recognized as a normal trait of man by the Siren-song which would allure to destruction with its cadences of promised knowledge. Homer's Achæans were absorbed with earth's eager life. But Hesiod's *Theogony* reflects a more contemplative desire to know those things anterior and transcendent which account for man and his environment. With the advent of historic times many Greeks appear wandering abroad simply from human curiosity to learn whatever might be of interest in foreign countries. In Herodotus, Crœsus says to Solon that he has heard how, from love of knowledge (*φιλοσοφέων*) Solon has travelled far to see what might be seen.[1] It was exactly what the Father of History was doing, and what was done by many of those early Greeks who afterwards were called philosophers.

Greek Philosophy Sprang from the Greek Spirit.

The fact that wise Greeks, from Thales on, were wont to travel in order to increase their knowledge, raises the question whether Greek philosophy was not in its origin largely an ingathering of thoughts from other peoples. Of a truth he was no Greek who would not learn from every one he met; and many a suggestion Thales, and those who followed quick upon him, took from non-Hellenic sources. But these men were Greeks; Greek were their faculties; Greek, the spirit of their inquiry, the mode of their investigation and their reasoning, and Greek were their deductions;—those broad results which have survived to represent the views of these early thinkers. Thales's opinion that the origin of things was water, like Anaximander's that it was undifferentiated matter, was an hypothetical explanation of the world.[2] We know of the results they reached; and time has spared just enough of their reasonings to show that these results were inferences, and not baseless guesses or borrowings. So, in general, whatever hints came from abroad, and they were unimportant, Greek philosophy was, like Greek art, a self-wrought thing, a matter of consecutive Greek

[1] Herod., i, 30.

[2] See Burnet, *Early Greek Philosophy*, Introduction, § x.

reasoning upon the content of Greek observation, a pure expression of the Greek discriminating and constructive intelligence.

Greek philosophy began in the Greek desire to know for the sake of knowing and the satisfaction brought. It stood for Greek desire to know and understand the visible world, to explain it in the sense of ascertaining its underlying and abiding reason—what is the primordial constituent and factor of the world ? This it sought to ascertain, to present, to picture. It was open-minded and objective, undistorted by wishes as to how things should be. Its initial motive was not the yearning to adjust the universe to man according to his personal desires, but to find out about it fundamentally. Yet the Greeks through their periods of growth kept their lives whole, the elements thereof related, unified. From the beginning Greek ethics had been inclusive of Greek practical wisdom and broadest views of life. Hence, as philosophy was a search for knowledge broad and fundamental, the philosopher would not be true to the wholeness of his character as Greek if he did not endeavor to relate his practical view of life, and his thoughts of conduct, to his view of the world's fundamental facts. Philosophy, moreover, the search for knowledge, was itself broadening to more complete inclusiveness of experience. Its borders must encroach on life's practical affairs. The two provinces of life, conduct and the search for knowledge, could not but join. Thus, with fuller maturity of thought, philosophy took life unto itself, and life took to itself philosophy; a process which was to complete itself when, with Socrates, philosophic investigation turned to man. Thenceforth more completely, with wider scientific wisdom, man should understand himself, and on that knowledge base his life. So comes it that at Delphi, in Apollo's temple, the precept, Know yourself, *γνῶθι σαῦτον*, was fitly set beside the broadest maxim of Greek conduct, *μηδὲν ἄγαν*,[1]

Its Nature.

[1] *Cf.* Plato *Protagoras*, 343.

nothing in excess, to wit, of you; for the which, know yourself. Philosophy became a part of life, a way of life indeed. Only when in later Hellenistic times is broken the full unity of human activity,—which is very life,—knowledge loses its final value as an element thereof, and philosophy becomes a thing of practical utility, a guide of life. It exists not for its own proper sake, as a high part of life, but only as a means of holding oneself poised amid life's storms.

So should philosophy ascertain the fundamental farthest facts of the world's constituency and of human life, and all its ascertainments it should recognize, and then discriminate the best, the most, the veriest, and sanction such for man. Herein in process it was art's converse, but in its goal, art's analogue. For art—sculpture, painting, poetry—presented Greek ideals in concrete exemplifications; while philosophy was the search critical therefor.

"The gods have not shown men all things from the beginning, but seeking in time they find out what is better."[1] These lines of Xenophanes tell the position which philosophy was to hold toward religion and the traditionary view of the world and man. Philosophy did not feel itself opposed to religion; its task was investigation. When that led to matters touching man's relationship to the gods, philosophy would consider popular views. In so far as these were disproved by broader consideration of the matter, they would be rejected. Tradition was itself a fact; accepted religious views and practices were not to be set aside without a reason. And it bears witness to the subtle Greek appreciation of the secrecy of life, that Greek philosophy remained conscious that its hypotheses were not exhaustive, and therefore bore itself reverently toward all which it could not explain. The Greek nature cared for life's myriad contents; Greek philosophers might not disregard whatever their natures recognized instinctively. Feeling these

[1] Xenophanes, *Frag.*, 16; Ritter and Preller, *Historia Philosophiæ Græcæ*, 87 b.

longings and interests within them, recognizing the complex manifold of life to which these longings related, they realized that as their speculation was born of wonder, so it still progressed amid mysteries. "Nature loves to hide";[1] man shall not exhaust her riddles. "The god whose oracle is at Delphi neither declares nor conceals, but suggests by a sign."[2] From Heraclitus to Plato philosophy fails not in hints that all may not be known, nor all of that be told. High its endeavor to know farthest knowledge, and grasp the secret of the universe. In the meanwhile it is no iconoclast.

Ionian School.

Greek philosophy begins with Thales of Miletus. As accounts remain he was the first to put the question: the world is what?[3] what is its source? For he did not distinguish between the source and moving cause. Thales knew that Homer had called Oceanus the source (*γένεσις*) of gods and men. Perhaps, being a philosopher as Homer was a poet, he divested Oceanus of his personality, and then said: water is the source—the world is made of water. It was an answer based on observation; for to a sea-dwelling Greek, water was exhaustless, boundless its reaches; and more palpably than anything else, water takes many shapes, descends in rain, ascends in mist, congeals in snow and ice, and moisture is wherever there is life.

Anaximander followed. The world is various, holding many elements in opposition to each other—wet and dry, hot and cold; and it is unlimited. Its source must correspond, must be unlimited; and cannot be any element which men perceive; for had any one of these opposing elements been unlimited, all else but it had ceased long since. The source then is just matter unlimited, infinite, undistinguished, unapposed to anything, imperishable—

[1] Heraclitus, *Frag.*, 10 (Bywater's edition).

[2] *Ib.*, *Frag.*, 11.

[3] See Burnet, *Early Greek Philosophy*, p. 43. Zeller's *History of Greek Philosophy* is not specially cited in the following pages because a study of it underlies them all.

τὸ ἄπειρον; whence by separation rise the distinguishable and opposite elements of the visible world and all things therein; into which again all things return, making reparation and requital to each other at the set time for the wrong done of temporary opposition and predominance. He held that there were innumerable worlds, and had hypotheses to explain the heavenly bodies, and the phenomena of thunder, lightning, wind, and rain. The earth hangs in mid-air, held by nothing, but remaining where it is because of its equal distance from everything. We walk on one of its surfaces, and there is an opposite side.[1] Living animals arose from moisture under evaporation by the sun. Man was something like a fish in the beginning.[2]

The third great Milesian was Anaximenes, who, like Thales, sought a source which could be perceived; for speculation might not yet free itself from the aid of sense. He saw this source in air, or more especially that thick mistiness wherein air makes itself visible. From out of its encircling boundlessness all things are formed by condensation and rarefaction, cooling and heating. The introduction of this latter thought offered an explanation of how a single substance might attain to manifold differentiation, and herein lay an advance upon the views of Thales.[3]

These Ionians of Miletus may have been the heads of a "school" whose members were connected by close ties of friendship and like interest. Their philosophy, nevertheless, has come down as physical speculation with no social or ethical bearing. Thereafter, however, philosophy should touch on ethical matters; though it was not to concern itself directly with the nature of man and the

[1] Ritter and Preller, 14 c.

[2] Ritter and Preller, 16 a; *cf.* Burnet, p. 47, etc. The same spirit of free investigation appears in the historian Hekatæus of Miletus, the contemporary of Anaximander. See Meyer, *Geschichte des Alterthums*, vol. ii, § 465.

[3] See Burnet, § 25.

validity of knowledge, until physical speculation was felt to be baffling and contradictory.

Pythagoras and the Eleatics.

This early speculation, which mainly regarded the visible world and its phenomena, appears to have been brought into more palpable relationship with social and political life by Pythagoras, and to have been connected with a religious basis of ethics by Xenophanes. Both men were of Ionia, the one from Samos, the other from Colophon. But both early left their homes, the Samian emigrating to Kroton in Magna Græcia, the man of Colophon wandering through European Greece and Sicily, leaving a name most closely connected with Italian Elea. In the sixth century, life and thought were freer in Ionia than in Hellas or Magna Græcia. On the Asia Minor coast and its adjacent islands there were fewer Dorians, and the Ionians had not been so sorely pressed upon by Dorian encroachment. Near them, back from the coast of Asia Minor, were ancient civilizations not antagonistic to their own and yet sufficiently distinct to afford standards of comparison and an outside point of view, from which these Ionians might consider their own institutions and opinions. Many strains of foreign influence mingled in Ionia, and at this time its cities were less provincial and more liberal-minded than those of European Greece. Speculation there was free, perhaps left undisturbed because it was sheer speculation, affecting neither politics nor religion; while in Athene's city, free thinking was not without its perils until the sacrificial death of Socrates liberalized Greece forever.

Of Pythagoras it is known only that he left Samos, and thereafter made his home at Kroton in Magna Græcia. It is not possible to separate the teachings of the master from those of the sect who reverenced him and bore his name. Certainly many Pythagorean doctrines grew up in the school long after the first forefather of the *ipse dixit* [1] had passed away. The master, however, founded

[1] Ἀυτός ἔφα.

such a philosophical, religious, close-banded school of disciples as could not long continue, without conflict, in the narrow compass of a Greek city. For the Pythagoreans were a society within a society—a *πόλις* within a *πόλις*. Hence there were troubles and expulsions.

The fact that such a sect owed its foundation to Pythagoras shows that his teachings embraced matters outside of physical speculation. This is confirmed by all accounts, earlier and later, of the school. Probably the master taught what very early his disciples held to, the doctrine of metempsychosis; and that the soul is confined in the body as a punishment. At death the souls of less worthy mortals enter other bodies, the worst passing to punishment in Tartarus; but the souls of the righteous go to a better world. Men therefore should strive to purify their lives, and better them. This school also had its answer to the central question of philosophy. The essence of all things is number, and all is number. What they meant by this enigmatical assertion cannot be ascertained; save that, inasmuch as they could have drawn no clear distinction between the corporeal and the incorporeal, they could not have regarded number as immaterial or abstract. Perhaps their "number" meant matter somehow thought of in modes of numerical relationship.

Xenophanes of Colophon passed his youth in that mingled Ionian atmosphere, where were many low views and customs vile, but where thought was free to shake them off and even to denounce them. He may have left his home at the time when the first united strength of the Medes and Persians descended upon the Ionian cities. Among others Phocis fell, and its fugitives, after a troublous time in Sicily, founded Elea in Italy, whither Xenophanes may have gone. Disgust with the practices of the religions which surrounded him influenced the thought of this earnest-minded man—moralist, poet, and philosopher. His hexameters loftily disavow the popular notions, and denounce all who impute lies, adulteries, and incests to divinity. With him God is one and not many, unchangeable and eternal, not created or born, like man in nothing, neither in form nor mind; but altogether, seeing, hearing, thought. Xenophanes' conception of deity had part of its roots in ethical motives, and also reacted upon ethical thought. He sought in God that unity which might be the source of all. Like God, if not God, the universe is uniform and eternal, thought Xenophanes. Parmenides, greatest of Eleatics, followed. All is one—Being; only Being exists, eternal and unchangeable. Apparent plurality and change, which is non-being, do not exist. Herein lay Parmenides' answer to the great question of philosophy. Being was the source, and all causation was absorbed in the universal absolute One, at once cause and effect, at once and indistinguishably All.[1]

Heraclitus.

Before the days of the Eleatics, in India Brahmans were teaching that nothing exists but the absolute One; all change is delusion. But even then Gotama had come to proclaim that all is a ceaseless flow, a passing flame; only "becoming" is. A similar revolution came in Greek philosophy, though in a different way and inspired by other motives. While Parmenides was teaching that everything was one eternal substantial being, in reality undistinguishable and the same, though appearing constantly to change to many forms, Heraclitus of Ephesus was holding that there was no such thing as permanent being, but everything is only in change; all things flow, all things constantly become. It is permanence that is delusion. Fire is the true expression of it all, and fire is the unseen soul of man. So the universe is one manifold of becoming, of union and separation, of transition from opposite to opposite. The life of the body is the death of the soul, the death of the body is the life of the soul. Strife is lord of all, yet in this strife and becoming lies the hidden harmony,

[1] It may be, as Burnet says, by "Being" Parmenides meant body, and his doctrine was a denial of void space; *Early Greek Phil.*, § 72 and § xi of Introduction.

the mighty order which is fate, the one pervading righteous permanence, *δίκη*, world-ruling wisdom. Dark is Heraclitus always, like Apollo's oracle, and speaking of this high order he becomes mystical. The Sun shall not unpunished overstep his bounds; God brings about the accomplishment of everything for the harmony of the whole. The best for man is to know this divine law, this order, this hidden harmony which is mightier than any heard by the ear. To be wise is the highest virtue; and this is to conduct one's life according to law, immediately according to human laws recognized by all, more remotely, yet even more necessarily, according to the divine law by which all human laws are sustained. Lowering are Heraclitus' moralizings; they proceed from his contempt of mankind in its ignorance, as well as from a sense of moral evil. Much did he despise men, their superstitions and reliance on the senses. He left one maxim which all men may observe: *ἦθος ἀνθρώπῳ δαίμων*, character is a man's genius. From the fragments which remain of Heraclitus, it is plain that this Ephesian philosopher greatly felt life's mysteriousness, and the utter babyness of human wisdom.[1]

Empedocles; Anaxagoras; Democritus.

The thoughts expressed by Parmenides and Heraclitus were diametrically opposed. But there came philosophers in whose doctrines may be seen attempted mediations.[2] First Empedocles, taking a middle course, announced four original substances,—each of which some philosopher before him had conceived as the sole primal substance—water, earth, air, fire. There is no essential change in these; hence there is no real becoming and ceasing. Yet the apparent continual change in the world is not mere illusion, for it consists in a real and never-ceasing movement of those

[1] *Cf. Frag.*, 96–99 (Bywater).

[2] Not that they were so intended. Many of the pre-Socratics were such near contemporaries that there is no agreement as to the priority of their doctrines; *cf.* Burnet, § 84.

underived and unchangeable substances, as they combine and separate, moved by the forces of Love and Hate.[1] So Empedocles perceived that to account for the visible world an efficient cause as well as a material source was necessary.

Though often baffled, the philosophic mind in seeking explanation necessarily seeks unity; if it abates the quest in one direction, it pushes on in another. Empedocles needed four material and two moving causes to account for the world. His contemporary Anaxagoras, who brought philosophy to Athens, conceived of the material substance as infinitely manifold in its original nature, conceived, that is, of an indefinite number of original substances, mingled at first in formlessness. In this formless composite existed the substance of all derived things, every one from the first stamped with the quality it was to bear forever. Hence there is no generation or destruction; but only combination and separation. So here was Anaxagoras, like Empedocles, half-way between Parmenides and Heraclitus.

If Anaxagoras abandoned unity in his material cause, he regained it in the great efficient cause which he announced, *νοῦς*, that is to say, force, self-moved and possessed of knowledge. This caused the motion and ordering of the primitive substances into the ordered universe. *Νοῦς*, the world-forming, all-pervading force, is the same everywhere, though more of it may exist in some bodies than in others. Anaxagoras formed his conception after the analogy of what was highest in humanity, not after the analogy of the passions as Empedocles had done. Empedocles had attributed no personality to his Love and Hate; and none apparently did Anaxagoras attribute to his Nous. But these philosophers' perception of the need of an efficient cause

[1] This combination is apparent coming into existence, this separation is apparent ceasing to exist. In his use of the term "Eros," Empedocles had Hesiod for a predecessor.

transcending matter represents the first steps of Greek philosophy along the way, where Plato farthest trod of any Greek, to the rehabilitation of an efficient cause as God.

The Atomists, Leucippus and his greater disciple Democritus,[1] regained unity in their conception of the original substance, the material cause; and they endowed it with such qualities that no efficient cause, no Love or Hate or Nous or god, was needed in the world. The original substance exists in the form of atoms, the same in essence, yet differing in size and shape, and from the beginning and forever severed from each other in space. This infinitude of atoms moving in the void constitutes Being; but the void, or non-Being, is also real, for otherwise there could be no movement of the atoms. There is no real becoming and decay, only continual combination and separation. Each atom is indivisible, impenetrable, contains no empty space, and the weight of each is in proportion to its size. So all qualities in things depend on the number, size, form, and arrangement of the atoms composing them. Hence in substance all things are alike, and possess primary qualities—weight, density, hardness,—which belong to the things themselves; and secondary qualities—heat, cold, color, and taste,—which exist only in our perception. The movement of the atoms is caused by their weight; in falling they collide, and the lighter are forced upwards by the heavier. Worlds are formed through the mutual adhesion and various arrangement of atoms in their infinite movement. Nothing happens by chance, but everything by mechanical necessity.

The soul is composed of fire-atoms, fine, round, smooth, capable of the liveliest movement. Sense-perception is the effect of the atoms composing the object, upon the

[1] Very little beyond the mere skeleton of the theory can be ascribed to Leucippus; all that relates to perception must have been developed by Democritus, perhaps influenced by Protagoras' doctrines.

fire-atoms existing in the organs of sense. Conditioned on the action of the latter atoms, it cannot be a true image of realities. Yet Democritus believed in the verity of knowledge arrived at through thought; and with him thought was but the smoothest movement of the finest atoms. So far as we know, he failed to distinguish thought from perception sufficiently to warrant his confidence in the former, while distrusting the latter. Yet in untroubled thought and in knowledge therefrom resulting —in this quiet movement of the atoms of the soul—he placed the highest human good, and so connected his ethics with his philosophy. Nothing is well for man which disturbs the harmonious movement of the atoms of his soul; therefore he should avoid sensuality and master his passions, discriminate between what is useful and what is injurious, and shun what is wrong and unseemly. Happiness is the aim of life, but that dwells not in herds nor in gold; the soul is its abode, and righteousness and intelligence bring it. Only the enjoyment of the beautiful and fitting is to be desired; the more a man covets the more he needs ; a little suffices for him who desires little, and moderation increases enjoyment. To conquer oneself is the best victory. Not only should a man do no wrong, but will none; he should be more ashamed before himself than before others ; only the consciousness of doing right brings peace of mind, and doing wrong makes a man more unhappy than suffering wrong. Ignorance is the cause of error, and as for knowledge, Democritus would rather know the causes of things than possess the Persian realm.[1] With Democritus apparently more fully than with any earlier philosopher comes the consciousness that philosophic knowledge must be held a part of the whole man, and especially must encompass and control his daily conduct. Democritus' ideal of knowledge is included in his ideal of life. Here his spirituality breaks through his material doctrines. His ethics are on as high

[1] *Fragments* of Democritus.

a plane as those of Socrates, but out of accord with a theory of the universe which reduces causation to the mechanical action of matter, and, in consciously excluding mind from all agency in the world, excludes all thought of purpose.

The Old and the New.

The element common to these earlier philosophers was the endeavor to know the causes or sources of the visible world. Their physical philosophy was the energizing of the Greek understanding as it arose like a strong man to run its course. The search for knowledge was a part of life, a part of Greek life at least ; and soon the philosophers came to have much to say of man and human lots. But structurally philosophy had not yet come to include ethics. Consequently the philosophers' views of life, their ethical opinions, were merely penetrating utterances of wise men, unrelated in systematic thought. Democritus first earnestly endeavors to bring his ethics within the justification and reason of his scientific hypotheses. Nor was philosophy as yet clearly conscious that it, philosophy, the search for widest knowledge, was the most comprehensive element of life's entirety, nay, that it was the unifying principle which made a man's life a whole.

To Democritus may be ascribed the last earnest attempt of philosophy to solve the problem of the universe, and without preliminary investigation of thought. Scornfully had Heraclitus and Parmenides been at one in deriding the testimony of the senses, yet in their opposing systems neither had uttered a doubt as to the power of the mind to grasp farthest verity. More systematically, according to the greater enlightenment of his time, Democritus taught that the senses could not be true reflections of the qualities of objects, and he did not distinguish in principle the action of thought from sensation. Yet he never meant to impugn the value of thought's subtler mechanism.

None other of Democritus' time had his hardihood.

Those who pursued physical inquiries gave up the great quest, contented themselves with following up the branches. Hippocrates advanced the science and art of medicine, and others less famous pursued each his own inquiry. Those whose physical inquiries were of a general nature were, like Diogenes of Appolonia, eclectics. Besides these, a numerous class of clever men, perceiving the contradictions of philosophic systems, abandoned serious investigation of such matters and turned to sensation as the guide of man. Inspired by lower motives they sought to teach things useful—for a price; and were called Sophists. None other of Democritus' time had his hardihood. Only one had his earnestness—Socrates. He, not content with Sophist views and Sophist teachings, was to institute a lowly search for the elements of a knowledge beyond sensation, which should be valid for all. Democritus stood the last of a line of mighty physicists. Socrates, older in years, came after him as the prophet of an era wherein the human mind, conscious of its aberrations and weaknesses, should strive to know itself, then turn this new knowledge into means of reaching the great verities more surely.

The Sophists.

The Sophists were men to whom the attainment of absolute knowledge or truth, and action right for all, had become unreal. They turned to a crass utilitarianism, seeking the apparent best for themselves, and seeing no higher standard of truth than as things seem to the thinker, no higher standard of action than its success. With a certain youthful pleasure in the newly perceived contradictions of unanalytic thought, they flaunted a callow agnosticism, and a positivism of the crudest sort. Recognizing the limitations of human faculty, they held extreme positions regarding the consequent relativity of knowledge; nor did they set themselves to the attainment of that which might be the truest and best under these limitations. Yet the Sophists played their part in the development of thought The temper of the times was soured by the Peloponnesian war, and any high hope of a united Hellas was shattered into enmities between those cities who followed Sparta and those whom Athens led. Men's characters deteriorated; but the knowledge and experience bequeathed by the past was not lost. The most serious Sophistic outcome of the conflicting views of philosophers was Protagoras' famous thesis: "Man is the measure of all things, of those which are, that they are, of those which are not, that they are not." As for the gods, said he, "I do not know whether they exist or not; many things forbid this knowledge, the difficulty of the subject and the shortness of human life." Each man's opinions or sensations were the measure of truth and right and wrong for him. The Sophists held this to be the law of nature, therefore more unquestionable than the laws and customs of society, a view following their assumption that knowledge comes from sensation. This they did not clearly state, for, not having analyzed thought or sensation, they could not clearly distinguish or relate the two. Possibly they were influenced by the doctrines of the Atomists, who had declared secondary qualities of things to be mere products of sensation.[1]

Socrates Begins a Philosophy of Concepts.

Many men were dismayed, and fell back on stolid adherence to law and custom. They could not in argument meet the Sophists, because they did not appreciate such truth as was in the Sophists' teachings. But Socrates, himself morally in earnest as was no other of his time, recognized what truth there was in these ideas, and then went on, seeking to analyze and know the entire nature of man. Was there not some human faculty operating in all men in the same way, which was capable of reaching truth that must be truth for all? This was the kernel of Socrates' inquiries,[2] the scope of which was to know him-

[1] It is hard to say whether Democritus or Protagoras was first here.

[2] Socrates must have been repelled from all inquiries into the operations of nature, by the apparent failures of the physical philosophers. He regarded nature as a system of means to ends, and from the adaptation of

self—and thereby other men as well—and his faculties and capacities for knowing; he sought to discover what it was he truly knew; what it was that, if explained to others, they must also recognize and know. In these inquiries he was on the way to discriminate sensation from thought, from reason, the faculty whereby man attains truth true for all men. Sense is particular, and each man's sensations are valid only for himself; thought is not particular, but necessarily grasps at the general concept, and concepts might be sifted of individual error until they became universal truths.[1] If this were so, there was a common ground of knowledge valid for all men, and human laws could be upheld against the law of man's nature, which merely meant his sensations, pleasures, pains, and passions.

So Socrates spent his life inquiring into the nature of man, chiefly devoting his inquiries to the determination of concepts of the virtues and the application of these concepts to life, in order to establish a system of scientific ethics. For moral questions were not to be treated as matters of custom and authority; but a clearly defined standard should be sought, that of knowledge tested by reason. "There are two things," says Aristotle,[2] "which must in justice be attributed to Socrates, the inductive method of proof, and the general definitions of ideas; both of which belong to the first principles of knowledge."

Virtue is knowledge; this was the basis of Socrates' ethics. Wisdom (σοφία) includes every virtue.[3] Right knowledge and right conduct are the same (εὐπραξία),

objects to their uses he inferred the existence of God, thus declaring the exhaustless argument from design. He regarded God as the personified reason ruling the world, yet often spoke of the gods in the popular sense, and his piety was deep.—Xen., *Mem.*, iv, 8, 11. In prayer and sacrifice he thought men should pray, not for special things, but simply for that which is good, believing that the gods know best what that good is.—Xen., *Mem.*, i, 3, 2.

[1] See Ferrier's *Lectures on Greek Philosophy*—"Socrates."

[2] *Metaphysics*, xiii, 4.

[3] Xen., *Mem.*, iii, 9, 5. He did not distinguish σοφία from σωφροσύνη, soundness of mind, *ib.*, 9, 4.

but quite different from good fortune (εὐτυχία).[1] Hence he argued on to the conclusion that no one intentionally does what he does not believe to be well for himself, which is to say, that no one intentionally does wrong. Socrates' argument appears personal to his character, and to his quiet consciousness that he could not know one thing to be right, and do the opposite.[2] His view, moreover, was the philosophic outcome of the tendency from Homer down to identify wisdom and virtue.[3]

So virtue in general is knowledge of the good.[4] Each virtue consists of the corresponding special knowledge; that one is pious who knows what is right towards the gods; that one is just who knows what is right and lawful towards men; that one is brave who knows how to act properly in danger.[5] Just as knowledge was necessary to virtue, or rather indistinguishable from it, so was knowledge the essential means of a man's well-being. Wealth alone brought it not, since it did not enable its possessor to distinguish life's good and evil.[6] Socrates taught and lived a life of mastery over needs and desires; without disapproval of moderate enjoyment,

[1] Xen., *Mem.*, iii, 9, 14.

[2] "He was so self-controlled that he never set the pleasant before the good." Xen., *Mem.*, iv, 8, 11. Socrates had defined justice as that which conforms to law, Xen., *Mem.*, iv, 4, 12, and by his death he vindicated his own consistency with his definition, showing that he would obey the laws even when they wronged him.

[3] The thought of Socrates that no one intentionally does what he thinks wrong, *i. e.*, bad for himself, in no way conflicts with holding intent to be the criterion of guilt or innocence. See *post*, p. 333. Socrates' whole system proves this, and more particularly such distinctions as that between εὐπραξία and εὐτυχία. *Mem.*, iii, 9, 14. So in the *Apology* he says: "If I corrupt the youth unwittingly, I ought to be instructed, not brought into court."—*Apol.*, xiii.

[4] Which is the advantageous, as the beautiful is the useful.—Xen., *Mem.*, iii, 8, 1–8.

[5] Xen., *Mem.*, iv, 6; all this reasoning is more or less from the analogy of the arts.

[6] *Mem.*, iv, i, 5. Socrates' ideal of virtue-knowledge is also seen in the sense of duty which he felt to examine and question men as to their knowledge, and free them from their ignorance of how little they knew.

he held him who is freest from wants to be nearest the divine.[1]

There was nothing good and real within his ken that Socrates did not prize and revere. He set reason and virtue and the needs of the soul above the needs of the body, impressing on his hearers the transcendent value of that freedom which consists in the possession of a will always able to will the best, and renounce the less important. Such a will must guide itself by knowledge of the best, without which freedom and virtue were manifestly impossible. It would have accorded neither with his temperament nor his philosophic position to attempt to formulate the supreme good for man; but from his life and doctrine it is plain that he thought it to consist in attaining the most complete knowledge of virtue, and in life according. Herein lay man's well-being, his happiness; the will perfectly free from bondage to wants and passions, able to use pleasure without regret at its absence, and guiding a life of virtue perfected in knowledge of what is virtuous.

In Socrates, philosophy became self-conscious, and conscious of its relationship with ethics and all human life, active and theoretical. The Greeks did not sacrifice the rest of their nature to the development of one faculty. According to temperament, one Greek would lay greater stress on one phase of life, another on another. A poet might cry out against the plague of athletes,[2] but what Greek would have been so impious, so untrue to his nature, as to decry the Olympian games, which educed all forms of human excellence, and crowned achievement of sinew with achievement of song? Homer had praised wisdom as well as valor, that wisdom which brings success in war and peace;[3] he praised virtue,—wisdom's self

[1] Xen., *Mem.*, I, 6, 1–10. Here was Socrates' *Hellenism*, *μηδέν ἄγαν*, nothing in excess, least of all the repulsive absurdities of asceticism.

[2] Euripides, *Frag.*, 284.

[3] Homer would have a youth *μύθων τε ῥητῆῤ ἔμεναι, πρηκτῆρά τε ἔργων*, as Phœnix taught Achilles, quick-witted and eloquent as well as valiant.—*Il.*, ix, 443.

—that absence of insolence and impious pride which brings overthrow. So down through all Greek literature, through Pindar, Æschylus, Sophocles, Herodotus, wisdom is glorified as well as might and beauty; virtue is praised, and temperance and righteousness. But the sense of the perfected unity of all these comes first in Socrates to glimmering consciousness, which becomes luminous in Plato.

The Platonic Parable.

An understanding of Plato is not to be had from any grouping and exposition of the metaphysical propositions contained in the dialogues which bear his name. This is true, not because Platonism is a mood, or anything so subtle, vague, or mystical as to elude apprehension. But rather because the philosophy of Plato is not essentially exposition, but consciously partial apprehension of life. The works elucidating it, the *Dialogues*, are not so much attempts to state or reason out facts sensible or transcendental, as they are modes of illustration and suggestion. This is evident as to the many myths and stories and other means of concrete illustration. But it is also true of Plato's direct statements and more formal arguments. They also are parables, parables of dialectic, argumentative suggestion of all that Plato realized as transcending the formulations of language as well as mortal comprehension. Plato is always conscious that the truth cannot be completely stated; his utmost endeavors are but to show "broken lights," half truths. And why? Not because life's phenomena are so complex and distracting; whereof he knows full well.[1] Rather because all truths are necessarily transcendent, touching mortal life, but one and all extending out beyond its range, beyond mortality, and so beyond man's comprehension. They are beams of light, only one end of which touches the mortal sphere.

This general characteristic of Plato's philosophizings is

[1] See Mr. Pater's suggestive chapter "The Genius of Plato," in *Plato and Platonism*.

in the way of form correlative to the fundamental substantial element of Platonism, the conviction of the absolute reality of things spiritual, an absolute reality not limited by mortal life, but of which mortality is a passing phase. Thoughts like these last are definitely pointed in the *Phædo*, as suits the formal topic of that dialogue. But all of Plato's writings are along this line. His view of life, his reasonings, his standards, his opinions, all make for, sustain, suggest, imply, assume, this reality absolute and immortal. With him any full view of life involves the soul's imperishable being.

Platonism Conviction.

Conviction of the reality of things spiritual is more than the foundation of Platonism; it essentially is Platonism, and the various Platonic arguments, discourses, and images are expressions of it. Plato knew, Plato felt, that these things were, and also that they were too much for mortal vision; not even he can know or tell them adequately. And so one notices in reading Plato that it is rarely the special argument that the master definitely believes or deeply cares for.[1] Readily he changes his expositions and his arguments. His conviction is as to that of which the argument is illustration and suggestion—no full statement ever; that could not be. Plato's fundamental convictions might not be completely stated without ceasing to be what they were. His object is to show or suggest how these spiritual entities, which he knows to exist, can be thought to exist or proved. But they do not stand or fall with the strength or weakness of each argument.

Whence sprang this fundamental conviction, which indeed was Plato? It sprang from no such arguments as illustrate or make it somewhat definite and detailed in statement. It was instinctive, that is to say, many-

[1] Take, *e.g.*, such a conclusion as that of the *Meno*,—virtue comes to the virtuous θεῖᾳ μοῖρᾳ. This is Plato's way of saying, he does not quite know, does not quite see, but must at least refer a good thing to a better cause.

sourced and myriad-rooted in all of Plato, in his whole nature and totality of experience. And in content it was a conviction that there existed complete and perfect and efficient prototypes of whatever he was immediately conscious of in himself. It was faith, rather than the outcome of reasoning; and yet a dialectic faith, inasmuch as it was constantly referred to argument for support.

Some of the factors of this conviction which was instinctive, yet sustained by dialectic, may be discovered in Plato's nature and education. All former Greek thought was taken up in him; he more than understands it. Plato's habit of thought contains the training of all previous thinking; his thoughts include the content, the reasons *pro* and *con*, and the analytic force, of previous opinion. His mind holds the power of thought, the weight of reasoning, the metaphysical insight, and all the speculative virtue of the definite philosophemes, of the Eleatic school.[1] The force of the contrary reasoning of Heraclitus is also his; and he has drawn mental clearness from the power of repellancy which lay for him in the materialistic doctrines of the Atomists. Likewise, not without its educational value, in enabling him to perceive as it were the severableness of thought from matter, was even Protagoras' extreme Sophistic view of the relativity and sense-perceptive character of knowledge. Combining and illuminating all of which was the dialectic training and the understanding of the nature of general definition, which was his from his own teacher Socrates.

Platonism Desire.

Then Plato was full Greek, caring for all of life, knowing all desire and the passion with which beauty fires the senses. Hotly in love with every form of beauty, he argued down the allurements of poetry and art which he felt so strong within him ; and felt also to be lures drawing his eyes from contemplation of the realities of which the poem or the statue was but the image of an image. And queening his

[1] See, *e.g.*, *The Parmenides.*

nature, holding all his loves and yearnings within its moulding, proportioning, beauty-giving power, was the intellect which searched and tested all he felt and loved and realized within him or without. His was the perfect Greek mind, clear-seeing and distinguishing, discriminating, choosing ever the greater and the better, the enduring rather than such fleeting things as leave a sting, the veritable rather than the accidental and apparent, and above all choosing the real. And the intellect of Plato, searching through his nature, through his desires and loves and his experience, for that which was the best, to wit, that which was most real, and weighing everything in reason,—the intellect of Plato approves the farthest instincts of his soul, and testifies that the real is the intellectual, the spiritual, and not the matter of sense-perception—sense-deception rather. So reason sanctions and dialectic shall illustrate and further prove the real and absolute existence of things spiritual.

With Plato mental conceptions become immediately matters of the soul, properties or desires of the human personality. He does not entertain them in his mind separate and apart, disjoint from his desires. It was incidental to his Greek artist-nature that as his reason forms its intellectual conceptions, they are visualized, beheld, seen clear and distinct as entities. But what is the motive of this intellectual and imaginative process? why builds he these conceptions? The motive is desire, intense and passionate, to apprehend, grasp, and verily possess and have them, and so share in their reality. Therefore Plato's thinking is ardent with desire to reach and gain and hold the ideal which he is seeking to conceive. So Platonism, the master's own philosophy, is always something more than mere mentality; it is of the whole soul rather than merely of the mind; for in it are emotion and desire, transformed to spiritual appetition. Platonism is philosophy in the real first sense of loving wisdom, desiring to possess it. And this love, which desires to possess wisdom and all the ideal conceptions of the mind, is the same love which is desire of fleshly beauty—Eros indeed—but purified in reason, mentalized, so rendered spiritual.

Thus with Plato love is the principle of appetition and advance unto the beauties seen by the soul. It is the principle of all life, motive all-pervading, desire inextinguishable, in the light of reason directing itself aright and aloft, purifying itself from passion's lower violence, bridling that passionate and slavish courser, dragging him back upon his haunches, lashing him onwards, upwards to the goal of beauty absolute. And so love is that which should strain on until it grasp and hold the highest, best, the eternal spiritual.[1]

Platonism Trust.

Thus the fundamental elements of Plato's yearning after wisdom, of his life which was desire of the best and a straining unto it, were the firm conviction of the reality of things spiritual, and then the always conceiving them as beautiful and good, and so to be desired with the entire strength of man. They are conceived and seen set always within the principle of their attainment, the vital principle of love. These two chief elements are supplemented by a third, vaguest of all and least supported by metaphor or illustrative argument ; this is the element of trust, personal trust in these realities which the mind conceives and the soul desires, the element of personal trust in reaching them through love. This element Plato feels as he feels the rest; it is the religious element strong in him, as in Socrates. But it might not address itself seriously to those gods of whom the poets sang, and other god no Greek ever quite reached. Plato can visualize all but God. Him he knows not, neither understands God's more than respondent love of that which, touched by it, strains thereunto. Plato reached the highest idea, that comprehensive of most reality, the Idea of the Good

[1] This is the matter of the *Phædrus* and the *Symposium*, see *ante*, p. 253.

—which is almost God ; and with a deep sense of the righteousness and the all-controlling wisdom of It, he often speaks of God, θεός and θεῖα μοῖρα ; but he does not know the personality of the Idea of the Good, the fatherhood of God.[1] He has no adequate conception of divine personality to form the basis of a conception of the divine yearning love, and consequently in his thoughts of God there enters no devotion, no giving of himself.

Yet though this last element be vague, the philosophy of Plato holds life whole ; clearly and consciously knowledge is no thing sought apart from life, nor sought with view to close advantage ; it is no mere guide of life. But the love of wisdom is life's formative element, being the spiritual love of all which intellectually seen is good, is beautiful.

The Metaphysics of Definition.

There are certain other general considerations to be borne in mind regarding Plato's *Dialogues*. Thales and other pre-Socratic physicists were in their methods nearer to modern science than Socrates and Plato. For the early physical philosophy investigated—largely and crudely to be sure—and then formed hypotheses to account for facts as observed. In the course of time contradictory opinions arose, and the Eleatics began to use crude, though possibly profound metaphysical argument to substantiate their physical hypotheses. Socrates felt the futility of such physical research, and the crudity of all previous metaphysical substantiations, which was also made apparent by the criticism and methods of Protagoras and other Sophists. Socrates perceived the need, which he made obvious to all men, to criticise and define general conceptions and examine into the means and nature of human knowledge. There resulted the general defini-

[1] Yet with Plato, God must be obeyed ; He is righteous ; to fly away and become like Him is to become just and holy and wise. See *Apol.*, 29 ; *Theætetus*, 176 ; *Statesman*, 171.

tions and the Socratic dialectic method, two enormous gains. Thereupon the great spiritual transcendentalist, Plato, took up the method of his teacher and applied it to the elucidation of that world of spiritual reality of whose existence his consciousness assured him. Thus were the Socratic definitions and dialectic transformed to metaphysics. Comprehensive was Aristotle's vision, but after him there was to be no longer any inductive forming of hypotheses to account for observed facts. Observation was consigned to a long repose. Only after many centuries there came a counter-revolution, and men reverted to methods of observation and induction, no longer crude, haphazard, and unanalytical, but clear and ordered, with modes of proof perfected, all because of the human mind's long exercise in deductive metaphysics.

With Plato, metaphysics was not barren. Incomparably clearer thinking, and more purely mental and spiritual conceptions of the mind and soul, came from it. So unformed were the ways of thought that definitions had still productive virtue; at all events, conceptions, when made clear through definition, helped knowledge to progress. Evidently Plato takes great delight in these new entities, these general concepts now for the first time marked off and definite, visible indeed.[1] He sees their many uses in philosophic elucidation, and employs them as elements of his metaphysical structures. They became direct representatives of reality, if not themselves real potencies. Herein his plastic artist-nature plays its part, and causes him to behold these reason's shapes almost as with the eye—with the soul's eye at least.[2] This indeed is indicated by the famous words so often used by Plato to express these things: *ἰδέα* and *εἶδος*, both signifying primarily shape or form which may be seen; and both

[1] The simple fun in these new ways of arguing and defining, and exposing fallacy, appears in early dialogues, the *Enthydemus* for example.

[2] Plato vizualizes, personifies the *argument* sometimes, as in *Protagoras*, 361, where it is said "For if the argument had a human voice," etc.

from the same root with the unused present εἴδω (*video*) to see, of which οἶδα, the perfect tense, meant I have seen, *i.e.* I know.

Modes of Plato's Teaching; the Ideas.

Plato discovered the human soul, in that he was the first Greek to apprehend clearly the human self in its essential spirituality. Within man and without, the spiritual was of the same essence. In man it lived as desire, courage or energy, and reason; throughout the universe it lived in the form of types, or general ideas, intangible, hardly imaginable, but intelligible to the reason. Material things, although not mere figments of the human mind, were real only as imbued with the corresponding idea, and in so far as they were transitory and changing partook of unreality or non-being. With Plato, the true spiritual life, the life of a lover of wisdom, consisted in contemplation and in reaching up to the attainment of spiritual entities, existing beyond the philosopher's personality. It was not thought of as an inner life, included all within the thinker's self. Subjective contemplation of spiritual things prevailed in later Hellenic times;[1] but with Plato spiritual life, instead of a retiring of the soul within its closet, was a flying forth to see the spiritual beauty of the universe and God.[2]

In source the Platonic Ideas were the Socratic concepts, which Plato elevated from defined general notions to principles of being.[3] The Idea was the general concept

[1] See *post*, chapter xi.

[2] While reading the following slight sketch of the forms taken by Plato's conception of spiritual things, it were well always to remember, as pointed out above, that the forms and modes in which he thinks them are not unchanging with him, and that with him argument, like metaphor, is largely illustration; not adequate statement of inexpressible realities.

[3] Plato was also influenced by the doctrines of Heraclitus as to the flux of all sensible things, and by the doctrines of the Eleatics, which were more to his mind; for he was repelled intensely by the application of Heraclitus' theories made by the Sophists. As against Protagoras and other Sophists, Plato held that sensation was not the source of knowledge, nor the sensible the true and real; the second negative being almost identical in its

necessary to all kinds of knowledge, indeed inherent in the activity of thinking. A sensation is always particular, but to think the sensation is to place it in a class, and this class or genus is the Platonic Idea. But the Platonic Idea was more than this. Since spiritual things were the truly real and knowable, the Idea was truly and objectively existent, an eternal reality which remained unaffected by the partial non-existence of its corresponding phenomenon, or by the contradictions contained in all concrete existence. Indeed the Idea was that reality through which the corresponding object became partly real and temporarily abiding. And since the Idea was reality, was true being, how could it be denied motion and life and soul and mind? Hence it should also be regarded as power.[1] Thus the Platonic Idea, which we must conceive as the abstract and absolute quality, like absolute beauty, or as the type of the particular thing, like the general concept triangle, Plato also held to be the cause of phenomena.[2] Yet as Ideas in their origin are general concepts or genera, they are related to each other so that the higher or more general contains the lower or more particular. Yet the lower are not so merged as to be identical with the higher, but remain separate entities. Above all is the one highest Idea, that of the Good. So there is unity at the apex of the system and correlation throughout. The highest Idea, that of the Good, is equivalent to God; and God, not man, is the measure of

consequences with the first. There can be knowledge only of the absolutely existent; of the non-existent there can only be the opposite of knowledge; of that which partakes both of Being and non-Being, *i.e.*, phenomena, there can be only that which lies between knowledge and ignorance, *i.e.*, opinion.—*Rep.*, 476 e. As against the Eleatics, Plato held that Being was not so one and indivisible as to preclude the existence of many distinguishable realities, to wit, different ideas. And Being, to be known, must be capable of being affected or acted upon by knowledge. True Being must have mind and reason, life, soul, and motion (Soph., 248), whereas the Eleatics denied it all these attributes.

[1] *Δύναμις*, *Soph.*, 247 e.

[2] *Phædo*, 100; *Philebus*, 26 e; *ib.*, 30.

.[1] The Idea of the Good cannot be compre-
ınder one term, as it at once manifests itself in
. It manifests itself in beauty, proportion, and
So Deity can only be known in some manifesta-
ruth, or reason, or beauty, or in the sum total of
deas.[2]

ne corporeal cannot be produced through itself, but its motion from mind. All things are due to a divine and intelligent cause.[3] The Creator "was good, and no goodness ever has any jealousy of anything; so he desired that all things should be as like himself as possible."[4] The motive of God's creative activity lay in divine love of Itself, of the Good, and the wish that all resemble It. The result is the universe, which is a live being, containing the totality of things created, and itself the most perfect of them all.[5] Matter is the substratum of indeterminate extension, which attains to partial reality by impregnation with Ideas,—creative moulding Forms.[6] God, thinking the intelligent better than the unintelligent, and that intelligence (νοῦς) could not exist in anything devoid of a soul, put the intelligence of the world into a soul, and this soul into the world as a body. This infusion of the soul brings order and proportion and beauty; reason imparts itself to the corporeal through the world-soul, which is

atonic hysics,

[1] *Laws*, 716 c; see Ritter, *History of Phil.*, vol. ii; Zeller's *Plato*, p. 285.

[2] *Philebus*, 64 e; see also *Laws*, 985 d.

[3] *Sophist*, 248.

[4] *Timæus*, 29 e; see also *Laws*, 896 e, etc. God, who is good, is the cause only of the good things in the world.—*Rep.*, 379 c. The statement from the *Timæus* cited in the text approaches the Christian conception of the divine love's initiative.

[5] *Timæus*, 30 c, 69 c. In it the stars are the noblest of created natures, created gods, as the universe is the one created God. From their unchanging courses man may learn to regulate the lawless movements of his soul. —*Timæus*, 40 b, etc.

[6] *Cf.* Zeller's *Plato*, p. 315. The mode of the combination of the Idea with matter, so as to produce the sensible, is not explained by Plato.

thus the indispensable intermediate principle between the Idea and the phenomenon.[1]

The object of Plato's philosophy was the knowledge and attainment of the supreme Good. His dialectic and physics form the basis of knowledge on which formally depends his ethics. Plato reasons that all men desire their happiness or well-being, which consists in the possession of the Good; the passionate longing for the lasting possession of the Good is Love. What is the Good? The real is evidently superior to the unreal; and the Idea alone is real. The real Good is the Idea of the Good, which is the absolute, self-existent Good. Man's well-being lies in the realization within himself of Ideas, above all the Idea of the Good; this realization consists in knowledge, more especially in dialectic.[2] And a life in accord with this conception of human good would be a life passed in contemplation of Ideas. But this, taking into account only dialectic or the science of Ideas, would disregard the more complete estimate of human nature; it regards the soul only as reason, and the soul consists also of courage and appetite, which are lower than reason, but cannot be ignored. Knowledge of the Idea, *i.e.*, the realization of it within the soul, is only the highest element of human well-being; the next element is the bringing of the Idea—the Type—to harmonious and fitting manifestation in the sensible world as it exists for men; this is effected through the right condition of the soul, which is virtue.

and Ethics.

[1] See Zeller's *Plato*, p. 341 *et seq*. The soul of man is self-moved, essentially the same as the world-soul, to which it is related as part to the whole. The human soul is almost identical with the Idea, has existed and will exist forever, for life is of its essence (*Phædo*, 105 d), and, like the world-soul, is the mediatizing principle between the Idea and the phenomenon. But its high position is lost by its union with the body, and the degrading environment of corporeality, which clings to it as sea-weeds to the divine visage of sea-god Glaucus.—*Rep.*, 611 c. After death the soul shall receive its deserts through cycles of reward or punishment.—*Rep.*, 614, etc.

[2] See *Protagoras*, 352 d.

Following Socrates, Plato identified virtue with knowledge, and at first held all virtue to be one.[1] Afterwards he admitted the value of practical and customary virtue, not founded on knowledge of conceptions; and, while continuing to recognize common elements in all virtue, he gradually came to distinguish, and at last settled upon a division into four cardinal virtues: Wisdom (σοφία), Courage (ἀνδρεῖα), Temperance (σωφροσύνη), and Justice (δικαιοσύνη).

Virtue.

To see the nature of these virtues clearly, Plato looks at them first in the large, as manifested in the state, for they must be the same in the state, which is a collection of men, as in individuals. In the state there is (1) wisdom or watchfulness in its rulers; (2) courage or spirit in its guardians, which is right opinion as to what is to be feared and what not; (3) temperance, which is unanimity between the rulers and the governed as to which of the two shall rule; and (4) justice, that principle which should exist in every person in the state, requiring each to do his own work and not meddle with many things. The human soul is composed of reason, courage, and appetite, and there are four cardinal virtues of the individual, as of the state: (1) The individual is wise in virtue of that small part within him, which contains a knowledge of his true advantage, and issues instructions to the courageous element as to what is to be feared and what not. (2) The individual is brave in virtue of the courageous element of his nature when, through pleasure and pain, it holds him fast to the instructions of the reason. (3) The individual is temperate in virtue of the friendship and harmony of the elements of the soul, when courage and appetite agree with reason in regarding it as the rightful sovereign, and do not oppose its authority. (4)

[1] In the *Protagoras* it is argued at first that virtue cannot be taught; but at last it is made apparent that the virtues, temperance, justice, and courage, are knowledge and therefore communicable. See *Protag.*, 361; *cf. Meno.*, 88, 89.

The individual is just when each of the three elements does its own work, and does not encroach on the provinces of the other two.

Thus temperance is the attuning of the three elements to harmony; justice is the consequent performance of its proper function or duty by each element, and the consequent due performance of whatever work the individual has to do in life. And the discussion as to whether justice or injustice is better for a man is as ridiculous as to ask which is better, health or disease.[1] Of these arguments from the *Republic* Socrates' closing words in the *Gorgias* afford, perhaps, a summary: "And of all that has been said nothing remains unshaken but the saying that to do injustice is more to be avoided than to suffer injustice, and that the reality and not the appearance of virtue is to be followed above all things, as well in public as in private life; and that when any one has been wrong in anything he is to be chastised, and that the next best thing to a man being just is that he should become just and be chastised and punished."[2]

Identity of Virtue and Knowledge.

Remembering that justice is primarily a harmonious and right condition of the soul, whereby each element duly performs its proper function, and that it is only incidentally dependent on performance of duties to others, we may advert to Plato's conception of the Socratic aphorism that no one does wrong voluntarily, which Plato reiterates in his latest works.[3] Virtue, with Socrates and Plato, consisted in the perfecting of one's own nature. The thought of duty to others was not germane, although it was only through doing no wrong to others that virtue, the perfecting of one's own nature, could be reached. The obliga-

[1] See *Republic*, 430 c to 446. Glaucon and Adymantus had demanded that Socrates should uphold the intrinsic value of justice to the possessor, and not argue that it brings more external advantage than injustice, either in this life or the next.—*Rep.*, 367.

[2] *Gorgias*, 527, Jowett's translation.

[3] *Laws*, 860; *Timæus*, 86 d.

tion of duty might have been antagonistic to the dictates of reason, which guides a man to perfect himself ; so Plato would have been loath to recognize it, even had he conceived it clearly.[1] Manifestly every man seeks his own well-being or happiness, his good as he conceives it; no one acts voluntarily against his own good, though he may erroneously conceive some pleasure or the satisfaction of some passion to be advantageous, and so act contrary to his good.[2] "When a man hates what he thinks good, and embraces what he knows to be evil, this disagreement between the sense of pleasure and the judgment of reason in the soul is the worst ignorance."[3] Although holding that the unjust man is bad against his will,[4] or through his ignorance, Plato recognizes that the legislator should distinguish between voluntary and involuntary hurtful acts, and punish as crimes only the former.[5] There is no inconsistency here. True, the unjust man is bad—acts contrary to his advantage—only against his intention. But that has nothing to do with the voluntariness of the act itself, and it is this voluntariness which the law regards as making a hurtful act a crime. Punishment with Plato is a deterrent from acting evilly in the future ; it is not vengeance, or even retribution;[6] no penalty of the law is designed for ill, but to make him who suffers it better.[7] So with Plato expiation becomes one with the good of the wrong-doer.

Philosophy is a purification of the soul from the affections of the body,[8] and wisdom and knowledge are best;

[1] See Ritter's *Hist. of Philosophy*, vol. ii, p. 387.

[2] The unwise man does not what he wills (βόυλέται), but what seems good to him (δόκει) ; and this is often bad for him, while of course he wills or purposes a good for himself.—*Gorgias*, 467, etc.

[3] *Laws*, 689 a.

[4] *Ib.*, 860.

[5] *Ib.*, 861, etc. Crimes committed in a fit of sudden passion, Plato places half-way between voluntary and involuntary acts.—*Ib.*

[6] *Protagoras*, 324 a.

[7] *Laws*, 854 e.

[8] *Phædo*, 67 c.

the exercise of virtue in human affairs is also part of what is good for man. And finally Plato recognized pleasure, although this, from its indefinite nature, its lack of measure and proportion,[1] was likely to be so unrestrained and wild that one might better occupy himself restraining than indulging it. And yet, since a life without any sensation of pleasure would be hardly desirable,[2] complete human happiness must be sought in the life which with wisdom combines pleasures, not the more vehement which trouble the soul, but true and pure pleasures of knowledge and art and those accompanying health and temperance ; such are the hand-maidens of virtue.[3] Plato loved youthful beauty. The reader still feels a thrill at the entrance of the beautiful youth Charmides, when the staid but enchanted Socrates says : "If to thy beauty is added temperance, then blessed art thou, dear Charmides, in being the son of thy mother."[4] So is the beauty of Lysis made lovely by his lover's telling Socrates that Lysis will surely come to him, as he is fond of listening.[5] And it was Plato's artist-nature that led him to make of Socrates' last hours a death-scene whose beauty may be compared with the steles in the old Athenian cemetery, which now after two

Pleasure.

[1] See *Philebus*, 28 a, etc. ; 646, etc.

[2] The *Philebus* discusses whether pleasure or knowledge is the highest good for man. Pleasure without knowledge is not, Plato establishes this clearly, but neither is knowledge without pleasure, *Philebus*, 20 e, 21 e, 60 e, 63 e ; neither knowledge nor pleasure has sufficiency and perfection ; but knowledge is ten thousand times nearer the good than pleasure, *Philebus*, 67 a. Plato felt that none of those opposites which stand out so prominently in life could exhaust the conception of Good.—Ritter, *Hist. of Phil.*, ii, p. 394.

[3] See *Philebus*, 61 b to 64 b. At the end of the *Philebus* Plato thus classifies the Goods for man : first, measure and the measured and suitable, wherein lies the eternal nature ; second, the symmetrical and beautiful and perfect ; third, reason and intelligence or wisdom ; fourth, sciences and arts and true opinions ; and fifth, pure and painless pleasures of the soul and senses.—*Cf. Laws*, 631 c.

[4] *Charmides*, 158 a ; see *ib.*, 154 c, and *cf.* Xenophon's *Symposium*, i, 8.

[5] *Lysis*, 206 d.

thousand years again shed beauty and peacefulness, and a quiet freedom from anxiety as to all in this life or beyond.[1]

Aristotle's Ethical Distinctions.

With Socrates philosophy became formally concerned with the well-being of man. He loved knowledge, but identified it with virtue; and one questions whether he would not have loved right-conduct more than knowledge, and knowledge rather as an aid to it, if he had seen distinctions between the two. So Plato, entranced with the vision of perfection, human or divine,—call it the Good, call it the Beautiful,—pierced with that divinest of love's pangs, the pangs of philosophy, the guide and way to God, the light making Beauty visible,—the blessed Plato saw as one this great love which was the love of knowledge, the love of beauty, and the love of everlasting possession of the good. Unlike Plato, Aristotle was not lifted above analysis by the very sublimity of his intellect; to analyze and systematize were his passions, for which he would, like his pupil Alexander, bring the whole world within his grasp. Just as fully as Plato did Aristotle regard every Greek object of desire; very far was he from confining himself to ethics. But while Plato's ardent genius fused all good things into a transcendental one, Aristotle's cool discriminating intellect saw their distinguishing traits, and, having analyzed them, systematized, yet never reaching the region of transcendent unity where his master dwelt.

Aristotle was the first to draw a line between knowledge and virtue, knowing the good and doing it. Whoever knows what is good and from passion fails to do it, is incontinent, weak of will.[2] For virtue is a matter of the

[1] Plato would have set his picture of Socrates above any work of plastic art, as having more of pure mind and greater freedom from the dross of matter. "To intelligent persons a living being is more truly delineated by language and discourse than by any painting or work of art; to the duller sort by works of art."—*Politicus*, 277 b; *cf. Rep.*, viii, 529 b, etc.

[2] *Nichomachean Ethics*, vii, i, 5.

will, not merely a matter of knowledge, although that is essential to the formation of a virtuous will. And virtue lies not in mere volition unrealized, but in action, habitual action in accordance with a virtuous will. Hence it is a habit depending on a steady preference of virtuous to evil acts.[1]

Virtue a Habit in the Mean.

More nearly Aristotle defined that habit wherein virtue consists, as a habit in the mean. This was a reproduction of the idea pervading all Greek life, *μηδέν ἄγαν*, which Plato brought into philosophy in the guise of measure or limit, or, more ethically speaking, moderation. Aristotle formally announced it as the criterion of all virtue, for virtue consists in the absence of excess and defect. He explains that it is not the simple equidistant middle point wherein virtue consists, but the condition or action forming a mean relative to the acting subject, *i.e.*, the condition or action befitting and proper to him.

Aristotle illustrates his conception by an enumeration of the different virtues: courage is a mean between cowardice and rashness; temperance, a mean between insensibility and intemperance; liberality, a mean between illiberality and prodigality; high-mindedness, a mean between humble-mindedness and vainglory, and so on through the remaining virtues, magnificence, self-respect, mildness, wit, sincerity, and friendliness.[2] Great-mindedness (*μεγαλοψυχία*), which may be regarded as a lofty and justified self-respect, is the crown of the other virtues, and cannot exist without perfect excellence of character (*καλοκἀγαθία*).[3] Aristotle's great-minded man cares not for the common objects of ambition, will attempt only great things, or remain inactive; he is open in friendship and hatred, but dissembles and shows not himself before the common herd; he cares more for truth

[1] See *Nich. Ethics*, chaps. iv and v, and *cf. ib.*, x, viii, 6.

[2] Of all these, courage appears to be the one containing the greatest proportion of duty.

[3] *Nich. Ethics*, iv, 3, 8.

than for opinion, and feels a just contempt for others; he prefers to confer rather than receive benefits; he wonders seldom, and is not disposed to praise, for nothing is great to him; he is not vindictive, forgetting small injuries; he cares not for personal talk; he prefers beauty and what is honorable, to what is useful and profitable; his step is slow, his voice deep, his language measured, for one who is anxious over few matters does not hurry; he neither loves nor shuns danger, and in all failure and success will act in moderation, caring for nothing too much.[1]

Wisdom a Knowledge of Final Causes.

The *Metaphysics* begins with the remark that all men are actuated by a desire for knowledge. This desire for knowledge for its own sake, for wisdom which does not relate to every-day life, Aristotle regards as springing from the feelings of wonder and curiosity which possessed men after their immediate wants were filled, and found its first satisfaction in myths. That knowledge is to be regarded as true wisdom which is desirable for its own sake, rather than that which men seek because of its utility. True wisdom relates to causes and principles, for through these all other objects of knowledge become capable of being known; and especially it relates to final causes, for the sake of which things are what they are,—

[1] Pride, selfishness, and contempt for others are prominent traits of Aristotle's high-minded man. The picture foreshadows the time when Greek patriotism became a name and public life an ignominy, and men sought through philosophy to sever themselves from the viciousness and trouble about them. After speaking of these virtues, Aristotle speaks of justice (*Nich. Ethics*, bk. v), which he first regards as law-abidingness, and as practically comprehensive of all the virtues. Justice in this general sense is virtue in practice in society, and relates rather to the good of others than to the good of the subject. See *Nich. Ethics*, v, 1, 13. Afterwards he discusses justice in its two forms of distributive and corrective justice, the first, awarding honors and rewards according to the merits of the recipients; the second, merely seeking to secure equality between the persons concerned. Strict legal justice, in order to meet the complexity of life, must be tempered by equity (ἐπιεικεῖα) which corrects the law where it falls short by reason of its universality.

since that for the sake of which a thing exists or an act is done, constitutes the good which is in the thing or act.

Aristotle views the investigations of the early philosophers as searchings for the cause of the world, and he sees their great shortcoming in this, that the only cause conceived by them all, except Anaxagoras, was the material cause. He held that four causes or principles entered into either the generation or existence or cognition of everything: first, the material cause, the elements out of which a thing is created; second, the efficient cause, or means by which it is created; third, the formal cause, which is the essential character of the thing or the expression or form of what it is to be; fourth, the final cause, the end or purpose for which it exists. The final, which tends to become one with the formal, most truly explains a thing; and the final and formal may both be identical with the efficient. Stating the matter in other terms, the object of philosophy is to know existence as such;[1] to know the causes of a thing, the primary matter, the formal nature, the moving power, and the final purpose, is to know the thing which they constitute.

Knowledge pleases in proportion to the grandeur of its objects; says Aristotle,[2] knowledge of the heavenly bodies is most sublime, even a little of it more fascinating than all science, as the smallest glimpse of a beloved beauty is more delightful than a full view of ordinary things; yet "we ought not to shrink with childish disgust from an examination of the lower animals, for there is something wonderful in all the works of nature; and we may repeat what Heraclitus is reported to have said to certain strangers who had come to visit him, but hung back at the door when they saw him warming himself before a fire, bidding them come in boldly, for that there also were there gods; not allowing ourselves to call any creature common or unclean, for there is a kind of beauty about them all. There is a pervading purpose in the

[1] *Meta.*, iii, i.

[2] *De Part. An.*, i. v.

works of nature, if anywhere, and the realization of this purpose is the beauty of the thing." Aristotle saw the beauty of the individual thing in the realization of its share in the purpose of universal nature. His passion for analysis and classification was most ardent; his genius therefor has never been equalled. His intellect yearned to grasp the sum total of existence in its adequate causes and complete concatenation, and he endeavored to systematize all the detailed phenomena it held.

Aristotle's View of Pleasure.

Life offered nothing better than this high and ordered knowledge. But what about pleasure? was that also desirable? and did it come with knowledge? Plato had shunned excluding pleasure from his complete view of good; yet he had regarded it for the most part as the mere abatement of some physical and painful craving. Aristotle thought his master wrong. Pleasure is rather the natural and sure accompaniment of the perfect exercise of any faculty, which comes whenever the faculty attains its end, reaches a more perfect existence, passes from potentiality to actuality. Thus, for example, reason is the highest, the most exclusively human faculty; acquiring knowledge is the mode of its exercise, and therefore in itself gives pleasure.[1] But pleasure is not the intrinsic perfection of a faculty, which rather consists in the habit acquired through continuous deliberate preference; pleasure is an end distinct from this, a good thing added to the attainment of some other perhaps greater good.[2] Some pleasures are better than others. Those which are only such to the evil man are unworthy of the name; and in every case the final standard is the judgment of the good man.[3] But Aristotle is no utilitarian; his conception of the highest good is not hung upon pleasure and pain. It must lie in the perfection of human faculties ; pleasure is merely a happy incident thereto. No one, says he,

[1] See *Poetics*, 4; *Nich. Ethics*, x, 7.

[2] *Nich. Eth.*, x, 4.

[3] *Ib.*, x, 5.

would care to live his life out with the intellect of a child, taking pleasure in childish joys ; nor would one delight in doing anything disgraceful, though no pain from it were ever to come to him. Men should be diligent in the pursuit of virtue, though it bring no pleasure.[1] But he sees no good in pain, nor even in toil, save in its results, for all toil is painful.[2] The virtuous man will make a moral use of poverty, disease, and other evil chances in life; still, well-being does not lie in these, but in their opposites.[3]

The Summum Bonum.

Man's highest good must evidently be an end in itself and not a means to something else; it must be intrinsically part of his nature, and not consist in circumstances nor depend on them.[4] Rather it consists in the unimpeded activity and realization of his highest faculty, his highest nature, which is characteristic of man alone and not shared with plants and brutes: this is reason, which is also the human faculty least dependent on circumstances, and capable of exercise in every station in life; and as it can be exercised more continuously than any other faculty, it promotes the man's happiness during the greatest length of time. Hence the highest life is the *βίος θεωρητικός*, the philosopher's life of thought ; which also is nearest to the divine ; for we cannot conceive of God as exercising the ordinary virtues, but only as contemplating and reasoning eternally. This "would be perfect human happiness, if prolonged through a life of full duration. Such a life, however, would be superhuman, for it is not as being man that one will live thus, but by virtue of a certain divine element subsisting within us. Just as this element far excels our composite nature, so does its operation excel action according to the moral virtues. Reason in comparison with man is something divine, and so is the life of Reason divine in comparison with the routine of a man's

[1] *Nich. Eth.*, x, 3.
[2] *Ib.*, iii, ix.
[3] *Politics*, vii, 13.
[4] *Cf. Ib.*, vii, 1.

life. One must not, however, obey those who bid us think humbly as being mortal men; nay, rather we should indulge immortal longings, and strive to live up to that divine particle within us, which, though it be small in proportionate bulk, yet in power and dignity far surpasses all the other parts of our nature, and is indeed each man's proper self. By living in accordance with it our true individuality will be developed, and such a life cannot fail to be happy above all other kinds of life."[1]

The next best life is one devoted to the practice of the ordinary virtues. This is inferior to the highest, inasmuch as the virtues are generally connected with men's passions and corporeal nature; and this life is too dependent on circumstances; for the liberal man will need money, and the brave and temperate man opportunities for the exercise of his virtue. But the philosopher, with a little of this world's goods, has enough wherewith to live a philosophic, which is the highest life. And living thus he is likely to be beloved by the gods, who may be supposed to take pleasure in what is best and nearest their own natures.[2]

The Coming Severance of Life.

Aristotle's works leave the impression that his convictions did not transcend his reasoned statements. He is always serious and rational, and his arguments seem to contain all his philosophy in a way entirely different from Plato's frequent use of argument to shadow forth what no man might express. Aristotle's analysis penetrates wherever his thought reaches; consequently he distinguishes and classifies what Plato, from a sense of the wholeness of life's transcendent reality, had seen as many-phased and many-colored, but as essentially one. Aristotle still cares, at least theoretically, for the manifold of Greek life, and his wide classifications comprise it all. But the whole is

[1] *Nich. Eth.*, x, vii, tran. by Sir Alex. Grant.
[2] *Ib.*, x, 8.

severed into parts, and his philosophy opens the way for men to select one part of life rather than another, rather than the whole. Perhaps life's inner inseverable wholeness is weakening with Aristotle ; and quite naturally after him come smaller men, missing life's completeness, content with following a part.

CHAPTER XI.

LATER HELLENISM.

IN the bounding strength that Athens felt after throwing off Persia, development was quickened. Her decades were as centuries. Rapidly she lived through phases of achievement and reflection ordinarily filling long periods in a people's life. The same men saw Æschylus, Sophocles, and Euripides. Some of the causes which made her decline as rapid as her growth are not far to seek. She broke her power in the Peloponnesian war; her citizens grew loquacious; their spirit of devotion to the city waned with their faculty of action; they were engrossed with pleasure, with their individual interests and thoughts. And when afterwards Thebes had roused herself for a mighty fling at Sparta's throat, and then sunk back to Bœotian lethargy, and there was no one but Athens to take the lead against Macedon, she had no capacity for such continuous self-denial and exertion, as were needed to uphold her freedom and that of her rancorous neighbors against the untiring king. As late as Philip's time, Athens understood strenuous exertion, she had still conceptions of the glory of civic achievement. When roused by the arguments of her last citizen who possessed elements of greatness, she could act with ephemeral energy; but enduring strength was hers no longer.

Athens and Demosthenes.

There was no lack of intelligence, no failure to appreciate the crisis, or at least the danger. Demosthenes foresaw it all, and urged many fitting measures. His countrymen understood his arguments,. But Demosthenes did not realize the weakness of the time, and thought it still possible, as in the days of Themistocles, by pointing out the wisest course, to persuade men to follow it. He himself had no great capacity for action, nor courage. He was open to bribery, except on the main issue between Athens and Macedon. After his death the Athenians inscribed on his monument: "Hadst thou for Greece been strong, as thou wert wise, the Macedonian had not conquered her." It was also necessary that Greece—Athens—should have been strong for herself.

There was a final flash of glory. Athens rose at Chæroneia; and after the event, when all was lost, Demosthenes struck the highest note: Athens has done nobly, she has not betrayed Greece; she has exposed herself for Greece at the point of danger. This was like the men of Marathon and Salamis. Here was her glory, in her high endeavor; that she did not succeed was the will of fortune, in whose hand lies the event always, strive a man never so strenuously. So Athens though unsuccessful was not inglorious nor unblest.[1] But the truth was, Athens had not striven as she needed to strive, she had not run the long course strongly, but had made a vain spurt at the end. And thereafter her efforts were slight as compared with Chæroneia. Perhaps she knew her impotence.

After Philip, Alexander; then the Diadochi. Nothing could be done against them; but Athens could flatter, and her flatteries, savored with the memory of the flatterer's great past, were grateful to these newly risen kings. Thirty-one years after Chæroneia, Athens paid her adulations to Demetrius Poliorcetes. He gave her large presents of food, gave her freedom, a gift which a people cannot hold unless able to grasp it ungiven. The freed city hails her deliverer:—" The other gods are far

[1] See Dem., *De Corona*, 261–266, and *passim*.

off, or have no ears, or do not exist; but thee we see before us, not in wood or stone, but in life. Guard and preserve us, dear one!" And they lodged the new god in the Parthenon, to indulge his lusts in Athene's temple. One Demochares, nephew of Demosthenes, was the last Athenian attached to the democracy. When he died his son asked the city to decree him a statue, relying on his public deeds, which were begging missions he had well performed, getting many presents of money and corn for the Athenian people from the Kings, Ptolemy, Lysimachus, or Antipater.

The Rest of Greece.

If such was Athens, what of the rest of Greece? Thebes was utterly crushed, and showed no courage after Chæroneia. There was some strength of obstinacy left in Sparta, who fought off Pyrrhus, as she had Epaminondas; and once more, under her hero-king Cleomenes, she made a short brave struggle. But the isolated endeavors of small Greek states might not prevail against powerful monarchs. Even had he not been beaten at Sellasia, Cleomenes could hardly have resisted Macedon after Egypt stopped her subsidies. It bears witness to the stanchness of the Spartan folk that its decline produced such men as he and his predecessor Agis. Yet the energy of a few is impotent to arrest a state's decay, and individual greatness often appears grotesque, or turns to evil amid the general sloth and selfishness. It was vain to expect Spartans to sacrifice their wealth, and return to the black broth of the public mess. The heroism of the young King Agis, the unselfishness of his mother, make a bright picture; for the results produced, it might as well not have been. Likewise in the end, Cleomenes could but gnaw his heart in Egypt, and fall on his sword.

The Achæan league promised more. The federal idea is not of early growth. In ancient times a city-state had been able to resist other cities or larger powers, as Tyre did, or it had not. In the latter case it was destroyed or incorporated into an empire. No thought had come of federating with other cities to gain the permanent strength of many without giving up the autonomy of each. In classical Greece, where there were only city-states, it was easier for each to preserve its liberty; and but slight indications of confederacy appear, as, for example, among the unimportant towns of Acarnania and Phocis.[1] The federal idea gained strength when Greece was in her decline, and surrounded by kingdoms against whom the united strength of her great days would have been needed. Then too late was adopted the expedient of federation, to drive out tyrants, resist Macedon, and preserve civic freedom. After Sicyon joined, the success of the Achæan league was considerable under the energetic leadership of Aratus; perhaps its aims were broader than was common with the city-states of Greece. Yet it was Aratus who, through hatred of Cleomenes, called on Macedon for aid against Sparta, and so dashed any hope there might have been for a free Peloponnesus. On the whole, the Achæan league is of interest chiefly to the student of comparative institutions.

So the decline of city patriotism throughout Greece left no idea in its place strong enough to preserve an efficient love of liberty. The frequent royal proclamations, inspired by policy or sentiment, declaring the Greek cities free, were mockeries. Greek city-states as such had ceased to be respectable.[2]

Hellenism and the East.

Happily the time has more to offer than the political degradation of Greek cities. Fruitful in many ways was the century following Chæroneia, during which Hellenic thought spread abroad, and was acted on by foreign influences. Even Hellas

[1] In those days the Bœotian federation meant mostly Thebes. The cities adhering to Athens were subject to her, and Sparta either ruled subjects or was followed by independent allies.

[2] For Greek history during these times, see Mahaffy, *Greek Life and Thought from Alexander's Time*; Droysen, *Geschichte des Hellenismus*; Holm, *Griechische Geschichte*, Band iv.

had much to learn from the rest of the world. Was there not something to gather from Asia, from Syria, from Egypt? Intercourse with the world outside might teach the kinship of men, and that some of her own thoughts were prejudices. And although the Hellenic city could do little against the power of the monarchies into which the world fell after Alexander's death, the Hellene himself could live and prosper, could learn new things, find new pleasures, and nerve himself with philosophy to enjoy or do without contentedly. If in the world he was powerless, there should be a peace within.

The bounds of Hellas were narrow, although spiritually they embraced the Greek cities in Italy, Asia Minor, and the islands. Beyond, all were barbarians, among whom towered the figure of the Great King. Hellas and Persia were set over against each other in thought and life, as in arms. This idea dominates the history of Herodotus, much as he found to admire in the non-Hellenic world. In time there were some slight interminglings. Persia surrounded, when she no longer ruled, the Greek cities of Asia Minor. Then came Greek inroads into Asia—Xenophon and his Ten Thousand, and Agesilaus. The Greek—witness Xenophon's *Cyropedeia*—found something to admire in the Persian past, if not in the Persian present. These matters, and especially the ease with which Greeks could overcome Persians in battle, were forerunners of the great opportunity which came to Alexander. Far was he from being a pure Greek. Above all, his regarding himself as superhuman on account of his great successes was non-Hellenic; that was *ὕβρις*, and countered the principle of *μηδὲν ἄγαν*. Alexander was less of a Greek than Philip would have liked to be. But he saw that the only way to make his empire permanent was to fuse Greek and Persian. This was his great idea; and his Persian garb, his requiring Persian servility from Macedonians and Greeks, his Persian wives, his desire to see his officers become Asiatic,—all these doings, which Greeks thought barbaric, had this end in view.

In a deep sense he was successful. It may be doubted whether, had he lived, he could have given such solidarity to his conquests as would have held them together as one empire for imperial successors. But he did extend Hellenic influence, and set such an example of cosmopolitanism to his officers as enabled them to hold his conquered world as huge Hellenistic kingdoms.[1] Macedonians and Greeks became such constituent elements of that world that indigenous populations of Asia, Syria, or Egypt might not at all events expel them as foreign. This was a gain for Hellenism. Alexander's generals and their successors, with their followers and advisers, from foreign conquerors became the ruling class of the country, and thus held their ascendancy.

Specialization of Occupations.

The city-states of classical Greece demanded many capacities in their citizens. An Athenian had to be judge and juryman and legislator, a speaker, and a soldier who might be called on to command on land or sea. His life gave him ready powers of judgment and decision, and made him good at need in every emergency. A citizen of Athens's great days got a complete education from his daily life. What was true of Athens was true of the other Grecian cities. The Greek ideal of developing the entire man, body and mind, is nearly connected with the requirements and opportunities of Greek civic life.

Progressive conditions caused a gradual specialization of faculties even in great Greek days, which also may be traced at Athens. Miltiades, Themistocles, and Aristides were statesmen as well as generals. So to an extent were Cimon and Pericles; yet Cimon was more of a mili-

[1] "No sooner had Alexander subdued Asia, than Homer became an author in high esteem, and the Persian, Susian, and Gedrosian youth sang the tragedies of Sophocles."—Plutarch, *Fortune of Alexander*. Alexander maintained his rule by changing his garb. *Ib.*

tary and naval leader, Pericles far more of a statesman. Then Nicias and the elder Demosthenes were even more exclusively generals, but Cleon a politician altogether, who was once made general by an accident. A little later Iphicrates and Chabrias were strictly professional soldiers; then Demosthenes and Æschines were orators, and never led an army. Phocian was the last Athenian to be prominent as an adviser and a general too, like Aratus, who for years was the leading statesman and general of the Achæan league.[1] The best warriors of these later times became mere fighters, like Philopœmen or Pyrrhus, despising the quiet pursuits they saw carried on by effeminate persons. No longer were they "Mars's and the Muses' friend," as Archilochus would have had men. One result of this specialization was the abandonment of war to professional soldiers. The growing disinclination of the better class of Greeks to fight caused the employment of mercenaries, with whom citizen levies could hardly contend; and the habitual employment of mercenaries increased the citizen's inaptitude for war. Moreover, the subjection of Greece by Macedon, Alexander's conquest of the eastern world, and the subsequent formation of great Hellenistic kingdoms, enormously increased commerce and international intercourse. Hence each city and each man was not called on to do so many things, but rather followed some single occupation. So everything fostered a specialization of human faculties, and the old Greek ideal of the completely developed man was lost sight of.

Individualism.

There was another effect of this growing intercourse, this formation of great kingdoms having so many elements of similarity, and this dropping of local prejudices and increasing recognition of a common humanity everywhere. Men's kindly curiosity widened, their loves narrowed. Heretofore the Greek had loved his city passionately and had been

[1] A very poor general he was.

engrossed in the life within its walls. Now he was interested in the world. Few can love anything so extensive; and since the city had become to the Greek merely his abode, he loved himself. Loyalty to a kingly house was hardly developed, while the kingdom over which the monarch ruled was too new, too broad, too vague and changing in its bounds to rouse a love of country. Nor could the new Hellenistic cities, like Alexandria or Antioch, develop it. They were not cities in the old Greek sense; there was no civic life in them, no political independence. They were merely centres, whither men from all parts and of all races thronged because they were pleasant or profitable to live in, utterly different from the old city-state, that greater unity of its citizens' lives and interests. Alexandria or Antioch might be a theatre for mob-passion or race-hatred; but they offered no ties, only advantages of residence. When these ceased, the resident moved elsewhere. There could be no citizens of a city which was merely the centre of a kingdom and the seat of its absolute monarch.

Thus private interests were gaining at the expense of broader devotion. It was not a time of fading spirituality; but rather a period when spiritual and intellectual conceptions were spreading among men. Scepticism existed; yet a thoughtful regard for the divine floated above the common polytheism. Following prevalent tendencies, the popular systems of philosophy were individualistic; for each man the standpoint of contemplation was himself. One result was a deepening of the self-conscious inner life of the individual.

The Literature of Love; the Alexandrians.

A maiden's love is never the main topic of the earlier and greater Greek poems; but always auxiliary to the heroic action of the piece. The narrative of Nausicaa is less for its own sake than to prepare for Odysseus' kind reception among the Phæacians and help on the main story of the *Odyssey*. The poet's mind is on the hero's adventures; very far is he from the thought of a love-tale. Likewise in the fourth Pythian ode, Medea's love is told as incidental to Jason's achievement. Pindar's heart was set on deeds endued with the universal significance of the heroic; his poems could not descend to those joys and comforts which, although common in life, seemed of importance only to the lovers.

Easily to dwell in regions of the ideal is not possible for mankind. That requires, even in those who love it, a conscious tension and reaching out of thought aloft and afar, away from home, as it were; for home consists of a man's own, what is not another's nor the world's. And when people have once beguiled themselves with little pleasures and interests and pictures suited to their narrow hearts, still more will it be difficult to leave them. When once an art or a literature contracts to specialization and realism, it will ever afterwards lack the far vision which discloses the ideal. When the Athenian people had been pleased with Euripides, never again as a people could they care for Æschylus and Sophocles. Aristophanes' complaint in the *Frogs* that Euripides had made love the great subject of tragedy, might have been shriller had he foreseen the long line of followers who should outdo the master. Aristophanes, forsooth, might not stem the tide. His own great comedies drew their interest from public matters; witty were they and bitter, and beautiful in their bursts of lyric song. Their popularity fell with the Athenian commonwealth; and their place was taken by the polished domestic comedies of Menander.[1]

Never had Æschylus shown the spectacle of a woman in love! That was Euripides to become famous for. Yet the recreant dramatist was a master, who could portray the passion of a Phædra, the hate of a Medea. But he often falls belows this height, and writes dramas like the

[1] Plutarch much prefers Menander to Aristophanes ; see his comparison between Menander and Aristophanes, *Morals*, vol. iii.

Andromache, wherein great names are used, while the characters are small, the interest domestic, and the plot turns on petty modes of passion. We notice the growing realism and elaboration of detail. The recognition of Orestes by his sister in the *Electra* is interesting. Euripides makes her reject the tokens by which the heroine of Æschylus and Sophocles had known her brother, and require new signs having a paltry probability. It was important that she should recognize him; the means were unimportant; but it was also important that a tragic heroine should not cross-question like a lawyer. Euripides writes also romantic dramas, the *Ion* for example, where the interest is in the intricacy of the plot and the picturesque pathos and prettiness of the play.[1] A clandestine love is the initial motive. Besides showing the individualistic, Euripides shows the spiritualizing tendencies of the coming time. He is the first to analyze the moods accompanying love's passion.

Euripides was one great forerunner of Alexandrian literature, and through it of Latin and later Greek romance. But the Alexandrians, besides caring for what was romantic and for the analysis of love's moods, wrote of its physical effect upon those on whom it came. Here they had forerunners who would have scorned to turn to trivial conceits and sensualities the mighty Greek emotion for beauty, which included love's passion within its greater compass. No one had expressed this more intensely than Plato in his *Phædrus*.[2] But hear Sappho: "At sight of thee speech leaves me, my tongue is broken, and straightway a subtle fire has run beneath my skin; with my eyes I see nothing, my ears ring, sweat pours over me, trembling seizes my frame, I am paler than grass and seem like to die." As the mountain wind falls on the oak, love bitter sweet shakes her. This is passion in the

[1] **The *Helen* is an inferior play of the same type. For comparison of Euripides with his predecessors see *ante*, p. 230, and p. 296.**

[2] See *ante*, p. 253.

glorified form of love of beauty. It will spurn the base. "Hadst thou felt desire for noble things, hadst thy tongue not framed some evil word, shame had not touched thine eyes, and thou wouldst have spoken out." So, tradition says, Sappho answered Alcæus when he addressed her: "Violet-weaving, pure, sweetly-smiling Sappho, I want to say something, but shame stops me." Sappho was of Æolian Lesbos, and she sings love's passion, not its mental side, its sentiment or sentimentality. Hers is burning desire, and the rapture of beauty—of beauty the vision, not beauty the thought. So with other lyrists. Anacreon, for instance, at banquets, would sing of wine and love. He has the vision of rosy limbs, not so passionate as the pure Æolian, but very beautiful.

Lyric poems expressing a mood, would naturally express this master mood of all. It cannot even be alleged —such is the wreck—that the prototypes of love stories may not have been found by the Alexandrians somewhere in the lost lyric poetry, most of which came not from Athens, but from those cities in Asia Minor or the islands, where love of pleasure had sapped strong civic life.

Alexandria had no past. It was the royal capital of a kingdom and a commercial centre; there met Greek, Jew, Egyptian, and stranger from any part of the world, and there could each imbibe the thoughts and learning and follies of the others. No patriotism towards the city was in the hearts of its inhabitants, and little love of anything except themselves. All took lively interest in the world about them, living as they did where news and commodities, exiles, princes, and prostitutes came from Carthage and Libya, from Babylon and Syria, from Asia Minor, the islands, from Macedonia, Greece, and Italy. As the Alexandrian soldiers and mob sought the goods and gossip of the present, so the Alexandrian scholars, grammarians, and learned poets sought the gossip of the past. Their serious occupations were learning and flattery of the king; their recreations were various; their most heartfelt passion was jealousy of one another.

Alexandrian literature is throughout minutely learned as to myths, stories, traditions, and all the poetic and scientific achievements of the Hellenic past. In their use of this studiously gathered mass, the Alexandrians show their love of all that might comfort or entertain the individual, and above all, their love of writing about love. They know every passion ever entertained by god or mortal; they know the little variations of all traditions wherein love enters; they can turn the most unloving characters to lovers and the direst myths into love poems. No small thing to transform Cyclops to a sea-nymph's lover, as Theocritus does in a pleasant idyl. But, although studying the past, they break from it. Much of their poetry could not, according to classical standards, be clearly classed as epic, lyric, or dramatic—forms which the Alexandrians mingled indiscriminately.[1] Many idyls of Theocritus are lyric in mood, but in form dramatic or epic; the *Hymns* of Callimachus, written nominally in praise of gods, really in flattery of Ptolemies, are epic in metre and structure.[2] The poems deviate from the past in substance also. Instead of great thoughts and achievements, they tell of love and domesticity. The lengthy *Argonautica* of Apollonius Rhodius was meant to be an epic. Its author knew every phase and detail of the myth, and sought to weave them all into the poem. But its real interest is not in the heroic achievement—quite stuccoed over with sorceries and magic. Rather the interest of the poem with its author, with his circle of con-

[1] See Couat, *Poésie Alexandrine*, p. 395, and the same work for Alexandrine literature generally; also Susemihl's exhaustive *Geschichte des Griechischen Litteratur in der Alexandrinerzeit.*

[2] Here they resemble the Homeric hymns, which are lyric in thought, epic in metre—hexameter. But those may have been composed before other metres had come into use, and so before the strict divisions of lyric, dramatic, and epic poetry, recognized by the great lyric and dramatic poets.

temporary admirers and detractors, and with such as have read it since, lies in the story of Medea's love for Jason and the masterly delineation of the emotions and thoughts it brought her. Viewing the epic as a whole, and considering what should have been its topic, the episode is bad art, drawing all attention to itself, sapping the rest of the poem of any interest the Alexandrian pedant may have given it. But this episode influenced literature; Virgil's story of Dido follows it.

Every lengthy Alexandrian poem, whatever its subject, has a love-episode. Eratosthenes' astronomical poem *Hermes* diverts itself with the love of Hermes and Cypris. And Callimachus' *Ætia*, a handbook of the reasons of sacrifices and other ancient customs, contains perhaps the initial story of its kind in literature, the simple love-story that begins with the sudden passion of a youth and maiden, and makes its plot out of obstacles to their marriage, with which it ends. In this early instance the tale runs thus: Acontius was a youth and Cydippe a maid of marvellous beauty. Neither, though often wooed, had ever loved. Eros in anger strikes them with love for each other. The maiden's parents would marry her to another; and thrice she falls sick from grief at her approaching nuptials, while Acontius, having fled the city, wanders unhappy through the woods, telling the streams of his love and writing her name on trees. At last the maid's father consults the Delphic oracle, is told the cause of her affliction and ordered not to thwart the lovers. And so they are married.

In these early love-tales, love comes suddenly. There is no subtle delineation of the passion's growth. That would have countered old traditions of the ways of Aphrodite and Eros, expressive of the common thought that love is something one cannot help, which comes suddenly, it may be like an overpowering bane. Theocritus puts this in an idyl.[1] Daphnis, happy in his wedded love,

[1] *Idyl*, i.

scouts at Aphrodite's power. She sends on him a bitter love for another. "Daphnis, methinks thou didst boast that thou wouldst throw love a fall; nay, is it not thyself that hast been thrown by grievous love?" Daphnis dies struggling against the passion. The Greeks are not the only ones who have thought thus of love; but, however this may be, with Alexandrian and Roman poets the idea of the sudden passion caused by the wiles of Aphrodite or the arrow of Eros is a convention, after which the poet begins the real story, and tells the feelings of the lovers, their love-burdened thoughts, and sometimes penetrates the psychology of the passion, displaying the doubts and fears and mental conflicts it may bring.

Another matter in these love tales is the maiden's chastity. Clandestine joys throughout the story would deprive the wedding of all interest; and such frailty would have lowered the greatness of a Medea and uncrowned her mighty passion. Beyond this, a conception of the beauty of chastity had place in the hearts of even these Alexandrians; and the use they made of it in their poems went to prepare the place which women's virtue has since filled in literature.

Though much of the love talk of Alexandrian pedants was frigid and artificial, there was one among them who, whatever else he may have been, scholar, pedant, courtier, was of his kind a poet always, the father of bucolic verse, Theocritus. His poems were whiffs of country air, a reason why the Alexandrians liked them. And one notices how a big city, built on ugly sand-hills, breeds strong imaginative love of the country. Till then men had not known the lack of country sights and breezes, so had not known how they loved them. The Syracusan in Alexandria soon comes to consciousness of country delights, and fills his poems with shepherdesses and goatherds, with the bleating of goats and the lowing of kine, the humming of bees and the low breath of summer breezes, with hours of sweet dalliance

Theocritus.

in reedy nooks: " Sweet, meseems, is the whispering sound of yonder pine tree, goatherd, that murmureth by the wells of water; and sweet are thy pipings."[1]

Many lovely pictures of nature are to be found in Theocritus. Indeed, the pictorial element is entering poetry,[2] which will now invade the field of painting. The more frigid poets describe their heroes and heroines elaborately, but produce no clear impression. A truer artist like Theocritus does better with a line; but perhaps his fellow-bucolic, Moschus, drew the most famous of all these pictures, in which human beauty is placed in a landscape, or rather sea setting: " Meanwhile Europa, riding on the back of the divine bull, with one hand clasped the beast's great horn, and with the other caught up her garment's purple fold, lest it might trail and be drenched in the hoar sea's infinite spray. And her deep robe was blown out in the wind, like the sail of a ship, and lightly ever it wafted the maiden onward."[3]

Theocritus has open eye and heart for the throng as well as for the secluded dell. A living picture of eager, thoughtless city life he gives in his famous fifteenth idyl; we can still hear the prattle of the women, and the noise of the streets, the prancing of bay steeds, and the irritated cries of pushed and crowded mortals; and see the splendid palace whither they throng, with its marvels of tapestry and its masses of treasure, the riches of great Ptolemy.

Of course Theocritus' idyls are erotic; all his shepherdesses, his goatherds, his youths, his city girls, are in love or loved; they burn with passion or jealousy; they toy with love, or bewail his flight, or lightly lament a fair one's death. Love may be light, love may be heavy, it may be sweet or bitter, bring gladness or sorrow; but

[1] Theocritus, *Idyl*, i, Lang's translation.

[2] It too has a beginning with Euripides. See the opening chorus of the *Ion*.

[3] Moschus, *Idyl*, ii, Lang's translation. Representations of this and similar pictures are seen in the wall paintings from Pompeii.

love it is always that fills the hearts of these rustics, who love each other as naturally as goats love the spring. There are echoes of Lesbian Sappho: "But I, when I beheld him just crossing the threshold of the door with his light step, grew colder all than snow, and the sweat streamed from my brow like dank dews, and I had no strength to speak, nay, not to utter as much as children murmur in their slumber, calling to their mother dear; and all my fair body turned stiff as a puppet of wax."[1] That lover was false, for which he shall knock at the gates of Hades, vows the maiden; for herself she will endure as Sappho might have borne: "But do thou farewell, and turn thy steeds to Ocean, Lady, and my pain I will bear even as till now I have endured it. Farewell, Selene bright and fair, farewell, ye other stars that follow the wheels of quiet night."[2]

As the bucolic poet can turn any myth into a love tale, so can he reduce marvellous deeds to charming scenes of domesticity.[3] "When Heracles was but ten months old, the lady of Midea, even Alcmena, took him on a time, and Iphicles, his brother, younger by one night, and gave them both their bath and their fill of milk, then laid them down in the buckler of bronze, that goodly piece whereof Amphitryon had stripped the fallen Pterelaus, and then the lady stroked her children's heads, and spoke saying: 'Sleep, my little ones, a light delicious sleep; sleep, soul of mine, two brothers, babes unharmed; blessed be your sleep, and blessed may ye come to the dawn.' So saying she rocked the huge shield, and in a moment sleep laid hold of them."

[1] *Idyl*, ii, Lang's translation.

[2] *Ib.* The girl has been invoking Selene to charm back her lover with magic rites.

[3] Of course in seeking the domestic, Theocritus was not alone. Callimachus had written a famous idyllic epic, *Hecale*, with Theseus' capture of the Marathonian bull for its nominal subject; but its most interesting matter was the story of her sorrows and domestic trials, told by an old woman, at whose cabin the hero seeks shelter for the night.

Then the poet tells how Hera sent the two serpents, how the babes wakened, Iphicles screaming in terror; how Heracles grasped them by the throats, and vainly they struggle in their pain. "Now Alcmena heard the cry, and wakened first,—'Arise, Amphitryon, for numbing fear lays hold of me; arise, nor stay to put shoon beneath thy feet. Hearst thou not how loud the younger child is wailing?' . . . Thus she spoke, and at his wife's bidding he stepped down out of his bed, and made for his richly dight sword that he kept always hanging on its pin above his bed of cedar . . . Then he cried aloud on his thralls who were drawing the deep breath of sleep: 'Lights! bring lights as quick as may be from the hearth, my thralls, and thrust back the strong bolts of the door! Arise, ye serving-men, stout of heart, 'tis the master calls!' Then quick the serving-men came speeding with torches burning, and the house waxed full as each man hasted along. Then truly, when they saw the young child Heracles clutching the snakes twain in his tender grasp, they all cried out and smote their hands together. But he kept showing the creeping things to his father Amphitryon, and leaped on high in his childish glee, and, laughing, at his father's feet he laid them down, the dread monsters, fallen in the sleep of death. Then Alcmena in her bosom took and laid Iphicles, dry-eyed and wan with fear; but Amphitryon, placing the other child beneath a lamb's wool coverlet, betook himself again to his bed, and got him to his rest."[1]

Pindar tells the same myth, shortly as is his wont, his heart burning with the thought of the deed. Theocritus tells of the mother's loving care, her blessings on her sons, their sleep, the terrified outcry of the younger, the mother waking first and anxious, rousing her husband, hurrying him to rise without his shoes,—and then the inrushing servants, and again the mother clasping the

[1] Theocritus, *Idyl*, xxiv, Lang's translation.

terrified Iphicles, and the father, after all the trouble, getting into bed again. The deed itself is but a little centre around which to group this domestic scene.

The Anthology.

Much that may be said of Alexandrian literature may be said of the *Anthology*, that huge collection of epitaph and epigram and varied verse which comes down to us, part of it from Alexandrian times. Happy, if often coarse, are the conceits of its love epigrams, and bitter too the sting at the tail of these caustic verses; and the pathos of the epitaphs carries the freshness of tears down these twenty centuries, teaching that centuries are nought, since the heart beats now as it did then. The great poems of Greece also taught that centuries are nothing; then the lesson moved in heroism, showing the perfect deed as a flash out of eternity. In the epitaphs of the *Anthology*, save the few old Greek ones, there are strains of pathos, the woe of the drowned mariner, tears for the lovely maid cut off, tears for the death couch of a mother:—the greatness is gone.[1]

Art: Scopas and Praxiteles.

The Phidian art of Periclean Athens was public art; its motives were the glory of the state and the honor of the gods, and public revenues defrayed the cost. After the Peloponnesian war, when the civic fervor of the great times passed away, tendencies toward individualism showed themselves in art, which was now to minister to the magnificence of princes and the luxury of the rich, and express the narrower motives of the times.[2] The age brought forth Scopas and Praxiteles, whose works were nearer its level, showed human acts and passions more palpably, and gave subtler expression to the moods and emotions of men.

[1] See Mackail's *Select Epigrams from the Greek Anthology*, and Introduction, xiii–xvi.

[2] Wherever after the period of the Peloponnesian war there was public spirit and achievement—as at Thebes or in Arcadia or Messene in alliance with Thebes—there followed a corresponding development of art; but never anything to be compared with the public art of the Athens of Pericles. See Overbeck, *Geschichte der Griechischen Plastik*, vol. ii.

Although Scopas was born at Paros he may have been influenced by the traditions of Phidian art as much as his younger contemporary Praxiteles, who was a native-born Athenian. At all events, there was such close relationship between the works of these two masters that in Pliny's time it was a question to which of them to attribute the Niobe group. The statues of Scopas express passion and emotion,—rage, fear, love, desire. His sculptured countenances express definite thought or feeling, or definite traits of character in action. No single figure from the remains of the Mausoleum can be surely attributed to him; yet, as he was its leading artist, its sculptures were probably executed under his direction. The action of the Greeks and Amazons of its frieze is energetic, even violent; many of their faces show the eagerness of battle or the pitifulness of danger and overthrow. Yet among them are youthful forms and countenances of ideal beauty.

Scopas also carved statues wherein was intensified some special element of humanity to the probable depreciation of the other traits which were required by the full classic ideal of complete perfection. Such were his three famous boy-forms at Megara, personifying *Ἐρός*, *Ἵμερος*, and *Πόθος*,—*Love*, its *Charm*, and the *Desire* inspired. Undoubtedly these three phases of human being were ideally presented, a result which must nevertheless have been reached through leaving imperfectly expressed other admirable youthful qualities, like strength and manliness. These statues represented an idealized human element, but not the ideal of full human being.

Perhaps one should regard sense-beauty as characterizing the sculpture of Praxiteles, though it was not the most prominent trait in all his works, which were various in character. We know from the *Hermes* found at Olympia that he invested his divine forms with lovely beauty, and the *Hermes* was not among his works most celebrated in antiquity, of which perhaps the most famous was his nude *Aphrodite* of Cnidos.[1] He was not always earnest with his marble gods, and seems in such a work as the *Apollo Sauroctonus* almost to play with thoughts of divinity. Praxiteles has grace and loveliness of form and feature. Far is he from realism. Yet in representing the human form he has become more natural, say than Polyclitus, for he gives his statues the softer and subtler suggestions of flesh and movement. Beyond all other sculptors, says Diodorus of Sicily, did Praxiteles express *τὰ τῆς ψυχῆς παθῆ*, the emotions of the soul, the movements of the spirit; and this too in their whole range from soft musing and gathering desire to violent passion. Yet judging from the notices of his works, it may be inferred that for the most part they expressed those emotions which are connected with sense-beauty.[2]

The grandeur of human quality bodied in the art of Phidias gave to its monumental creations a loftiness of intellectuality which no later art could equal. The statues of Scopas and Praxiteles more palpably exhibit spiritual life in play of thought and motive and desire. Had Phidias in the features of his gods displayed vivid play of thoughts and sentiments appropriate to each, he would have given them more palpable individuality; for it is in action rather than in repose, in specially directed mental exertion or sentiment, or in passion and emotion, that characteristic traits more plainly show themselves. Yet no such transient phase of thought or passion can exhibit the personality so completely and permanently as repose, when the face wears that expression which is, as it were, the sum of the man's past life. Particular expression in a statue usually exists at the expense of deeper truth and permanence.

From the broad Phidian ideal of setting forth entire and

[1] An idea of which may be given by the *Venus* of the Vatican.

[2] The Choregic monument of Lysicrates, 334 B.C., affords examples of the lighter sculpture of the Praxitelean time. Its sculptures have life and beauty, humor and grotesqueness too, and exquisite technique.

complete being at its noblest, the art of Scopas and Praxiteles was a deflection in its specialization of Phidian idealism by creating beings who did not contain the whole range of human attribute, but stood rather for one or another side of human nature, like Eros or Desire. The creations of this latter art are of a lesser beauty because they do not set forth the full round of human excellence, and thus moreover will lack complete physical and intellectual proportion. Again, this latter art lacked the highest beauty, because it did not give due pre-eminence to the grandest traits. Its gods were not as great gods as Phidian *Zeus* and *Athene*. And its creations lacked ethos, that ethical impressiveness, that free and intellectual nobility, springing from the union of great and universal qualities in a self-directing personality.[1]

Lysippus.

As Scopas and Praxiteles were, in a measure, the successors of Phidias, so their younger contemporary, Lysippus of Sicyon, though calling himself self-taught, was the successor of Myron and Polyclitus. The art of the Argive masters expressed the strength and completeness of physique. Polyclitus' *Doryphorus* had become the canon of the human athletic form. With this statue as a model, Lysippus sought farther to elevate the body by refining its baser traits, its every superfluity of flesh, and by raising those elements which gave it grace and power and nobility of aspect. The *Apoxyomenus* was a glorified *Doryphorus*. The complete, fully developed, and formally correct work of the ancient master received its apotheosis in the nobility of bodily strength and beauty created by Lysippus. And withal the latter statue is the more natural, in that it expresses the subtler traits of physical life.

Lysippus also executed colossal statues and portraits

[1] See *ante*, chap. ix. The course of Greek painting was similar. Aristotle says the pictures of Polygnotus had ethos, those of Zeuxis had not. —*Poetics*, vi.

whose fame has been enduring. The chief of the latter were his portraits of Alexander, on one of which was written the epigram,—"It looks up as if saying, 'Mine is the earth, thou rulest, O Zeus, in Olympus.'" These preserved certain of the conqueror's peculiarities, as carrying the head on one side; and with insight Lysippus presented such individual traits in their proper relationship and common effect, so as to give the impression of the very Alexander.

Imaginary statues of past literary worthies, *Homer*, for example, also came from his hand, a mode of art which seems to have been original with him. He also carved gods and allegorical statues, as of *Opportunity*, the favoring instant. This was an allegory, lacking true personality and making one of the first of this type of statues; for now and afterwards Cities and the Fortunes of Cities were personified, and Poetry and Music and the other arts. All of which were again forerunners of the still more lifeless personifications of abstract ideas, *Æquitas*, *Salus*, *Pax*, *Securitas*, *Concordia*, and the like. In the great Greek period such personifications were made more sparingly and only of ideas like *Victory*, which had long possessed personality in common thought. *Eros* and *Youth* were also represented in art; but these were human qualities, naturally offering themselves for personification. The great creations of Greek art, the deities, were true personalities, or, if we choose, proper personifications of personal attributes; that is, of attributes like strength and wisdom, bravery and self-control, which exist only in persons. It was a different matter to take impersonal circumstances or conditions, or their abstract ideas, such as "peace," "wealth," "liberty," "concord," and represent them in human forms. Such art errs because these are not elements of human being, and have no genuine personality; but merely constitute its environment or condition. They are abstract notions of circumstances, not of personal qualities; and art resorted to them only when the vision for sublime and universal personalities was passing from men. This tendency of art was not the animism of early times. When Phidias placed the *Ilissus* on the west pediment of the Parthenon, he represented in human form the river-god, the personal spirit, who in old Greek thought animated the river and made it flow. It was no abstract idea that he was endeavoring to embody in marble, such as the waning idealism and growing sentimentality of the later time affected.

Pathos in Greek Sculpture.

The highest plastic art makes sparing use of pathos to enhance its interest. Phidian art felt no need to point its ethical worth by pathetic elements. There was no pathos in the Olympian *Zeus* or in the *Athene Parthenos;* nor is there any in the sculptures from the pediments of the Parthenon which have been preserved, nor any in the frieze. In the metopes which show the conflict between Centaurs and Lapiths, pathos enters of necessity, for a battle implies wounds and death. Hence there is great pathos in the expiring Lapith form of the famous metope; there is pathos in the agony of the Centaur whose back is pierced by a sword. Yet in these Parthenon metopes there is no heightening of pathos for its own sake; such as exists is necessary to the general theme and its main thought, a great and ethical thought, the ruin involved in lawless crime.

Pathos became a very prominent element of art when men's motives were narrowing to their individual desires. Then the pathetic came to be greatly valued for its own sake; for it represented the appeal of individual to individual, which, with the increasing individualistic tendencies of the times, was taking the place of broader ethical motives, such as the greatness of the citizen in the glory of his state. The pathetic in Greek art grew at the expense of ethical and intellectual qualities. It impaired the full ideal of beauty and of excellence when it led to the creation of specially emotional natures. Such were Scopas's yearning sea-gods, hippocentaurs, and mænads; such were his statues *Eros* and *Desire*. These were all creations in which the emotional side was so prominent as to impair their full personality. Besides, they were beings representing the pathos of unfulfilled desire and the yearning of individuals towards one another, matters which the Greeks rarely treated in a lofty way.

Two groups may be referred to as examples of the pathetic in Greek sculpture. The first is the *Niobe*, a work either by Scopas or Praxiteles. *Niobe* is essentially a pathetic creation, yet possessing great character and intellectual qualities,—ethos. She is an agonized mother; she is also a beautiful woman and a great queen. She does not grovel and shriek out in vain fear, but would interpose her body between her children and Heaven's vengeance. Beyond this, she does not impotently resist or blaspheme the cruel retribution of the gods. Her pride and loftiness of mind control her grief, and will sustain her till her form stiffen to stone. Moreover, the ethical import of ruin brought by overwhelming pride of greatness is clear and impressive.

The pathos of the *Niobe* is exceeded in intensity by that of the *Laocoön*, a work of Rhodian sculptors of at least a century after Praxiteles' time. Every one knows it to be a marvel of plastic composition and skill, perhaps the most difficult work left by antiquity: one can hardly see the statue without thinking of the skill of the artists —no praise, to be sure. The mortal agony of the group is intensified with consummate technical and dramatic skill. In the elder son there is the beginning; he is only held in fear, is not yet pierced by the poison of the serpents, nor crushed by their folds. In the younger son there is the end; his sufferings are over, and he is swooning in death. These two set off the climax of agony in the father, the incarnation of struggling pain, overmastering, absorbing. As the physical pain contorts his features, so does it also obscure his mind; indeed, a noble mind, one may think, if only the physical agony would let the mind clear itself.

Niobe feels the anguish of a mother, feels it clearly, her mind and soul possessed by the despairing hope of protecting her children. But the mind of *Laocoön* is so obscured by his own agony that such mental anguish as he feels is not clear and definite, is only vague despair. Intense physical pain deadens thought and mental woe. *Laocoön's* mind would seek its woe in thought for his sons, in thought for the doomed city; but the pain obscures clear thought of anything, so that there is actually little more in *Laocoön* than physical agony. Consequently the *Laocoön* is a less noble work than the *Niobe;* the pathos in it is more the pathos of physical pain, presenting no great quality brought to expression in a concrete form, as the *Niobe* expresses the anguish of a mother's love. The *Laocoön* shows the tendency of the pathetic in Greek sculpture towards the narrow and the individual; shows how higher themes were losing their hold on men. And if in sculpture, how much more in painting, which lends itself more readily to the pathetic and the little. When reading Æschylus' *Prometheus,* the Titan's greatness, his resolve, his strength of will and far vision fill the mind to the exclusion of thoughts of physical pain. In these later times admiration for these qualities had shrunk, and we read the story of Parrhasius torturing a captive to get the very utmost expression of agony to copy in his *Prometheus.*

The Later Realism.

The pathos of the last bloom of Greek sculpture, while it acquired no higher motives than those of the *Laocoön,* became even more individual because it became realistic. In the art of Pergamon, from the time of Atallus I, about 200 B.C., on through the next fifty years, the sculptors chose often contemporary historical events, and carved their statues with close attention to historical and ethnographical accuracy, all of which is shown in the many carvings of Gauls and other barbarians dating from this period. This sculpture was nearly all pathetic, representing the overthrow or suicide of these barbarians, and in addition to its almost exclusive pathos, with no high motive rendered prominent, the growing realism of detail and feature further detracted from its breadth of human significance. These Gauls were Gauls, rather than broad human beings, and their frequently carved suicides represented a special phase of barbaric despair which had no such universal human significance as *Niobe's* anguish.[1]

A splendid example of realistic sculpture is given by the reliefs around the great altar of Zeus built at Pergamon for Eumenes II, who reigned from B.C. 196 to B.C. 157. They represent the Gigantomachy. Their art combines inherited tradition with the tendencies of the time. The conceptions of the gods are of great nobility and power; but realism enters in the minutely careful carving of their garments, the texture of which is shown in the marble. Further realism appears in the detail of the animals—dogs, lions, eagles—which attend the gods and rend the giants. Likewise the mode of representing the combat is realistic; the eagle of Zeus with its claw seizes the lower jaw of one of the snakes forming the monstrous extremities of a giant; another giant of completely human form is agonized, his thigh transfixed with a flaming thunderbolt from Zeus's hand. Some of the giants are of ideal beauty, while others are but half human, with snaky extremities or bestial heads. In their faces appears the pathos of struggle, suffering, or overthrow. The technique is admirable, and the composition is skilful, although it will seem confused to those who love the harmony and order of the Parthenon frieze. These large reliefs of the Zeus altar are all in true relief

[1] An example is afforded by the statues which remain (in the museums of Naples, Venice, Rome, Paris, and Aix) of the gift of Atallus I to Athens. The *Dying Gaul* of the Capitol is of the same school.

style. But some smaller reliefs, probably from an interior bit of frieze representing the myth of Telephus, are pictorial, with landscape background and other suggestions of painting.

After this strong art of Pergamon, sculpture seems to have had no further original impulse. Probably all the great Hellenic statues are earlier. The *Samothracian Nikè* was probably dedicated by Demetrius Poliorcetes about B.C. 300; the *Venus of Melos* cannot be much later; nor the *Apollo Belvedere.* There is something final in these last periods of Hellenic sculpture. Its proper limits have been reached; beyond them there is nothing for the sculptor but to attempt to narrate or depict. Henceforth sculpture must overstep its bounds or reproduce. If it does the former, it loses its proper greatness in mistaken attempts to accomplish what poetry or painting can do better; if the latter, it degenerates through loss of originality. In both modes of degeneration sculpture was now rapidly to decline.

The Drift to Philosophy.

The life of the Greek city-states had been often hard and cruel; and in the third and second centuries, living was perhaps more comfortable than it had been in the greater days. But formerly, whatever life actually was, there always seemed possibilities of bettering or upholding or controlling it. External powers were not so palpably overwhelming. Now the crowd might take what pleasure it could get day by day. It had no longer public duties to perform nor public spirit; why should not each man take his pleasure? And many did. But those who looked before and after could find no satisfaction thus. Feeling themselves powerless over life about them, they sought a refuge and a peace within; such men turned to philosophy. That had been a search for knowledge loved for its own sake; it had meant keen investigations and grand imaginative systems. Now it meant a means of guiding one's life in the best way; and knowledge was sought as yielding surer rules of conduct. So philosophies became practical systems, with thoughtful men supplying the place of religion, and superseding those ethics which public opinion had sanctioned; and though, from lack of prayer and worship, Stoicism and Epicureanism were not religions, they tended to become philosophic creeds. In former times, only men with yearning intellects would devote themselves to philosophy; many other matters filled noble minds. Heraclitus, Democritus, Socrates, Plato, and their few disciples might be philosophers, formal seekers after knowledge and an accordant life; but the full and eager life of the same times made Pindar, Æschylus, Sophocles, poets; made Solon, Themistocles, Aristides, Pericles, Epaminondas, statesmen and soldiers. Had these men lived in the third century before Christ, they had been neither poets nor statesmen; what else could they have been than Stoics, Epicureans, and Sceptics? In this century, philosophy, because of the number of its votaries, who possessed a large part of the intellectual energy of the time, became of general importance as never before.

Cynics and Cyrenaics.

However useful Socrates' teachings may have been to the individual, they had public motives and predominant regard for the state. So had Plato's philosophy shown a grand spiritual objectivity, wherein the individual was of less importance than the ideal community, and wherein spirituality was far removed from any ideal of self-centred inner life. But even Socrates had disciples who represented tendencies which were to become the master motives of the Hellenic world, tendencies born of waning public energy, and growing as men centred their desires in themselves. Chief among these were the austere Antisthenes and Aristippus, master of the art of self-content. Each professed to see the true Socratic doctrine in those opposite elements of the master's teaching respectively most congenial to the rude Cynic and the voluptary from Cyrene. Madness were better than pleasure, said the one; sense-pleasure is the only good, said the other. Both, anticipating the waning intellectual energy of the coming times, laid aside the care for knowledge. Antisthenes, Diogenes, and other Cynics, with their congenial friend Stilpo the Megarian, fell into a nominalism so extreme and material as to render knowledge impossible. They would not hear of abstract qualities, would hold to nothing but particulars, and only to those particular things which could be seen and felt. Virtue was enough for man; that was his whole well-being; *ἀρετή* and *εὐδαιμονία* were the same. External goods were useless, marriage and a home, encumbrances. Let a man wander a homeless beggar, blessed with his virtue. Virtue was also reason, wisdom; a few wise men there are, the rest are fools; and the wise are sufficient to themselves, which is enough.

Cynicism was brutal negation. It would cast off all ties, all bonds, all decencies. Virtue lay in austerity and suppression of pleasure, intellectual as well as sensual; though it was sense-pleasure that predominated in the festering Cynic imagination. They called themselves citizens of the world, yet had no sense of the brotherhood of man; they were cosmopolitan only in having no civic loves, and recognizing no civic duties. They did recognize the propriety of promulgating their doctrines, from vanity perhaps, and the pride which Plato saw through the rents of Antisthenes' garments.

Opposed as the doctrines of Aristippus were to those of the Cynics, they represented the same abandonment of duty to the state, the same centring of the individual in himself. Thinking there was no sufficient reason to deem sensations true images of the external world, he held physical science impossible, and regarded sensation as the only matter important for man. All that men can surely do is to occasion sensations within themselves, beyond which they know nothing; hence the farthest rule of conduct is for each man to give himself pleasurable sensations and avoid unpleasant ones, the former being good without regard to their source, the latter unconditionally evil. What the morrow may bring is uncertain; the present with its sensations only is ours; these alone afford assured good and an unerring guide to life. Yet, since it is known that certain pleasures bring greater pains, men may wisely avoid the one to escape the other; at least men know that abandonment to sense-pleasures results in dulness and pain. So the wise man will control himself and walk the ways of temperance, following pleasures always, but content with those that bring no pain. In such a life of temperance wherein pleasures and pains were weighed, it was impossible that mental elements should not enter, even though they might not be emphasized in expression. Pleasant mental elements, at least, would be the contemplation of past pleasures and a gentle looking forward to pleasures to come, yet without building too much on the future's uncertainties. So, at all events, both as to the present and the future, the rule of life should be self-control and contentment. Thus, through an opposite course, Aristippus reached the same goal with the Cynics,—freedom from the bonds of circumstances. This was the goal so many were to seek; but as for Aristippus' views, they were soon departed from, his followers first abandoning the pleasure of the moment as a guide, then giving up the hope of getting positive pleasure at all, seeking only freedom from pain, and in the end doubting whether pleasure and pain were after all the great matters.

Cynics, Cyrenaics, Megarians too, were forerunners along the way over which multitudes of Stoics, Epicureans, and Sceptics were to travel more knowingly. The crudities of the earlier doctrines were discarded, and their incompleteness supplemented by the broader and more positive teachings of the Stoa, and Epicurus' more adequate exposition of the nature and limitations of hedonism. Zeno and Epicurus had the opportunity of deriving such illumination as their characters permitted from the systems of Plato and Aristotle. And as for Scepticism, that might never have advanced beyond the narrow doubt of Pyrrho, had not Carneades used Plato's dialectic to establish an academic despair.

Stoicism.

Stoic philosophy falls into Logic, Physics, and Ethics. The object of the first was to obtain a criterion of truth and some formal scheme of ratiocination whereby to base Stoic ethics on Stoic physics. For Chrysippus declared that he could see no foundation for justice except in the nature of Zeus and the universe. Which is to say he could see no sure basis for a system of ethics, of human conduct—the great matter—except in principles rooted in the nature of man and the world about him. This idea is still admirably Greek.

These later philosophies begin with some preliminary discussion of human knowledge. It was especially necessary for such a positive system as the Stoa to establish a theory of knowledge and a criterion of truth. The endeavor of Stoic logic was, through analysis of the forms and general nature of mental presentations, to obtain a criterion whereby their truth or falsity might be determined. All presentations (φαντασίαι) arise from the impressions made by objects through sensation upon the soul, which is at first as a piece of white paper; sensation, perception, is the origin of all mental presentations. From sense-perception comes memory, from many like memories comes experience, and from the comparison and combination of multiform perceptions, rendered possible by memory and experience, ideas are formed which transcend sensation.[1]

Although the contents of ideas are derived from sensa-

[1] Those ideas which are formed without artifice, and according to nature, constitute the προλήψεις or κοιναὶ ἔννοιαι which the Stoics regarded as the principles of truth and virtue and as the mark of rational beings. See Zeller, *Phil. der Griechen* (3d ed.), 3[1], p. 63, *et seq.*

tions, the Stoics did not regard sensation in itself as true. Truth depends on the relation of sensations to thought; for truth and error are not predicable of disconnected sensations, but only of the conclusions drawn from them through the formative activity of the mind; and as like can be known only by like, so only the reason within can know the reason of the universe. Yet thought and sensation differ only in form, for in substance thought must be the same as sensation from which it derives its entire content. Thought is merely a classifying and generalizing of the contents of experience.[1] Practically, however, the Stoics based the validity of thought on its own convincingness, the greater certainty of the conclusions of reason and the irresistible conviction which they carry. That is true which after careful consideration carries conviction; and the Stoics alleged that there must of necessity exist a cognition of truth, for otherwise no one could act with conviction and on principle.

Stoic physics sought to determine the nature of the universe and man in order to find a sure rule of human conduct. Physical knowledge was not sought for its own sake; indeed, Chrysippus had declared that to pursue studies for the sake of knowledge and its delights was to lead a life of pleasure. It accorded with the practical aims and character of Stoicism that in matters of science it seized upon what lay nearest and most apparent. So, perhaps starting from the every-day life of man which moves among things tangible and visible, the Stoics declared that only the material was real.[2] Hence all properties, attributes, and qualities can only be material —produced by air-currents. The relations of all things to each other, of body and body, body and attribute, body and soul, are simply mutual interminglings. Force,

[1] Thus inconsistently the Stoics ascribed greatest truth to that which had no real existence according to their extreme materialistic and nominalistic views, which found reality only in particular material things.

[2] *Cf.* Zeller, *ib.*, 3^1, p. 123, *et seq.*

the efficient cause, is the part of the universe which acts; matter is the part which is acted on. This efficient cause is God, who must possess all attributes which he produces. Formless matter is the material cause; it is passive, God is active; in substance both are one. This is Pantheism, finding in God the primary matter as well as the primary power.

The human soul is also material, as are its qualities, vice and virtue for example. It may be regarded as warm breath diffused through the body, as the soul of the world is diffused throughout the world. The soul is one in substance, reason (*τὸ ἡγεμονικόν*) being its primary activity. Reason, moreover, constitutes a man's self, determines his identity. The human soul is part of the world's soul, and will be resolved into it at the end of this world's course, though as to its lot until then Stoic philosophers differed.

The Stoic conception of God was fervent rather than original. Cleanthes's famous hymn to Zeus, though its devout tone is almost unequalled in Greek literature, contains no thoughts he might not have gathered from Æschylus or Sophocles. Stoic expressions as to the divine are diverse, often vague, often emotional, and seem to spring from a reverence for all-ruling law, call it destiny or nature, Zeus or the universal reason, or call it Providence, a term which came into use. The world is ruled by Providence; everything is produced by divine power, and with a purpose interweaving its existence with the rest of the universe; plants are produced for animals, animals for man, men for mutual intercourse.

There were many contradictions in the Stoic theory of the universe, connected with the character of Stoicism as a system of materialism with spiritual aims. That was its noble inconsistency, from which, however, sprang many of the special questions of its "physics." For example: how reconcile the apparent presence of evil in the world with its perfection? They answered, physical evil is nothing; moral evil is man's fault; in the end God will turn it to good. And they emphasized the Socratic aphorism—no evil can come to a good man. Again, another Stoic problem: how reconcile moral responsibility with an all-ruling Providence? They answered, though the human will may not be free to act, it is free to will; man is responsible for what he wills, without regard to whether the act is within his power or not. So they solved these problems with a certain lofty insufficiency; and how a spiritual system was reared upon a basis not its own more strikingly appears in Stoic ethics, the noblest outcome of the time. The reasoning was faulty; but these ethics were profoundly felt.

Stoic ethics start from a vague and general conception —nature—inherited from the Greek past. The primary impulse of every one is toward self-preservation and gratification; that is, toward a preservation and furtherance of his own well-being. Such an impulse is right because according to nature, and because his own well-being is man's highest good. From this it was an immediate inference that only what suited man's nature—furthered his well-being—was good for him. Stoicism might now proceed in any direction: the particular direction it would take depended on what was meant by nature, especially by man's nature. In determining this, the Stoics evolved a doctrine, which in its form and application must be regarded as original with them, although they might have gathered its elements from Heraclitus and Plato. Man is a reasonable being; reason is his peculiar characteristic, his essential nature. Hence nothing accords with man's nature, or can be a good for him, which is not consonant with reason; speaking more explicitly, consonant both with man's reason and the universal law, the reason of the universe, of which human reason is part. Hence only acts which spring from man's reason, recognizing and acquiescing in the universal reason, conduce to his well-being. Such action is virtue. Only virtue is good; only virtue brings happiness; well-being, happiness, consists only in virtue.

The Stoic conception of good often bears the aspect of law—the law "universal and eternal in righteousness" of which Cleanthes sings.[1] With this accords the law of man's nature, and the laws of the state are a recognition and reflex of the divine: hence obedience to them is man's duty, and a natural impulse as well.

Zeus, God, the universal law all-ruling, is wholly reason. But man is not; he has emotions and passions arising from lack of self-control and errors of judgment. These are: pleasure, which arises from an irrational opinion of what is good, and refers to the present; desire, arising from the same source, but referring to the future; care, which arises from an irrational opinion of evil, and refers to the present; fear, arising from the same source as care, but referring to the future. These emotions should be suppressed; the wise man is free from them, suffering no affliction, feeling no fear nor anger nor pity.

Besides this apathy, virtue has a positive side, which consists in acting according to the universal law through rational self-control; and virtue becomes that theory and practice which bases action on knowledge of the good and has right conduct for its aim: it resolves itself into power of will based on reason and knowledge. Following Plato, the Stoics recognized four cardinal virtues, which differ among themselves only in their special aspects: he who possesses wisdom will show temperance, bravery, or justice when circumstances call for them. So virtue being essentially a unit, the virtuous man must necessarily be altogether virtuous; every one who is not so—and this includes all men—is altogether evil. There is nothing between the two. The rare change from wickedness to virtue is instantaneous and total. Virtue and wickedness are always and exclusively such through the intention and will of the doer, irrespective of the out-

[1] *κοινὸν ἀεὶ νόμον ἐν δίκῃ.*

ward act and its consequences. A wicked desire which would be carried out if opportunity offered is as evil as if carried out. Every good act is unconditionally and absolutely good; there are no kinds and degrees of goods, and external or bodily matters, like health, wealth, or life itself, are not to be reckoned among them. A virtuous will is the only good; every thought or act which infringes the moral law is absolute evil; all else—riches, honor, life, and their opposites—is indifferent, *ἀδιάφορον*. Least of all can pleasure (*ἡδονή*) be a good. Even the pleasure accompanying virtuous conduct is indifferent. Pleasure is no part of virtue; it is often had by wicked men; is of no value whatsoever.

In the conviction that nought beyond a man's own will is a good or evil for him lay the wise man's refuge; in this he might repose amid the storms of life, unshaken, serene, blessed. This was the dominant motive that made the Stoics illogical with all their logic, and led them on. Focusing their thought upon this inner spiritual life, the Stoics developed the idea of conscience, the inner recognition of a moral law applying uniformly to every individual. Each man determines the rightness of his conduct by reference to the universal reason, regarded as uniform moral law and recognized by that part thereof which exists within him and constitutes his moral judgment.

The Stoic conception of conscience came to its full development only with Roman Stoicism, when the system became even more practical and religious than it had been among its founders. But from the first the practical ethical purpose of Stoicism bent its doctrines from their logical severity. And difficulties soon appeared in the doctrinal part of the system. To restrict the notion of man's nature to his reason, to say that reason alone accorded with his nature, was palpably forced. The natural instinct of self-preservation includes the well-being of the body, and before long a practical system would recognize health and a reasonable enjoyment of physical faculties as matters not entirely indifferent; but they must never conflict with man's absolute good, which lies in the activity of a virtuous will. So the Stoics admitted bodily well-being and harmless enjoyments as conditional goods for man, which under proper circumstances he might desire and pursue. These were matters preferential, and might be regarded as man's secondary duty, wherein he carried out subordinate instincts of self-preservation, and acted at least not in disaccord with his true nature. It followed, too, that soon the Stoics would modify their demand of apathy—entire freedom from emotion—and substitute therefor a mastery over self amid pleasures as well as pains, and a subordination of the whole man to his higher will. Still another ethical modification of their system lay in the admission that a man not completely wise might not be wholly wicked, and that a condition of progress towards virtue was better than an absolutely wicked state. And finally they abandoned the harsh Cynic doctrine that the wise man was all in all to himself; truly the wise man might be, but where was he to be found? Ordinary men, even good men, were not. This admission, combined with the proper Stoic doctrine of universal citizenship of the world, which recognized the common nature of mankind, —the brotherhood of man as Roman Stoics more lovingly thought it—led the Stoics to recognize fully duties towards others and towards the state, and this notwithstanding that the individual was always paramount in Stoicism. Likewise Stoics approved of marriage and the family ties springing from it, though as to these matters there was divergence of opinion. They were loath to break altogether from the popular religion, holding to its traditions and to divination. Their deeper religious thought was monotheistic, and regarded the popular divinities as manifestations of the supreme Zeus, whom they endowed with all divine attributes.[1] And further,

[1] As in Cleanthes's hymn.

deferring to their truer religious feelings while endeavoring to observe tradition, they sought to bend mythology to monotheism through symbolical and allegorical interpetrations.

The significant elements of Stoicism were its convictions: that in the poise and noble calm of inner life, set in a virtuous will, lies a beatitude which can be shaken by nothing from without; the virtue wherein lies the wise man's peace is a part of the will of God; man's inner nature is a part of the divine, his reason part of universal law, his prerogative to yield to fate, follow the righteous law, obey God.

Epicurus.

The system of Epicurus had the same aim as Stoicism. With both, man's happiness was the object of philosophy, and knowledge was sought only as a guide to happiness. Both systems show the individualistic tendencies of the time as well as thoughts which break through materialistic doctrines. Both see man's happiness in temperance and self-control and mental poise. But in their views of the essential nature of human well-being the two systems were opposed, and in their opposition the Pagan and Christian world recognized the difference between good morals and bad. Whatever were the doctrinal differences between them, whichever of the two had the better logic, and whatever likeness in practice might logically have resulted from them, the fact is incontestable that Stoicism fostered nobility of character, that Epicureanism had an opposite effect.

The disciples of Epicurus clung to the letter and spirit of his teachings, making no important additions to doctrines which the master fully developed. His teaching did not stimulate to inquiry; upon a statement of his borrowed facts often came the words: this may be so or it may be otherwise, what difference? With him philosophy was an activity (ἐνεργεῖα) helping men to happiness (εὐδαιμονία) by words and reasonings. As a support for his philosophy, and deferring to the demands of the age, he stated a theory of knowledge. His Canonic, or test-science of truth, held that no truth could be had beyond sensation; which therefore must be taken as true in itself, though not necessarily giving true images of objects. Every sensation is ultimate truth for the subject. Thoughts are sense-perceptions or sensations remembered and transformed by the mind.

Epicurus sought from natural science an hypothesis to obviate the need of supernatural causes, and free the minds of men from anxieties about God and death. Such he found in Democritus' atomic theory, which explained the universe mechanically and excluded thought of purpose. He distorted this theory in one respect. Free will was needful to his ethics, and might be imperilled were the atoms allowed to fall perpendicularly in parallel courses. He thought to exclude fatalism by letting them deviate a little; what matter if the consistency of Democritus' theory was thereby destroyed! The soul of man consists of the finest, quickest atoms; it is composed of fire, air, vapor, and a fourth nameless element. More significantly speaking, the soul consists of two parts, the rational and irrational, the former residing in the breast, the latter dispersed throughout the body. Mental activity, sensation, perception, movements of the will, belong to the rational part. Epicurus denounced religion and belief in Providence, yet set up a number of serene, do-nothing gods which served to illustrate his idea of happiness.

Such was Epicurus' general notion of the nature of things. The object of knowing even this much lay in his ethics. Pleasure is the absolute good, pain the absolute evil. There are varieties and degrees of the pleasures and pains entering a human life; to secure the greater pleasure, often the lesser pain must be endured, or again pleasure must be treated as evil because entailing some greater pain. It fell in with Epicurus' temper to think more of immunity from pain. So he followed Plato in holding that every positive pleasure presupposes some want, and is but the removal of a craving. Broadly considered, pleasure is freedom from pain. Consequently the beatific state is perfect repose—*ἀταραξία*—which implies no want and brings no pain, but is a matter of the mind arising from intelligence. Nature provides for the little that men need; bread and water suffice for the wise. Pain, though an evil, need not disturb; for changeful bodily conditions are slight matters compared with mental repose; this is pleasure pure and abiding, and may be as independent of circumstances as the Stoic's apathy.

Epicurus—more Greek in this respect than the Stoics —sought not to crush, but to control, the senses. Sense-pleasure in itself is good. Enjoy what offers, only with due regard to the avoidance of consequent pain, and crave nothing. Beware of entering on situations that may bring anxieties; hence, avoid turmoil and be chary of undertaking social obligations; all ties are dangerous. Yet virtue may be a good, not in itself, but in the pleasure it may bring. Perhaps the sweetest thing on earth is friendship based on wise selfishness. And the humane spirit of Epicureanism, which taught compassion and forgiveness, culminated in the thought that it is sweeter to do well than to be well done by.

The good of Epicureanism was limited to its slight fostering of the milder virtues of humanity. Its theories ran parallel with all the frailties. Wise had been Plato's thought, that whether pleasure was a good or not, men had better not cultivate it. Pleasure might safely be left to inspire its own seeking. The practical results of Epicureanism were ignoble. If the accusations of its enemies are to be doubted, if in truth it did not encourage all sense indulgence in its votaries, nevertheless it stood for the weakness of the age. It was a form of unbelief in the worth of virtue and accomplishment. It meant withdrawal from that eternal conflict which is progress. It was no creed to help on the world.

Sceptics and Eclectics.

The weakness of the time took another form in Scepticism. That also sought to give repose of mind and make its followers independent of circumstances. But it starts from no positive assertion as to the nature of human good; but rather with a forced indifference as to what it could not surely know. While neutral between Stoics and Epicureans, Scepticism opposed the dogmatic assertions of both, and for itself remained unconvinced of anything.

Pyrrho [1] gave form to its germ. Nothing can be known of the nature of things; hence judgment should be suspended; an imperturbability of spirit will result, while in practice the philosopher will act on probabilities. It was left to the New Academy to develop the philosophic denial of the possibility of knowledge. Arcesilaus argued against the Stoic view that truth lies in irresistible impressions. And Carneades [2] skilfully opposed a number of the Stoic doctrines, using many now familiar arguments against their theory of design. He also developed the positive side of scepticism, the theory of probabilities: a notion is probable when by itself it makes the impression of truth; it is probable and undisputed when that impression is confirmed by the agreement of all notions relating to it; it is probable, undisputed, and tested when an investigation of all these notions produces the same corroboration for all. Practically, men may act on such probabilities. This was an answer to the Stoic and Epicurean argument that knowledge must be possible to make certainty of action possible.

Scepticism is a natural halting-place between one set of doctrines and those which shall supersede them. From time to time it rises and directs itself against some special phase of dogmatism, overthrows it possibly, and clears the way for men to advance. The scepticism of the Sophists showed the faulty methods of the physical philosophers, before the philosophy which founded

[1] A native of Elis; he accompanied Alexander to India; died about B.C. 270, leaving no writings.

[2] B.C 210–129.

thought upon itself came to consciousness in Socrates. The far more advanced scepticism of Carneades might in turn have been succeeded by some great positive doctrine, had philosophy continued creative. As it was, philosophy could make reply only with Eclecticism, which amounted scarcely to a novel application of time-worn doctrines. Scepticism had denied the possibility of knowledge; Eclecticism was a practical admission that knowledge could not be found unless among existing systems. It was no organic system growing from itself by virtue of some proper vital principle, but a patchwork of many-sourced opinion. It added nothing to human thought, although suggesting modes of comparing and reconciling doctrines apparently adverse, yet always with the chance of introducing more insidious inconsistency through glossing over what could not be reconciled.

There were palpable causes for the spread of Eclecticism. Zeno and Chrysippus, Epicurus, Pyrrho, naturally laid stress on the distinguishing traits of systems which they founded. The three schools, however, started near the same time, under the same influences, led by like aims, and continued to exist side by side. Points of comparison and coincidence would be noticed, and the habit of comparing doctrines and borrowing from each other would grow among philosophers whose powers of origination were scanty. The sceptic theory of probabilities made for Eclecticism; and the demands on Greek philosophy arising from the practical characters of the masters of the world impelled philosophers to gather from any ready source whatever appeared plain and serviceable. So men of all the schools, and especially those who dwelt at Rome or occupied themselves instructing Romans, were eclectics, whatever name they bore. Finally appears the prince of eclectics who shall compose philosophic treatises in noble Latin out of opinions indifferently taken from the Stoics, the Academy, the Peripatetics, or even from the Epicureans on whom he looks with most unfriendly eye.

CHAPTER XII.

THE GENIUS OF ROME.

ALTHOUGH, in the great days of Greece, the Greeks set above all the glory of the state, their own lives were too intense to be merged in social and political organization.[1] Sacrifices for the city might be made with fervor; but they were always conscious sacrifices, the rational surrender of a smaller thing for a greater. The Greek's instinctive nature pressed towards the satisfaction of his own desires, the fulfilment of his own life, the free and complete development of himself. So, whenever a public crisis was passed, he turned naturally to other affairs than building up the state. The few Greek cities that gained some breadth of power did not hold it long. Empire exacts such entire devotion as was found at Rome.

Roman Characteristics.

Roman life brought no such free development of the individual. Purpose and energy in Rome had few and definite objects. There, as elsewhere, environment, character, and institutions worked upon each other; the environment and character fashioning fit and characteristic institutions, the latter, in their working, preserving and strengthening the character. For example, at Rome, an office originally of narrow powers, created to relieve the consuls from the charge of numbering and assessing the citizens, broadened its compass to an authoritative supervision of the lives and conditions of men, and became

[1] Sparta appears as an exception here.

the most revered of Roman dignities. Conversely, the Censor's functions reacted on the community which had acquiesced in them, working good, yet hampering free growth and individuality.[1] Fundamental traits of Roman character are suggested by the words *bonus*, *gravis*, *tenax*, *dignitas*, *severitas*, *fides*, all of which had somewhat different meaning from the derived or corresponding terms in modern use. There was early a temple to Fides at Rome, and the word, as expressing the principle of steadfast holding to the performance of what has solemnly been promised, corresponded to the more idealizing Greek qualities indicated by the word αἴδως, and sanctioned by the thought of νέμεσις.

To order well his house and serve the state was the compass of the duty, the compass of the life, of a Roman. To order well his house with respect to things divine and human, to accumulate wealth in his family and civic honors through the discharge of public office, made up his life within the walls of Rome; beyond those walls life meant defence of the city and all its hearths, and the increase of its power and possessions. To the fulfilment of this life all qualities and principles approved in a citizen contributed—energy, gravity, self-control, valor, fortitude, tenacity of purpose, adherence to his solemn word, insistance on his rights, intelligence, and definite conception of ends as well as means, order, obedience, and stern command, and insatiate desire to conquer and acquire for the city and himself. These traits, which made Rome great, are exhibited by her history; they constituted her morality and religion; they were exemplified in the Roman family and stamped upon the Roman law. It may be that they were shown most marvellously in the ability of self-government under a constitution containing palpable elements of deadlock and overthrow; for Roman co-ordinate magistrates could act without their colleagues, as well as forbid their colleagues to act;

[1] See Mommsen, *Hist. of Rome*, vol. i, p. 551 (bk. ii, ch. viii).

the function of the Roman tribune was to interdict, and the Roman dictator had absolute power. When this ability failed the Romans, despotism came; but, before then, the Mediterranean world was subjected to the imperial self-governing Republic.

Rome was the strongest community of Latium. She fought her way to leadership among her Latin kin, and with added power advanced to the conquest of neighboring cities, and so, continually gathering strength and impetus, to the subjugation of all Italy. Her site was one of natural strength, with the advantages without the dangers of a seaport,[1] for merchant vessels could come up the river. The Tiber was also a protection against the Etruscans; but Roman armies could always cross bridges overhung by the city's walls. The situation was central, adapted for conquest in all directions. The Romans could not have conquered or held Italy from Neapolis or Tarentum; and after Italy was united under Rome, and the agonies of the war with Hannibal had been sustained, Rome would not have acquired universal empire—or had it thrust upon her by circumstances—but for the central situation of the Italian peninsula among Mediterranean lands. It made for the rise and continuance of Roman empire over other countries, that the nations having greatest powers of resistance were nearest Italy, or, at least, most exposed to Roman attack. Mighty Carthage lay just across the Mediterranean, nor did Rome finally conquer in Africa until the Punic power had been broken in Sicily and Italy. The exigencies of the Punic wars called for the conquest of Spain, a country which offered resistance without end, but never resisted unitedly. The Gauls possessed the north of Italy; Rome conquered them in self-preservation. And to the east, had the situations of Macedonia and Greece been interchanged with those of Asia Minor and Syria, Rome might not have overthrown the kingdom of Philip. Rome conquered

[1] See Cic., *De Republica*, ii, 4.

Macedonia which lay near, and there was little power of resistance in the countries farther to the east, till Parthia was reached, which Rome never conquered.

The ancient songs of Italy, comic ribald verses, or barbarous lines of chant, have passed away. They seem never to have risen above their occasional character and primitive rudeness. The periods of Rome's growth and greatest native strength produced no literature.[1] At a remote period, archives of the temple of Capitoline Jupiter were kept. These "Fasti" contained the names of the magistrates, and gradually events of the year came to be entered, till they grew to be annals; but they never became connected narrative. Rome was in the sixth century of her existence before history was written. Slight also was the native impulse toward sculpture, though the Romans early became great builders. Appius Claudius (Censor 312 B.C.) built the Appian Way and the first great aqueduct. Many colossal undertakings followed, deepened channels for draining districts of country, military roads, and fortresses. The Romans made wide use of the arch, which they may have borrowed; but they did not borrow the energy and toil which made their works mighty and enduring. That the fifth century of the city brought some artistic impulse, is shown by the bronze she-wolf of the Capitol.[2] But the direct thought, the stern ideas, the energy, the courage and fortitude of the Roman Republic are not to be sought in artistic or literary accomplishment.

The Family.

The strength of character by which Rome achieved empire, and the clear narrow mental vision of the Romans, their logic and reliance on its conclusions, appear in domestic institutions. The Roman family consisted of all the members, past, present, and

[1] See Teuffel-Schwabe, *History of Roman Literature* (1891), vol. i, p. 118 of English translation; and Mommsen, *Roman Hist.*, bk. iii, ch. xiv. Compare Prof. Nettleship's somewhat different view, "Earliest Italian Literature," in *Lectures and Essays.*

[2] Probably cast in 296 B.C.

future, except daughters of the house who by marriage had entered other families.[1] Its ties were blood relationship, the worship of the same household gods, and common sacrifice to the same ancestors, whose images gave glory to the solemn funeral of each warrior laid in his grave. That the members should pass away was natural; that this great religious and social entity should be blotted out, and all its gods and spirits be left unappeased, was a calamity, to be guarded against by adoption if natural members failed.[2] The living members were made one under the absolute authority of the head of the house.

The *patria potestas* was a power quite different in principle from a master's over his slaves. That existed for the master's good; slaves were his chattels. But the *patria potestas* was to be exercised for the good of the entire house—herein lay its ideal justification—and for the good of the state. It was a duty[3] not to be renounced, a power of life and death, which a sense of justice in its possessor and his love of child and wife should preserve from abuse. If the father could take the life of the son, it might still be that he would sooner die for him; he was free to accept or reject a child at birth; the right of exposure was his;[4] but what stronger desire had he than to continue his family, what clearer duty towards the state than to bring up warriors and the mothers of warriors for his country's service? He could sell any member

[1] Nor did daughters' sons belong to the family, because, if born in wedlock, they belonged to another family, if born out of wedlock, they were *spurii*, belonging to no family.

[2] Adoption brought the adoptive son into the position of a son born in marriage. This principle was carried out in all its consequences, *e.g.*, he inherited equally, and he could not marry his adoptive father's daughter any more than if she were his natural sister.

[3] It bound the father to educate and so rear his son as to fit him for his position in the community. For flagrant neglect of this duty a father might be publicly prosecuted.—See Livy, vii, 4, 5.

[4] Mommsen, *ib.*, bk. i, ch. 5. But the right of exposure was soon restricted. See Dion, 2, 15; Bruns, *Fontes Juris Antiqui*, 4th ed., p. 7.

of his household;[1] but though no punishment was attached to the act, a father who sold his wife or married son was held accursed.[2] Of course neither wife nor child had rights of property as against the father. Only the later law recognized the separate rights of the son to property acquired as a soldier or otherwise in the service of the state.[3] The son owed the father obedience and respect. He who struck or reviled his father became forfeited to his father's gods;[4] and the early law had no punishment for parricide, because, as was said, the crime was not conceived.[5] But the *patria potestas* did not exist solely for the sake of the family; and, moreover, direct public duties were always paramount at Rome. Hence the father's power ceased when incompatible with the exigencies of the state. So long as the son held a high magistracy, he was free from the *patria potestas*, and, by virtue of his office, had command over his father as over other citizens.[6]

The wife's position was one of dignity. Her duties lay within the house, to rear her children, direct the maid servants, and spin. She was subject to the jurisdiction, not of the state, but of her husband advised by a council of relatives, hers as well as his; and to him was she answerable. So the unmarried daughter was subject to her father, and the fatherless unmarried daughter to her nearest male relatives, tracing the relationship through

[1] By law of XII Tables, if the father sold the son three times, on the third emancipation by the purchaser the son did not return to the *patria potestas*, but became free from it. See Bruns, *ib.*, p. 20; *cf.* Gaius, i, 132.

[2] Mommsen, *ib.*, bk. i, ch. 5; but according to Dion, ii, 27 (Bruns, *ib.*, p. 9), a law of Numa forbade the sale of a son whom the father had permitted to marry and establish a separate household.

[3] *Peculium castrense* and *quasi castrense*.

[4] Law of Servius Tullius, see Bruns, p. 14—*puer divis parentum sacer esto*. There was the same provision as to a daughter-in-law, Bruns, p. 7.

[5] See Plutarch, *Romulus*, 22. All murder seems to have been called *parricidium*.

[6] *Cf.* Livy, xxiv, 44. So likewise was a daughter free on becoming a vestal virgin.

males (*agnatio*).[1] Woman's virtue was chastity, which the Romans, according to their character, esteemed more seriously than the Greeks, with whom it was as a tale that is told.[2]

Thus, within the house, all human beings were bound by duties, which with wives and children might appear more palpably in the guise of obedience. None the less was the father bound by duties in the exercise of his authority, moral obligations to the members of his family, and formal obligations to the state respecting them. From beside the hearth arose the sternest of Roman ideals, which, as the guiding genius of every Roman, was to control him in the forum and inspire him on the battlefield,—the duty to obey, the duty to command aright.

The State.

The most primitive tribe or state differs from a family in that it is composed of a number of grown men whose wives and children have no separate political existence, while a typical family consists of one strong man, and a wife and children dependent on him through their inferior strength and wisdom. Another necessary difference is that the position of the house-father arises by nature, while the position of the *rex* is based on some form of selection. The original constitution of the Roman state was that of the Roman family modified by the two facts, that a state is composed of a number of grown men, and that the position of the king is based on convention.[3]

[1] The wife or unmarried daughter inherited equally with sons, though she held her property under the guardianship of her relatives. See Gaius, iii, 1–4; i, 44, 45.

[2] Great respect was shown to women at Rome, nor were they kept secluded within the house. Sons respected their mothers; and still the memory endures of Cornelia the mother of the Gracchi; a woman, however, not born in the early times of the Republic nor educated after its traditions.

[3] This last was strictly true at Rome (where the notion of the divine right of kings did not exist) and was implied in the principle that, though absolute, the *imperium* of the king was an *imperium legitimum*—*i.e.*, related to or based on law or agreement.

The ultimate power of an early community, however slight the ordinary functions of this power may be, resides in that body of men from whom the authority of the king originally emanated. Hence, at Rome, although after the analogy of the family and in accordance with primitive usages the king was invested with absolute authority in peace and war over every individual, the supreme power was in the assembly of the housefathers, where it lay latent usually, restricting itself to changes in the fundamental constitution of the city. As the city grew,—probably by a union of kindred and contiguous communities,—a smaller circle of advisers gradually made a third among its constitutional factors. According to the old tradition, the community was composed of ten curiæ, each composed of ten clans or gentes, each one of which in its turn consisted of ten families. As the greater assembly would consist of the housefathers, so each clan might have an elder, and one elder from each of the hundred clans would constitute the assemblage of elders (senatus). And whenever the three traditional communities of the Ramnes, Tities, and Luceres united in the City of the Seven Hills, there would be three thousand householders, and three hundred clan elders, forming respectively the greater assembly of the people and the senate. Even this uncertain outline of the primitive Roman constitution illustrates the characteristics of the people. They chose their king, and with grand obedience, reasoning clearly from the analogy of the family, they gave him absolute power. Equal freemen as they were, they would obey the one of themselves whom they set over them; they would endure harshness and cruelty in him—these were traits of their own character—so long as he ruled as a leader of the state, and not as a tyrant for his pleasure.

The early condition of affairs at Rome portended a threefold political and social struggle.[1] The authority of

[1] See Mommsen, *ib.*, bk. ii, ch. i.

the king was too absolute to suit the character and circumstances of a race growing in power and in consciousness of might. Kingships among Hellenic and Italian communities usually ceased as the people became more conscious of political rights and conceived other schemes of government. As soon as men were capable of devising further forms of election and better adjusted modes of delegating authority, a revolution was prepared and would occur at the king's first flagrant outrage.[1] Hence the first constitutional struggle at Rome was to abolish kingship and bring the powers of the chief magistracy into compatibility with political liberty. This did not mean a diminution of the sovereignty of the government, but rather enhanced the devotion of the citizens to a commonwealth which was now more palpably theirs. Nor was this a revolution which promoted the free development of individuality, for it bound the citizens by duties that became sterner and more engrossing as the citizen rose to influence and command; the consul must be prepared to punish even his son with death for disobedience, or formally to sacrifice his own life for Rome.[2]

The Threefold Revolution.

The expulsion of the kings, the creation of the consulship, and the consequent reorganization of the government were the acts of the *Populus Romanus*, that is to say, the body of burgesses or *patricii*. Besides these, there were other residents of Rome, who did not belong to the old Roman clans, but had placed themselves under the

[1] See *ante*, p. 240 *et seq*.

[2] The introduction of the principle of plural and co-ordinate magistrates holding power for a limited period was the great measure which restricted the magisterial power. For example, each consul had full power by himself; they need not act together; but the equally supreme power of one—to use a phrase as inconsistent as the theory of the consulship—prevented danger from the other. The formal conservatism of the Roman character is illustrated by the revolution which overthrew the monarchy, as well as by that which established the empire under Augustus. The restrictions on the consuls' powers were practical, while formally the kingly prerogatives remained.—*Cf*. Livy, ii, i. The consul was elected for a year, yet in law

patronage of some Roman house, as *clientes*, or simply dwelt in the city without political rights (*plebs*). As the Patricians had no thought of sharing their rule with these, a further and distinct phase of revolution consisted in the gradually enforced demand of the Plebs for a share in the government and for social equality before the law. During two centuries of refusal and persistence, the magistracies were opened to the Plebs, marriage between Plebeians and Patricians was allowed, Plebeians obtained full equality with the Patricians, and decrees of the assembly of the Plebs acquired force of law. Mark the Roman qualities which this struggle displayed, obstinacy on the one side, persistence on the other, and a self-control and power of self-government, which through many bitter years kept within the bounds of peaceful civil contention that struggle which in a Greek city usually meant the sanguinary expulsion of one party by the other. The fortitude which upheld Rome through crushing defeats by Gauls, Epirots, and Carthaginians, had its counterpart in the forbearance of the bloodless secessions to the Sacred Mount.

The equalization of the orders within the city did not end this struggle, the last phases of which were to be bloody. The demands which the Plebs had enforced for themselves, they agreed with the Fathers in refusing to the Latins. Hot was the wrath of Rome at the demand that one consul and half the senate should be taken from the Latin cities;[1] and not even the exhaustion of the city after Cannæ overcame the government's repugnance to

might hold over and could not be deposed; he named his own successor like the king, but in fact the election lay with the people. The Roman conception of a magistrate of every kind was derived from the conception of the monarchical chief magistrate, the *rex*. Consequently, whatever might be the occasion of a magistrate's appointment, whatever special function he might be created to fulfil, it was only through gradual republican education that the Romans reached a clear conception of limited magisterial powers. —See Mommsen, *ib.*, vol. i, p. 401, etc.

[1] 340 B.C., Livy, viii, 5, etc.

grant senators to the Latins, who equally with Rome had sustained the war: "Let us forget this proposal has been made," said Fabius Maximus.[1] The demands thus refused were afterwards extorted for all Italy by the terrors of the Social war,[2] when Rome's existence was threatened by the equal strength and arms of her Italian subject-allies. Though the sword of Sulla preserved the honors of the war for Rome, she yielded to the unveiled necessity, and the Roman franchise became the common right of all Italians. Thus Italian nationality gained political unity, and the intellect and strength of all Italy were more than ever at the service of the Republic whose hours were even then numbered. Free institutions which had been developed through the exigencies of a civic community, might not, when that community's power of self-government was waning, be expanded to the government of an empire.

The remaining phase of domestic contention was economic rather than political, merely the particular form taken at Rome by the universal struggle between the poor and rich. The rich creditors asserted their strength in severe laws for the recovery of debts, while the poor never gave up the struggle for equitable distribution of conquered public lands and for legislation to prevent the rich from monopolizing the possession of them (*leges agrariæ*).[3] This naturally was the mode of contention exhibiting fewest noble traits. The Roman character was grasping in all respects; Romans were a wealth-getting race. Through the agrarian struggle the rich were insatiate, the poor dogged; the struggle became demoralizing to both; and distributions of the public

[1] Livy, xxiii, 22.

[2] 91–88 B.C.

[3] Conquered land and other spoil belonged to the state. The state, at least so far as concerned conquered land, was regarded as the continuing owner, the citizen as having only the use. This land was *ager publicus*, the citizen acquired *possessio* thereof through *concessio* from the state.—Puchta, *Institutionen*, i, 40.

land—not in themselves unjust—and the manner in which they were brought about, went to prepare the way for proletariate customs and legislation tending to pauperize the masses.

The Final Political Development.

In view of the character and circumstances of the Romans, what form was the government likely to assume in the culminating period of the Republic, the period of the second Punic war? Rome was not likely to produce individuals of overshadowing greatness; her institutions tended towards moulding her citizens alike. Every citizen was bound by duties and enveloped with customs, which made of him a useful member of the commonwealth, but hampered his individuality. It was likely that the government of Rome would be strong in its entirety, but not brilliant through the genius of individuals. Further, though the Roman was obstinate, he could recognize necessity, and forbear. It was likely that all classes at Rome, that which stood for dignity and ancestral honor, that which stood for wealth, and that which represented strength through numbers, would be given representation. And finally, since the Romans had clear perception of worth and ability, and strong capacity for abnegation when required, it was likely that, so long as Roman character stood firm, the government would be left with those best able to carry it on.

The course of the Republic accorded with these probabilities. The greatness of the government always towered above its members; it long continued mainly in the hands of those best fitted to govern, and, to use the ancient modes of expression, it combined and held in equilibrium the elements of royalty, of aristocracy, and of democracy. Such certainly was its ideal, as shown by the language of Cicero, who loved the Republic as one might a dear friend dying before his eyes.[1] And it so impressed a keen observer, the Greek Polybius, friend of

[1] *De Rep.*, ii, 33; *cf. ib.*, i, 29.

the younger Africanus. Speaking with reference to the time of Cannæ, he says: "As for the Roman constitution, it had three elements, each of them possessing sovereign powers; and their respective share of powers in the whole state had been regulated with such a scrupulous regard to equality and equilibrium, that no one could say for certain, not even a native, whether the constitution as a whole were an aristocracy or democracy or despotism. And no wonder; for if we confine our observation to the power of the consuls, we should be inclined to regard it as despotic; if to that of the senate, as aristocratic; and if finally one looks at the power possessed by the people, it would seem a clear case of democracy."[1] Polybius then gives a description of the powers of consuls, senate, and people, faithfully reflecting, even in its inconsistencies, the characteristics of a government which, as the slow outgrowth of custom, circumstance, and occasional legislation, presented many contradictions. Yet he fails to set forth the fact that the government of Rome had become above all a government by the senate.

Senatorial Government.

It may be that the Roman senate was at first an assembly of clan-elders. But whatever its composition in times of which nothing is known save by inference, admission to the senate in early historic periods depended on the choice of the king, then on that of the consuls, then, though in a more circumscribed mode, on the discretion of the censors.[2] The Ovinian law,[3] which substituted the censors' confirmation for the consular power of nomination, made the choice of at least some of the senators dependent indirectly on the vote of the people. For it seems to have given provisionally a seat in the senate to every consul, prætor, or curule ædile. But it authorized the censors to exclude any one for cause; and further, since these

[1] Polybius, vi, ii, Schuckburgh's translation.

[2] See Mommsen, *Römisches Staatsrecht*, iii, 2, 854, *et seq.*; ib., *Roman History*, book ii, ch. iii (vol. i, p. 407).

[3] *Circa* 312 B.C.

offices might not suffice to keep up the number of the senate to three hundred—a number traditional as well as practically needful—the censors were given the power to name further senators. Thus the larger and more influential part of the senate came to owe its choice—for life—to an indirect mode of popular election. In the course of time a life-senatorship was also attached to the offices of quæstor and tribune.

At first the consul's choice of senators had undoubtedly been restricted to Patricians. The senate appears to have been opened to Plebeians as they gradually made good their eligibility to the magistracies. Nevertheless, as it had been a Patrician body, so it continued aristocratic, and was composed principally of Patricians and members of prominent Plebeian families, which had become ennobled through their wealth and the attainment of the higher magistracies, which brought the right to exhibit on public occasions the images of ancestors. The senate was never an hereditary body, nor, during the Republic, self-perpetuating. Not only was admission to it open to all citizens who had reached the requisite age, but its membership would necessarily include all those who, through position, wealth, or individual ability, had attained the magistracies. Thus, practically, all leading citizens became members. Their life position as senators was more to them than their short possession of magisterial powers; and even while magistrates, they would be under the influence of that body which included their relatives and friends and natural peers. So the senate combined with its aristocratic spirit an *esprit de corps,* rising from the consciousness of permanent power as a body. It was continually recruited with fresh blood and strength; and if it represented primarily an upper class, that class had to be, through the conditions of its existence and recognition as such, the best and strongest in the community.[1]

[1] *Cf.* Cicero, *Pro Sestio*, 65.

So, by the general operation of circumstances, by the strong conservatism of the Roman character, by Roman forbearance and desire that the ablest should rule, and finally through the broad tendency of Roman life and institutions to evoke a high average of character and ability in its citizens, and control exceptional individual genius, the powers of government, during the great periods of the Republic, centred in the senate. It was a broad, silent principle of Roman constitutional law, sprung from reverence for authority, that the edict or command of a magistrate, though based on no formal law, and therefore exceeding his conceded powers, should be valid in itself, at least during his term of office. This principle would foster the growth of senatorial power. A decree of the senate, irrespective of contents, carried the weightiest authority, and on its face was entitled to obedience. It was, however, the senate's most significant formal right to consider previously the decrees to be proposed by the magistrates to the assemblies of the people. This was the constitutional basis of its power, the growth and maintenance of which it justified by its corporate greatness and the mighty mode in which it administered the affairs of Rome. Nowhere else were Roman traits shown more grandly—Roman courage, fortitude, persistence, insight of affairs, and energy; and Roman forbearance too; for the senate neither sought to deprive the people of their ultimate sovereignty, nor to reduce the magistrates to lifeless tools of a bureaucracy.

Military Organization.

The Roman power of obedience, perfected by discipline and made efficient through the practical genius of the race, was shown in the army. Under the Servian military constitution, the infantry unit was the legion,[1] a body of three thousand heavy-armed men, formed for battle in the old Doric style, six in file, with a front of five hundred. To

[1] See Mommsen, *Hist.*, vol. i, p. 132, *et seq.;* and *cf. ib.*, pp. 108, 332, 559, *et seq.*

these were attached twelve hundred light-armed. The completely equipped holders of an entire hide of land made the first four ranks, the less completely equipped members of the second and third classes made the two rear ranks; while the light-armed troops were made up from the poorest classes.

From the earlier form, the manipular legion was developed, the line of which in front was divided into ten bands of two maniples each, while in each maniple every soldier occupied a space of six feet square. These bands were separated into three divisions, *hastati*, *principes*, and *triarii*. Only the *triarii* retained the thrusting spear, while the first two divisions were armed with the pilum, a heavy javelin, to be cast in volleys into the hostile ranks, after which the legion charged, sword in hand.[1] The legionaries were now classed according to length of service, the recruits forming the bands of skirmishers, from which they were advanced to the first, second, and third divisions of the legion. To know his place in the ranks and keep it in every danger was the first duty of a legionary, to which he was trained by constant practice and strict discipline enforced by the severest punishments. Yet because of the free internal order of each legion, the line of battle could be drawn to meet any circumstances, and as rapidly changed, and reinforcements could be pushed to the front through the files of the legions engaged. The principle of the Roman battle was absolute obedience, with sufficient freedom of action to render the obedience more effective.

If the legionary knew his place in the march and battle, he knew it also in the camp, which was always laid out on the same plan, so that at the end of a day's march,—a military tribune with centurions having gone before and

[1] Marius finally abolished the distinctions between these classes and reduced the legion to greater uniformity. He divided the legion into ten cohorts, instead of thirty maniples. See Mommsen, *Hist.*, book iv, ch. vi (vol. iii, pp. 242–245).

selected the location, fixed the consul's tent, and drawn the lines for the tents of the tribunes, —each legion on arriving, and every soldier, knew where to go as in his native town.[1] Roman camps were drawn and fortified with the same care whether in friendly or hostile territory. No feature of the Roman military system is more impressive than the efficiency of the legionaries as workmen and the enormous labors undergone by them.[2]

The Roman military organization would have been impossible, as it would have been useless, but for the character of the Roman people. It could not have been attained without such unabated devotion through centuries to the art of war as only Rome was capable of, and an army wherein each soldier, fighting as it were singly, with free space between himself and his comrades, unimpeded by them and unsustained by the strength of shield to shield, shoulder to shoulder, would, without the unyielding valor and mighty obedience of the Roman citizen-soldier, have become a mob at the first onset of battle. Rome was obedience, Rome was sternness, Rome was devotion. Manlius Torquatus, before going out to kill the insolent Gaul, asks the consul's permission; afterwards, when himself consul, the same Manlius executes his son for a like feat done in disobedience to orders, and with his colleague Decius, the great Plebeian, is ready to devote himself to the infernal gods for Rome. It was on Decius that the fortune came to accomplish this self-sacrifice.[3] And as for Roman fortitude, Livy might truly say of his people, who never spoke of peace after Cannæ, "Nulla profecto alia gens tanta mole cladis non obruta esset."[4] True are the words which he puts into the

[1] Polybius, vi, 41. For the strict discipline of the camp, see *ib.*, vi, 27, *et seq.*

[2] *Cf.* Polybius, vi, 42.

[3] This was in the Latin war, B.C. 340. See Livy, viii, 6, *et seq.* The son of Decius, when consul for the third time, followed his father's example in battle with the Gauls.—Livy, x, 28.

[4] Livy, xxii, 54. See the latter part of his twenty-second book generally. The Romans refused to ransom the prisoners captured by Hannibal at

mouth of Scipio Africanus taking command of his soldiers in Spain: "It is ever our fated portion that, conquered, we conquer. I pass over ancient matters—Porsenna, the Gauls, the Samnites. I need mention only the Punic wars, in the first of which what fleets, what leaders, what armies have we lost! and why recall the present war? Trebia, Trasimenus, Cannæ,—what are they but monuments of Roman armies and consuls slain? Add the defection of Italy, of the greater part of Sicily, of Sardinia, and that final terror, the Punic camps and Hannibal before the walls,—amidst this universal ruin has stood single, erect, and immovable the courage of the Roman people, till it has raised its fortunes from the ground."[1]

International Ethics.

The rules of conduct which the Republic set itself to observe regarding other peoples illustrate Roman character. The state's aggrandizement was the dominant motive. Rome's function in the world was to conquer and subdue and civilize,—the last wrought out without much conscious intent on her part. Her imperial purpose was conceived only with the gradual fulfilment of her destiny. Rome under the kings, Rome under the Republic, at least until after the Punic wars when the world came hurrying to bow down before her, had always some near object in view, some strenuous defence against a pressing foe, some town or country to subdue in order to satisfy her vengeance or secure her safety. But whatever the end, she willed it strongly, she willed it persistently; if baffled, she did not falter, and she always conquered at last. The safety, the welfare, the glory of her city, as it sanctified the pouring forth of her own blood, so did it justify the slaughter of her foes.

Roman ethics demanded a definite justification for aggression, and set the mode in which war should be begun and carried on. A war should be *justum* and

Cannæ, and even those soldiers who escaped were treated as disgraced.—Livy, 25, 31; xxv, 5–7; Polybius, vi, 58.

[1] Livy, xxvi, 41.

pium: in some way the fault must lie, or be made to lie, with the enemy.[1] The Romans and other Italian peoples felt that a war rising from an unrighteous cause would prove unfortunate.[2] That was a just war which was undertaken for revenge, or to repel an enemy or protect an ally.[3] "Our race," says Cicero, perhaps not without irony, "has mastered the whole world by defending allies."[4] Besides needing a good cause, a war, to be *justum* and *pium*, should be formally declared,[5] and truces or treaties, if made with due formality, must be strictly adhered to; *fides* must be observed,—Regulus must return to Carthage.[6] But it was just as essential that a pact should be concluded with all formality,[7] as that it should be made by officers having authority.

Sometimes the Romans, or a Roman general, chose to act up to higher principles of honor, as in the story of Fabricius sending bound to Pyrrhus the king's physician who had offered to poison him.[8] But often it accorded with their statecraft or necessities to make use of the rule that pacts informally concluded need not be observed. An extreme instance of this is the disavowal of the treaty made by the consuls and officers of the army with the Samnites at the Caudine Forks.[9] The consuls, Livy says, had declared to the Samnites their inability to make a

[1] "The Romans were wont to take great care not to appear to be the aggressors, or to attack their neighbors without provocation; but to be considered always to be acting in self-defence, and only to enter on war under compulsion."—Polybius, *Frag.*, xxviii (157), Schuckburgh's trans.

[2] See the speech of the Samnite Pontius, Livy, ix, 1.

[3] See Cicero, *De Rep*, iii, 23.

[4] *Ib.*

[5] *Ib.*, ii, 17; *De Officiis*, i, xi, 36.

[6] *Ib.*, i, xiii, 39–41.

[7] This idea is related to the technical and strict observance of religious rites. Archaic gods punished only formal breaches of faith, and acquiesced in crafty literal performance.

[8] The war with Pyrrhus was carried on in an exceptionally high-minded way; each side adhering honorably to its undertakings. It was not a life-and-death struggle.

[9] See Livy, ix, 1–12.

treaty (*fœdus*) without authority from Rome, nor could a treaty be concluded without *fetiales*, the priests whose formal office it was to conclude a treaty or declare a war. Hence, argues the historian, the consuls made no *fœdus* but a *sponsio*; that is to say, they and the officers of the army bound themselves under the surety given of six hundred hostages and their own faith, that Rome should ratify what they had agreed to.[1] Afterwards, at Rome Postumius, one of the consuls, freed the government from its dilemma by proposing that he and the others who had joined in the pact should be given up to the Samnites as guilty. Accordingly they were carried to Samnium and delivered to the enemy by the *fetiales*, with these words: "Since these men, unauthorized by the Roman people, have promised that a treaty should be made and have been guilty of that crime, therefore, that the Roman people may be freed from this guilt, I deliver you these men."[2]

If the Romans had caught the Samnites in such a snare as the Caudine Forks, probably they would have exacted no severer terms than those Rome had set before herself to obtain as the object of the war, and which she was prepared to adhere to in victory as well as defeat. When Rome entered on a war with the purpose of utterly crushing the enemy, as in the Veientine or third Punic war, she carried out her purpose relentlessly and undeterred by disaster. The senatorial government of Rome, during its strong periods, always seems to judge beforehand what lay within the power of Rome to exact. Up to this limit, the senate would persist; but they did not let fortunate accidents lure them into demanding more than they had previously decided on. This was another phase of

[1] In concluding a *fœdus* the *fetiales*, representing the people, prayed that Jupiter would smite the people as the *fetiales* were about to smite the swine they were sacrificing, unless the people observed the treaty.—Livy, ix, 5.

[2] Livy, ix, 10. The Samnites refused to accept them, and sent them back to the Roman camp and demanded that, if the treaty were not ratified, the legions should be put back in the Caudine Forks.

Roman forbearance and self-control, based on political foresight. So it was that after overthrowing Antiochus, Scipio demanded no more than before the battle;[1] while in another instance when, after a victory over the Roman cavalry, Perseus tried to make peace, he found the Romans inexorable. "For this is a peculiarity of the Romans, which they have inherited from their ancestors, and are continually displaying, to show themselves most peremptory and imperious in the presence of defeat, and most moderate when successful."[2] There was political justice, *fides*, in this stern insistance on that to which their power entitled them, and on no more.

Religion.

All Roman life was permeated with religion.[3] According to the tradition, Romulus's supreme authority over the community of the Seven Hills was declared by flight of birds;[4] and from the beginning the city's life was enveloped in religious observances. Romulus himself, as tradition says, was no less prominent in establishing these than in war. To him are ascribed two "excellent props of the Republic," the *auspicia* and the senate.[5] *Auspicia* was a broad term covering every manner of observing signs and portents indicative of the future. The kings, after them the consuls and other high magistrates, represented the people before the gods as well as before men; their full authority was expressed by the words *auspicium imperiumque*, and the word *auspicium*

[1] Polybius, xxi, 17.

[2] Polybius, xxvii, 8, Schuckburgh's trans. Given more rhetorically in Livy, xxxvii, 45.

[3] Livy, v, 51–54, gives a grand speech to Camillus dissuading the people, after the destruction of the city by the Gauls, from moving to Veii. The religious element is dominant in the speech: the gods of Rome had there signified their favor to the people; they could not be moved. Roman fortune could not be plucked up and set in another place; the worship of the gods in their chosen locality must be continued if the Romans would prosper.

[4] Livy, i, 7. Plutarch, *Romulus*.

[5] Cicero, *De Rep.*, ii, 10. Numa added further observances and priesthoods, and tempered the minds of the people. See Livy, i, 19, 20; *cf.* Cicero, *De Rep.*, ii, 14.

stands first.[1] Only the magistrates might take the auspices for the people, the *auguria* from observing the flight of birds, entrails of birds and beasts, and appearances of the heavens, and the *signa ex diris*, the extraordinary portents; all of which came under that most important part of the magistrate's authority, his *auspicium*, which in the case of the consul enabled him to control the popular assembly as well as the times of setting forth on military expeditions, since no public act was done at Rome without a previous authoritative declaration of the favor of the gods.[2]

That all Roman life, in the house, the forum, or the field, was ordered with reference to superhuman approval, hardly makes the Romans peculiar, since the lives of all ancient peoples moved in an environment of the superhuman or divine, scarcely severable from things strictly human, if there were such.[3] Yet the characteristics of the Roman people, their virtues, what they approved in men, were impressed on their religion, and moulded it as they did other matters at Rome.

The word *religio*—that which binds men through their fear of the gods—is distinctly Latin. It brought home to the Romans the element of obligation[4] developing into the conception of duty. *Religio* imposed formal, unvarying duties, extending through the man's entire life as he grew from youth to manhood, as he rose from private citizen to consul. In obedience to rule, in normal fulfilment of his duty, let the citizen serve the state; so let him serve the gods and obey them. The Roman religion was one of observance, sacrifice, and outward act, that in

[1] So also as Cicero phrases it, *Leg.*, iii, 3, 10, "Omnes magistratus auspicium judiciumque habento."

[2] One reason for withholding the consulship from Plebeians, was that the consul took the auspices, which no Plebeian could take in early times, as no one not belonging to the original Roman families could represent Rome before the gods.—See Livy, iv, 6.

[3] The all-pervading religious elements in ancient institutions are well brought out in Fustel de Coulanges' *La Cité Antique*.

[4] *Obligatio*, also distinctly Latin, and related to *religio* etymologically.

no way searched the heart of the worshipper,[1]—a system of rules which covered the circumstances of Roman life and bound the man to act so and not otherwise, bound him neither to fall short nor exceed. Even in worship he should be frugal and self-controlled; his sacrifices to the gods should be what was strictly due them; he should not act the prodigal towards them any more than among men. And yet this religion, which called for only what was due, might call for all. Rites were to propitiate the gods, and the gods in angry mood might demand a year's produce of the flocks and the special consecration of children born within that time (*ver sacrum*); might even signify by yawning chasms or impending conflicts their demand for noble lives; whereupon the duty to propitiate the gods to the state calls on a citizen to leap into the gulf, calls on a consul to sacrifice his life in battle.

A system strict and definite and all-embracing needed special expounders.[2] These were found in the sacred colleges of the augurs and pontifices, close corporations of men handing down among themselves sacred lore, especially knowledge relating to the *auspicia*.[3] As interpreters of the will of the gods, they attained great influence in the state, where they could affirm an election to be inauspicious, or declare the divine will to forbid or require, as party interests might demand. But Rome did not become a hierarchy nor approach it. Priests, augurs, pontifices, never composed a distinct mediating class or obtained political power. Not they, but the magistrates represented the people before the gods, with authority to take the auspices.[4] The augur stood by, and at the

[1] See the introductory chapters to Boissier, *La Religion Romaine*.

[2] See Boissier, *La Religion Romaine*, chap. i, § 2.

[3] Besides these, there were priests and priestesses (*e. g.*, vestal virgins) devoted to the special worship of some god.

[4] Frequently, perhaps usually, the magistrates—consuls or prætors—were also pontifices or augurs. This preserved the lay or political spirit of the Roman religion. There never could be any conflict between religion and the state, because those who presided over religion were not a separate

request of the magistrate, gave him explanation or advice. So the priest did not represent the private worshipper before the god. The Roman appealed directly to the Penates or Lares within his house, or to Capitoline Jove. The priest might advise him how to appeal successfully. Thus, with all their religiousness and formalism, the Romans kept their government secular.

Roman worship was practical, unimaginative, as appears from the earliest table of festivals—the *feriæ publicæ*. These included the day of the full moon (*idus*) sacred to Jupiter, and the festival to Mars at the beginning of the year.[1] Then came festivals relating to the cultivation of corn and wine, the April festivals, when sacrifice was made to Tellus, the nourishing earth, to Ceres, goddess of germination and growth, to Pales, fecundating goddess of the flocks, to Jupiter as the protector of vines, and to Robigus (Mildew) the enemy of the crops. Then came the late summer festivals of the harvest, and festal days in winter to commemorate the blessing of well-stored granaries. There were also sailors' festivals to divinities of the sea and port and river, and festivals of handicraft; and many were the festivals of household life,—to the spirits of the storechamber, to the goddess of birth, and to the dead. So besides the blessings of his home, the Roman desired wealth and increase of flocks; and with the spread of the city grew the mercantile spirit, entering the religion, and taking gods from the market-place—*Deus Fidius*, god of good faith, *Fors Fortuna*, goddess of luck, *Mercurius*, god of traffic.[2]

As the spirit of Roman religion helped to mould its votaries in normal types, so its own creations were typical divinities.[3] The plastic spirit of the Greeks had no coun-

caste, and had always political rather than sacerdotal interests at heart. See Boissier, *La Religion Romaine*, Introduction, chap. i.

[1] The first of March. [2] See Mommsen, *Hist.*, bk. i, ch. xii.

[3] The Romans were given to worshipping the gods in groups, *e.g.*, the Penates, or Lares, or Vesta and the Penates grouped as tutelary spirits of the household.

terpart at Rome. As compared with the manifold beauty and color of the Greek religion, the Roman is a dim picture in the gray. The personalities of its gods were vague. Yet it gained in dignity and reverence. Neither crime nor weakness existed in the Roman pantheon. The Greek, sacrificing, looks up to heaven, the Roman sacrifices with veiled head.[1] And yet it is the Greek that feels the mystery, not the Roman, whose mind in religion, as ever, is fixed upon the furtherance of some set thing. His religion knows no mystery, contains no secrets, except the names of tutelary gods, kept secret lest some enemy call them from his household or from Rome. The religion of the Greek might rise or sink, though never drop from beauty's sphere. But the Roman religion remains bound to the recognized needs and prescribed objects of the Roman state and the Roman household.

The Law.

As the characteristics of the Roman people appeared in their religion so were they also shown in the law, which partly grew out of it, and vividly exemplified the strict, logical spirit of Roman affairs. Likewise Roman respect for authority and wisdom was shown by the formal recognition of the *responsa prudentium* as a source of law.[2] The Roman law as first known in the code of the Twelve Tables, has already passed those primitive stages where the main object of law is to substitute legal procedure for blood. It is a system strict and formal,[3] and already in the stage of development where the law seeks to enforce the intention of contracting parties if duly expressed. It allowed freedom in

[1] *Cf. Æneid*, iii, 406.

[2] The *responsa* were published in a collection before 100 B.C.

[3] The following remarks relate to private civil law. The Roman criminal law of the Republic sprang from the *provocatio*, the right of the convicted to appeal from the sentence of the magistrate to the assembly of the people. The decisions of the people would naturally be swayed by party feelings or by passion or pity; and consequently a regular and unvarying system of criminal law hardly came into existence.

contracting,[1] nor were the formal modes, prescribed for entering into contractual relations, cumbersome. Yet they had to be strictly followed. For example, the words—*Dari spondes?* *Spondeo*[2]—created an obligation to perform as promised, which did not arise if the equivalent was uttered in Greek.[3] And the old mode of sale (*mancipium*) was a formal matter; the purchaser in presence of five witnesses declared the slave or other object to be his according to the law of the Quirites (*ex jure Quiritium*), "purchased by this copper and copper scale"; whereupon with a piece of money he struck the scales held by the libripens.[4] These forms of transaction gave strict rights, which could be enforced with formal exactitude by the *legis actio sacramento*, a form of action in which the proof must correspond exactly with the demand, or the suit would fail.[5] In the old law the plaintiff had no further rights than what the law expressly gave him;[6] but these it would enforce with a severity only stopping short of wanton cruelty.

The main features of the law of debtor and creditor as contained in the Twelve Tables are known, and afford apt illustration.[7] The debtor, summoned before the magistrate, must go; if he went not willingly, the creditor brought witnesses and again summoned him in their

[1] "Cum nexum faciet mancipiumque, uti lingua nuncupassit, ita jus esto." —*Frag. of XII Tables*; Bruns, *Fontes Juris*, p. 23.

[2] The usual form for transacting a loan.

[3] Gaius, iii, 93. Yet the contracts made in other forms gradually acquired validity.

[4] Gaius, i, 119, 120.

[5] See Gaius, iv, 30. The strictness with which the letter of the remedy had to be adhered to, was illustrated by the action for cutting vines, which had to be stated *de arboribus*, as the law of the XII Tables mentioned only trees.—Gaius, iv, 11. The English common-law forms of action afford a parallel in technicality.

[6] That is, he had no equities arising from the requirements of good faith (*ex bona fidei*), such as the later law gave him.

[7] See Bruns, *Fontes Juris*, *Leges XII Tables*, Tab., i–iii; Puchta, *Institutionen*, i, 150, etc; Gaius, iv, 11–29.

presence. If he was still obstinate, the creditor might lay hands on him, and lead him before the magistrate, though if the debtor through age or sickness was unable to walk, the creditor must provide a wagon.[1] The debtor need not follow before the magistrate if he furnished a *vindex*, a person of his own station and condition, who in his stead should accompany the creditor and substitute himself as defendant.

The proceedings which took place before the magistrate brought out the most prominent feature of the Roman civil procedure, a contrivance illustrating the legal aptitude of the Roman genius, and admirably conducive to the definite and logical development of the law. As already remarked, the prototype of Roman magistracy was the king, and a considerable period passed before the Romans reached the conception of a magistrate with limited and definite functions. At no time under the Republic did there exist a magistrate whose functions were exclusively judicial. Even the prætor, who became the ordinary judicial magistrate, had always other duties to perform. The magistrates with their varied powers and duties were ill-fitted to hear and determine private causes between citizens. So, as early as the Twelve Tables, proceedings before the magistrate were limited to the ascertainment and precise expression in legal form of the claim of the plaintiff and the defendant's defence, if he interposed one. Thereupon, the issue having been rendered precise and the pleadings regularly drawn, as we might say using the language of the English common law, the cause was sent to a *judex* or college of *judices* to be fully heard and determined.[2]

[1] "Si morbus ævitasve vitium escit, que in jus vocabit jumentum dato."—*XII Tab.* (Gellius, 20, 1, 24).

[2] The proceedings before the magistrate were termed *in jure;* those before the judge, *in judicio.* Similarly, the object of the English common law system of pleading,—the "declaration" of the plaintiff, the "plea" of the defendant, and the plaintiff's "replication" when there was one—was to render the nature of the dispute legally precise, and bring it to an

The usual form into which the controversy was turned before the magistrate in the early times was the *legis actio sacramento*,[1] so called from the sum of money which each party deposited in a sacred place (*in sacro*), engaging respectively to make good his allegation or denial, or forfeit the sum to the state. The Twelve Tables provided that this penal sum should be five hundred *asses* if the matter in dispute amounted to one thousand; if less, the penal sum was fixed at fifty.[2] The smaller sum only was required when the dispute concerned the freedom of a human being, a provision intended to facilitate a man's defence of what was priceless to him.

The issue having been reduced to precise statement within the recognized technical form, and the deposits having been made, the parties appeared before the judge who was to ascertain the facts and finally determine the controversy, rendering upon proof a judgment in accordance with the nature and form of the action. If he decided in favor of the plaintiff, the debtor had thirty days in which to pay. Failing to do so, the creditor might lay hands on him,[3] and again take him before the magistrate. Then if he did not pay, and no one in his place satisfied the claim, the creditor could take him to his house and keep him there for sixty days, bound with fetters of fifteen pounds weight. During this time the creditor must supply him daily with a pound of meat,

issue, *i.e.*, the allegation and denial of a specific matter. The function of the Roman *judex* approaches that of referee appointed by the court "to hear and determine."

[1] The *legis actiones*, of which the *sacramento* was the chief, continued in use long after the time of the XII Tables, till superseded by the *formulæ* sometime before the time of Gaius.

[2] The formula ran thus in an action *in personam*:

Creditor. Aio te mihi x milia æris dare oportere.

Debtor. Denial in the same words.

Creditor. Quando negas, te sacramento quingenario provoco.

Debtor. Quando ais neque negas, te sacramento quingenario provoco.—See Keller, *Römisches Civilprocess*, § 14.

[3] *Manus injectio*. See Gaius, iv, 21.

unless the debtor chose to live on his own substance. On each of the three last market-days during this period the creditor had publicly to produce the debtor before the prætor, and cause the amount of the debt to be announced. If no one paid it, the creditor on the last day could kill his debtor or sell him out of the city as a slave, for no Roman might be a slave in Rome. If there were more than one creditor, they might divide the debtor into as many parts.[1] This was the furthest conclusion, logical, unmitigated, that could be drawn from the principle of responsibility for incurred obligation.

The qualities of character found in Roman institutions made Rome's history. Throughout persists the race's energy and fortitude. Unlike Spartan valor, aroused only through emergency, Roman energy required no rousing and needed no repose. To all nations comes the courage of the rush of victory: Rome's rose sterner from defeat. Hers also were other qualities of fortitude, capacities for self-control and self-denial and endurance of long labor for the gain. During centuries of devotion to the state's aggrandizement, Roman qualities grew in strength, culminating in the period of the Punic wars. The fruits came after Zama, when, with the ease of fate, Rome moved on to empire.

The strength of Rome had its Assyrian side. Such strength, in its advance and self-accomplishment, must often commit cruelties, must usually be unfeeling. The only tenderness ever shown by Rome was towards Greece, a country which she admired and despised; and within Rome these mighty qualities when unemployed might need to assuage themselves with the blood of the arena and with debauchery. These were incidental accompani-

[1] See Bruns, p. 19; Keller, *Röm. Civilprocess*, § 83. These extreme measures were abolished after a while, and an execution against the debtor's goods given, which was not provided by the early law. The *lex talio* also existed: "Si membrum rupit, ni cum eo pacit, talio esto."—*XII Tab.*, Bruns, p. 27.

ments of a character which should have the enduring strength to conquer the ancient world and mould the nations of the west to the forms of its own partly borrowed civilization.

The Greek ideal of the noble enjoyment of leisure was lacking at Rome. The thought that leisure could be made the crown of toil might have checked the current of Roman achievement; in its stead the higher Roman self-consciousness was filled with unbending dignity and pride and sense of personal worth. Their character impelled the Romans to incessant practical occupation; and Roman ideals, until the influence of Greece suggested that leisure was for culture, remained ideals of toil and valor, of unremitting endeavor for some end, iron obedience to stern command, ceaseless energy in all things.

CHAPTER XIII.

THE REPUBLIC AS INFLUENCED BY GREECE.

PROBABLY at no time was Rome unaffected by Hellenic civilization. Numa was said to have been taught by Pythagoras; but the wise king lived many years before the sage of Magna Græcia. More credible is the tradition that the elder Tarquin conversed with exiles from Corinth before leaving his Etrurian city.[1] It is certain that there had been intercourse between Etruria and Greece. Etrurian culture was peculiar, but not original. From what cities of Hellas or Magna Græcia came its inspiration is not known. So the currents of Greek influence which touched Rome cannot be traced to their sources; but the general fact remains that there was intercourse between Romans and Hellenes from times preceding certain history, and that Greek influence came from Hellas itself, as well as from Greek colonies in Italy, and also through turbid Etrurian channels.

Early Currents.

At some early period the Romans took their alphabet from the Greeks, and their system of weights and measures; they formed their games and festivals after Greek models, they borrowed Greek gods, they accepted for a while Greek weapons and tactics; even jurisprudence, the only great and original Roman science, was in the time of the Decemvirs influenced by the laws of Solon. Naturally in matters trivial or material, domestic utensils, habits of eating and daily life, modes of build-

[1] Cicero, *De Rep.*, ii, 19.

ing, as well as early attempts at fine art, the influence of Greece was never absent. All this was but the beginning. The first Punic war[1] brought the Romans into contact with Greek culture in Sicily; the second Macedonian war[2] and the war with Antiochus[3] carried them into Greece itself as well as to the Hellenic East; and from the battle of Pydna, which ended the third Macedonian war,[4] Polybius dates the establishment of Rome's power over the civilized nations of the Mediterranean. So Rome's expanding activities brought her into the midst of Greek civilization, and she found herself the political mistress of the Hellenic world before she realized it or had any definite imperial intentions. It was a natural consequence of the extension of Roman power, that many Greeks came to Rome through diverse political exigencies or to seek their fortunes at the source of power and wealth.

Comprehensiveness of Greek Influence.

From early times the Romans were a grown-up race. Youth is marked by a spirit of playfulness, a spirit of adventure and hope of strange things and new, by an idealism not yet dashed by experience, and often by a shifting purpose setting itself towards one goal or another as inspiration comes. But manhood means fixed purpose, practicalness, limits set to scope of endeavor, steady endeavor within those limits, definite conception of means, and, instead of playfulness, seriousness and gravity. The Romans were always men; the Greeks never lost their youth—*Ἕλλενες ἀεί παῖδες*. How was this race ever young, in its age still touched with youth's idealism, this race ever ready for new hope, ever ready to embark on new seas, be they the actual seas laving the shores of earth or seas of novel knowledge,—how was this race, with all its manifold cleverness and genius and its perfect culture, to affect the stern, practical, narrow Roman character?

At the time when the Greek tree of knowledge of good

[1] 264–241 B.C. [2] 200–197 B.C. [3] 191 B.C. [4] 168 B.C.

and evil was offered to Rome, Rome had realized her own ideals. Her ideal of obedience had been realized in the Roman family, her ideal of fortitude, in the war with Hannibal; her conceptions of government had found their goal in the senatorial government of the Republic, her ideal of a good citizen had been realized in Portius Cato, and her craving for power and wealth was about to satiate itself in mastery over the fortunes and resources of the Mediterranean world. Left to itself, as no great people ever is, what further progress the Latin race might have made is a question one need not try to answer. In practical, immediate, material matters, the Latins had great aptitude and would in time have developed further material civilization. Yet of themselves they had never shown capacity for broader scientific knowledge, and still less for abstract reasoning on life, which is philosophy; they had slight understanding of beauty or love of it, and there is no likelihood that they would have developed any noble art, except perhaps in building, where their practical sense and industry produced solid results. They had developed the beginnings of a rude literature and a native mode of versification, the Saturnian measure, which might in time have produced high poetry, and they had an inborn genius for oratory. Their destiny of world-wide empire which was to remove barriers, civilize the West, and mould the spiritual as well as political fortunes of men, they had not conceived,—indeed Cæsar was the first Roman to whom came this great vision. And, in fine, they had reached no adequate thought of how to apply or use or enjoy the power and wealth which their mighty qualities had brought. They were rude provincials in thought and aim; they needed further knowledge, broader vision, and more manifold desires in order to conceive broader and finer ideals; and how far, when this knowledge and wider vision had come, they were to realize these ideals, was perhaps to be a question of how far they still retained their own strong traits.

On the other hand, Greek culture was all-embracing, it

could render whatever the human spirit might demand; it had all knowledge and attainment; it could teach science, philosophy, statecraft, ethics; it had a splendid literature—poetry, epic and lyric, the tragic and the comic drama, and noble compositions of all kinds in prose; and it had art,—architecture, sculpture, painting, forms of the arts as noble as the world has seen, and others ministering to the descending wants of men. And Greek culture had within its universal scope modes of frivolity and sensual vice. Moreover, Greek thought and character from the time of Alexander had gradually laid aside provincial and even national coloring; Greeks were no longer Athenians or Corinthians, Thebans or Spartans; indeed they were no longer Greeks, but Hellenic citizens of the world, and this whether living in Asia or at Rhodes, at Alexandria, or at Athens. Hence, having few provincial prejudices, no overpowering national thought and interest, but universal culture and appreciation of life and understanding of men, they were fitted to teach mankind, and with impartial hand deliver from their store whatever their scholars might ask for. Consequently the Romans, having power and opportunity to ask whatever they would, and the willing Greeks possessing all that could be asked, the influence of Greece upon Rome was to be unique in its completeness and manysidedness.

First Literary Quickenings.

The Tarentine Greek, Livius Andronicus, was brought a slave to Rome at the end of the first Punic war. There he educated his master's sons, and, when freed, devoted himself to the reproduction of Greek plays in Latin, and translated the *Odyssey* into Saturnian verse. He was no poet of original genius, but he heads the line of Hellenic and Italian men who introduced Greek literature at Rome. So Romans had a glimpse of literature and a taste of the theatre. Literary productions addressing themselves to the pcople, or more especially to the upper classes, never thereafter ceased.

Few men at Rome could have understood Æschylus or

appreciated Sophocles. They might understand the universal pathos of Euripides; but it was amusement that the Roman crowd sought in the theatre; comedy was to its taste. Thus the matter may have seemed to Plautus, an Umbrian. He wrote no original plays, but freely adapted Attic comedies, and being a man of native wit, he recast his Attic originals into Latin plays excellent for acting and full of rough humor. The plays of Aristophanes, with their local allusions and Athenian political spirit, would not have been understood at Rome. So Plautus chose the artificial society comedies of Menander, which, slightly changed, would be appreciated by the Roman populace. Menander's delicate touch was lost in the Plautine reproduction, and his keen appreciation of the universality of human foible may have been passed by; but the Latin plays amused the audience. There was no serious morality in them. In fact, the Roman comic stage never presented much besides a frivolous treatment of forms of social dissoluteness. Plautus produced one play, the *Captivi*, the prologue of which announced that it was to be decent and improving to the morals of the good. Unique in its decency, it continued a stage favorite through the merits of its plot. The Roman government indeed would not permit such matters as formed the plots of Plautus's plays to be represented as taking place at Rome or among people wearing the whitened toga; but here the government held its hand, unmindful of the perniciousness of vice even when clad in a Greek pallium.

Theatre of Plautus.

Yet these plays exerted one beneficent effect. The Athenians of Menander's time were a kindly people, and Plautus's adaptations could not but reflect that humane spirit which, for instance, recognized a human being in a slave.[1] Plautus indeed felt that he must apologize for

[1] C'est dans une pièce de Plaute que Rome entendit pour la première fois un esclave dire à un homme libre, "Je suis homme comme toi." (Tam ego homo sum quum tu.)—*Asinar.* ii, 4, 83.—Boissier, *La Religion Romaine*, livre ii, ch. iii.

letting a slave bandy talk with his master: the actors explained that they were all Athenians. Nevertheless, the Roman audience could not leave the theatre without a sense of good-nature toward those unhappy beings who Cato thought should be used and thrown away, like worn-out tools.

Besides the theatre, all kinds of public games after Hellenic models became frequent in Rome. The cruelty of the Roman character transformed them from harmless modes of wasting time into wild-beast butcheries and gladiatorial combats. But there was little good in these borrowed amusements, akin to the luxury which increased as Rome grew richer and learned how people lived in the Hellenic communities of Asia. The Roman women, perhaps, led in their craving for luxury of garb, overpowering the outcry of Cato, who would have kept unrepealed the decree of the times of Cannæ forbidding women gold ornaments and chariots. But the cultivated gluttony of the men did not lag behind, and Greek cooks brought a higher price than Greek philosophers.

The More Serious Trend: Nævius.

More earnest purpose than moved Plautus, lived in Nævius and Ennius. Nævius was probably a Campagnian by birth. He served through the first Punic war and died towards the end of the second. In character he was a true Roman, and the fragments of his verses breathe Roman bravery and strength. But he had neither knowledge nor imagination, nor the sense of form needful for finished poetry. Judging from the names of the plays attributed to him, he adapted Greek dramas and also composed original plays with subjects from the Roman past. His great work was a long poem on the first Punic war. As a partisan of the popular party, he did not hesitate to spice his plays with attacks on the nobles; in consequence of which he died an exile and a warning to subsequent playwrights to abstain from political allusions. One reason why the Roman drama never became much more than an adaptation of the Greek, was that Greek subjects were the only ones which could safely be brought on the stage. But although Nævius was Roman in spirit, and took his subjects from Roman history, even he could not avoid forming the first part of his great poem on the Punic war from Greek legend. The natural prelude to the story of the war was an account of the origin of the two rival peoples, and Nævius, in accordance with what must have been the prevalent story of his time, deduced the origin of Rome from Trojan Æneas. Nevertheless so far as was possible in view of the scantiness of Roman myth and story and the crude condition of Latin verse, Nævius with a Roman heart wrote Latin poetry, and for the most part in the native Saturnian metre, rough and unformed as it was. He stands for the final, yet primitive and rude effort of Latin poetry to find for itself original form and metre.

Ennius.

As great-hearted and patriotic as Nævius was his younger rival Ennius. Born in Calabria, he served in Sardinia in the second Punic war, came to Rome with Cato, and there became a friend of the elder Scipio. Ennius was Italian by birth, Greek by education, Roman in sentiment. He reproduced in Latin a number of Greek tragedies, mostly those of Euripides; he even occupied himself with comedy and occasional poems; but his fame rests on his annals, a poetical narrative of Roman affairs down nearly to his own time. Feeling the need of finer form than the Saturnian metre, he wrote these in hexameter, and boasted that Homer's spirit dwelt in him. Ennius's work is filled with Roman respect for Roman strength of character, and reverence for the example of the past. Patriotism and sympathetic understanding of the Roman temper breathe in the famous praise of Fabius; and a grand expression of Roman conservatism is his monumental line:

Moribus antiquis stat res Romana virisque.

The Two Ideals: Portius Cato.

Ennius's work suggests what were to be the two main currents of Roman ideals during the last centuries of the Republic: the native Roman conservative ideal of fortitude, sternness, obedience, and strength, and abiding by the customs of the fathers; and the desire fostered by Hellenic influence for broader knowledge, broader culture, broader humanity in fine. This was the growing cosmopolitan ideal of taking what was best wherever it lay, whether within or without the ancient Roman institutions.

There was no man of mind and heart at Rome who did not prize Rome's native virtues. The division rather lay between those who prized Roman virtues with such exclusive spirit as to deem all foreign influence pernicious, and those who would also learn of the Greeks. Portius Cato represents the first class, a man of tireless energy, ability, wit, entire bravery and self-control, a born orator, and an upholder of the constitution; but narrow in his views, harsh in his treatment of his slaves, selfish and heartless towards the outside world. His reiteration: "Carthage must be destroyed," was as cruel as it was shortsighted. Wiser was the reflection of the man who was to be the instrument of her destruction,—what was to become of Rome when she had no one to fear? Cato's heartlessness comes down to us in his scornful remark closing the debate on the release of the Greek hostages,—have we nothing better to do than waste time talking whether these old Greeks shall be carried to their graves here or in Achaia? Cato passed his old age in literary activity as tireless as had been the military and political activity of his youth and manhood. He was the first great Latin prose writer, composing history — his *Origines* — and works on every topic within the scope of Roman economy, public and domestic. But such were the tendencies and needs of his time, that even Cato learned Greek in his old age.[1]

[1] Cicero, *De Senectute*, i.

The ideal of a broader humanity was represented by men the best and highest in Rome, some of whom had rendered incalculable service to the state. There was the great Africanus, patron of Ennius, who showed his understanding of the Greek spirit of culture by the phrase attributed to him: "Numquam se minus esse otiosum quam cum otiosus esset,"—by which he meant that he devoted his leisure to self-culture. Of far less weight, but showing how far a knowledge of Greek had progressed among the Roman aristocracy, were Fabius Pictor, the first Roman writer of his country's history, and Publius Scipio, son of Africanus, who also wrote history. Both wrote in Greek, assuming that it could be read in the cultivated and high-born circles for which they intended their works. Besides Africanus, two other famous men stood for Greek culture, T. Quintius Flamininus, who had ended the second Macedonian war, and L. Æmilius Paulus, the final conqueror of Macedon, a man who possessed Roman virtues tempered by his own humane disposition. He saw that more knowledge was needed by those men whom fortune called to guide the affairs of a state which was to control the Mediterranean world. So he had Greek tutors for his sons. He was allied by marriage with the house of Scipio, and one of his own sons adopted into that house was to become the second Africanus.[1] No nobler figure has Rome to show than the younger Scipio, a man free from the foibles and overweening self-esteem of the elder Africanus. He led the higher spirits among the Hellenizing aristocrats, and about him were grouped the men of intellect and culture of his time, Romans as well as Greeks. There was the younger Lælius, hereditary friend of the house of Scipio; there were many other Roman consulars; there was Lucilius, writer of bitter satire; and, of the Greeks, there was Polybius, the first man to grasp the thought of an interconnected world history, Panætius

The Scipio Circle.

[1] B.C. 185–129.

the Stoic, and Punic Terence, the perfect adapter of Menander.

The aspects in which the work of Terence differs from that of his genial predecessor Plautus, reflect the differences between the audiences for whom these playwrights wrote. Plautus had made the subtle wit of Menander more rollicking to suit the popular taste. The plays of Terence, intended for the Scipio circle, were more skilful translations of Menander; their Latinity was finer; they preserved the Attic polish as well as the cosmopolitan Hellenic appreciation of humanity. Such a line as: "Homo sum; humani nil a me alienum puto,"[1] Plautus might have dropped, and certainly would not have preserved, in the mouth of one country neighbor justifying his well-meaning interference in the concerns of another.

Lucretius as Poet.

In the last century of the Republic lived Lucretius and Catullus, both true poets but very opposites. The main motive of the former, his point of repulsion as it were, was scorn of popular beliefs; his philosophy was that of Epicurus, his lofty vision, his intense nature, his capacity for sustained reasoning, was his own. He was indeed a poet. His intense feeling is ever fusing into living images the dry atoms of his argument. He could not expound his theme in quiet prose, and loose his heart in lyrics. For his nature was too intense for prose, and his unbent intellect and yearning vision held ever his thoughts and convictions in their linked sequence and entirety, with all their woof of feeling. He must express himself in one great poem. He found his model in the poem *On Nature* by Empedocles, the poet-philosopher of Agrigentum, whose thoughts burned within him too, and whose vision of universal life and decay, consisting in the strife of elemental love and hate, appealed to the Roman poet around whom raged the violence of mobs presaging bloodier war, and in whose inner thought the atoms clashed unceasingly.

[1] *Heauton. Tim.*, 77; or, quot homines, tot sententiæ, *Phormio*, 454.

As Lucretius could not help writing one great poem, so Catullus could not but have written just such pieces as he wrote. His sensitive, passionate nature demanded the immediate expression of whatever moved him, and his feelings spontaneously took lyric form. His nature was an Æolian harp touched to melody by every air, responsive in tones tender, violent, sad. He did not think, he felt; nor did he contemplate or muse upon his feelings. The young Catullus—he was an unthinking child, with a great range of feeling, strong affection, tender love, writhing insatiate passion too, lofty reproachfulness, scorn and contempt, and bitter reviling hate. He is never ethical, never thoughtfully good or bad, never anything on reasoned principle; yet withal of noble instincts.

Catullus.

A temperament so sensitive was naturally saddened. He did not apprehend the broad, intellectually conceived pathos which comes to Virgil or Horace. Catullus feels the pathos of the particular event, however little, happening before him. The death of Lesbia's sparrow touches his heart. That wee piping thing,

> Qui nunc it per iter tenebricosum
> Illuc, unde negant redire quemquam ;[1]

it also has to go the dark way, whence they say no one returns. To think of that speck 'midst the huge darkness, which shall envelop the world's great ones, brings further pathetic thoughts,—the sparrow is so little, its fate seems too large for it, as a babe in a tomb prepared for Cæsars. But all this pathos, added through thought, is not Catullus, but the reader. Catullus saw only the dead sparrow and the weeping girl. There also comes home to him the pathos of his and Lesbia's short day of love!—"Let us live, my Lesbia, and love. Suns set and rise; for us, when our short light has set, we must sleep an eter-

[1] Catullus, iii, 11–12.

nal night.—Give me a thousand kisses, then a hundred, then another thousand, then a second hundred.[1] "

Catullus's quivering passion for Lesbia was maddening, insatiate, despairing, just the wild sensual madness the thought of which inspired Lucretius' horror-stricken diatribe against love.[2] Lesbia was a doubly faithless wicked woman, false to her husband, false to her lover. And her lover reviled her with revilings vile and brutal beyond the words of other men. Yet his love had its lofty moods, its tender phases; at her worthlessness it falls dead as a flower cut by the plow.[3]—" I loved thee with no vulgar passion."[4] Always must he love her though her deeds have been so vile. Odi et amo—such is the fact; he himself cannot understand it. In the end he reaches a mood of passionate introspection;—he has been guilty of no crime, broken faith with no man ; why should he torture himself ? Alas,—Difficilest longum subito deponere amorem! Yet to put this old love aside is his only deliverance.—" Ye gods, if it is yours to pity, look on me miserable, and if I have lived a blameless life, free me from this bane. I ask not that she should love me or—what cannot be—that she should be chaste. I seek only to be well of this foul disease. O gods, grant me this for my piety ! "[5] Even this bit of introspection and prayer shows what a thoughtless creature was Catullus. He is still a child that can only feel its pain.

But he could picture what he had not experienced, sweet, faithful, loving love, as in his *Acme*,[6] and beyond Venus's pale, he felt pure and unselfish sentiments. He loved his home, his Sirmio, sweet rest from cares, and spoke to it such words as seldom have been uttered.[7] He loved his friends,—" the dulces comitum cœtus,"[8]—and for a friend's neglect had nothing bitterer than a sad re-

[1] Catullus, v.

[2] *Cf.* Couat, *Étude sur Catulle*, p. 74.

[3] Cat., xi, 22.

[4] *Ib.*, lxxii.

[5] *Ib.*, lxxvi.

[6] *Ib.*, xlv.

[7] *Ib.*, xxxi.

[8] *Ib.*, xlvi.

proach.[1] Above all, he loved his brother, and was faithful to him in the grave, passing over many seas to pay a tribute of hopeless grief at his tomb :

> Multas per gentes et multa per æquora vectus
> Advenio has miseras, frater, ad inferias,
> Ut te postremo donarem munere mortis
> Et mutam nequiquam adloquerer cinerem,
> Quandoquidem fortuna mihi tete abstulit ipsum,
> Heu miser indigne frater adempte mihi.
> Nunc tamen interea hæc, prisco quæ more parentum
> Tradita sunt tristes munera ad inferias,
> Accipe fraterno multum manantia fletu,
> Atque in perpetuum frater ave atque vale ![2]

This lovely elegiac poem of hopeless sorrow may suggest Catullus's formal poetical qualities. His feeling, his sentiment, was his own. Never was there a more spontaneous poet; but if he is called the young Catullus for his sad life and early death, he is also called *doctus* Catullus,[3] the learned and skilful; for he had complete knowledge of the metres he used. These he was not born to; they were not the native metres of Italy; yet, as emotion was his nature, so a perfect sense of form and metrical facility, from his intimate acquaintance with Greek poetry, was second nature. His mind consisted of a sense of form, and no poet ever wrote with more perfect control of metre and expression. With him, art was very artlessness in effect. Whatever Greek metre took his fancy, he used, and always with entire facility; but his favorite was the eleven-syllable verse of Phalæcus.

When Catullus was not expressing his spontaneous feelings, but was rather writing poems for the sake of verse, he turned for his borrowings to the Alexandrians[4] rather than

[1] Cat., xxxviii. [2] *Ib.*, ci. [3] Tibullus, iii, vi, 41.

[4] See Teuffel-Schwabe, *Rom. Lit.*, § 214, 6 and 9; and for instance, his *Marriage of Peleus and Thetis*, or his *Comæ Berenicis*, which last was a translation from Callimachus.

to the national poetry of Greece. There was nothing in his nature to enable him to feel the value of the greater Greek spirit. That spirit was deep and strong, inspired with lofty thought and patriotism. Catullus felt no patriotism; his heart reached not to such wide love. What came more home to him was his hatred of Cæsar and his satellites, and disgust for the course of things at Rome.[1] Such were not the feelings to prompt an appreciation of great Greek models. Hence, whenever Catullus looks beyond his own heart, he cares more for style than substance. This is Alexandrianism.[2] When he was *doctus*, it was from the artificial poets of Alexandria that he borrowed. So he, as well as other Romans, took from Hellenism according to his capacities and tastes.

Roman Art.

The Romans comprehended the greatness and idealism of Greek art far less than they comprehended the greatness of Greek literature. It could not be but that such a mighty, toilsome people should have been great builders, should have built strongly and enduringly; it could not be but that a race so intelligently practical should have built most usefully. Strength and utility were the native and never-failing traits of Roman architecture. It were trite to speak of the military and political utility of the Roman roads; and as for their lasting qualities,—travellers still drive over the ancient paving-stones of the Appian Way. So it were trite to speak of Roman sewers and Roman aqueducts; the former still drain Rome, the latter still span the Campagna. And the concrete of the old Roman arches, in temples, baths, and palaces, is found by the restorers of the kingdom of Italy to be too hard for pick-

[1] Quid est Catulle? Quid moraris emori?
Sella in curuli struma Nonius sedet,
Per consulatum peierat Vatinius.
Quid est Catulle? Quid moraris emori?—lii.

Catullus's pieces reviling Cæsar and his friends are among the filthiest from antiquity.

[2] *Cf.* Couat, *Étude sur Catulle*, p. 129.

axes; and modern streets are laid through ancient ruins by the help of dynamite.[1]

When the Romans wished to adorn their structures or to introduce more beautiful architectural features, they took from the Greeks. In nothing did they make greater abuse of what they borrowed. With Greeks, all architectural style, features, and ornament had intellectual meaning and rational justification. So, native Roman architecture had its meaning and justification in its utility and strength. But the Romans applied the borrowed Greek forms, with no regard to the order and import they had borne in Greek temples. There is no Greek harmony in the Hellenized buildings of Rome; Doric, Ionic, and Corinthian features are confused, till there emerges the composite style of capital and plinth and architrave, which is neither flesh nor fowl, nor hot or cold, but inane and tasteless. Yet a Greek column was of such beauty that if the Roman imitator would but follow a pure model, as he sometimes did in Corinthian columns, he could not fail of making something beautiful in itself.

Withal, however, the architects and builders were Romans, and down through the Empire bear genuine Roman names.[2] But there was no Roman sculpture or painting: that was all Greek, tinctured with Etruscan realism; and sculptors and painters were Greeks, or Tuscans perhaps in early times. As the Romans took the fashion for sculptural and pictorial ornamentation from the Greeks, it was natural they should follow the Greek taste of the times when Rome came to care for these matters. Then Greek art had forsaken its high ideals, though retaining many elements of loveliness. For the most part, it was a rich man like Lucullus who wanted statues to adorn his villas; and from the first, sculpture and painting were used by the Romans mostly as means of private luxury and cultured ease, though the height-

[1] For the uses of this concrete and its extraordinary strength, see Middleton, *The Remains of Ancient Rome*, chapter ii.

[2] See Friedländer, *Römische Sittengeschichte*, sixth edition, vol. iii, p. 302.

ened national feeling of the Empire employed these arts in the adornment of the many new public buildings. But the thought was not conceived of embodying an expression of the glorious achievement of the state in a great building, or in great sculpture—in the mode in which the Parthenon, with its statue of *Athene*, stood for the glory and might of Athens, and the *Zeus* of Phidias stood for the sum and climax of Hellenic intellectual grandeur and beneficence. So sculpture and painting became the fashion[1] in Rome, and with few Romans were more than the fashion. Hardly before the time of Hadrian did sculpture so become a part of Roman life as to represent a genuine widespread love. Plastic art stood for no ideal at Rome as it had at Greece.

Greek Influence on Religion.

At an early period Roman gods became identified with the Greek, and some gods were taken bodily from the Greek Pantheon. The first effect of Hellenism on Roman religion was to fill out the characters of the Roman gods and furnish the barren Roman imagination from the fulness of Greek myth. But it is hard to see how there could have been at Rome deep respect for the Greek gods. Many a story of divine doings must have scandalized the decorous Roman. He could not respect the Jupiter of Plautus's *Amphitryon*. With a rational, unimaginative race, clothing the gods with full personality might tend to cause inward denial of their actual existence. However this was, observance of rites, sacrifices, and auspices continued, while the natural conservatism and prudence of the Romans tended to turn the prayerful or deprecatory words and acts of primitive times into formalistic mummery. Hence arose the condition which made Cato wonder how two augurs could meet without laughing; yet Cato himself would not have omitted a single formal act prescribed by the customs of his country.

[1] Possibly Cicero has at times a gleam of art's higher functions. See *De Fin.*, ii, xxxiv, 115. Seneca would not include *pictores*, *statuarii*, or *memorarii* among the *liberales artes*.—Sen., *Epist.*, 88. 18.

These religious conditions, made up of enlightenment from without, further reflection, and an increasing formalism, which intrenched itself in new complexities of form, affected differently the habits of the common crowd of men and women, the conduct of men of affairs and statesmen, and the views of poets.

It is possible to regard observance and form in ancient religions as a mode of obedience and discipline and self-control — obedience to prescribed form, discipline in carefulness and prudence, self-control in doing what is prescribed and in not permitting fear or hope or feeling to carry one astray or lead to superstition, which with the Romans meant a going beyond what was prescribed. But there come crises when public misfortune or anxiety is such that men, in turning their beseeching hearts to the powers above, will cry out passionately, nor be satisfied within the limits of set form. They may demand new and more emotional forms of worship. A time came in the city when stress forced the self-control of the multitude and drove them to more impetuous and, from the Roman standpoint, extravagant if not pernicious devotions. Probably at all times surreptitious devotions were practised. But the dragging strain of the latter part of the second Punic war so unnerved the people that the Senate was obliged to authorize the reception of Cybele, the Phrygian mother of the gods, in whose orgiastic cult pent-up feelings might find vent. Such novel sense-emotional worship having been once admitted, men, and more especially women, did not afterwards hold themselves within the old observances, but kept seeking strange and extravagant modes of worship. Not twenty years later the government found itself taking measures as severe as they were ineffectual to suppress the abominable Bacchic rites which were ruining the morals of Rome and Italy.[1]

But what effect would the growing enlightenment of

[1] Catullus in his *Attis* pictures the fascination and horror of these Eastern practices.

the times have upon the conduct of public men, officials of the state and of the state-religion? Ancient religions of observance did not make it their office to probe beliefs. The Roman religion, so long as appropriate forms were observed and set acts were performed, took no thought of the worshipper's mental attitude. The religion was part of the government of the state. Although there were distinctly priestly offices like that of Chief Pontiff, nevertheless most offices at Rome were at once civil, military, and religious. It was impossible to change the religion without affecting the government, and all conservative and reverent feeling at Rome combined to uphold the two which were so nearly one.[1]

Another influence contributed to make the Roman statesmen stanch upholders of religion. They might have doubt or disbelief, but they were also superstitious. Even the sardonic Sulla wore a wooden image suspended from his neck, to which he addressed prayers and vows; even that freethinker, Julius Cæsar, never mounted a chariot without uttering magical words to ward off accidents. All these reverential, deferential, superstitious instincts made men shudder at the thought of omitting any service of the gods under which the greatness of Rome had risen.

Nevertheless many Roman statesmen of the last centuries of the Republic had certainly come to disbelieve in the living, ruling presence of their country's gods; such was the effect of a little thought on their part, and a little Greek philosophy and sneering. These men in familiar conversation usually allowed themselves to question freely and disbelieve when so inclined; yet they duly performed all rites and ceremonies which fell to the offices they held. There was no objection in a Roman's mind to his being a pontifex like Cotta, or an augur like Cicero himself, and yet discussing the existence of the gods and the validity of divination.[2] The value of observance and outward

[1] See opening chapters of Cicero's *De Natura Deorum*.

[2] *Cf.* Boissier, *La Religion Romaine*, bk. ii, ch. vii, § 1.

act might present itself to the minds of educated Romans as a matter quite independent of underlying truth. If the ritual, the auguries for example, were technically observed, that was sufficient. A Roman general might with all sincerity employ a trick to prevent unfavorable auguries when the opportunity for battle was manifestly favorable. He might even go further. Religion existed for the welfare of the state, so did the auguries. Anything which contravened that welfare should not be observed. To Fabius Maximus was ascribed the saying: "Optimis auspiciis ea geri quæ pro rei publicæ salute gererentur; quæ contra rem publicam ferrentur contra auspicia ferri."[1] Polybius does not tell the whole truth, saying that the rulers of Rome upheld religion because it served as a check on the people; that it undoubtedly did, and aristocratic consular or augurial chicane often served to frustrate the popular will. Rather, these men from the combined influence of statecraft, conservatism, and veneration for the past, and through their own religious or superstitious feelings, deemed that the maintenance of religion and the observance of the auspices were for the well-being of the state. So Cicero need not be thought a hypocrite because he insists on maintaining the regular worship handed down by the ancestors;[2] and it was with a touch of genuine feeling that he makes his Stoical friend end the argument for the existence of the gods with these words: "Mala enim et impia consuetudo est contra deos disputandi, sive ex animo id fit sive simulate."[3] The evil in such courses reverted on the heads of these formal observers, depriving them of the strength of religious belief; throughout Cicero's correspondence, in times of his deepest depression, no faith in the gods comes to console him.[4]

There were, however, thoughtful Romans without pub-

[1] Cicero, *De Senectute*, iv, ii; *Cf.* Hector's saying, *Il.*, xii, 243.

[2] *De Natura Deorum*, iii, ii, 5. [3] *Ib.*, ii, lxvii, 168.

[4] *Cf.* regarding these matters, Boissier, *La Religion Romaine*, Introduction, ch. ii.

lic responsibilities, but devoted to literature and familiar with Greek myth as well as Greek philosophy. Such men, as a class, during the last two centuries of the Republic did not believe in their country's gods, and took no pains to conceal it. Plautus expresses no serious religious feeling or belief. Ennius was a more earnest poet, and it was impossible that in his *Annals*, when his heart was burning with the great deeds of his country, he should not have breathed occasionally a reverence for those gods with whose cult the entire history of his country was impressed. But when not telling of his country's history, he is outspoken in contempt of astrologers and soothsayers, and, in his plays, admits Epicurean passages utterly opposed to all active religion. His freethinking subversive frame of mind further appears from his translating into Latin the writings of Epicharmis, an old Sicilian physicist, and the works of Euhemerus, that shallow Greek freethinker who taught that the gods were bygone men, who had been deified openly or around whose lives legends had formed. The satirist Lucilius ridiculed unsparingly the more foolish kinds of superstitions; but more earnestly he shows how little present were the gods to him by a passage characterizing virtue (*virtus*), which markedly omits any reference to the worship of the gods as part of the conduct of a good man.[1]

Mood and Opinions of Lucretius.

These slighting allusions of the earlier poets are as nothing, compared with that scorn and hatred of religion and the people's gods which sends a shudder through the reader of Lucretius. This is the first characteristic of his extraordinary poem on *The Nature of Things*, the initial motive of which is to dispel from men's minds infatuate dread of supernatural evil in this world or after death:

> Primum quod magnis doceo de rebus et artis
> Religionum animum nodis exsolvere pergo.[2]

[1] See this fragment in Sellar's *Roman Poets of the Republic*, ch. vi.

[2] *De Natura Rerum*, i, 931.

"When human life to view lay foully prostrate upon earth crushed down under the weight of religion, who shewed her head from the quarters of heaven with hideous aspect lowering upon mortals, a man of Greece [Epicurus] ventured first to lift up his mortal eyes to her face and first to withstand her to her face. Him neither story of gods nor thunderbolts nor heaven with threatening roar could quell; they only chafed the more the eager courage of his soul, filling him with desire to be the first to burst the fast bars of nature's portals. Therefore the living force of his soul gained the day; on he passed far beyond the flaming walls of the world, and traversed throughout in mind and spirit the immeasurable universe; whence he returns a conqueror to tell us what can, what cannot, come into being, in short on what principle each thing has its powers defined, its deep-set boundary mark. Therefore religion is put under foot and trampled upon in turn; us his victory brings level with heaven."[1]

It is religion that often has given birth to sinful and unholy deeds, and Lucretius illustrates by the story of Iphigenia:—

Tantum religio potuit suadere malorum.[2]

"This terror then and darkness of the mind must be dispelled, not by the rays of the sun and glittering shafts of day, but by the aspect and the law of nature."[3]

Lucretius proceeds point by point, arguing against the religious beliefs and observances of his day, and the fear of a future life, for existence after death presents itself to him only as something to dread. Throughout, he bases himself on the physics which Epicurus borrowed from Democritus, and on the ethics of the later philosopher. Ever and again his heart breaks through his argument in lofty scorn and pity: "O hapless race of men, when

[1] i, 62–79. **The English of these passages from Lucretius is taken from Munro's translation.**

[2] i, 101.

[3] i, 146–148.

that they charged the gods with such acts and coupled them with bitter wrath! what groanings did they then beget for themselves, what wounds for us, what tears for our children's children!"[1]

Lucretius' mood may be partially understood. Some years had passed between the death of the younger Scipio and the manhood of Lucretius,[2] years during which all things seemed to have grown worse. Hardly another city has been the prey of such continuous anarchy as filled Rome during the days of Catiline, Clodius, and Milo. Times of passion, running riot, bear in their dark the seeds of further good. There was but one man, however, who could see the coming good, and he was not Lucretius, but Julius Cæsar, who was subjugating Gaul while the poet was uttering his high note of protest and despair. Lucretius felt only the turmoil of the political and social situation. In his nature three elements may be discerned: he had the moral sternness of a Roman, he was gifted with the imagination of a poet, and he had a mighty gift of reason. This stern and bitter and grandly rational Lucretius turned his gaze to the state-religion, composed of the emptiness of Roman formalism supplemented by the immoral mythology of Greece, upon all of which from time to time burst blasts of passion from the East. The sight filled him with scorn and horror of the whole evil delusion, and pity for the poor deluded mortals who terrified their lives with it.

A Roman might temper and apply Greek thought, but to originate a new system of philosophy lay not within his genius. When Lucretius turned with loathing from the state religion, he must needs look to the Greeks. Why then did he not become a Stoic? his heart was Stoical, the tendency of his moral views was Stoical. But he loathed religion and the gods and all popular concep-

[1] v, 1194.

[2] The younger Africanus died B.C. 129; Lucretius was born B.C. 99 or 95 and died B.C. 55.

tions of life beyond the grave. Stoicism respected the gods and religious observances, and entertained doctrines of a future life. Lucretius would have none of it. No god for him, no truce with false pernicious rites, no troubling thought of Tartarus. He would have a universe coming to its present form by the inherent laws of its own component parts, with no interference of capricious gods. The atomic physical system of Democritus was made to his mind. But Lucretius, with all his intense desire for knowledge, was still a Roman, and no Roman could love knowledge severed from practical advantage. It was Epicurus who had taken Democritus' physical system to use as a basis for a practical philosophy. This practical philosophy of Epicurus, though calm and self-controlled, was not austere; yet a stern and austere Roman might transform it to an austere system, by laying exclusive stress on its principles of self-control and freedom from disturbing desire, principles which with most Epicureans were more than tempered by a wish to get all of sense pleasure that could exist with self-poise. Lucretius, having in sweeping lines invoked Lady Venus,[1] and having once for consistency's sake uttered the words, Dux vitæ dia voluptas,[2] turned from the voluptuous side of Epicureanism with a horror-stricken cry against the madness of love.[3] Here was a Roman follower of Epicurus, whose heart was more burningly austere than any Stoic's mind.

Lucretius stood above life's mimicry,[4] and, as from the great shore,[5] his mind beheld the infinite turmoil, the conflict and the quiet, the life and death of elements of being.[6] Yet he could also see the fire kindled in the Trojan's breast by the beauty of Tyndareus' daughter,[7] hear the moans of wife bereft of husband, and the eternal

[1] i, 1, etc.
[2] ii, 172.
[3] iv, 1050, etc.
[4] See ii, 323–333.
[5] ii, 1.
[6] v, 365–379; v, 493–508; vi, 647, etc.
[7] i, 472.

strife of first-beginnings in the newborn infant's cry mingling with the funeral wail.[1] All this touched him, but his great bursts of pity are for those held in the darkness of delusion, the purblind race of men, for whom peace is best.[2] He had argued point by point against the existence of such gods as his people believed in, he had argued against all divine activity or interference in the world,[3] he had argued against purpose in the world's creation, against the thought that things were made for man;[4] he had argued against all foolish fear of ills to come hereafter,[5] and had tried to show that annihilation was no ill, for then we shall have ceased, and know no fear or want or pain; "as in time gone by we felt no distress when the Pœni from all sides came together to do battle, and all things, shaken by war's troublous uproar, shuddered and quaked beneath high heaven."[6] Beyond all this, his steadfast thought is that the universe contains within itself all-pervading, undeviating law, in accordance with which everything takes place:—nothing arises from nothing; nothing takes place without a cause; nothing comes into being or perishes; but all things change and pass.[7] He whose reason recognizes and submits is the equal of the gods.[8]

Philosophy at Rome.

With no taste for speculation, at no time would the Romans have cared for the full Greek gospel of universal knowledge which Plato and Aristotle followed. Nor was it the great Greek gospel that the Hellenic teachers of the second century before Christ brought to Rome. Enthusiastic love and hope of

[1] ii, 569–580. See v, 223–226. He feels even for the cow whose calf is taken for sacrifice, ii, 530.

[2] Yet he recognizes a hope of progress in the splendid simile of ii, 77–79.

[3] Lucretius seems almost wilfully to have limited his conception of deity to the popular unworthy notions of the gods; see, *e.g.*, ii, 1092, etc.

[4] v, 195, etc.

[5] iii, 31, etc.

[6] iii, 830; see also the remainder of the third book.

[7] *Cf.* the account of Lucretius' philosophy in Sellar's *Roman Poets of the Republic.*

[8] See i, 79.

knowledge great and true existed no longer. The spirit of the Academy was not the spirit of Plato, nor did the mind of Aristotle live among the Peripatetics. Both schools had turned to the discussion of details and subtle points; they borrowed principles from one another; yet, from a sense of mutual contradiction and common weakness, they had become sceptical, and, more than knowledge for knowledge' sake, loved quibbling for the sake of argument. Nor were they always earnest in endeavor to find in philosophy a guide of life and a refuge under adversity. The more sincere Greek thought of the time was to be found among Epicureans and Stoics. It was in these schools that men were seeking firm rules of conduct and the knowledge on which these rules were based.

Apparently the stanch Romans of the time of Cato Censor saw no good in philosophy. For, despite the growing interest in all things Greek and the thought which had come of further breadth and culture, the senate in the year 161 B.C. decreed that all philosophers and rhetoricians should leave Rome. Though this decree was vain, many Romans must have sympathized with it when five years later Carneades, one of the philosopher-ambassadors of Athens, who had come to Rome in a cause as paltry as it was unjust, displayed his dialectic skill before a Roman audience, arguing one day for the great superiority of justice over injustice, and the next showing that injustice was the better, and that the Romans, through their superiority in unjust conduct, had made their state the power it was. Well might old Cato urge the Fathers to finish quickly the business of these strangers, to whom the Roman youth were flocking. Neither was there a lack of Epicurean teachers to teach their simple rules, by which the problem of how life might pleasantly be led was solved in a way likely to make men useless members of society. Epicureanism had in time its Roman followers who applied its doctrines according to their individual tempers: Lucretius thought and felt not at all like the restless Cassius, who also professed to be an Epicurean; and both differed in their lives and principles from Cicero's friend Atticus, perhaps of all Romans of the Republic the most consistent Epicurean.

Stoicism.

Stoicism was the one philosophy fit for Rome. Never a system of thought devised by men of other race was so adapted to the men of its new home. It was practical, it was reverentially religious, respectful of the past, and it was formal; it taught fulfilment of social duties and duties to the state, and in every way fell in with the strongest temper of Rome. Panætius, a Rhodian Greek,[1] did much to introduce it. Coming to Rome, he was accepted as a companion by the younger Africanus. Like all philosophers of his time, he was eclectic. He cared for all the old philosophers, and did not hold strictly to the Stoic system, and denied the immortality of the soul.[2] His follower Posidonius helped on the cause of Stoicism, himself following the tenets of the school somewhat more strictly than his master. Yet in the time of Panætius, philosophy was but getting its first foothold. The Romans had still their native strength of character; they could lead their lives without the aid of philosophy. Cato Censor was an uncut Stoic. Philosophy was hardly domiciled at Rome before the time of Cicero, whose writings spread a taste for it. The civil wars drained the *vivida vis* of Rome. Under the Empire men began to feel their weakness, and turned with more heartfelt searchings to find in philosophy a strength whereby to live. Nevertheless, in Cicero's time there may have been others besides the younger Cato who looked to philosophy for guidance.

The effect of the Greek enlightenment, and more especially the effect of Stoicism on those who represented the old virtues of Rome, may be seen by comparing this

[1] Born B.C. 180. There was a Stoic, Diogenes, in the embassy with Carneades B.C. 156.

[2] See Zeller's *Philosophie der Griechen*, 3d ed., vol. 3^1, p. 557, etc.

man with his great-grandfather. The younger Cato is a nobler character, less harsh and cruel, devoted to his country, only perhaps, through failure to understand the resistless tendencies of affairs, rendering her less service than his ancestor. Altogether a man of less sense and ability, he may have seemed what perhaps he was, a school-bred dreamer. But he had the old Censor's strength of character, and through a study of Greek philosophy, especially its more earnest ethical side as exemplified in Stoicism, he had conceived higher ideals of conduct. He stands for the severe, stern, harshly strenuous Roman character, enlightened and refined by Hellenic thought. Moreover, the increasing corruption of the time, the unfitness of Rome to rule the world and herself as a free state, and the tyrannies of Marius and Sulla which she had already known, gave thoughtful men a clearer conception of that freedom which was passing from the world and of the character and conduct in citizens needed to retain it. By contrast men then, as ever, were learning. So the younger Cato's conceptions of virtue and of what was right conduct for him as a citizen of Rome were always clear in his mind, and the power of corruption and disintegration which he was powerless to check, and the course of events which only the masterful intellect of Cæsar could guide, while they rendered Cato's life grotesque, also made clear that he acted always on principle and that his principles were good. He was incorruptible, he was untiring in public affairs; he opposed every measure threatening Rome's free constitution; nor did he push his own affairs, or seek to advance the cause which he had at heart, by servility or bribery; and when the civil war broke out, though he did his military duty on what he thought the least unconstitutional side, he held his hand from cruelty, sparing as best he might the blood of citizens. At the last in Utica, when no hope was left, he insisted on his friends escaping; but for himself he had

The Younger Cato.

the sterner way of freedom. It was characteristic of Cato's sense of duty that he first despatched such business as had call on him, and then characteristic of the eclectic Stoicism he professed, that he passed his last hours reading no work of Zeno or Chrysippus, but Plato's *Phædo*.

The careers of the two Catos are of especial interest, for perhaps more generally than any other of Rome's worthies they were regarded as models of republican conduct; their lives were realized Roman ideals. While they lived they were respected, and their memory became hallowed:—

> Audire magnos jam videor duces
> Non indecoro pulvere sordidos,
> Et cuncta terrarum subacta
> Præter atrocem animum Catonis.[1]

All Romans pursuing Greek culture acquired some idea of Greek philosophy. What school each Roman might affect would often depend on the tenets of the philosopher whom chance made his preceptor. One thing the natures of the Roman learners demanded, that philosophy should be practical, and that all its teachings and store of knowledge should be such as taught men how to live, evilly or well, at any rate in some way satisfactory to themselves. Abstract speculative discussion seemed to most Romans a foolishness unworthy of sensible men. Why not come to accord at once, as proconsul Gellius thought when at Athens he offered himself as arbitrator to adjust the disputes of the schools?[2] So Greek philosophy, as adapted by its facile preceptors to the demands of their imperious pupils, was practical, enabling the younger Cato to set before him a clear ideal of virtue, and enabling many others who desired lives of

[1] Horace, *Carm.*, ii, i, 21. Cato's suicide at Utica was the great example followed by men protesting in the same way against imperial tyranny.

[2] Cicero, *Leg.*, i, 20, 53, about B.C. 72.

cultivated ease or pleasure to find sound philosophic grounds therefor. Philosophy might while away the time of those who, like Lucullus and Crassus, devoted themselves to their fishponds careless of the Republic, to Cicero's scorn, who calls them fish-fanciers—*piscinarii.*[1] Nor should be overlooked the influence of Greek social and ethical speculation on earnest political reformers. Tiberius and Caius Gracchus, Livius Drusus, had a Greek education, and found examples in Greek history to stimulate their hopes, and clear political reasoning in Greek literature, by which they might render definite to themselves the objects of their endeavors.

The Romans were orators; Cato Censor relied on his native genius for speaking; Caius Gracchus, an orator unsurpassed in passion and power, was indeed an orator born, but he had also Greek culture, and his careful purity of Latin diction had arisen from his ability to use his own language as an educated man. After his time a knowledge of Greek rhetoric was necessary, though the orator might seek to conceal the source of his eloquence, as did Marcus Antonius of the generation before Cicero.[2] Cicero speaks of this man and Lucius Crassus, to his mind the great orators of the elder generation, as both affecting to despise the Greeks and their rhetoric, or in the case of Antonius affecting even entire ignorance of it; yet both were trained rhetoricians.

Cicero.

Cicero himself is the finest example of what a Roman might be through Greek culture, for it was through his complete Greek education that this gifted man became a splendid orator, a charming didactic and philosophic writer, as well as wide in his interests, quick in his sympathies. Closely following the Greeks in all his intellectual ideals, he gained a broad *humanitas* such as the ancient world had hardly seen. His assimilation of Hellenism is so complete that it is not easy to distinguish his inborn genius from his Hellenic culture,—

[1] *Ad Att.*, i, 18, 6.

[2] Cicero, *De Oratore*, ii, 1.

beyond indeed this palpable fact, that Cicero's natural oratorical and literary gifts were marvellous, and among them not least his capacity for making others' thoughts his own. Sympathetic, rhetorically passionate in his nature, he had wit and sarcasm, and a power of language so facile and exhaustless that with him emotion and thought brought always fit expression. These powers he cultivated with the unremitting diligence of genius, keeping always in view that ideal of a perfect orator which he has described in his rhetorical treatises.

In these one notices that Cicero treats his subject oratorically, enhancing its importance by arguments to prove all human virtues, faculties, and knowledge essential to perfection in the art of oratory.[1] It goes without saying that the orator should show those qualities of style which are not so much praised as their absence is condemned. The orator must speak with a true Roman pronunciation,[2] with pure diction, and perspicuously; there should be a rhythm, flow, and proportioning to an oration, both in the sound of words and the arrangement and presentation of thoughts, all of which contribute to make the discourse elegant. Through these qualities an oration becomes elegant (*ornatur*) in its general character (*genere*), and in its tone (*colore*) and spirit (*suco*).[3] But oratory's highest merit lies in amplifying the argument through that which beautifies it (*amplificare rem ornando*),[4] a principle excluding every kind of embellishment that is not germane to the subject.

[1] See Cicero, *De Oratore*, i, *passim;* also ii, 5. Philosophy is necessary for an orator, *ib.*, iii, iv. So Quintilian, following his great model, says: "Non posse oratorem esse nisi virum bonum."—*Ins. Or.*, i pr., § 9.

[2] Cicero has a good deal to say about the peculiarly fine and harmonious pronunciation and manner of speech at Rome. One could always tell a stranger, as at Athens, by peculiarity of pronunciation. See, *e.g.*, *Brutus*, 46. No one at Rome was so *rusticus* as not to dislike the sound of hiatus.—*De Oratore*, xliv, 150; *cf. ib.*, xlv. The Latin ear must have been acute; a whole theatre would stamp at a false quantity.—*Ib.*, li, 173.

[3] *De Oratore*, iii, xxv; see also *ib.*, iii, xiv, and lv.

[4] *Ib.*, iii, xxvi, 104.

Although Cicero's rhetorical training was mainly acquired at Rhodes, it is the great Attic orators that he admires. With him, to speak well is to speak *Attice*.[1] Atticism is perfect conformity in all respects to the judgment of the best taste, that very perfection of oratory to which not even Demosthenes attained.[2] For there is no actual oratory but that the mind can conceive more perfect, as in thought we can always conceive what is more perfect than anything actually seen or heard.[3] Plainly, Cicero is forming his ideal of oratory after the analogy of Plato's *Ideas*,[4] and he delivers himself over to the Platonic mode of reasoning, which proceeds by referring the subject of discussion to its Idea and comparing it therewith. He adds that when he seems to state novelties, he is only telling what is very old, though unknown to most people: "And for myself, I say, that I have come forth an orator or whatever I may be, not from the workshops of the rhetoricians, but from the groves of the Academy."[5]

Cicero's philosophic position accorded with his temperament. Practically he was convinced of many things, though his was not that set and forceful character which, through success and adversity, holds fast to fixed principles of conduct or of thought. Yet he shows no deep-principled scepticism; he merely is not sure, and his usual philosophic standpoint is that of the later Academy. "I am not one," says he, speaking in the person of his friend Cotta, an Academician, "to whom nothing seems to be true, but one who thinks that to every truth there enter certain falsities so like the truth itself that they cannot by any sure mark be distinguished from it."[6] A genial eclecticism fell in with the temperament of one whose mind was a guest-chamber for other men's philoso-

[1] *Brutus*, [illegible]; *cf. Orator*, xxiii. [2] *Orator*, vii–ix. [3] *Orator*, ii, 7.

[4] Has rerum formas appellat *ἰδέας* ille non intelligendi solum, sed etiam dicendi gravissimus auctor et magister, Plato.—*Orator*, iii, 10.

[5] *Orator*, iii, 12; *cf. Ad Quintum F.*, i, 1, 28.

[6] *De Nat Deorum*, i, v, 12. See *De Off.*, ii, ii, 7; and *cf. De Nat. Deorum*, ii, 1, 2.

phies. His courtesy to all these guests is equal, except those from the Epicurean sty. Eclectic habits of thought, and perhaps the fact that his mind was not deeply penetrating, often led him to minimize differences between various systems. He thought the Peripatetics differed from the Academy *nominibus* rather than *rebus*,[1] and looked on Zeno's system as a "correctionem veteris academiæ potius quam aliquam novam disciplinam."[2] It was a man's view of the *summum bonum* that determined the school to which he belonged. This would be the main influence leading him one way or the other.[3]

One opinion common to all philosophies, though well lost sight of in Epicureanism, he held with firm conviction, that reason is man's highest part. "Men differ from beasts in many things, but most in this, that reason is theirs by nature and a mind sharp and strong, quickly devising many things at once, and so to speak keen-scented, which perceives the causes and sequences of things, discovers common features, joins things remote, links the future to the present, and brings all life's course within its view. The same faculty of reason has made man desirous of his fellows and congruous with them through nature, speech, and custom, so that, starting from the love of his own household, he takes wider range, and embraces in fellowship first his countrymen, then the human race."[4]

The first part of this extract characterizes the office of reason; the second part, making use of Stoical ways of thinking, taken from the old Greek germ that like-minded men are naturally friends, refers the principle of universal good-will to the reason implanted in man.[5] Cicero continues, saying that reason gives man desire for truth and hatred of deceit, and then follows with one of his untranslatable sentences, in which one notices, however, that

[1] *Acad.*, i, iv, 17. [2] *Ib.*, i, xii, 43. [3] *De Fin.*, v, vi, 15.

[4] *Ib.*, ii, xiv, 45; *cf. De Leg.*, i, 7.

[5] Cicero lays stress on the essential likeness of all men.—*De Leg.*, i, 10: *cf. ib.*, i, 12 and 15.

there is no thought not borrowed from Plato or the Stoics: "Eadem ratio habet in se quiddam amplum atque magnificum, ad imperandum magis quam ad parendum accommodatum, omnia humana non tolerabilia solum, sed etiam levia ducens, altum quiddam et excelsum, nihil timens, nemini cedens, semper invictum." [1]

Being also a thoughtful jurist, Cicero applies these philosophical ideas to legal conceptions, arguing that the conceptions of *lex* and *jus* spring from man's nature: "Natura propensi sumus ad diligendos homines quod fundamentum juris est." [2] He also states the principle that the object of government is the greatest possible happiness of the governed,[3] and holds it just that the stronger and better race should rule the lower, that being for the good of the lower, just as it is well that reason should rule the body.[4] As for the Romans, it was unnecessary to show by argument that they were the best and strongest race, and that they should rule themselves as a free Republic. Other nations might be able to bear servitude, but not the Romans, for servitude contradicted their inborn and inherited nature, which judged the worth of all counsels and acts by reference to manly virtue.[5]

Cicero, who cared for all the arts and sciences and spoke of liberal studies as the noblest bonds among men,[6] is very near to loving knowledge for its own sake.[7] Yet he finds something lacking in all knowledge that bears no fruit in action; ethics is of greater value than any other science.[8] For himself, late in life, weighed down by the misfortunes of the Republic and prevented from discharging more active duties towards his country, he had turned to philosophy for comfort and with the hope of instruct-

[1] *De Fin.*, ii, xiv, 46.
[2] *Ad Quin.* F., i., 1, 24.
[3] *De Leg.*, i, 15; *cf. ib.*, 12.
[4] *Rep.*, iii, 24, etc.
[5] *Philippic*, x, 20; *cf. De Rep.*, i, 46; *De Leg.*, i, 8.
[6] *Pro Archia Poeta*, i; *De Oratore*, i, 3.
[7] *De Fin.*, v, xviii, 48.
[8] *De Off.*, i, xliii.

ing his fellow citizens.[1] "As medicine is the art of health, as steersmanship is the art of navigation, so wisdom (*prudentia*) is the art of living (*ars vivendi*)."[2] Through philosophy men should learn how best to live in the activity of public life or in the quiet of old age, or when public affairs become such that self-respecting lovers of their country can take no part in them, as when freedom has passed from a community ruled by its master. So had men in Greece turned to philosophy for refuge when Greek freedom had become a name.

In life, Cicero was humane and kindly. In the Pompeian party,[3] he, almost alone with Cato, had noble unwillingness to make war on Italy or join with eastern barbarians against his countrymen; tender was his solicitude over the illness of Tiro, his talented, faithful slave;[5] affectionate was he towards his friends, refined in his nature, hating obscenity,[6] possessed of fine sensitiveness in matters of social intercourse and obligation.[7] His faults, his errors, his tergiversations, his adulation of the living Cæsar, his change of tone towards him when safely dead, arose from the pressure of distress and peril on a character lacking fortitude.[8] Constitutionally timid, it was harder for him than for other men to stand firm in that time of blood. He judges Cicero most justly who

[1] *Acad.*, i, 1, 3. [2] *De Fin.*, v, vi, 16; *cf. Tus. Dis.*, ii, iv, 11.

[3] Of which he said "Nihil boni præter causam."—*Ad Fam.*, viii, 3, 2.

[4] *Ad Att.*, ix, 10.

[5] See *Ad Fam.*, xvi, 1–9.

[6] See *De Oratore*, ii, 253.

[7] In a letter to Curio, *Ad Fam.*, ii, 6, he says: "A man of sensitiveness hates to ask a great favor of one whom he regards as being under an obligation to himself. He fears that he may seem to demand a right, not to beg a kindness, and to regard the granting of his request as the payment of a favor; but . . . a man with feelings of a gentleman, where he owes much, would fain owe more."—Trans. from Tyrrell's edition of *Cicero's Correspondence*.

[8] His exile broke him for the time completely. Even his pro-consular sojourn in Cilicia was unendurable. See *Ad Att.*, v, ii, i. To him Rome was still the centre and the orbit of the world. "Urbem, Urbem, mi Rufe, cole, et in ista luce viva!"—*Ad Fam.*, ii, 12.

judges him most leniently. No finer words have been spoken of this high-intentioned man than those of Augustus, finding a grandson of his furtively reading a work of the great orator. The emperor took the book which the boy would fain conceal, read for a while, and gave it back, saying: "My child, this was a learned man and a lover of his country."

Tendencies of the Popular Party.

From early times in Rome the vindicators of the people's rights came forward as reformers of the existing order of things, or, as was alleged by their aristocratic adversaries, as subverters aiming at despotic power. And, since popular leaders had stood for the economic, social, or political rights of the Plebeians, who were not members of the ancient body of Roman burgesses, they necessarily had advocated the extension of political and social rights, and almost from the first had endeavored to bring at least the Latins within the compass of benefit intended by proposed measures. For example, Spurius Cassius, himself a Patrician, in his third consulate, B.C. 486, proposed certain distributions of the public domain among the poorer classes at Rome, and also among the Latin confederates. His adversaries alleged that he aimed at regal power; and though the accusation probably was unjust, it may be said of him, as certainly may be said of later democratic leaders, that from the exigencies of their positions they assumed to exert what, from the point of view of conservative constitutionalism, was an unconstitutional exceeding of the powers of such magistracies as they happened at the time to fill.

Spurius Cassius failed and met his death.[1] After two centuries of struggle, the Plebs obtained civil rights. Nevertheless the rich and noble continued to rule Rome. In course of time, in generous defence of popular rights, arose Tiberius Gracchus and after him his brother Caius,

[1] See Livy, ii, 41, and compare the case of Sp. Mælius, Livy, 14, 13.

such a man as Rome had not hitherto seen.[1] In regard to Caius Gracchus, these same three points are noticeable: in his endeavors to overthrow the oligarchy and make the people at least nominally supreme and relieve their economic distress, he was a subverter of the existing order; he palpably exceeded his tribunician powers, and ruled Rome with a generous, short-lived despotism; and finally, looking beyond Rome, he instituted a system of Roman colonies which should carry with them the Roman franchise. And as Gracchus looked upon the Roman crowd, and thought of relieving its necessities by feeding it at home and colonizing it abroad, and let his mind expand to the thought that the condition of all Italy might well be made equal with Rome, he naturally thought other thoughts as well, and realized that this enlarged imperial democracy must attain its rights and govern through one supreme leader, and that man was Caius Gracchus. So, whether he thought to be king of Rome, he certainly thought to continue what for two years he was, its ruler; and if a ruler, why did he not stand in the same relation of superiority to Romans as to Italians, and why should he not rule for the benefit of all his subjects? So his being absolute ruler in Rome would lead him to view Romans and Italians as alike in rights and entitled to equal standing in the broadened commonwealth.[2] Thus Caius Gracchus, as enemy of the aristocracy, as leader of the people, and as ruler of the commonwealth, was the forerunner of Julius Cæsar.

Factors of Cæsar's Statesmanship.

The statesman's vision of the latter sprang from three factors: his own perfect genius, his Greek culture, and the general views and tendencies of the popular party at Rome, of which he became the leader. The second and third of these

[1] As to Caius Gracchus see Mommsen, *History*, bk. iv, ch. iii.

[2] What has been said of Gracchus applies in principle to Marius, at least in so far as he had political understanding. And Sertorius after him, making head in Spain against the restored oligarchy, saw in the Spaniards the making of Roman citizens.

factors may be analyzed and their results accounted for. The first may only be characterized.

The oligarchy of wealth and position, which was overthrown by Caius Gracchus, shortly recovered itself, taking advantage of the unpopularity of his proposal to extend the franchise to the Italians. Some decades afterwards came the bloody onslaughts from the popular party under Marius, and then followed the formal restoration of the oligarchy by the dictator Sulla. The doings of the Sullan restoration showed the imbecility of the oligarchical party. Manifestly it had not the strength and energy to rule the Republic and the subject nations, nor, in its narrow selfishness had it the intelligence to see that for its own interest it should not treat Rome as a field for corruption and violence and the provinces as fields for plunder. On the other hand, the people could not govern except under a leader with unlimited power. Yet in all its lack of self-control, in all its unbridled passion and corruption, the people, because it was the people and not a class, stood for the diffusion of Roman institutions and for the clearing away of barriers between Rome and her dependencies. He only was fitted to be a leader of the people,—to be the people's king—who realized these tendencies, and should also see that if Rome was to continue to rule, she must become part of her own Empire and unify the interests and institutions of the Mediterranean world. In some such mode as this, the fact that Cæsar was the leader of the popular party was an element of his statesman's vision.

Another element of Cæsar's vision was his Hellenic culture. He was born a Roman with all the strength of the Roman character; his Hellenic education made him broadly human. A knowledge of the law, literature, philosophy, government, modes of life of another people gives a man outside vantage-points from which to view himself and the institutions he lives under. Greece gave her Roman scholars data for comparison and trained them to compare. It is hard to conceive what the mighty mind of Cæsar took from Greece. His Greek education, got at Rome, in travel, and at Rhodes, was complete. There was nothing he might not learn, for he was all-capable and Greece was all-affording. We know how he perfected himself in oratory,[1] and we may imagine with what grasp he would seize Greek theories and experiences in matters political and military. Above all, he gained the conception of the greater likeness of men everywhere and the function of Roman world-rule, world self-rule it might almost be, so thoroughly might the ruling state become organic with the rest, the ruling principle throughout its Empire. And, finally, he had from Greece an example of a man who conquered the world, and in a manner after Cæsar's heart set to work to constitute it into one Empire, applying in his royal way principles which Cæsar after him should bring to more enduring realization.

Cæsar's genius—his discernment, his persuasiveness, his winning personality, his power over men, his magnanimity, his readiness of resource and aptitude for all manner of business, his capacity for clear purpose within himself, and his ambition—would have made him leader in any state. His strength of will, his perfect courage, his self-reliance and belief in his star, his unparalleled generalship, his constructive political genius, his far vision of the outcome, made him the master of the crises and catastrophes he moved among, the master who should force the warring elements along the course whereby might be reached the ideal dark within the blind tossings of the time and the thwarted endeavors of other men.

Rome was unrestrained in Cæsar's time, Rome was insatiate, Rome was corrupt. The world pampered her; she was crazed with power and indulgence. Her rich had

[1] Cicero, in *Brutus*, 72–75, praises Cæsar's eloquence, and the exceeding purity of his speech, and the simple naked beauty of his *Commentaries*.

every luxury; her poor maddened for them. Men set themselves no rein. Those men of talent and position who lacked fortunes, borrowed; never did such colossal indebtedness exist, the fruit of mad extravagance in private debauchery and public office-seeking. Morals were far to seek. Honesty, temperance, chastity, were the virtues of a quixotic few, and won enmity for their possessors.

In all this there was a strength, a *vivida vis*, which was to bring partial regeneration. There were many strong and able men in Rome displaying their forcefulness in various ways. The meteoric energy of a Lucullus got him such riches in Asia that afterwards he might live in royal ease. Atticus was able and alert in all kinds of commercial money-making; Crassus was tireless in the pursuit of wealth through political banking and intrigue; it meant something that a farmer of the revenue of no great prominence would shut up and besiege the elders of a delinquent city till five of them had died of hunger.[1] That was energy at least. Better men displayed force and activity in nobler ways,—Cicero was tireless; Cato was ever at his post, ready to harangue through the livelong day. Curio and Mark Antony were tireless in debauchery, yet with brilliant talents that should display themselves in action. The noble ruffians Clodius and Milo had at least ability and bravery, in which qualities Catiline had not failed. And the people too, the mob, had the energy of restlessness, surging in turmoil, demanding distraction, public games, and public bread, unceasingly asserting its right to ride through life on the neck of the world. Everywhere we find strength, whether we look for it in the burning reasonings of Lucretius, in the revilings of Catullus, or in the orations of Cicero, or seek it in the mad graspings of lower natures; or whether we look where strength of every kind is to be found, in the personality of Julius Cæsar, who in the way

[1] See Tyrrell, *Correspondence of Cicero*, vol. iii, Introd., p. 28.

of seeming folly had indulged in the caprices of the time and owed more millions of sesterces than other men.

Cæsar's Career.

A great man realizes the purpose of his life as events and his own growth disclose it. Yet his nature is displayed in acts of youth as well as manhood. Cæsar had disclosed himself to Sulla's eye when he had refused to put away his wife at the despot's command. He showed himself still further when he redeemed his promise to the pirates by crucifying them every one. Still further he showed himself, pursuing his Greek studies, for it was his nature to absorb and use all knowledge. He did not especially disclose himself, but only illustrated the times, by leading for a while an extravagant and dissipated life. He did disclose himself, however, by coming through this life unscathed, showing that indulgence had never dominated him; and he announced himself emphatically when as ædile he restored to the forum the trophies of Marius. In these times and afterwards when with difficulty he got himself elected Pontifex Maximus, he could hardly have been conscious of the imperial purpose which events were to unfold in his mind. Even when he went as proprætor to Spain, he had been only the ablest leader of the popular party; he was forty years old and had never led an army. But he must have felt his unequalled aptitude for generalship, which his successful proprætorship in Spain confirmed. He did in very truth disclose the man he was, when on his return he waived the vanity of a triumph in order to enter the city and grasp the reality of consular power. Now he began to know himself Cæsar. He was consul. He had become such by boldness and by management of the two most powerful men of the still so-called Republic. He knew his superiority to them. As consul, with their aid, he did his will, passing an agrarian and such other popular laws as he saw fit. At the end of his consulship, again by arrangement with the plutocrat and the supposed ruler of Rome's armies, he obtained the province of Gaul for five years, with authority to levy legions there and subdue farther Gaul.

For there was a surrounding barbarian world. This Cæsar had always known, and must have come to realize in Spain. He also knew that, in order to maintain his influence in Rome, he must lead an army and hold it devoted to himself. He could train an army against the Gauls. But the man in whom abode the thought of Rome's majesty had no idea of fighting Gauls merely to train an army. Rome always knew herself in danger from the barbarians of the North; and it was Cæsar who, with a marvellous far vision, set himself to conquer the semi-barbarians of Gaul, make Gaul a province truly Roman and a wide barrier against fiercer German tribes beyond the Rhine. When it was done, he held his hand and recognized boundaries of the Roman power: he did not seek to do more than awe the Germans; he never sought to carry through the conquest of Britain. Gaul was barrier enough, and Cæsar had no purpose of conquering farther then, even if affairs in Rome might have stood still. As it was, Gaul was completely pacified before the infatuation of Cæsar's opponents called him to fulfil his destiny.

Cæsar's victory in the civil war was a romance of genius. His force was apparently so slight, and the resources of his opponents seemed to include most of the strength of Rome and her dependencies. The heart of the people may have been with Cæsar, but the people did not conquer for him. It was the power of greatness,—it was Cæsar. And after he held sole mastery in the Roman world, the task to order that world was still before him, a threefold task, no part of which could be effectually accomplished if the other two were left undone. The first part was to introduce social, economic, and political order into the affairs of Rome and Italy; the second was to regulate the provinces, assimilate their condition to that of Italy as far as might be, and order their relations to the centre of the Empire; the third part was to complete and define the Empire's boundaries, and give them permanence as against the outside, for the most part barbaric, world.

The fact that one man had become the absolute ruler of the commonwealth closed forever the strife of political parties, which before Cæsar's time had become a struggle of misrule with anarchy. Cæsar now in every way endeavored to make men lay aside the anger of the civil war and become reconciled to his imperial order. His purpose to be Rome's ruler was justified by the palpable impossibility of a free Republic. He united republican offices and functions in himself, and the senate devised and granted him new powers. A large part of Cæsar's followers, men of extravagance and broken fortunes, as well as the Roman mob which had been ready to shout and riot for him whom it thought its leader, looked for the wiping out of all debts, if not for the distribution of the property of their creditors and political opponents. Cæsar confiscated little beyond the property of Pompey and public funds, which he took as the head of the state. In regard to debts he struck a middle course, cancelled arrears of interest, leaving the principal debt valid, but permitting the debtor to compel his creditor to accept the debtor's property in payment at its value before the civil war. And, in the spirit of his own and Greek humanity, he abolished the right of creditors to enslave the persons of debtors who could not pay; debtors might cede their property and be free. In other matters Cæsar showed himself the master of the mob. He reduced from three hundred and twenty thousand to one hundred and fifty thousand the number of recipients of public grain. But he remained mindful that it was as a democratic leader he had risen, and the interests of that democracy included the people of Rome as well as those far and wide beyond the city's walls. Within Rome and without, his great building enterprises were for the public use. He built a new comitium for assemblies, and new court-houses to relieve the overcrowded forum, and he supplied the baths with oil. Then he projected a new senate-house, a new theatre, a public library, and proposed to turn the Tiber's course, whereby the city's available area would have been enlarged, the marshes drained to the coast, and Rome provided with a safe seaport. He issued ordinances regulating the municipal affairs of Rome, requiring the repair of street pavements, restricting the carrying of litters and the driving of wagons within the city, reorganizing the police, and making stricter the administration of criminal justice. He attempted to restrain the extravagance of the table and extravagance in dress; he tried to raise the morals of the people by stringent laws upon adultery and divorce; and finally he sought to check the depopulation of Italy by keeping Italians at home.

Cæsar's care extended to all Italy, following the tendencies of the democratic party, but with world-wide views and measures of his own. The city of Rome was no longer to stand on an isolating elevation; the rest of Italy was to be raised to the same status, nor were the provinces forgotten. Cæsar's municipal ordinances formally applied to all Italy; they were plain announcements of his policy to maintain the superiority of Rome only in so far as it was necessary because she was the capital city and the seat of the imperial rule. And when Cæsar raised the number of senators to nine hundred, he made senators of many able men who were not even Italians, thus introducing fresh blood with fuller representation of the Empire.

During the last century of the Republic, in the provinces, Roman governors, officials, farmers of revenue, and capitalists had been autocratic plunderers with power of soldiery to enforce their extortions. Even before regulating Rome, Cæsar visited the provinces, lessened their burdens, and entirely changed the existing order by substituting imperial for republican officials. These were responsible for good administration to a master at Rome who cared for the provincials, intelligently recognized that in their welfare lay the welfare of the Empire, and who was even then founding an imperial house which, however ill it might conduct itself at Rome, was to be a lasting boon to the provinces. He also checked the doings of Roman capitalists, and provided measures for the liquidation of debts similar to those instituted at Rome. He placed many towns on the same footing with Italian municipalities, gave Roman citizenship to Cisalpine Gaul; and, proving to all the world that Rome was no longer to rule for her own enriching, he carried out Caius Gracchus's project of a colony on the site of Carthage, and rebuilt Corinth, the other site which might commercially rival Rome. Even in respect to the presence of troops, the provinces were brought nearer to the condition of Italy, for the troops were gradually stationed on the frontiers of the Empire.

To make firm these frontiers was the third part of Cæsar's task. His conquest of Gaul was the great establishment of the frontier on the northwest; it may have postponed by centuries the overthrow of the Roman Empire,—until the conquering barbarians had themselves become capable of profiting by the civilization of the conquered. Cæsar, in conquering the Gauls and Germans, had borne in his heart as well as on his banners the majesty of the Roman people. All his battles and sieges, his marches and incursions into Germany, his fortress building and establishment of camps, had in view the dignity and safety of the Republic. While proprætor he had pacified Spain; even during the civil war he had established frontier fortresses in Africa; and at the time of his assassination he was preparing for a decisive conquest of Parthia, which should avenge the slaughter at Carrhæ and establish firm frontiers in those Syro-Mesopotamian regions. He had in mind, moreover, plans for establishing the Danubian frontier, and, had Cæsar lived, Dacia might not have been left for Trajan to subdue. These were all farseeing plans for the establishment of the boundaries of the Roman Empire. Schemes for the conquest of the unknown east and farther north, which have been attributed to him, probably he never entertained. He had no Alexander-thought of conquering the world, and well he knew that Rome and her provinces had reached the climax of their strength. It lay not within the capacities of Roman power and civilization to conquer and assimilate the untold barbaric races who roamed without the Empire's boundaries. Cæsar had recognized this by turning back voluntarily in Britain and on the Rhine. His object now was to give endurance to Roman power within its existing bounds.

These were all mainly military matters; and by the sword had Cæsar come to sovereign rule. But he had been and sought to remain the democratic leader, or democratic king it might be. At least he would hope to rule through law and popular support, not through a standing army. Yet when a people ceases to have power to govern itself, so that the only possible government is monarchy, the monarch cannot safely base his power solely on popular support. Cæsar may have known this; its recognition was soon forced on his successors. Nevertheless, he did his best to establish an empire which should be self-sustaining and neither upheld nor controlled by soldiery. He disbanded his Gallic legions, tried and disciplined as no other soldiers in the Empire. They were too military in spirit. He might still have held them loyal to himself, but perhaps could not have kept them as soldiers loyal to such a state as he sought to found. So he settled them as colonists throughout Italy. Further to show himself the people's king, he would have no body-guard, a carrying out of principle which cost him his life.

Cæsar's monarchy realized the ideals pointed to by the

tendencies of the popular party at Rome, so far as was possible. It was an imperial rule considerate of the welfare of human beings who were not Romans, and it recognized all men as men. The leaven of Greek thought had fitted the world for it. Much of the native Roman force of character remained, and was to show itself in the maintenance of the Roman Hellenic Empire now to be completed on the foundations laid by Cæsar. But it was a force no longer peculiarly Roman; for the purposes and personalities of its possessors had become the purposes and personalities of denizens of a Græco-Roman world. Cæsar is the ideal example of the great Roman man enlightened, not corrupted, by Hellenic thought. Through the genius of Cæsar, Rome touched the destiny which the influence of Greece enabled her to conceive.

END OF VOLUME I.

DATE DUE